KINGSTON
Building on the Past

Butternut Press Inc.   Westport, Ontario, 1988

KINGSTON
Building on the Past

Brian S. Osborne and Donald Swainson

© Copyright Brian S. Osborne and Donald Swainson, Kingston, 1988

Canadian Cataloguing in Publication Data

Osborne, Brian, S., 1938 –
 Kingston: building on the past

Includes bibliographical references and index.
ISBN 0-921575-05-x (bound) ISBN 0-921575-04-1 (pbk.)

I. Kingston (Ont.) – History. I. Swainson, Donald, 1938 –   . II. Title.

FC3099.K5082 1988   971.3'72   C88–093820–x
F1059.5.K5082 1988

ISBN 0-921575-04-1
Printed and bound in Canada

Butternut Press Inc.
P.O. Box 166, Westport
Ontario, K0G 1X0

Editor: Peter Smith
Graphic Design: Peter Dorn
Typesetting: Typesetting Systems Inc.
Printing: Gagné Printing

To Ann and Eleanor

Contents

Foreword

Kingston. The Limestone City. City of Old Fort Henry, of Queen's University and the Royal Military College; of grand and elegant mansions and grey, forbidding penitentiaries. Tourist haven, institutional mecca, and flourishing centre of commerce and industry.

Today, Kingston is at long last comfortable with its own identity, with its role, with what it is and where it is: a community in which the quality of life is cherished as much as, if indeed not more than, its abundant variety. But it was not always so.

It is said that a city is what its people make of it. In Kingston's case, however, the city we see today is as much what its people have *not* made it, whatever their best efforts over many generations. Throughout its long history (long in North American, even longer in Canadian terms), Kingston has had great expectations. But as is often the case they have remained largely elusive and unachieved.

The pattern was set by the first masters of the site; and for much of the next three hundred years, through Canada's history as a settlement, colony, province, dominion, and finally full and sovereign nation, Kingston was to prove doggedly consistent in seeing its great expectations – some would say its great pretensions – burst forth in a flourish of high energy and even higher spirits, only to evaporate even more spectacularly.

Founded on the orders of Louis de Buade, Count Frontenac, the fort that was to bear his name was to be a major strategic element in controlling both the fur-trade and the often troublesome Iroquois. La Salle's seigneury was to be the spearhead of a thriving community of settlers. However, by the time of its capture by British forces almost a century later, in 1758, the French military presence had been reduced to only fifty soldiers who, along with some sixty dependants and civilians, constituted the whole community. Among the loot and plunder "liberated" by the victors were no fewer than 178 gold- and silver-laced hats and other such finery, eloquent symbols of the post's faded importance.

With rebellion in the Thirteen Colonies, however, all was to change. The coming of the Loyalists marked the settlement for new and important things; and with the creation of Upper Canada in 1791, the recently-named Kingston could look forward to a bigger and brighter future. The village became a town. Commerce grew. Ship-building and the military garrison became more important still with the War of 1812-1814. No wonder its citizens developed a sense of deep satisfaction and self-assurance, and had it reinforced by the Imperial government's acceptance of Colonel By's plans for a waterway on the Rideau, defended at its point of departure by five great redoubts of which Fort Henry was to be but the first. Kingston was to be a citadel of the first magnitude.

But that destiny was already unravelling. By 1834, the naval yards were closing. As Reverend Herchmer was to discover, the Imperial purse was not bottomless: Fort Henry was to remain splendid in its solitude. Neither rebellion from within nor quixotic forays from without by so-called Patriots would halt the slow decline in Kingston's strategic importance. Political importance, however, was something else.

What Mars could not grant, surely Mercury, patron of commerce, would. In terms of early-nineteenth-century travel, Lord Durham's visit was indeed a flying one, but his report would have a lasting impact: union of Upper and Lower Canada. And with anglicization, westward expansion, and the growing industry and wealth of Upper Canada, there was little doubt the capital of the new Canada would be in the younger province. For whatever lucky town was chosen, and for its inhabitants, the future would hold unlimited opportunity.

Fortune smiled brighter and more gloriously than ever: Kingston was to be that town. Yet, once again, its victory was to be transient, this time brutally so. Between the official proclamation of Kingston as capital in February 1841 and the resolution of the Assembly declaring it unacceptable as the capital just twenty months elapsed. Kingstonians fought with every weapon at their disposal to keep their status, but to no avail. On Midsummer's Day, 1844, Governor-General Metcalfe departed for Montreal, and with him went "Kingston's age of greatness."

In *Kingston: Building on the Past*, authors Brian Osborne and Donald Swainson explore the origins and growth of this city, and how, by design or misadventure, it was transformed into the multi-faceted community we know today. Through their examination of Kingston's commerce and economy over its long history, we come to see the city's development not only in terms of many of the great figures and issues of Canada's past but also in terms of our ongoing growth and development today. We see that the struggle to create a broader economic base, to attract new industry, to sustain the institutional presence – all so familiar in our recent history – are nothing new.

Here are the forwarders of an earlier day, transshipping cargoes to or from small ships built for the rapids-ridden St Lawrence. Here, too, are the entrepreneurs of the great age of railways, the era of the Grand Trunk and the Kingston and Pembroke (the "Kick and Push") and of the Canadian Locomotive Company, once Kingston's largest employer. Under the direction of William Harty, Liberal member of parliament for Kingston, it was to win many a lucrative government contract. Conflict-of-interest rules were still, in Laurier's day, a thing of the future!

Transport, of course, has always played a major role in Kingston's economy. The passionate and persistent determination of the city, its leaders, and its inhabitants during the early years of this century to win designation as the foot-of-the-lakes transfer terminal of the grain-trade should therefore come as no surprise. For twenty years, the issue was of consuming interest. Study followed study. Lobbying was intense. And even following the award of the plum to rival Prescott, Kingston could not and would not give up the fight. The citadel of stone was now a citadel of belief. But as so often in the past, events would overtake brave hopes. A generation later, the Seaway would open and make the whole issue redundant.

But whether on the winning or the losing side, Kingston has been blessed with an exceptional cast of unique and colourful personalities who have brought their own particular riches to the city: the "Little Gentleman," the Reverend John Stuart, who methodically amassed an estate of 7,000 acres; the Honourable Richard Cartwright, who went Stewart 20,000 acres better; the extraordinary Molly Brant; Governor-General Sydenham, who shocked the citizenry of his new capital with his "sacrifices to Venus," and who vowed never to set foot again in St George's, only to be buried there to this day; John Sandfield Macdonald, "Sweet William" Draper, Louis-Hippolyte LaFontaine, and of course a canny lawyer and even cannier politician, one John Alexander Macdonald. All have passed through the city's history, along with thousands whose names are not known, among them the many immigrants who ended their journeys and their lives in the fever-haunted sheds on the old waterfront. All have left their mark, large or small, all have contributed whether intentionally or not, to making Kingston what it is today.

Kingston: Building on the Past is a work of solid scholarship, an invaluable resource for the serious student of the city's, the province's, and indeed Canada's economic growth. It has equal worth as a case-book study of urban development. But it is of no less value to the ordinary reader interested in the history of the Limestone City, and concerned for its future. Indeed, if we are to build upon the past with any degree of reverence and respect for the unique heritage that is the city of Kingston today, this volume is required reading.

The Honourable Flora MacDonald, MP for Kingston and the Islands.

Acknowledgements

Both of the authors of this book began to publish material about Kingston, Kingston-ians, and the Kingston region some twenty years ago. While much of the research for *Kingston: Building on the Past* is new, the authors would have been very foolish indeed not to have used the extensive materials accumulated during two decades of research. One of the results of such a protracted enterprise is a very large intellectual indebtedness. Repeatedly we have benefited from the generosity and assistance of a large number of individuals and institutions. Physical space denies us the opportunity to thank all of those who helped to make this book a reality. Some, however, must be given particular credit.

The relevant research units at Queen's University were endlessly patient and responsive. Anne MacDermaid, George Henderson, Shirley Spragge, and Mario Creet at the Queen's University Archives were always willing helpers and advisers. In Douglas Library, William Morley, Barbara Teatero, Donna Dumbleton (Special Collections), and Doreen Rutherford (Information Services) provided much assistance. Robert Swain and Michael Bell at the Agnes Etherington Art Centre educated the authors on various aspects of Kingston's artistic heritage. Valuable research assistance was also provided by the Government Documents unit of the Douglas Library.

Within Kingston, research assistance was also forthcoming from the staff of the Kingston Public Library (and particularly from Deborah Dafoe), the City of Kingston's Planning Development, the researchers at Fort Henry, and Maurice Smith and his ever co-operative colleagues at the Marine Museum of the Great Lakes at Kingston.

Ian Wilson, David Russell, and Chris Norman at the Archives of Ontario were of material assistance, as were Richard Brown, Pat Kennedy, Betty Kidd, Carl Vincent, and Glen Wright at the National Archives of Canada.

Several members of the Queen's University Department of Geography provided expert assistance: Ross Hough and George Innes did sterling service in producing maps, diagrams, and illustrations; Joan Knox merits special praise for long hours of typing and generally shepherding the manuscript for us.

A variety of individuals gave us information and advice that was most appreciated. This group includes Rose Mary Gibson, Kathy Waugh, Douglas Heath, William Westfall, Douglas Fetherling, Neil Patterson, and Gerald Tulchinsky. Margaret Angus, Alan Artibise, Sally Barnes, and Richard A. Preston read the manuscript in draft form and gave us the benefit of their advice. Bogart Trumpour provided wise counsel and legal advice at a crucial point in the evolution of the manuscript. Nor can we fail to appreciate the professional guidance of our publisher, David McGill, our very knowledgeable editor, Peter Smith, and our creative and imaginative designer, Peter Dorn.

Over the years both authors have taught courses and supervised theses that relate to Kingston to some extent. We have learned much from out students and thank them for their assistance. Of particular help were Duncan McDowell, Walter Lewis, Richard Harris, Sally Drummond, Bradley Rudachyk, Randy Widdis, Jay Nuttal, James Eadie, Quentin Chiotti, William Teatero and Kathryn Bindon.

The un-captioned profiles of Kingston that appear throughout the book are from the Queen's University Archives (title page), the National Archives of Canada (p. 5), Queen's University Library, Special Collections (pp. 144–145) and Ross Hough (pp. 242–243). Other illustrations are captioned and cited where they appear. The ornamentation throughout the book consists of details of the decoration in City Hall. A detail from David B. Walkely's *The Market Square, Kingston* appears on the front cover. It is part of the permanent collection of the Agnes Etherington Arts Centre, Queen's University, and hangs in the office of the Principal. We also acknowledge the assistance regularly received from the Kingston *Whig-Standard* and its staff and in particular the permission to publish Frank Edwards' cartoon on the back cover.

This volume is a private-sector enterprise, unsubsidized by any agency of the Crown. However, over the years, the authors have been assisted in their work by the Social Sciences and Humanities Research Council, the National Museum of Man, the Ontario Department of Culture, the Ontario Arts Council, the Advisory Research Committee (Queen's University), and the Queen's University School of Graduate Studies. Two former deans of the Graduate School, R.L. McIntosh and Maurice Yeates, were particularly supportive. For their generosity and faith in our project we are very grateful.

All of this assistance notwithstanding, the authors do, of course, take full responsibility for what has finally appeared in print.

Finally, we must refer to our wives, who have for years put up with our crazy work schedules – sometimes in Kingston and sometimes away. Without their support this book would not have been written. Therefore *Kingston: Building on the Past* is dedicated to Ann and Eleanor.

Brian S. Osborne
Donald Swainson
Kingston, 15 June 1988

KINGSTON

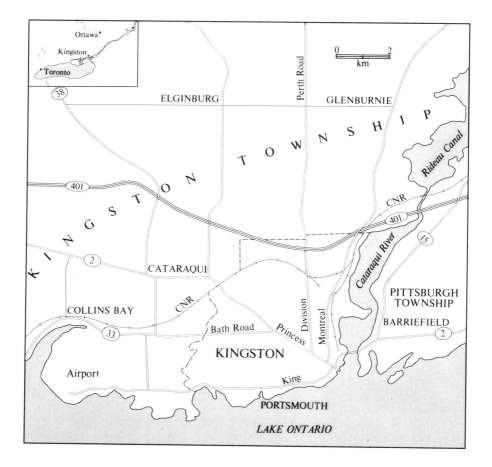

The site of Kingston.

The Personality of Place

Cities are the focal points for the economic, social, and political life of the region in which they are located. They are also communities in which families live, pursue a livelihood, and interact with kith and kin in a complex network of social links. The nature of the activities within a city and its associated hinterland is an important factor in the city's size and significance, and contributes much to the character and personality of the urban community.

One of the characteristic features of contemporary urban communities is their loss of identity in a process of standardization and homogenization; they become undifferentiated from many other urban environments. Fortunately, this process is incomplete for some cities, and a distinctive, if not unique, sense of place continues in the midst of the trappings of the modern urban society.

What is Kingston's "personality"?[1] Indeed, does it exist at all? For some it is "The Limestone City." But this epithet is, after all, a reference to the fabric of the architecture, albeit a dominant and striking element of the total urban image. Perhaps the essence of Kingston's personality can be better summarized in one word, "continuity" – in particular, continuity of function and continuity of form. Kingston's origins go back some three hundred years, although its formal establishment as a townsite dates to the late eighteenth century. And over the last two hundred years of considerable political, economic, and social developments in Ontario, few cities have changed as little as Kingston.

THREE CENTURIES OF DEVELOPMENT

The specific site over which modern-day Kingston has expanded is quite circumscribed. Bounded by the Great Cataraqui River to the east and the Little Cataraqui Creek to the west, it constitutes a flat limestone plain, rising gently to the interior. It is fronted by some nine miles of shoreline, much of it amenable to development for wharfage.

From 1673 to 1763, this site and the surrounding area were part of New France.

In 1673, Louis de Buade, count de Palluau and de Frontenac and governor-general of the French colony, met with the Iroquois at Cataraqui and established a fort and trading post there. This act initiated the three centuries of subsequent occupation. Developed as a seigneury, and with a more prominent military role assigned to the improved fortifications of Fort Frontenac, the site passed from French control effectively by British conquest in 1758, and legally by the Treaty of Paris in 1763.

Two decades later, a new hegemony was established with the arrival of the British military in 1783 and the provision of a new home for Loyalist settlers and Loyalist institutions. This toehold of settlement in Britain's newest colony grew slowly into the nineteenth century, was stimulated by the War of 1812-1814, and by the 1830s had become established as the primary centre of Upper Canada's commerce, military and naval might, and political establishment. This preeminence was marked by the selection of Kingston as the capital of the newly-constituted United Province of Canada, consisting of Canada East (Quebec) and Canada West (Ontario), on 10 February 1841. The loss of this seat of government a mere three years later was a major economic and psychological blow. It was accompanied, moreover, by other setbacks that affected Kingston's economic structure. The waning of the St Lawrence traffic in grain following the repeal of the British Corn Laws in the late 1840s diminished Kingston's port activity. Also, the improvement of navigation along the St Lawrence in this period allowed more traffic to by-pass Kingston. The completion of the Montreal-Toronto rail connection in the 1850s was another blow to Kingston's shipping function. And with the closing of the British naval station at Point Frederick in 1834 and the formal termination of the British military presence in 1870, another important dimension of Kingston's economic base was lost.

From the mid-nineteenth century to the 1930s, Kingston strove to achieve a new economic rationale and sought new initiatives for growth – a growth that was always energetically pursued and yet never achieved at the rate experienced by cities elsewhere at this time. The sponsorship of new rail corridors and linkages, the luring of industries by the bait of bonuses and tax exemptions, and the prospect of a revitalized transshipment function in association with the enlarged Welland Canal – all these failed to serve as the elixir of growth.

Not until the outbreak of the Second World War was Kingston at last to experience accelerated development. The war stimulated the traditional manufacturing industries and shipyards, and the city added the new metallurgical and textile technologies of Alcan and Du Pont to its economic base. But even these long-awaited industrial contributions could not diminish the essential mainstay of Kingston's economy – the institutions. The several penitentiaries, Queen's University, the Royal Military College, and other institutions constituted important symbolic and economic presences that continued to dominate the ethos of the community.

Indeed, it is also the relative failure to achieve significant industrial growth and associated demographic growth that has allowed this ethos to develop. In 1830, Kingston was still the premier town of Upper Canada, with a population of 3,587 –

York (Toronto) having a mere 2,800, London only 2,415, and Hamilton a scant 2,031. Toronto (30,775) had taken the lead by 1851, however, and Kingston with its 11,585 had fallen to third place in the urban hierarchy, behind Hamilton (14,112). The ensuing decades were telling. By 1901 Kingston's population had increased only to 17,961 whereas Toronto was now a metropolis of some 208,040 people. And by the end of the Second World War, Kingston's mere 33,459 was dwarfed by Toronto's ever-accelerating growth to 675,754!

In consequence, Kingston will enter the 1990s as a city of some 60,000 people, the functional centre of the adjacent townships, which together with Kingston will contain some 130,000 people. It is a city-size that allows a continued sense of community and a townscape of diverse domestic and institutional architecture of the nineteenth century. And it is a city that is replete with open spaces bequeathed by past military and government functions and never far away from surrounding countryside and lakeshore vistas. It is an ethos to be cherished.

The situation of Kingston.

CONTINUITY

From the first organization of the site by the French, through the advent of the British and their several responses to perceived American threats, to the more complicated pressures of modern *realpolitik*, Kingston has been a military town. Military personnel, military society, and military land-use have affected the look and feel of the town, while the garrison's economic contribution has been no less significant. Similarly, various institutions and agencies located in Kingston have included penitentiaries, universities, hospitals, asylums, and – the ultimate institution – government itself. Finally, for much of its history, the transport and handling of incoming commodities and outgoing produce have been more characteristic of the city's economy than the manufacturing of goods. While this commercial function has weakened, it has been replaced by the dominance of service functions rather than by the growth of industry that has come to typify the life of other Canadian cities since the late nineteenth century. With this continuity of function, therefore, and with the absence of growth to metropolitan size, Kingston's downtown still retains much of its nineteenth-century atmosphere. Perhaps it is not surprising that for many this "continuity" is also characterized by a Kingstonian conservatism that expresses itself in the day-to-day affairs of the city.

If only one element of place can be identified to help better understand this continuity, it is perhaps the location of the town. Generalizations of Canadian historical development have placed emphasis on east-west movements. Located as it is on the main artery of Canada, the Great Lakes-St Lawrence route, Kingston has been very much integrated into the flows of people, goods, and ideas between the interior and the east coast. But this emphasis must not be allowed to detract from the significant north-south connections that also existed and became better developed with the advent of rail. Thus, any attempt at understanding Kingston's development must consider its links with New York and Buffalo, as well as its links with Montreal and Toronto; a hinterland that included the counties of upper New York State as well as those of eastern Ontario; and American villages like Clayton and Alexandria Bay that were as much a part of its social interactions as Canadian communities like Bath, Sydenham, and Gananoque.

With these generalizations in mind, this study will attempt to demonstrate the "personality" of Kingston. In form, the study will take the approach of an urban biography. Its structure will generally follow the chronology of Kingston's "life-history," but it will occasionally deviate to allow an underscoring of distinctive themes in the ways in which the city developed its own physical morphology and society. Fundamentally, this book is concerned with the emergence of Kingston as a community with a distinctive sense of place.

PART ONE

ORIGINS

Point Peninsula pot, some one to two thousand years old, probably dropped from an over-turned canoe. Indians traversed the area for centuries. It was found off Wolfe Island. (Brian Gammeljord)

ONE

The French and Cataraqui

THE FRENCH AND THE IROQUOIS

Unlike many other European settlements in North America, Kingston was not established on the site of an Indian settlement. However, it was a need to interact with the native population that first focused European attention on the region. By the mid-seventeenth century, the trappers and traders who were energetically prosecuting the fur-trade from their bases in New France had already pushed up the Ottawa River and west to the upper Great Lakes. Here they actively traded with the Algonquin, Ojibwa, and Huron peoples and established a lucrative enterprise. The French, however, did not enjoy similar relationships with the powerful League of the Iroquois to the south. Champlain's support of, and active participation in, Algonquin and Huron raids into Iroquois country in 1609 and 1615 in fact ensured Iroquois hostility to his countrymen. The subsequent series of retaliatory raids on Huronia during the 1640s resulted in the assertion of the League's control over the hunting and trapping country to the north of the lower Great Lakes.[1]

Prior to the 1660s, the Iroquois were confined to their historic homeland to the south of Lake Ontario. By 1670, however, no fewer than six villages had appeared on the north shore of Lake Ontario: Ganestiquiagon, located at the mouth of the Rouge River, was a Seneca settlement; Ganaraské, at the mouth of the Ganaraska River, Quintio on Rice Lake, and Quinté at the neck of the Quinte peninsula were all Cayuga; while Ganneious, at the site of modern Napanee, was Oneida. Whereas the Iroquois villages to the south were large, often with some one hundred long-houses and close to a thousand people, the north-shore villages were smaller, with only twenty to thirty long-houses and some 500 to 800 people. But they all strategically dominated the major water routes from the interior to the lake. From these bases they could not only extend their own hunting territories into the Georgian Bay-Ottawa River region but also interdict the French fur-trade with their allies, the Ottawa. This state of affairs was noted in 1671:

The Iroquois ... live on the lands on the south shore of Lake Ontario, and it is by those chiefly that one could obstruct the French trade, for having few beaver and other

Louis de Buade, count
de Palluau and de
Frontenac and governor
of New France, built
the first fortifications at
Cataraqui in 1673.
(QUA)

animals in their country which is too temperate, and also their country being too much
overrun with hunters to let these animals multiply rapidly, the Iroquois are compelled
to go hunting in the northern countries where there is a prodigious quantity of beaver,
otter, etc., and to cross Lake Ontario for that purpose. As they dare not cross it in the
middle with their bark canoes because it is twenty-five leagues wide, they travel along
the shore to the end where it is narrow and where there are islands which they cross
from one to the other.[2]

Predictably, the French were much concerned with the potential the Iroquois
had for blocking the movement of their traffic in furs along the St Lawrence route
to Montreal and Quebec. Indeed, it was estimated that beaver skins to the value
of over one million *livres* (old French pounds) were being diverted south to Dutch
and English traders on the Hudson River.[3] While the French monarchy and the
minister for the colonies, Jean-Baptiste Colbert, were opposed to western expansion, the economic and military implications of the Iroquois threat were not lost
on Jean Talon, intendant of New France. As early as 1670 he had advised his masters
in the mother country that,

In addition to what I had been told, orally and in writing, about the Iroquois threatening a breach of the peace, I realized that they were ruining French trade, hunting
beaver on lands belonging to the Indians under our protection, and using violence to
steal their skins. I am firmly convinced that if an establishment be made on Lake Ontario, which I planned to do before my departure for France, the Iroquois would more
easily be kept in duty, respect, and fear with a hundred men.[4]

Earlier that year, Daniel de Rémy, sieur de Courcelle, negotatiated the St
Lawrence rapids upstream from Montreal and arrived at Lake Ontario with a force
of fifty-six volunteers. This feat sufficiently impressed the Iroquois that they entered
into a peace treaty with their Algonquin neighbours.

This interlude of peace was but a brief one, and soon after his arrival in Quebec
in 1672, the new and dynamic governor of the French colonies Louis de Buade,
Count Frontenac, heard of renewed Iroquois threats to French allies and the French
fur-trade. Accordingly, he directed his attention to the site of Cataraqui at the
junction of the Great Lakes, the St Lawrence, and the route south to Hudson River
country. Champlain had passed this way in 1615, during his participation in a raid
on the Iroquois to the south; in 1668 the Sulpicians had established a mission to
the Cayuga at Quinté; and, as has been seen, Rémy de Courcelle had reconnoitered
the area two years later. In 1673, following preliminary contacts with the Iroquois
by his emissary René-Robert Cavelier, sieur de La Salle, and backed by a force of
the Carignan-Salières regiment, Frontenac travelled to the meeting place at the
mouth of the Great Cataraqui River. Here he treated with the north-shore Iroquois
and gained control of the routes and territories crucial to the successful pursuit of

the fur-trade. A fort, Fort Frontenac, was established with appropriately impressive pomp and ceremony in 1673, and a century of French control of the region was initiated. In the words of one scholar,

Fort Frontenac might best be view [*sic*] as a catalyst which in spite of all royal policy to the contrary helped to turn the French away from the lower St. Lawrence region and hastened the economic development of a unique society of soldiers and fur traders who for the next century turned the North American interior into their private fiefdom.[5]

In his report to his superiors in France, Frontenac had commented on the qualities of the site at Cataraqui. Apart from the "meadows half a league wide by almost three long where the grass is so good and so fine that there is none better in France," Frontenac paid particular attention to the harbour:

the pleasantest harbour that can be seen; it is more than three quarters of a league in depth [that is, inland]; its bed is only mud and there is more than seven or eight feet of water in the shallowest places.

The river which forms it has six or seven fathoms at its mouth and for a distance of nearly three leagues which it runs up into the land to a fall, it is of such a kind that quite big ships could easily enter it. A point situated at the entrance puts the harbour which is thereby formed so much under shelter from all winds that boats could lie there almost without cables.[6]

Favourably impressed, Frontenac pushed ahead with securing the site, and despite the complaints of the "habitants" whom he directed to the task of clearing the site and erecting a fort, the project was completed within six days.[7] Frontenac was further impressed, advising Colbert that

there is still no fort in this country built like this one, or a settlement so advanced, since there are now two sides of buildings each forty-six feet long and a store twenty feet long; since I have already had cows, pigs, and poultry sent there; since by spring more than twenty arpents of land will be ready for sowing; and since eight days after the fort was finished I stored there provisions for a garrison of thirty men for a year from the ship-ments which I had brought from Montreal.[8]

While the primary purpose of the fort at Cataraqui was to oversee the fur-trade in general and the Iroquois in particular, the military role was accompanied by some limited settlement and agriculture, with the seigneurial rights and privileges being awarded in 1675 to La Salle. La Salle's grant extended some four leagues along the lakefront, a half a league inland, and incorporated two islands offshore, Grande Île (now Wolfe Island) and Île de Tonti (now Amherst Island). In return for his seigneurial rights and trading monopoly, La Salle was required to strengthen the

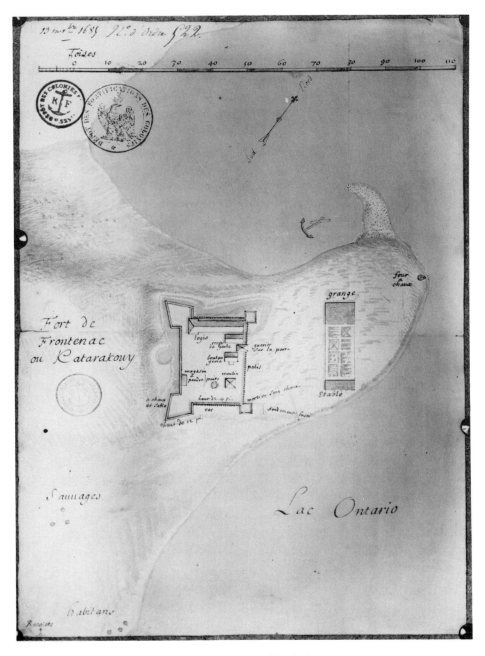

Plan of Fort Frontenac and associated features, 1685. (NA)

fort, bring in settlers, construct a chapel to serve the spiritual needs of the settlers, and establish a mission to the native population. These obligations appear to have been discharged expeditiously. La Salle rebuilt much of the original wooden pallisade, enhancing it by incorporating a stone wall on one side and stone bastions at each of the four corners. By 1682 a visitor reported on the fortifications at Cataraqui:

Three quarters of it are of masonry of hardstone, the wall is three feet thick and twelve high. There is one place where it is only four feet, not being completed. The remainder is closed in with stakes. There is inside a house of squared logs, a hundred feet long. There is also a blacksmith's shop, a guardhouse, a house for the officers, a well, and a cowhouse. There is a good amount of land sown round about, in which a hundred paces away or almost there is a barn for storing the harvest. There are quite near the fort several French houses, an Iroquois village, a convent and a Recollet church. [9]

From this base, the French actively prosecuted the fur-trade. Indeed, during this stage of the "fur-trade frontier," the north-shore villages served as bases for Iroquois groups passing through to the northern hunting grounds as well as rendezvous for French, British, and Dutch fur-traders. [10] This proved to be a mixed blessing for the natives. By the mid-1670s it was recorded that traders from Cataraqui were trading liquor for furs as far west as the Seneca village of Teyaiagon. The entire village was inebriated for some three days, all participating in the "Ganiary" – running around naked, except for a keg of brandy under one arm! [11] Here, and also at Ganestiquiagon and Ganneious, numerous incidents of violence were recorded. [12] Contacts such as these did little to ease French-Iroquois tensions.

At the fort itself, some progress was being made in clearing the land and making it productive. Father Louis Hennepin was a missionary at the site from 1676 to 1679, and his description of this, the earliest European settlement in the region, is of some interest:

The Ground which lies along the Brink of this Lake is very fertile: In the space of two Years and a half that I resided there in discharge of my *Mission*, they cultivated more than a hundred Acres of it. Both the *Indian* and *European* Corn, Pulse, Pot-Herbs, Gourds, and Water-Melons throve very well. [13]

Hennepin reported that apart from these crops La Salle kept thirty-five head of cattle at his settlement.

But La Salle's interests centred on grander ventures than the prosaic achievements of clearing land and increasing agricultural production. He had four ships constructed in the sheltered waters of the Cataraqui estuary, the largest, the *Griffon*, being a respectable forty tons in size. Armed with cannon, these ships added further weight to the French military presence at Cataraqui; but their primary use was for La Salle's explorations and surveys to the west. Indeed, his preoccupation

with extending the western frontier of New France caused him to neglect his seigneurial duties, and his estates at Cataraqui were seized by Frontenac's successor,
Governor Joseph-Antoine Le Febvre de la Barre, in 1683.

Despite the presence of the much-improved fortifications, this isolated outpost
of French authority was very vulnerable to attack, especially from the Iroquois. Accordingly, in an attempt at resolving the Iroquois threat, in July 1684 La Barre led
a force of 1,100 Troupes de la Marine, Canadian militia, and allied Indians to Fort
Frontenac – only to retreat in disgrace after disease and discontent debilitated his
force.[14] His successor Jacques-René de Brisay, marquis de Denonville, launched
his own campaign, and on 1 July 1687 he reached Fort Frontenac with his force of
832 Troupes de la Marine, 900 Canadian militia, *coureurs de bois*, and allied Indians.[15]
Invited to the fort for peace talks, the north-shore Iroquois were deceived, and fifty
braves and 150 women and children from Quinté and Ganneious were treacherously
taken prisoner.

Not surprisingly, subsequent years witnessed renewed hostilities, and in 1689 the
commandant of the fort withdrew to Montreal. The defence works were abandoned
and destroyed; it was argued that "it would be better that the house be burned and
all the walls thrown down than to learn one day that the enemy are in possession
of it or that the English are settled there."[16] The destruction was far from complete,
however, and Fort Frontenac was reoccupied in 1695, rebuilt as a stone fortification, and reestablished as a French military base. In 1696, Count Frontenac, who
had returned to New France in 1689, mounted an attack on the south-shore Iroquois from the refurbished fort. By that date, the reconstruction was well in hand:

The masons who had been left there had built during the absence of M. le Comte a
building 12 feet [high] along one of the curtain walls which is not as high on that side as
the parapet. The framework is attached there and loopholes run along the attic as in the
rest of the fort. This long building contains a chapel, the lodging of the officers, a
bakehouse, magazines which are now filled with provisions. ...[17]

In 1701, the French and Iroquois negotiated a peace treaty. By this date, the north-
shore settlements had been abandoned and the Iroquois had retreated to the south.
Some of the sites came to be occupied by their successors in the region, Algonquin-
speakers from the north. Increasingly, the lands fronting on Lake Ontario came
to be the resource lands of the Mississauga, albeit still nominally recognized as the
domain of the Iroquois.

FORT FRONTENAC AND THE BRITISH

From 1700 to 1758, Fort Frontenac's new role was that of an element of the line of
fortified centres along the French-British military frontier. A plan of 1740 shows a
considerable fortification. Each of its four corners boasted bastions whose names
were possibly more imposing than the armaments present: Bastion St-Claude

Profile of Fort Frontenac, 1738 (NA)

(southwest), Bastion St-Michel (northwest), Bastion St-Philippe (northeast), and Bastion St-Louis (southeast). Within the walls, the fort was equipped with officers' quarters, a forge, bakery, wells, magazines, stables, ice-houses, and sundry other facilities. And outside the walls were extensive gardens of vegetables and grain, cheek by jowl with the fourteen "cabannes des sauvages," or long-houses of their Indian allies.[18] It was this establishment that played an important role in the Marquis de Montcalm's advance on Oswego by acting as a base for his three-thousand-man expedition in 1756. He was not impressed with what he saw, commenting somewhat sardonically that it was "an ill located fort, which must be preserved because of its existence."[19] One of Montcalm's engineers provides a more detailed critique of the strongpoint, which had been built "contrary to all the rules of fortifications":

The fort has a simple revetement of masonry, with poor foundations of small stones badly set, and the lime is bad; one could easily damage it with a sledge or a pick. The wall is about three to three and a half feet thick at the bottom and two at the top; it has been necessary to build walls for cover. The walls are from 20 to 25 feet high; there are no moats. The trees have been cut down within cannon-shot north and west and about two cannon-shots from the west to the south. ... As for the interior, a wooden scaffold has been built all around except along the north curtain where the commandant's house and chapel are, where the buildings are against the wall. This scaffold is too high; battlements have been let in on a level with the scaffold only eight inches high, which makes them useless. There are two openings for cannons on certain faces of the bastions and one on the flanks. There are some places where the scaffold and even the wall would not stand cannon-fire long.[20]

With the departure of Montcalm's force, the fort's standing garrison was as modest as were its defences. A skeleton force of only fifty men under the command of Sieur Payen de Noyan et de Chavoy, a sixty-three-year-old officer of the Colonials, was left to face the British.[21]

On 13 July 1758, Lieutenant-Colonel John Bradstreet had been directed by General James Abercromby, the British commander-in-chief in North America, to "attempt the reduction of Fort Frontenac, and destroy the Shipping at Cataraqui. ..."[22] Bradstreet's force of some 3,100 troops comprised, for the most part, colonial levies, and they did not impress him. He complained that "Sickness, Discontent, Disertion [sic], Reluctance and want of Spirit ... hath prevail'd throughout the whole of the Provincial Troops ordered to serve this way, except the Yorkers."[23] By 21 August Bradstreet arrived at Oswego, and the next day his force embarked for Fort Frontenac in a motley fleet of 123 batteaux and 95 whaleboats.[24] Bradstreet did not sight his objective until 25 August, and commenced landing his artillery and reconnoitering the terrain around the fort.[25] Bradstreet's artillery was positioned within 150 metres of the fort; shelling commenced against the fragile defences, and the British

threw a number of shells into the fort, with great success; they did considerable damage to the inner part; one burst near the magazine, and fired a quantity of gunpowder, which scorchid [sic] some of the Indians almost to death, and greatly intimidated the garrison.[26]

On 27 August 1758 de Noyan surrendered his garrison of fifty men and some sixty dependants.[27]

The significance of the settlement at the time of its capture may be measured by the estimates of the personnel and the quantities of materials captured and destroyed:

It was a square Fort of 100 Yards the exterior side, and had in it 110 Men, some Women, Children and Indians; sixty Pieces of Cannon Small Mortars; with an Immense Quantity of Provisions and Goods, to be sent to the Troops gone to oppose Brigadier General Forbes, their Western Garrisons, Indians. We have likewise taken 9 Vessels from 8 to 18 Guns, which is all they have up on the Lake. ...[28]

The British force burned provisions, vessels, crops, and buildings and demolished the walls of the fort. Bradstreet estimated that his force had destroyed provisions valued at some £35,000,[29] while plunder shared by the force included 178 hats laced with silver and gold, 33 pieces of gold lace, 16 pieces of silver lace, 3,690 men's shirts, 1,978 woollen caps, and "a great variety of other clothing."[30]

With a 1,300-man French relief force en route to Cataraqui from Lachine, Bradstreet sent his prisoners on their way, reembarked his force on 28 August, and, after

The London Gazette
EXTRAORDINARY.

Published by Authority.

TUESDAY, *October* 31, 1758.

Whitehall, October 31.

YESTERDAY a Mail arrived from New York, with Letters from Major General Abercromby to the Right Honourable Mr. Secretary Pitt, dated from the Camp at Lake George the 8th and 10th paſt, giving an Account, That Lieutenant Colonel Bradſtreet, having propoſed a Plan againſt Cadaraqui or Fort Frontenac, had been detached to make an Attempt on that Place, with a Body of Men conſiſting of 154 Regulars, 2491 Provincials, 27 of the Royal Regiment of Artillery, 61 Rangers, 300 Batteau-Men, and 70 Indians, in all 3103 Men, including Officers : And the following Copy of a Letter from Colonel Bradſtreet to Major General Abercromby, dated Oſwego, Auguſt 31, contains the Account of his Succeſs in that very difficult and moſt important Enterprize.

" I Landed with the Troops within a " Mile of Fort Frontenac, without " Oppoſition, the 25th : The Garriſon " ſurrendered Priſoners of War the 27th, " between Seven and Eight in the Morn-

" ing.—It was a ſquare Fort of 100 Yards " the exterior Side, and had in it 110 " Men, ſome Women, Children, and " Indians; fixty Pieces of Cannon, " (Half of which was mounted ;) Sixteen " ſmall Mortars ; with an immenſe Quan-" tity of Proviſions and Goods, to be " ſent to the Troops gone to oppoſe " Brigadier General Forbes, their Weſtern " Garriſons, Indians, and to ſupport the " Army under the Command of M. " Levy, on his intended Enterprize " againſt the Mohawk River, valued by " the French at 800,000 Livres.—We " have likewiſe taken 9 Veſſels from 8 to " 18 Guns, which is all they have upon " the Lake, two of which I have brought " here ; one richly laden ; and the reſt " and the Proviſions I have burnt and " deſtroyed, together with the Fort, Ar-" tillery, Stores, &c. agreeable to your " Excellency's Inſtructions, ſhould I ſuc-" ceed. The Garriſon made no Scruple " of ſaying, that their Troops to the " Southward and Weſtern Garriſons will " ſuffer greatly, if not entirely ſtarve, " for Want of the Proviſions and Veſſels " we have deſtroyed, as they have not " any left to bring them Home from " Niagara.

" The Terms on which the Garriſon " ſurrendered were Priſoners of War, un-" til exchanged for equal Numbers and " Rank."

(Price Two-pence Half-penny.)

Printed by *E. Owen* and *T. Harriſon* in *Warwick Lane.* 1758.

The London *Gazette* announces the fall of Fort Frontenac, 1758. (QUA)

camping on an island opposite the fort, was back in Oswego by 30 August 1758. Later in the same year, a more portentous battle was fought on the Plains of Abraham, and the defeat of the French under Montcalm by General Wolfe marked the end of a major French colonial presence in North America. With the formal recognition of this *fait accompli* by the Treaty of Paris in 1763, New France, and with it the now-abandoned outpost of Cataraqui, became part of the colony of Quebec in British North America.

Despite much commercial, spiritual, and military enterprise throughout the general region, the French left little evidence of their presence. Their numbers were always few and no French settlers remained after the British conquest. Although the French had been present for the better part of a century, only a few hundred acres were ever effectively occupied, and even at that their settlement was interrupted from time to time. Apart from a few place-names and relics of military activity at Fort Frontenac, the contemporary landscape has little to show of the French period of occupancy and control. Indeed, for some scholars, the fort and settlement at Cataraqui were anachronistic:

the outpost proclaimed the French presence but most of the fur traders, missionaries and explorers passed it by, often following other routes west and north. In the immediate region, the fort also proved ineffective. It was the site of a minor mission and an unsuccessful seigneury, and was soon neutralized by the Iroquois who merely avoided it sending their brigades around the western end of Lake Ontario.[31]

But the simple recognition and use of the site by the French was important to the eventual history of Kingston: they constituted the first stage in what was to become continuous European settlement. The British military's knowledge of the five hundred acres of land cleared by the French at Cataraqui, and of its suitability for settlement, occasioned its survey and eventual preparation for settlement by the Loyalists in the following period of development. Rather than entering a wilderness, the Loyalists were occupying a site that had already experienced nearly a century of European presence, however sporadic.

TWO

"A Poor Happy People":
Establishing Loyalist Kingston

ORGANIZING A NEW COLONY

In 1783 the site of the former French fort at Cataraqui was selected for the establishment of a town to be the centre of the region that was to receive a small minority of the displaced Loyalists from the former American colonies. For some twenty years following the defeat of the French, British occupation of the area had been nominal only, although the naval base at Carleton Island, located about ten miles to the southeast, on the south side of Wolfe Island, had witnessed some considerable military activity. The arrival of military surveyors in 1783 was the overture to a process of developing a permanent settlement, a settlement to accommodate displaced Loyalists and a naval base to replace Carleton Island, which by then had been ceded to the Americans.

In 1783 General Sir Frederick Haldimand, governor-in-chief of the Province of Quebec, addressed himself to the problem of establishing settlements along the St Lawrence and Bay of Quinte for Loyalist settlers moving into the region. He originally conceived of the site as a location for resettling loyal Mohawk Indians, and in May 1783 he directed Major Samuel Holland, surveyor-general of Quebec, to "proceed to Cataraqui; where you will minutely examine the situation and site of the Post formerly occupied by the French, and the land and country adjacent; considering the facility for establishing settlements."[1] Holland travelled from Carleton Island to the proposed site at Cataraqui, which "in every part surpassed the favorable idea I had formed of it."[2] His report went on to detail the "advantageous Situations" of the site:

The Vaults still remain entire with part of the Walls of the Fort, Barrack etc. etc. are in such a State as will contribute to lessen the expence of its reistablishment [*sic*], the Works or Lines began by the French on the Commanding grounds near the Fort, will cover a Sufficient space for a Town: the harbour is in every respect Good and most conveniently situated to command Lake Ontario.[3]

On 30 June 1783 Major John Ross was appointed to the command of the proposed "Post at Cataraqui, on the North side of Lake Ontario" and was ordered to "Repair thither, with all convenient speed, taking along with you, all the Troops & Artificers of your present Garrison of Oswego [and] such stores, planks &c from thence, as may be usefull [sic] at Cataraqui."[4] He was to be joined there by the garrison retreating from Oswegatchie (Fort La Galette; later, Ogdensburg). Ross had some previous experience of the task before him, having been complimented by Haldimand for the "Rapid Establishment of the Post" at Oswego, and on 30 July 1783 he arrived to commence the works at Cataraqui.[5] His force consisted of twenty-five officers and 422 men, the detachments being drawn from no fewer than four regiments of the line, the Royal Artillery, and the King's Royal Regiment of New York.[6]

Before the British could organize the land for settlement, however, some accommodation had to be made with the Indians who laid claim to the region as part of their traditional domain. Originally the domain of the Iroquois, the Cataraqui back country had witnessed the gradual penetration of newcomers from the north during the eighteenth century. But rather than displace one cultural system by another, the newcomers occupied their new lands only at the pleasure of the Iroquois. Thus, a prudent treaty of this period between the Iroquois and Mississauga was recorded by an English fur-trader from New York:

We have come to acquaint you that we are settled on Ye North side of Cadarachqui Lake near Tchojachiage [Teyaiagon] where we plant a tree of peace and open a path for all people, quite to Corlaer's house [house of the English Governor] and desire to be united in Ye Covenant Chain, our hunting places to be one; and because the path to Corlaer's house may be open and clear, doe give a drest elke skin to cover Ye path to walke upon.[7]

By 1700 the Mississauga had moved to the south and southeast of Lake Huron and Lake Simcoe, and were soon well established along the north shore of Lake Ontario. Pierre Charlevoix encountered them at Cataraqui in the early 1700s and reported that they had brethren at three other locations throughout Ontario.[8] Major Robert Rogers describes two parties of Mississauga along the Bay of Quinte in 1769. Rogers camped at the mouth of the Moira River "and found about 50 Mississauga Indians fishing for salmon"; and the next day, some fifteen miles to the southwest, at another river called the "Life of Man," Rogers' party met with another thirty Mississauga "who were hunting there."[9]

The British decision to occupy the former French site at Cataraqui, and to develop it as an agricultural settlement for the thousands of Loyalists waiting to be assigned lands, required some form of arrangement with the Mississauga. In July 1783 there was concern that "the Missisagys seemed displeased at our taking Possession of Fort Frontenac."[10] By 2 October, Ross reported that the "Indians have

Cataraqui or Mississauga Indians, sketched by James Peachey, 1784, (NA)

not as yet been advised. ... I am doubtfull [*sic*] they will make more difficulty than Sir John Johnson imagines but still I hope of no great moment or importance – I have had no Rum to give them since my arrival to which they are absolutely devoted."[11] A week later Ross communicated to Haldimand from Cataraqui that the

Indians are collected at the Island [Carleton] for the Purpose of Purchasing their Land. I hope it will be easily accomplish'd but I take the liberty to say that (as this place [Cataraqui] is by far the greatest Resort of the Indians) if Sir John Johnson had placed the Officer of their [Indian] Department here instead of the Island, it would have pleas'd them more.[12]

This problem was resolved by the signing of the Crawford Purchase, or "Gunshot Treaty," of 9 October 1783. But the precise extent of the territory referred to by this agreement was vague. According to Captain William Crawford's correspondence, the Mississauga had relinquished title to all the lands from Toniata or Ongara River to a river in the Bay of Quinte within eight leagues of the bottom of the said Bay including all the Islands extending from the lake as far back as a man can travel in a day, the Chiefs claiming the land at the bottom of the Bay could not be got together at the present. I believe their land can be got nearly on the same terms.[13]

The Mississauga recollection of the terms of the "Gunshot Treaty," however, was that they had surrendered their rights to an area determined by how far the sound of a gunshot could be heard. (The musket of the day was notable for its production of as much noise as smoke!) Despite the confusion over the interpretation of these descriptive but vague designations, the actual extent of land severed from Mississauga control and organized for the resettlement of the Loyalists extended from the vicinity of Gananoque in the east to the Trent River in the west, and approximately thirty miles into the interior. In return, the Mississauga received gifts, but no guarantee of a perpetual annuity:

The consideration demanded by the chiefs for the land granted is that all the families belonging to them shall be clothed and that those that have not fusees shall receive new ones, some powder and ball for their winter hunting, as much coarse red cloth as will make about a dozen coats and as many lace hats.[14]

A "Requisition for Presents Proposed for the Mississagas and Indians Near and About Kingston for the year 1796" was even more comprehensive. An inventory of goods worth £118 11s 4d included not only the ubiquitous pairs of blankets but also a veritable check-list of contemporary textiles including "Cloth Broad," "Callico," "Callimanco," "Cadies," "Linnen," "Molton," "Pennirtons," "Serge Embossed," and "Strouds." The Indian Agency largesse also included a miscellany of ivory combs, gartering, guns, powder, shot, hoes, kettles, butcher knives, looking-glasses (mirrors), cod-lines, mackerel-lines, needles, shoes, vermillion, and tobacco.[15]

Subsequent transfers were of a more pecuniary nature. In 1816 the Mississauga ceded their title to some 428 acres at the mouth of the Moira River for £107 and an annuity of five shillings.[16] Three years later a further 2,748,000 acres were acquired from the Mississauga – an area that was subsequently surveyed into no fewer than forty-six townships. By this treaty, an annuity worth £642 10s 0d was to be paid in kind to the 159 Indians in the Bay of Quinte area and the ninety-eight "Kingston Mississauga."[17] Dispossessed of their lands throughout Kingston's back country as far north as the Ottawa River, the majority of the Mississauga moved to the Bay of Quinte *en route* to their ultimate destination, a reservation in Alnwick Township. But others appear to have claimed lands in Bedford Township, and for many years some Mississauga continued to pursue their traditional subsistence economy throughout the as-yet-unorganized back country.

With the Indians' claim to the site resolved, settlement could proceed. Certainly, the surrounding lands appeared to be conducive to settlement, and on 14 October spy-master-turned-surveyor Justus Sherwood reported from Cataraqui that "I think the Loyalists may be the happiest people in America by settling this country from Long Sou to Bay Quinty [sic]."[18] John Collins, Holland's deputy, echoed this opinion in his laudatory report on the lands of the adjacent Kingston Township, which he had surveyed on 27 October 1783:

[The] greater part of which appear to be of an Excellent Quality fit for the production of Wheat, Oats, Indian Corn, Hemp, Timothy and Clover. The Woods in general are Maple, Bass, Hickory, Ash, Elm, Pine and White Oak etc., the two latter are in many parts from two and a half to three feet Diameter.

This Township hath great advantage on account of its Situation, having Lake Ontario on its front – all the Small Bays afford good Harbours for Boats and the lake abounds with great Variety of Excellent Fish and Wild Fowl, the little River Cataraqui is navigable for Batteaux from its Entrance into the Lake to the upper bountary [sic] of the Township in which space are many proper stations for erecting Mills.[19]

With a good harbour, a townsite, and productive lands nearby, Cataraqui seemed an ideal site at which to relocate the Loyalists.

The basic conceptualization of the townsite had not waited on the negotiations with the Mississauga. As early as July 1783 Holland sent a sketch of the proposed plan to Haldimand, having taken "the Liberty to adopt names to the several Places." His original plan called for a town and fortifications on Point Frederick, arguing also that "a common for the feeding of the Cattle of a Town is of the greatest benefit to its Inhabitants."[20] Ross demurred at this, however, arguing that Point Henry would be a more suitable location.[21] In October 1783 Deputy Surveyor-General John Collins surveyed the farm lots for the first township to the west of the Great Cataraqui, and, in November, a townsite was surveyed by Lieutenant John Frederick Holland – also on the west bank of the Cataraqui.[22] The decision to abandon the east shore was probably influenced by the Collins survey, the suitability of the terrain for laying out a town, the existence of a clearing established by the former French settlement, and proximity to a good harbour. More importantly, the decision had already been anticipated. Robert Hamilton and Peter Clark (merchants), John Howell (sutler), and Lieutenants John Howard and Oliver Church had established themselves at the site of the ruined French fort.[23] By the following year the site had been transmuted from cadastral concept to an actual, albeit nascent, community. Three buildings had been floated across from the abandoned naval base on Carleton Island, and work had commenced on a wharf, a saw mill, a grist mill, and a navy store. More importantly, Joseph Forsyth and Richard Cartwright, merchants involved in the infant forwarding trade, had also recognized the importance of the new site and moved to the post at Cataraqui.

These various facilities were well enough established to be included in James Peachey's view of the post in 1784, at the time of the arrival of the Loyalists. Guy Carleton had reported to Haldimand in July 1783 that Loyalists wishing to travel to Fort Frontenac had been organized into eight companies of militia. The second company of some 106 men, women, and children was under the command of Captain Michael Grass who, having been a prisoner of the French at Fort Frontenac, claimed some prior knowledge of the district.[24] By the winter of 1783, an advance party of seventeen men from Grass's company had arrived at Cataraqui. These, together with the merchants from Carleton Island, and the men of the King's Royal Regiment of New York and their dependants who were preparing the site with Ross, constituted the first Loyalist contingent.[25]

Throughout the summer of 1784, settlers moved through Cataraqui, on their way to their promised lands. By 9 October 1784 the muster of "disbanded troops and Loyalists settled in Township No 1 Cataraqui" could report a population of 220 (93 men, 42 women, 43 boys, 37 girls, and 5 servants), with some eighty-six acres cleared.[26] Settlement proceeded apace in the other four Cataraqui townships. Fortunately for the limited reception facilities at Cataraqui, the thousands of new arrivals were rapidly distributed throughout the concessions and lots of the adjoining townships, and the population at the townsite quickly dropped to about four hundred people. By the end of 1784 this small nucleus served as the administrative and economic centre for the 3,776 settlers distributed along the shores of the Bay of Quinte.

However, the process of locating the settlers on the land was to prove to be more problematic than the conceptualizing of the new colony on paper. Collins reported in August 1784 that he had administered oaths to the disbanded British and German troops who had drawn their lots for land, received certificates for their new properties, and appeared to be "well pleased" with them.[27] He was not unaware of the problems facing his new charges and observed that "the poor people have set themselves down half a dozen together in different parts of the Townships not knowing where to find their Lots, except those in the front, nor can it be expected until the several lines between the different Concessions be drawn and Boundaries fixed."[28] Not surprisingly, Collins could not stop himself from expressing his longing to bring this "troublesome business to as speedy a conclusion as possible."[29] A year later, the Loyalist settlers were found to be

extremely well satisfied with their present Situation and have made much greater Improvements than could be expected in so short a time, they have all Comfortable Houses and their cleared Lands sown with different Kinds of Grain, all those that received more grain than they could make use of in their own Lands have lent the overplus to their Neighbours and are to be paid in the Fall of the Year. The only complaint at present is the want of Grist Mills which should be Provided for against the Spring when they will be much wanted.[30]

Another problem continued to be the unmarked – even if surveyed – lots, but it was noticed that "as the New Settlers are too much occupied in improving their Home Lots, few or none of them are pressing to have their land laid out at present."[31]

Writing to Lord North, secretary of state for the Home Department at the end of 1783, Haldimand reported on the routine details of the resettlement project and also imparted his sense of mission in thus preparing an "Asylum from the Tyranny and Oppression" to the south.[32] He was optimistic for the future of the new colony:

> I foresee great advantages from this Settlement. The Six Nations wish it, the Royalists settled together in numbers will form a respectable Body, attached to the Interests of Great Britain & capable of being useful upon many Occasions. Their Industry will in a very few years raise in that Fertile Tract of Country great Quantities of Wheat and other Grains and become a Granary for the Lower Parts of Canada.[33]

At the end of 1784, Haldimand left for Britain declaring that "Nothing further remains to be done for them in a military line, and as inhabitants of the province they come under the Immediate protection of the civil power, except in such cases where further occasional reliefs may become necessary."[34] The transplanting of a Royalist and Loyalist culture into the northwestern limits of what was left of British North America had been achieved.

THE LOYALISTS

Kingston has long been known as a major Loyalist centre, and the history of the town cannot really be understood without some knowledge of the origins and nature of the United Empire Loyalists.[35] They have often been romanticized as the educated, cultured, wealthy, and civilized upper echelons of American society, who rejected the American Revolution and remained loyal to King George III because of high principles combined with honour. Some Loyalists met these elevated criteria, but for most the reality was grimmer and far more complex.

Perhaps the most basic single characteristic of the Loyalists is that they were the losers in a civil war. The American Revolution was not merely a conflict between colonists and Britain. It was also a conflict between Americans who differed about the future of the Thirteen Colonies and Britain's role in that future. The Loyalists supported the Crown, and they lost. There is no single explanation for their royalism. Some were idealists; others enjoyed British patronage. Some simply adhered to a prominent leader who opted for loyalty; others were caught in a loyal community and had no option but to conform to majority opinion. There were Anglican priests who remained loyal because it was their duty to pray for the king. Some minority groups – Palatine Germans and Quakers, for example – supported the Crown because the Crown had respected their desire to pursue their distinctive ways of life. Numerous Indians remained loyal because of their traditional alliance with the British and because they knew that they would be dispossessed of their lands if the American settlers were triumphant.

Whatever their reasons for loyalty, these people shared a common fate: they lost the war and were forced either to conform to the wishes of the victors (should they be so permitted) or to become refugees and find new homes.

It is obviously difficult to know how many Americans remained loyal to George III during the Revolution. Many maintained a low profile and simply blended into post-revolutionary society. However, it is known that between 80,000 and 100,000 Loyalists left the United States. Some 45,000 went to the British North American maritime colonies, while about 9,500 emigrated to Quebec. Of this latter group approximately 7,500 settled in what was to become Ontario.

At a later date these Ontario Loyalists were able to submit claims for losses. By studying these claims (along with other evidence) scholars have been able to paint a portrait of this group that founded both Ontario *and* Kingston. Some 90 per cent were "pioneer farmers."[36] Roughly 80 per cent came from two New York counties – Tryon and Albany. In addition to the farmers, there was a handful of shopkeepers and artisans. The Ontario Loyalists could boast of a single medical doctor, and only "five ... had held public office, three in relatively modest positions. ..."[37]

Ethnically the group was hardly homogeneous, including as it did Germans, Irish, Gaelic-speaking Highlanders, blacks (most of whom were slaves), and Indians. Roughly half were Scots and 8 per cent were "English by birth."[38] A very large percentage of the Loyalists had emigrated to America shortly before the Revolution. The Loyalists were no more homogeneous religiously. The group included Baptists, Quakers, Mennonites, Tunkers, Roman Catholics, Lutherans, and Methodists. Anglicans were there, too, but in spite of the prominence of many Anglican leaders, they were a distinct minority.

It should not be assumed that the Loyalists, in spite of their general frontier and humble origins, were docile and deferential. They saw themselves as British citizens with the rights and privileges that accompanied that status. They expected to hold land in the British way, and they assumed that they would in due course be provided with British law and British political institutions. They also wanted adequate educational facilities and a societal infrastructure that would enable them to function in a frontier land. And, of course, while most Loyalists had been far from rich in the United States, many had owned land and other property. They had lost that: the revolutionaries had confiscated their lands and goods. They wanted the British to compensate them for their losses.

A substantial percentage of Loyalists bound for Canada left the United States by ship from New York. It goes without saying that these often-destitute people, who had lost everything – including their country – were angry and filled with despair. But they had a case to press, and they were vigorous in demanding compensation, free land, and aid. Larry Turner comments: "The migration was burdensome and disturbing. Refugees were bitter, resentful and suspicious. To the

Loyalists, the authorities were rigid in their demeanor and insensitive to their sacrifice. The authorities saw the Loyalists as stubborn and demanding."[39] Their campaign for aid and compensation was highly successful:

Historians have calculated Great Britain had spent £1 million start up costs in Upper Canada by 1787, not including the disbursement of free lands and that the grand total for all expenditures on Loyalists, including compensation, was a phenomenal £30 million! Many people have benefited from the spoils after winning a war, but no people in history ever did so well by losing one.[40]

As the major Loyalist centre in Ontario, Kingston and the adjacent districts derived substantial benefit from this British largesse. Kingston's intimate relationship with the public purse is clearly as old as the city.

The Loyalist phenomenon of the eighteenth century was enormously complicated, but Bruce Wilson, a recent historian of Ontario's Loyalists, has presented some sensible and defensible conclusions:

They were the founding group in our province; its political, social, religious and economic systems were put in place to meet the needs and desires of those who wished to continue to live under the crown, the Loyalists. ... Without them, there probably would not have been a Canada. ... If we owe our geography to the Loyalists, we also owe to them our political tradition of "evolution" rather than "revolution," our ideal of steady progression towards constitutional democracy. Likewise, in their diversity and heterogeneity we can find one origin of our "tossed salad" society with its stress on pluralism and tolerance, as opposed to the American "melting pot."[41]

Given the hundreds of Loyalists who settled in Kingston during the eighteenth century, it would be invidious to focus on a small handful of individuals. At the same time, a discussion of a limited number of people can illustrate several aspects of the Loyalist experience and explain some of the manifold ways in which Loyalists made their mark on Kingston. Four have been selected: Michael Grass, Molly Brant, the Reverend John Stuart, and the Honourable Richard Cartwright.

MICHAEL GRASS was "hard-nosed, strong-willed and suspicious of those who fomented change."[42] He was born about 1735 in Strasbourg, the chief city of Alsace, which has been a province of both France and Germany. Ethnically, Grass was a Palatinate German who, with many of his fellows, emigrated to America. In 1752 he settled in Philadelphia, where he worked as a saddler. Subsequently he moved to New York City and then to Tryon County in New York, a huge county that bordered on the upper St Lawrence and included a substantial stretch of the Mohawk River. Tryon County, which became a Loyalist centre, attracted a large number of Palatine Germans. Grass continued his vocation of saddler and in addition became a farmer.

There is little evidence concerning Grass's life before the Revolution, but there is some "oral history and folklore of succeeding generations. ..."[43] According to this kind of evidence, Michael Grass served the British during the Seven Years War, was captured by the French, and was held prisoner at Fort Frontenac in 1756 or 1757. As we have seen, it has been claimed that this imprisonment made Grass aware of the potential of the Kingston area, and convinced him in the 1780s that Cataraqui was the ideal settlement place for the Loyalists. Unfortunately no hard evidence exists to place Grass at Fort Frontenac in the 1750s.[44]

However, we do know that he became a militia captain and remained loyal to the Crown at the outbreak of revolution. Tryon County became unsafe for the loyal Grass, and he moved to the safer Loyalist centre, New York City, in 1777. As a result, his farm, valued at £1,200, was confiscated and sold. For the remainder of the war Grass was in New York, where he served as a lieutenant in Company 39, New York City Militia.

The bulk of the Loyalists who emigrated from New York City went either to Nova Scotia or to the territory that was to become New Brunswick. Michael Grass rejected this plan and "for reasons unknown... explored the possibility of going to Fort Frontenac and anticipated that others would join him."[45] He announced his decision in the *Royal American Gazette*, 27 May 1783:

Those Loyalists who have had a meeting at the house of Michael Grass ... & have signed their names to form a settlement on Fort Frontenac. ... The only eligible place left by the late treaty for the King's subjects, to carry on the Indian & fur trade, etc. are hereby notified, that their request has been communicated to his Excellency the Commander in Chief ... & that his Excellency was pleased to give them the encouragement they desired. A list of the names of those who may be inclined to settle in this new country, is opened at the house of the said Mr. Grass, in Chatham Street, near the Tea-Water Pump, New York.[46]

His Excellency Sir Guy Carleton (the future Lord Dorchester) pressed the scheme on a very reluctant Sir Frederick Haldimand, the governor of Quebec. Haldimand, who opposed settlement in the interior, finally agreed, and Grass's plan went forward.

Grass was given charge of a company of intending settlers, and he and his people left New York in July 1783, arriving at Sorel on 12 August 1783. The Loyalists wintered there. Grass proceeded to Cataraqui, where he left a group of men to prepare for the arrival of the main body of Loyalists in 1784.

Grass and his fellow-officers petitioned Governor Haldimand in January 1784, in a remarkable and revealing document. At the material level the captains asked for massive aid of every sort. They demanded building supplies, farming equipment, tools, seeds, livestock, arms, ammunition, blacksmiths, teachers, clergymen, and transportation. They specified the lands they wanted. Moreover, they explained in reasonably precise terms their political and constitutional vision of Cataraqui:

And in as much as the said Associated Companies have for years past nobly contended for the support of that Constitution or Form of Government under which they have long enjoyed Happiness, & for which they have at last sacrificed their All, Tis therefore their Earnest Wish & desire that his Excellency for their Better Government & Good order when they arrive at the Place destined for their Settlement would be Pleased to Establish among them, a Form of Government as nearly similar to that which they Enjoyed in the Province of New York in the year of 1763 as the Remote situation of their new settlement from the seat of Government here will at present Admitt of And that Persons Chosen of their own Body be appointed & vested with Power before their departure from hence to carry the same into Execution when there. [47]

Clearly Governor Haldimand had had enough of Loyalist demands and unhappiness. His reply was singularly testy. He concluded,

If His Excellency's endeavours for the happy settlement of the Loyalists ... do not suit the views of Mr. Grass and the other Loyalists in Question, He is pleased to desire Sir, that you will acquaint them that a passage will be provided for them to Nova Scotia as early as the season will permit. ...[48]

Grass had depleted his credit with the administration of the Province of Quebec, and thereafter was in eclipse. Of the one thousand Loyalists who left New York with him in 1783, only some fifty families made it to Cataraqui during the summer of 1784. They settled in the first township and thereby became charter members of the Kingston community.

Haldimand continued to find Grass to be a problem and was convinced that the Loyalist leader claimed to have much more control at Cataraqui than was the case. Grass was forced to apologize but "maintained that he did not presume to take the claim as founder himself but only meant that he was the first of the Loyalists who before they left New York, pointed out [Cataraqui] as the most desirable place to go."[49]

Grass lived quietly in Kingston until he died in 1813. For a brief period he served as a magistrate, but he never gained much prominence in the town he helped to found. Michael Grass published a letter in the Kingston *Gazette* in 1811. It could well serve as his epitaph. He referred to his creative years and said "strong in my attachment to my fellow subjects, I led the loyal band, I pointed out to them the scite [*sic*] of their future metropolis, and gained for persecuted principles a sanctuary[,] for myself and followers a home."[50]

MOLLY BRANT had, as her Mohawk name, Konwatsitsiaienne, which means "someone lends her a flower."[51] She was born about 1736 into a Mohawk "Family of Distinction."[52] Molly Brant's younger brother was the powerful and famous Mohawk chief Thayendanegea, known to Canadians as Joseph Brant. Her father, an important chief, attended the Court of St James and was received by Queen Anne in 1710.

It is unknown whether she officially married Sir William Johnson, the superintendent of Indian Affairs for the Province of New York. Certainly, she lived with Johnson as his wife from 1759 until his death in 1774, and she has been referred to as his wife and as his consort. In his will Sir William described her as his "prudent and faithful Housekeeper."[53] They had numerous children, eight of whom survived infancy. As was the custom among Mohawk nations, Molly Brant retained her maiden name during and after her liaison with Johnson.

Sir William Johnson was one of the most influential men in British America. He occupied an all-important place in Anglo-Indian diplomacy and was able to exercise substantial authority over Britain's Indian allies. Johnson was also a businessman and landowner. He was enormously wealthy: Sir William and Molly Brant lived on an estate of some 130,000 acres in the Mohawk country in upstate New York.[54]

Sir William died on the eve of the Revolution, leaving Molly Brant in a comfortable situation. She was left a house, some additional property, a black slave, and £200. She used her money to set herself up as a trader with the Indians. A description by an Englishwoman makes it clear that Molly Brant was a striking presence: "Her features are fine and beautiful; her complexion clear and olive-tinted. ... She was quiet in demeanor, on occasion, and possessed of a calm dignity that bespoke native pride and consciousness of power. She seldom imposed herself into the picture, but no one was in her presence without being aware of her."[55]

Molly Brant's importance escalated with the outbreak of revolution. She was the "head of the Six Nations matrons" and as such was a major leader of the Six Nations.[56] These Indians were central to British military operations on the frontier during the Revolutionary War. Molly Brant had tremendous authority among them. There was never any doubt about how that authority would be exercised: she was instinctively and immediately loyal to the British Crown.

As early as 1777 she supplied intelligence to the British that enabled a group of Indians and Loyalists to secure a victory over the rebels near Fort Stanwix. Her loyalty was known to the revolutionaries, and she suffered harassment and lost her property. She was forced to move, first to Onondaga, then to Cayuga, and in the fall of 1777 to Niagara. There she worked effectively to keep the Indians loyal to the British cause. A senior British official, Daniel Claus, described her influence: "one word from her goes farther with [the Iroquois] than a thousand from any white Man without Exception. ..."[57]

In 1779 she moved again, this time to Carleton Island. Again she played a key role in keeping the Indian warriors gathered there quiet and loyal to the British. The British commander on Carleton Island referred to "Molly Brant's influence, which is far superior to that of all their chiefs put together."[58] Her final move came in 1783 when she moved to Kingston, where she lived until her death on 16 April 1796.

A recent biographer of Molly Brant concluded that "Unquestionably she was one of the most devoted United Empire Loyalists."[59] British authorities recognized her devotion and value. She had lost her property during the Revolution, and quite properly received compensation. Haldimand awarded her a not-inconsiderable pension of £100 per year. She was also granted land at Niagara, Fredericksburgh, and Kingston. The British military built houses for both Molly and Joseph in Kingston: "The site of the two houses was near the Cataraqui on land [later] occupied by Anglin's Lumber Yard. Both have long since been torn down and not even the foundation stones remain to mark their place."[60]

Molly Brant was a devoted Anglican and was the only woman among the fifty-four benefactors who contributed money for the erection of the first St George's Church.[61] She was regular in her attendance at church, where she was described by a traveller shortly before she died:

In the church at Kingston, we saw an Indian woman, who sat in an honourable place among the English. She appeared very devout during Divine Service and very attentive to the sermon. She was the relict of the late Sir William Johnson ... and mother of several children by him, who are married to Englishmen and provided for by the Crown. When Indian embassies arrived, she was sent for, dined at Governor Simcoe's and treated with respect by himself and his lady. During the life of Sir William, she was attended with splendor and respect and since the war, received a pension and compensation for losses for herself and her children.[62]

JOHN STUART, who was (unusual for his day) well over six feet tall, was jokingly dubbed "the *little* Gentleman" by Charles Inglis, who became the first Anglican bishop of Nova Scotia.[63]

Stuart was born near Harrisburg, Pennsylvania, in 1740 or 1741. He married Jane Okill there in 1775; they had eight children. Stuart attended the College of Philadelphia where he obtained a BA degree (1763) and an MA degree (1770). He converted from Presbyterian to Anglicanism, and in August 1770 the bishop of London ordained him first deacon, and later priest. The Reverend John Stuart then received an appointment from the Society for the Propagation of the Gospel; he was assigned to Fort Hunter, New York, where he became missionary to the Mohawks. Stuart was "a missionary of almost boundless energy," one who concerned himself with most aspects of the spiritual and physical needs of his congregation.[64] Among his other achievements Stuart, in collaboration with Joseph Brant, translated St Mark's gospel into the Mohawk dialect. The work was published in 1787.

Stuart was not particularly inclined to politics and displayed no great interest in the events that led to revolution. But he was an Anglican priest and remained loyal to the Crown. The revolutionaries suspected him and turned on him. He was nearly arrested in 1777, saved only by Joseph Brant and his troops. Then his house was looted, his property (worth some £1,200) confiscated, and his church occupied and desecrated. Stuart described the fate of his church:

I cannot omit to mention that my Church was plundered by the Rebels, & the Pulpit Cloth taken away from the Pulpit; – it was afterwards imployed [sic] as a Tavern, the Barrel of Rum placed in the Reading Desk. – the succeeding Season it was used for a Stable; – And now [1781] serves as a Fort to protect a Set of as great Villains as ever disgraced Humanity.[65]

Finally, in 1781, Stuart was given permission to leave the United States. In October of that year he went to Canada, where he settled at Montreal with his wife, children, and black slaves.

Montreal had its attractions, but John Stuart wanted a secure position and land. Hence, in December 1783, he petitioned Governor Haldimand:

As your Memorialist has been informed that a Garrison is established & a Colony of Loyalists intended to be settled at Cataraqui; He humbly presumes that ... he will be thought a proper Person to reside there as a Clergyman. ... Your Memorialist therefore humbly begs ... That he may be appointed Chaplain to the Garrison of Cataraqui, with the same Allowances & privileges as are enjoyed by the Chaplains of the Garrisons of Quebec & Montreal. And that your Memorialist may have his Proportion of Land assigned to him contiguous to that Garrison. ...[66]

Stuart was successful, receiving his appointment in 1784. He paid a scouting visit to Kingston later in 1784 and settled there permanently with his family in August 1785. He was delighted that he "found every thing agreeable to, and even beyond any Expectation the Situation pleasant, the Climate wholesome, and what was still more flattering, the People expressing, unanimously, their Wishes that I wou'd [sic] settle among them. ..."[67]

Clerical responsibilities required immediate attention. Stuart visited the neighbouring Mohawks and dealt with the spiritual needs of his fellow-Kingstonians. He was the only clergyman in town, and his flock consisted of Christians of a variety of hues. His first church was a room in the garrison above the mess. It was for use by both troops and townspeople. This woefully inadequate space sufficed for seven years, until the first St George's Church was available for use in 1792. Bishop Mountain described St George's as it was in 1813: "The church is a long, low, blue, wooden

Reverend John Stuart, rector of St George's Church and founder of Anglicanism in Upper Canada (Ontario). (QUA)

building, with square windows, and a little cupola or steeple, for the bell, like the thing on a brewery placed at the wrong end of the building."[68] Stuart was a dedicated and loving clergyman whose contribution to Anglicanism was well recognized. Lieutenant-Governor Simcoe appointed him chaplain to the Legislative Council in 1792, and in 1799 his *alma mater*, the College of Philadelphia, awarded him an honorary doctorate of divinity. The Reverend Doctor John Stuart was Ontario's first Anglican priest, and John Strachan, the first bishop of Toronto, was correct when he described Stuart as "the Father of the Episcopal Church in the Province."[69]

Education was another of Stuart's concerns. As soon as he arrived in Kingston he campaigned for a school and was quickly successful. A school opened on 1 May 1786 with thirty pupils. Stuart ran it until 1788.

When Stuart served as missionary to the Mohawks in New York State, he had also farmed, and he was anxious to follow the same pattern in Kingston. Clearly his interest in the acquisition of land became highly developed, and over the years he acquired much more property than he could farm himself. His initial grant, obtained in 1784, was within a mile of his first place of worship, and was a choice morsel of property, bounded on the north by Union Street, on the west by University, on the east by Barrie Street, and on the south by Lake Ontario. This lot totalled two hundred acres, and Stuart built his house by the waterside. By 1798 this initial grant had been enormously expanded. Stuart explained to a friend, "we have now in the Family more than 7,000 acres, and I hope to make it ten, before the present year expires."[70] James Carruthers was no doubt correct when he noted that "after 1795 Stuart could claim to be a wealthy and landed gentleman-farmer."[71]

The Little Gentleman, the Reverend Doctor John Stuart, died on 15 August 1811, in a comfortable and contented old age. Clearly this was a man who had very nicely recovered from the pain, anguish, and dislocation of revolution.

RICHARD CARTWRIGHT might well have been the most important of the Kingston Loyalists. He was born in Albany, New York, in 1759. His father was an English immigrant, his mother was of Dutch origin. Cartwright's father was a successful businessman able to send Richard to a private school. Richard Cartwright was a devoted Anglican, anxious at one phase of his youth to enter the clergy. He married Magdalen Secord in Kingston about 1784. They had eight children.

Cartwright seems to have been an instinctive Loyalist. As revolutionary activity proceeded in the 1770s, his father managed to avoid conflict with the rebels. The same was not the case with the son, whose views became well known. It was probably as a result of Richard's loyalism that "his father's tavern was attacked twice by republican mobs in 1776."[72]

New York State was not a safe place for Richard Cartwright, and in 1777 his father secured permission for him to leave American territory. Cartwright later explained why he left his home:

The distinctive Condition of my native Country, where all Government was subverted, where Caprice was the only Rule and Measure of usurped Authority, and where all the Distress was exhibited that Power guided by Malice can produce, had long made me wish to leave it. ... I set out ... notwithstanding the tender Feelings of Humanity which I suggested at Parting from the fondest of Parents, and a Number of agreeable Aquaintance it gave me a sensible Pleasure to quit a Place where Discord reigned and all the miseries of Anarchy had long prevailed.[73]

In 1778 and 1779 Cartwright served the British Army and was involved in a number of military operations in the frontier war in New York State. This military experience was useful as Cartwright learned a great deal about how the British military were provisioned, and how one went about making a profit therefrom.

Cartwright gave up the military life in 1780 to commence a career in business. Initially he was based on Carleton Island, but along with the military and other traders he moved to Kingston in the mid-1780s. He became one of Kingston's most important businessmen and participated in a large variety of business activities: the fur-trade, provisioning the military, importing goods from Britain, exporting Canadian produce, ship-building, retailing, manufacturing, milling, and land speculation. He was so successful in this latter activity that he owned 28,632 acres of Upper Canada when he died in 1815. Cartwright had extensive interests in the Napanee area. The extent of his activities is made clear by this description:

In 1801 more than 25 per cent of all the flour shipped to Montreal from Kingston was Cartwright flour. The Kingston merchant was also very much involved in the salted pork trade. In 1794, for example, 800 barrels of pork were produced in Kingston – 75 per cent more than 1793. The remarkable increase was traced to one man – Richard Cartwright.[74]

Richard Cartwright, "Honourable" after his appointment to the Legislative Council in 1792, was a militia officer, a justice of the peace, "and he served as chairman of the magistrates in his district once the court of quarter sessions began meeting in 1788. ..."[75] Also in 1788 he accepted the post of judge in the court of common pleas that had been declined by the Reverend John Stuart.[76] Cartwright also had an abiding commitment to the importance of adequate educational facilities in Upper Canada and brought John Strachan to Kingston to serve as tutor to his children.

It would not be fair to treat Richard Cartwright as a systematic political thinker, but he did have some defined political views that he articulated from time to time. Since he was a leading figure in the emerging society of Upper Canada, these views carried weight.

He might best be described as an adaptive conservative. He had had enough of

American mobs and democracy. At the same time, he fully understood the fact that Upper Canada was a frontier society inhabited by a very mixed population. He recognized that economic growth was a key to stability, and to that end he was willing to have free trade with the United States *and* substantial government intervention in the economy if such intervention would improve the transportation system and stimulate trade.

Cartwright saw Britain as Upper Canada's appropriate trading partner and as the province's societal model. In 1794 he explained some of these views in an address to the grand jury:

We are happily exempt from those political dissentions that are now covering Europe with crimes and blood. Happy in a liberal constitution, and reposing under the protection of a Government from whose bounty we possess a soil that furnishes the industrious every necessary of life – a Government that both liberally assisted us in converting our forests into comfortable habitations and fruitful fields – we seem little disposed to forget, and base would we be if we could forget, the ties of gratitude as well as duty by which our allegiance is secured.[77]

A deferential society was desirable, but Cartwright himself refused to defer. He was, for example, convinced that Lieutenant-Governor Simcoe's main policies were wrong. Simcoe wanted to replicate English society and government in Upper Canada in detail, but Cartwright knew that slavish adherence to such a program would produce alienation and unrest. He wanted deference, but he understood that compromise was necessary in a frontier society. Cartwright opposed Simcoe's policy and, ultimately, he was proved correct. Marilyn Miller's assessment is apposite: "Cartwright's conservative sense of an organic, layered community was based on his belief that Loyalists had rejected the American type of society in favour of an older system of loyalty and deference. ..."[78]

Unlike John Stuart's, Richard Cartwright's exit from life was less than pleasant. In 1811 James and Richard, his two oldest sons, died. Finally, his third son Stephen died. A grief-stricken Richard Cartwright died on 27 July 1815, aged fifty-six. John Strachan delivered Cartwright's funeral sermon and concluded:

His anxiety was only for his family and his friends; for himself he was ready, nay, joyful, as going from a world of pain and suffering to another of infinite happiness and duration. In a letter addressed to his friend, but not to be opened till after his decease, he says: "My infirmities are increasing so fast upon me that it would be infatuation in me to expect to live long, and I may very possibly be called away in a few days. To me this is no otherwise an object of anxiety than as it may affect my family. Adieu, my dear friend; before this **reaches** you I shall have finished my earthly career, which has been shortened by the **afflicting** events which have in the three last years prostrated my fairest hopes. I shall, without dismay, resign my soul into the hands of its Creator, trusting to the merits of our Saviour for all the blessings which Christianity offers to her friends."[79]

Thus ended the life of a great Loyalist, a great Kingstonian, and a great Canadian.

FROM MARTIAL LAW TO A NEW CONSTITUTION

Apart from certain natural advantages of site and situation, political decisions served to reinforce Kingston's centrality in the affairs of the country. Of most importance was its function as the centre for the very establishment and organization of the new colony. When the Loyalists arrived at their locations along the front of the upper St Lawrence and the Bay of Quinte, they settled in one of the westernmost districts of the Province of Quebec. For generations this area, which is now eastern Ontario, had been the monopoly of Indians, fur-traders, and soldiers; and the immediate concern of the settlers was the task of establishing themselves in an environment that could be as threatening and hostile as it was promising.

Initially, local affairs were administered by the military, and in July 1784 Haldimand appointed Major John Ross and Neil McLean, the assistant commissary and storekeeper, as justices of the peace.[80] Sensitive to the needs of his civilian charges, Ross exercised his authority "under the Sanctions of Civil power,"[81] confident that "no disputes of Consequence have as yet Happened, [and] when they do I presume they will be managed with General Satisfaction and the moderation which a new settlement requires."[82] It was not all peace and harmony, however, and Ross advised Haldimand

some daring plunderers infest this place, the Gardens and all the little agriculture which was made at Your Excellency's recommendation in the Spring are totally destroyed. Shingles, boards, and other materials are frequently stolen, without the smallest discovery of the Guilty persons.[83]

During these years, Major John Ross was in many ways the leading figure at Cataraqui. When his sterling services in preparing the first base are added to his subsequent efforts in trying to administer his troublesome flock, he clearly merits recognition as a key figure in Kingston's early years. For R.A. Preston, "Ross was largely responsible for the success of the loyalist settlement at Cataraqui. He, rather than Michael Grass, captain of the loyalists who settled there, should be called the 'founder of Kingston'."[84]

But despite Ross's well-intentioned efforts and benevolent stewardship, discontent with military control soon emerged. At first certain benefits were to be derived from the military overseeing of the community, and initially most settlers were not interested in the form of politics and administration of the new settlement. However, major issues emerged to provoke political discussion and controversy. The Loyalists were accustomed to a degree of self-government and to substantial control over their everyday affairs, and it is understandable that they soon became irked by military control and representation by Loyalist army officers. By the late 1780s this system was in advanced decay, in major part because many settlers convinced themselves, quite erroneously, that the officers were conspiring to perpetuate feudalism.

Of more fundamental concern was that Cataraqui and her sister-settlements were governed by the laws of Quebec. Land ownership was of primary importance to the settlers. They were particularly dissatisfied at being subjected to the customs and law of seigneurial tenure, even if King George III was now established as the "master seigneur." Each township was technically a seigneury, and settlers were feudatories who could not obtain their land grants in freehold tenure. Very quickly this became an issue for the Loyalists, who wanted the same rights to land enjoyed in most of the Thirteen Colonies and feared that land tenure in Quebec would prove even more restrictive than it had been in the old royal colony of New York.

Other, less pressing issues also emerged. For example, there was no popular assembly in Quebec, and not surprisingly, the Loyalists expected to have available the same kind of representative government that operated in Britain and several other parts of North America. The administration of justice also created problems. The system was centralized in the older parts of the province. Justices of the peace were present in various settlements, but they had such limited jurisdiction as to be more or less useless.

Lord Dorchester met some of the aspirations of the Loyalists in his proclamation of 24 July 1788. He established civil administration in place of military control, divided the upper settlements into judicial districts, and allowed for the appointment of judges, justices of the peace, sheriffs, clerks, and coroners, and for the establishment of courts of common pleas and of quarter sessions. The proclamation also established administrative centres throughout this western portion of the colony of Quebec and confirmed Kingston as the regional capital of the new District of Mecklenburg. The first court of quarter sessions for the District of Mecklenburg met in Kingston on 14 April 1789. Richard Cartwright was the most influential among the judges from 1788 to 1815, and like his fellow-judges in the court of common pleas, he was a layman without legal training. The whole province, in fact, was mercifully short of lawyers, and the legal system was obliged to rely on such prominent worthies as Cartwright.

As the decade ended, a new order was emerging. Township meetings were authorized, and the settlers drew up a large-scale petition to London to ask for "the blessings of the British constitution," freehold tenure, improved communications, aid for schools and established churches, and some economic protection against the competition of primary producers south of the line. These demands illustrate the rapidity with which the political system emerged from the subsistence phase of settlement life. The subsequent Constitutional Act of 1791 established Upper Canada, the progenitor of the present Province of Ontario, as a separate entity. Sir John Graves Simcoe was appointed to the post of lieutenant-governor.

Upper Canada was proclaimed a separate constitutional jurisdiction in St George's Church, Kingston. W.R. Riddell described the event:

Simcoe appointed the Protestant Church (St George's) as a suitable place for opening the Royal Commissions, and on Sunday, July 8, 1792, repaired thither, accompanied by Osgoode, Russell, Baby and White, the Attorney-General, together with the principal inhabitants – the Commissions were read and Simcoe took the required oaths. The Executive Council did not function until the following day, July 9, when Simcoe, now fully clothed with his office, formally appointed Osgoode, Robertson (still absent), Baby, Grant (still absent) and Russell, Executive Councillors.[85]

Mrs Simcoe's diary entries were more laconic: "The Gov. went to Church & took the Oaths preparatory to acting as Governor."[86] The good lady devoted more words to her new-found hobby of the previous day – forest fires:

I walked this Evening in a wood lately set on fire. ... Perhaps you have no idea of the pleasure of walking in a burning wood, but I found it so great that I think I shall have some woods set on fire for my Evening walks. The smoke arising from it keeps the Musquitoes [sic] at a distance & where the fire has caught the hollow trunk of a lofty Tree the flame issuing from the top has a fine effect. In some trees where but a small flame appears it looks like stars as the Evening grows dark, & the flare & smoke interspersed in different Masses of dark woods has a very picturesque appearance a little like Tasso's enchanted wood.[87]

Fortunately, Kingston's surrounding forests were spared Mrs Simcoe's attentions because of her other bucolic pleasures: her diary records that she "sailed ½ a league this Evening in a pretty boat of Mr. Clarke's, attended by music to Garden Island."[88] The Simcoes together were determined to transform the Canadian wilderness by order, fire, and a modicum of culture.

With the Constitutional Act in place, Kingstonians were represented in the Assembly of Upper Canada by the member from Leeds and Grenville counties from 1792 to 1800, and by the member from Frontenac County from 1801 to 1820. Not until 1820 was Kingston recognized as a separate constituency. None of these early assemblymen was a powerful figure, and turnover was rapid – especially during the early parliaments. During these twenty-eight years, four members represented the town and adjacent areas: John White (1792-1796); Solomon Jones (1797-1800); John Ferguson (1800-1804); and Allan McLean (1804-1820). McLean, in fact, held Frontenac until 1824. Kingston's real political weight was felt not in the Assembly but in the Legislative Council, where Richard Cartwright sat from 1792 until his death in 1815. During his entire period in office, he represented Upper Canada's largest town and strove to maintain Kingston's position as one of the key political centres in early Ontario.

The first St George's, opened for use in 1792. Here, that same year, Lieutenant-Governor Simcoe proclaimed Upper Canada a separate constitutional jurisdiction. (QUA)

THE EMERGING TOWN

Until 1788, official government correspondence still referred to the small community of log and frame houses and buildings clustered around the barracks on the site of Fort Frontenac as "Cataraqui." In that year, however, a proclamation recognized "Kingston" as the capital of the Mecklenburg District, which comprised the Bay of Quinte settlements in the westernmost reaches of the old Province of Quebec. In time, Kingston increasingly became the popular as well as official name of the new community. It was not the only centre servicing the Loyalist settlers along the river and lakefront townships. Buell's Bay or Elizabethtown (later, Brockville), Ernesttown (later, Bath), and Adolphustown all functioned as centres for their respective communities. Indeed, though the difference was measured in a few families, Bath and Adolphustown were located in townships that were more populous than Kingston's immediate surroundings, and both rivalled Kingston itself in size. Kingston, however, had several advantages that benefited it in its competition with these early rivals.

Kingston's location at the junction of the St Lawrence and Lake Ontario ensured it an influential economic role. In the emerging commercial system of the day there were two distinct transport elements: the river and the lake. Commodities travelling along Lake Ontario were conveyed by sailboats and were transferred to smaller batteaux and, in some cases, rafts for movement along the St Lawrence. Kingston, located at the junction of the two systems, and upstream from the rapids and shoals of the St Lawrence, was one of the principal sites for this transshipment.

Further, merchants had quickly recognized the advantages of this crucial location from the early days of the Loyalist settlement and had moved there from Carleton Island. The passage of the Inland Navigation Act of 1788 opened the lakes to commercial vessels and further stimulated mercantile activities. Richard Cartwright early appreciated the demand for more vessels to engage in this trade, and by 1789 he had constructed the first ship to be built at Kingston since the departure of the French, the *Lady Dorchester*.

This early momentum favoured Kingston's continued progress, and Patrick Campbell, writing in 1791, argued that "everything is inviting, and it seems by nature intended for emporium of this new country, capable of being extended to a considerable empire."[89] By 1794 Sir John Graves Simcoe, the new lieutenant-governor of the province, could comment

On my arrival at Kingston, I found it improved beyond my expectation; many stores for merchandize and wharfs had been built and new ones were in contemplation. I also found the language of the merchants very much altered. The Fur Trade, as I had hoped, seem'd no longer the principal object of their attention. They looked forward to the produce of their country as the true source of their wealth.[90]

Increasingly, the "produce of their country" consisted of wheat, flour, peas, pork, butter, cheese, lard, together with that particular indicator of the advance of settlement and the retreat of the forest, potash. The return cargoes represented those exotic products not cultivated or otherwise available in the local region: sugar, molasses, tobacco, and salt – together with textiles, tools, domestic utensils, and general haberdashery. Small though the initial cargoes were, the increased volume and diversity of the trade on the St Lawrence allowed the forwarders to flourish.

Kingston merchants continued to be prominent participants in this commerce throughout the first generation of Loyalist settlement. Richard Cartwright and Joseph Forsyth were soon joined by others, and by 1815, some nineteen merchants and forwarders had constructed wharf facilities along the waterfront of the new settlement. But the sheltered harbour of the "cannotage" or canoe landing behind the old French settlement on the Great Cataraqui River was abandoned. Instead, the merchants located their activities along the adjacent Lake Ontario waterfront and thus committed Kingston to an investment in a harbour that was to compromise its effectiveness as a port over the next century.

And as commerce flourished, so did Kingston. Within a decade of the first settlement, the Simcoes found Kingston had grown to a cluster of some fifty houses. In 1795 the *émigré* Duke de La Rochefoucauld-Liancourt reported 130 houses, albeit of varying quality:

Many of them are log houses, and those which consist of joiner's work, are badly constructed and painted. But few new houses are built. No town-hall, no court house, and no prison have hitherto been constructed. The houses of two or three merchants are conveniently situated for loading and unloading ships; but, in point of structure, these are not better than the rest.[91]

Apparently, some progress had been made by the time of Sir David William Smyth's visit in the late 1790s, as he listed "a barrack for troops, and a house for the commanding officer, an hospital, several store houses, an episcopal church, a gaol, and courthouse."[92] In 1815, Joseph Bouchette reported that Kingston "now presents a front of nearly three quarters of a mile, and extending in depth about six hundred yards. The streets are regularly planned, and running at right angles with each other, but not paved."[93] By this date, therefore, Holland's 1784 simple plat of three blocks containing thirty-six lots had been much enlarged.[94] An 1815 plan demonstrates how the town had grown to some 336 lots bounded by "Front" (Ontario) Street on the waterfront, "Rear" (Bagot) Street on the landward side, and "North" and "West" streets to the northeast and southwest, respectively. The main thoroughfares were "Church" (King) Street, "Store" (Princess) Street, and "Grass" and "Quarry" streets (which together were later renamed Wellington Street).

Despite such developments, European visitors must have been struck by the exotic sights of a frontier town. The Kingston Mississauga may have ceded their lands to the British government, but for years they continued to be actors in the townscape. On 16 August 1801, the order book of the Royal Canadian Volunteers expressed concern over "the Conduct of some men of the Garrison to wards [*sic*] the Indians particularly toward the Women has been equally unsoldier like and unmanly" and threatened the "most examplary [*sic*] punishment."[95] Three days later two privates of the 41st Regiment were accused of various charges including "abusing, and beating, several Indians" and were sentenced to the punishment of "Six hundred Lashes each, in the usual manner"![96]

That these Indians were Mississauga is unclear, but certainly we know they were viewed with less than universal approbation by contemporary visitors. To Mrs Simcoe, the wife of the first lieutenant-governor of the province, the Mississauga were "an unwarlike, idle, drunken dirty tribe," and she made the ironic observation that "these uncivilized People saunter up & down the Town all the day, with the

"Mississauga Indians" [*sic*], sketched by Captain Basil Hall, *c.* 1816. (NA)

apparent Nonchalance, want of occupation & indifference that seems to possess Bond street Beaux."[97] Whether the Mississauga of this period were "London Beaux" or "noble savages" is difficult to determine, although a careful scrutiny of Peachey's early watercolours reveals the local native population peacefully fishing on the lake and sojourning on the lakeshore, viewing the newcomers to their lands.

Whatever the contemporary opinion was of the Mississauga, they certainly played an important role in supplementing the supplies of the military commissariat in the early years. Kingston was the market for several of their traditional commodities, and contemporary visitors record them trading their produce with the inhabitants of the small community. Thus, in the 1790s, the Duke de La Rochefoucauld-Liancourt noted that "In the month of September the Indians bring wild rice to Kingston, which grows on the borders of the lake, especially on the American side. The Indians bring yearly from four to five hundred pounds of this rice, which several of the inhabitants purchase for their own consumption."[98] Other visitors reported that "the Mississaguis [*sic*] keep the inhabitants of Kingston well supplied with fish and game" as well as maple sugar.[99]

Indeed, Kingstonians must have been very grateful for the supplements provided by the Mississauga. Certainly, they could not rely upon their own immediate back country because of the inadequate communications. One contemporary wit was prompted to advocate the "many good purposes to which the Air Balloon might be applied in a country like this, where the roads are in general so extremely bad."[100] A few years later, Kingstonians were required to consume potatoes from upper New York State at 3s 6d, while local potatoes at 1s 6d per bushel could not get to market because of the "badness of the Roads ... and the poor devils in the rear can only get to town with their produce about three months out of twelve which is a shocking encouragement for actual settlement."[101]

Not surprisingly, because of the prominent role played by Kingston in the early affairs of the colony, because of the continued evidence of its material progress, and because of the need for it to overcome some of the deficiencies of its frontier-town existence, leaders like Richard Cartwright consistently advocated some form of special status for Kingston. The Constitutional Act of 1791 had established British civil law, and a bill passed in the following year allowed for the nomination and appointment of various town and parish officers. Accordingly, Kingston continued to be governed by magistrates and the District quarter sessions that met four times a year. While this system of municipal government was, in relative terms, somewhat unsophisticated, the justices of the peace possessed considerable authority because they were in no way limited by any "American" notions concerning the separation of powers.

This embryonic form of local administration was suitable to an embryonic society, although some like Cartwright champed at the bit and were anxious to acquire some more grandiose recognition of Kingston's potential, if not existing, achievements. As early as 1794, in his capacity as chairman of the quarter sessions, he proposed the incorporation of the "Town of Kingston." His concept was as simple as it was ideologically flexible. A council of four persons, to be elected or appointed by the lieutenant-governor, would concern themselves with "regulating the Police of the Town." They would provide fire protection, regulate markets, control the price and weight of bread, keep the streets clean, and monitor the rates charged by carters.[102] In the same year, Simcoe wrote to the Duke of Portland that he favoured the incorporation of both Kingston and Niagara as, "from their situation [they] must be places of great resort," and recommended a Corporation of mayor, six alderman, and "a competent number of Common Council."[103] That these concepts were not implemented meant that the magistrates and courts of quarter sessions would continue as the dominant agency of town management for a generation. They exercised both judicial and executive authority. As justices, they enforced the law and maintained the peace. In their executive guise, they appointed local officials who controlled, or rather tried to control, the large number of domestic animals living in a quasi-urban area, the licensing of taverns, and the maintenance of the streets.

Thus, the guaranteed provision of foodstuffs was crucial. Even though communications were deplorable, the town had taken steps to provide a central market place where town consumers could trade with farm producers, and served as the principal mechanism for the distribution of food for the inhabitants. Accordingly,

The town of Kingston and its fortifications, 1796, (QU Special Collections)

the early informal sale of produce by farmers to townspeople had been regularized by the establishment of a formal market in 1801. On 13 May 1811, the clerk of the peace for the Midland District announced the rules and regulations of the "New Kingston Market." Stalls were provided for the farmers and eight butchers were accommodated in the market house. The market was to be open daily, except Sundays, between 6 am and 4 pm, and the regulations established that "the square between St George's church and the river, in the Town of Kingston, should be the market place, where all butcher's meat, butter, eggs, poultry, fish and vegetables should be exposed to sale."[104] It was a beginning.

The maintenance of law and order was to be a major problem as the town grew. But initially, because of its small size, Kingston was a place where personal problems and social stress could be alleviated by direct and forthright mechanisms. Thus, for the unfortunate Patrick McDallogh, an advertisement in the Kingston *Gazette* served at least to air his complaint if not seek redress for his grievance:

Whereas my wife, Mrs. Bridget McDallogh is again walked away with herself, and left me with five small children and her poor blind mother, and left nobody else to take care of the house & home and I hear she has taken up with Tim Ghigan, the lame fiddler the same that was put in the stocks last Easter, for stealing Barney Doody's game cock. This is to give notice, that I will not pay for bite or sup on her account to man or mortal, and that she had better never show the mark of her ten toes near my house again.
P.S. Tim had better keep out of my sight. [105]

As long as Kingston continued to be nothing more than a village in size and social complexity, the courts of quarter session could adequately monitor the needs of inhabitants like Mr McDallogh. But as the community increased in size, complexity, and diversity, new pressures appeared requiring new structures of control.

The settlement of Kingston emerged, then, from the initial 1783 encampment on the site that had accommodated the Loyalist refugees and the military personnel charged with organizing them. Such material, economic, and social developments reflected Kingston's transformation from a town plot occupied by a few settlers to a community that had aspirations to become something truly urban. And the rhetoric of local residents and visitors during this period refers much to Kingston's aspirations and promise for the future. Patrick Campbell had promised that Kingston would be the "emporium of this new country" and foresaw it "extending to a considerable empire." Twenty years later, Joseph Bouchette also recognized progress and potential:

For the last fifteen years the town has obtained considerable mercantile importance; wharfs have been constructed, and many spacious warehouses erected, that are usually filled with merchandize; in fact, it is now become the main entrepot between Montreal and all the settlements along the lakes to the westward. [106]

But these fictions of what Kingston could be must not distract us from what Kingston actually was at the close of this first stage of settlement. A community of less than a thousand residents hardly constitutes a town, let alone a city. But certainly the presence of offices of government and key public figures, the development of a commercial function, and the emergence of a social and economic infrastructure serving the needs of the local inhabitants merited recognition of Kingston as the settlement most advanced along the way to urban dominance of the new colony of Upper Canada. While not incorporated as a town, Kingston continued to grow and maintain its position as the most populous and economically dominant settlement in Upper Canada. And more importantly for future events, the character of the evolving centre was already much influenced by the presence of the military, preoccupation with its role in government, and participation in the nation's developing commerce.

A view of Fort Henry, by Maj.-Gen. Phillip Bedingfeld, *c.* 1857. (QU Agnes Etherington Art Centre)

THREE

Citadel Kingston

If Kingston was recognized early as an important place of trade and as a centre of regional government, its initial growth was also much associated with the presence of the military who contributed a great deal to both its economy and social structure. Indeed, merchants like John and Joseph Forsyth and Robert Macaulay were soon to recognize the commercial benefit to be derived from the military presence. It was commented upon by one of the principal beneficiaries, Richard Cartwright:

To what is to be ascribed the present State of Improvement and Population of this Country? Certainly not to its natural Advantages, but to the Liberality which Government have shewn towards the Loyalists who first settled it; to the Money spent by the numerous Garrisons and public Departments established among us; and the Demand for our Produce which so many unproductive Consumers occasion on the Spot. As long as the British Government shall think proper to hire people to come over to eat our Flour, we shall go on very well, & continue to make a Figure.[1]

This was to be a constant theme over the next century of military presence in Kingston.

A MILITARY POST AND NAVAL STATION

Kingston was one of the few places in Upper Canada to maintain a permanent garrison. With the continuation of British-American sensitivity, if not hostility, following the American Revolution, the derelict French fortifications at Kingston, together with Haldimand's preliminary works there, attained a new importance. As has been seen, in 1783 Major John Ross had been ordered to establish a military post at Cataraqui. By October of that year he reported that the ravelin and north curtain-wall of the old French fort had been restored, and that barracks for officers and men, provision stores, a bakehouse, a hospital, and a kiln were ready for use.[2] Ross also recommended the fortification of Point Henry, which commanded Point Frederick and Haldimand Cove, later to be renamed Navy Bay.

In 1794, Lord Dorchester, concerned about the "appearance of Hostilities with our Neighbours [Americans]," directed Simcoe to appoint "a proper Person to make a Survey of this [Point Frederick] & the opposite Point [Point Henry], with the adjacent Country and Coves, taking in whatever may lye near enough to affect the Security or convenience of the Port."[3] Lieutenant Alexander Bryce of the Royal Engineers was charged with this reponsibility, and having surveyed the possibilities from Gananoque to the Bay of Quinte, he recognized the potential of Haldimand Cove – if defended by fortifications on Point Henry. Simcoe forwarded Bryce's report to Dorchester but argued against developing the base at Kingston because of its vulnerability and the excessive cost of fortifying it. His own recommendation for the defence of the frontier called for a system of blockhouses – ideally located on islands – and gunboat patrols. And he favoured York over Kingston as the centre for this defence for several reasons:

The distance which Your Lordship observes in respect of York or Toronto, as applicable to present purposes, I humbly apprehend may be its preservation. It is also powerfully protected by our Indian Allies, and the Militia combined with the Troops in the district of Niagara, [i]n a Military view, the most important part of his Majesty's possessions. I therefore am of the Opinion, that this place (York) ought to be the refitting port and Winter deposit of all Naval & Military Stores under existing circumstances.[4]

The easing of frontier tensions with the signing of Jay's Treaty in 1794 lessened the urgency of the question. Neither York nor Kingston was developed as a fortified naval base, although by 1800 Point Frederick could show stores, workshops, and a sail loft, and sundry buildings and several gun boats had been constructed at Navy Bay.[5] Renewed tensions in 1809 and news of the development of an American naval base at Sacket's Harbor prompted the commencement of the construction of the corvette *Royal George* at the Point Frederick dockyard. However, the question of Kingston's suitability for this role lingered on, and in April 1812 Major-General Isaac Brock, the civil and military leader of Upper Canada, was advised that because of the "exposed situation of Kingston," it was "an extremely unfit situation for our Naval Establishment on Lake Ontario." This report went on to recommend that the base should be removed to York, "a situation in every respect more eligible for the security of the Navy Yard and Shipping, and where its safe and commodious Harbour, is capable of affording shelter at all times to any number of Vessels."[6] The rivalry between Kingston and York was continuing, but the outbreak of the War of 1812-1814 found the naval base still at Kingston, and the events of that war were to confirm its appropriateness there.

The fortifications at Kingston itself had received little attention since the original preparations made by Ross and his men. A report on the state of the military establishment in 1802 presented a dismal picture of neglect and disrepair: even the garrison gates needed replacement.[7] Apart from a small garrison, the defence depended upon the local militia who were not found wanting in enthusiasm and patriotic fervour. Rallying to the colours in response to a fear of invasion in 1807, Richard Cartwright donned his uniform of colonel of the militia and exhorted his troops to the defence of the realm:

Listen not to those who talk of our scattered Settlements, & Slender Population, as incapable of resistance. These are the Suggestions of Cowardice or Treachery. Our Population affords Thousands of brave Men to arm in the Cause of their Country; and supported as we shall be by a regular Military Force, what have we to fear from any Attempt to invade us? ... If ever Men were bound by Honour, Duty, or Gratitude to exert themselves in the Cause of their Country, we are so bound to Great Britain. If ever Men had peculiar political Advantages to contend for, we are the Men. Or if ever Men had Injuries, Insults & Degredation to dread from being Subdued, we certainly have them to dread from Subjugation to the American States.[8]

With such rhetoric from local worthies and with the more material evidence of the preparations at Navy Bay, Kingston looked to the south with some apprehension in the years prior to the outbreak of the War of 1812-1814.

THE WAR OF 1812-1814 AND KINGSTON

The War of 1812-1814 had a powerful influence on Kingston and on Canada, but Canadians were little involved with its origins. The conflict came late in the Napoleonic Wars that had convulsed Europe for over a decade. It emerged from long-standing tensions between the United States and the United Kingdom, tensions massively exaggerated by the war in Europe. Canada, and primarily Ontario, became the main theatre of operations because of its loyalties and location: it was British and it was thought to be vulnerable to American attack. This war, in which we were little more than a pawn, heightened anti-Americanism and strengthened Loyalism, especially in Ontario towns like Kingston. It reconfirmed Canada's desire not to be American and was instrumental in defining Canadian political culture.

Of course, had the American strategy succeeded, Canada would have had no distinctive culture, political or otherwise, because the country would have been absorbed by the United States. This did not happen, and the ultimate explanation for our survival was probably a result less of British initiatives than of American ineptitude. As Sir James Lucas Yeo, commodore and commander-in-chief of the Lakes, explained:

The experience of two years active service has served to convince me that tho' much has been done by the mutual exertions of *both Services*, we also owe as much if not more to the perverse stupidity of the Enemy; the Impolicy of their plans; the dissensions of their Commanders, and, lastly between *them* and their *Minister of War*.[9]

The war boosted the fortunes of Kingston directly by expanding the military presence in the town, and indirectly by devastating other parts of the province. Prior to the war, the military presence had been limited. At the outbreak of hostilities, Kingston's defences were meagre and deteriorating, and apart from the refurbished fortifications at Fort Frontenac, there was only a small dockyard establishment at Point Frederick. What garrison there was consisted of some ninety-eight men of the 10th Royal Veteran's Battalion who, it was said, "suffered from rheumatism and hammer-toes, from syphilis and hernia, and from every disease which seems to come with advancing years."[10] By 1814, the situation had changed, and Kingston's one thousand civilians were joined by a garrison that for a short time consisted of as many as four thousand troops. Moreover, while there had been no fixed fortifications other than the crumbling facilities at Fort Frontenac, Kingston was surrounded by the end of the war by a picket wall and five blockhouses on its landward side and several batteries and blockhouses on the lakeside. Point Henry and Point Frederick were also fortified. Point Henry received the most attention, its log-and-earth fortifications being improved throughout the war until they constituted a formidable system of earth and stone ramparts, complete with barracks, magazines, a system of semaphore signal towers, and support batteries. Fortified outposts were established to command the approaches to Kingston at Amherst Island, Snake Island, Lemoine's Point, and Lake Ontario Point.

While the attention of the military was directed to the defence of the principal community in Upper Canada, it was the strategic significance of the general location and its naval facilities that were of paramount concern. In his analysis of the War of 1812-1814, the American naval strategist Rear Admiral Alfred Thayer Mahan commented on the significance of Kingston: "No other harbour was tenable as a naval station; with its fall and the destruction of shipping and forts, would go the control of the lake, even if the place were not permanently held. Deprived thus of the water communications, the enemy could retain no position to the westward because neither reinforcements nor supplies could reach them."[11]

This strategic importance may have been recognized by later Americans like Mahan, but the British at the time had invested as little in their naval establishment as they had in their military one. The geriatric garrison was matched by a geriatric naval force: one captain of the Provincial Marine was reputed to be in his eighties and another commander, in his seventies. The naval base consisted of storehouses and work sheds on Point Frederick, while the fleet was comprised of two corvettes, three schooners, several gunboats, and some 230 officers and men.

In 1813, Sir James Lucas Yeo arrived in Kingston with a further 437 officers and men. Together with this increase in naval personnel, Yeo also developed the facilities at Point Frederick, and commenced a program of shipbuilding. Apart from an abortive and ineffectual attack on Kingston in 1812 by Captain Chauncey, the dominant naval activity took the form of a nineteenth-century armaments race, a "shipbuilders war." By April 1814, the Kingston yards had launched the fifty-six-gun *Prince*

HMS *St. Lawrence*, launched at Kingston, 1814. Her 112 guns made her the most powerful warship on the Lakes. Conjectural reconstruction by C.H.J. Snider. (QUA)

Regent and the forty-two-gun *Princess Charlotte*. On 10 September of that year, the 112-gun *St Lawrence*, the most powerful warship on the Great Lakes, was launched. As is typical with the logic of arms races, this massive British naval construction program was matched by the Americans at their naval base of Sacket's Harbor as they attempted to keep up with the British. This, in turn, prompted more activity at Kingston and by the time of the Peace of Ghent in 1814, two more ships were on the stocks at Point Frederick, and several other vessels had been planned. Quite clearly, whatever the outcome of the British-American naval race, the War of 1812-1814 served to consolidate Kingston's role as an important naval and military centre.

All of this occasioned much activity in Kingston, and while other sections of the province experienced considerable economic depression, the Bay of Quinte region was relatively unaffected and actually benefited from the war. Contemporary opinions support this view. The diary of David Wingfield, a naval officer on the Great Lakes during the war, notes that

previous to the war [Kingston] was a place of no great importance; but a large Naval Establishment being formed, and York having lost all its former advantages ... from its laying so open to the incursions of the enemy, all the trade flowed to this place, and York was nearly deserted, though the seat of Government for the Upper Province; consequently building became the rage, and at the conclusion of the war Kingston had risen into a large Town, with many handsome and substantial houses, forming several streets.[12]

Gourlay later echoed this opinion. "Though the war destroyed Niagara, checked the progress of York and made Ernest[t]own a 'deserted village,'" argued the itinerant Scottish radical, "it doubled the population, the buildings, and business of Kingston."[13] Apart from the abortive American raid in 1812, Kingston was spared too close a contact with the realities of war, while experiencing the benefits of economic growth and consolidating its primary position in the affairs of the colony. Ironically, despite Simcoe's forebodings, it was York – not Kingston – that had proved to be vulnerable to invasion and depredation.

The substantial military and naval activity centred on Kingston generated a considerable demand for supplies, labour, and services. As early as 17 October 1812, the Kingston *Gazette* called for tenders for the supply of five hundred barrels of pork and another five hundred barrels of flour "for His Majesty's troops stationed at Kingston and its dependencies." As the garrison grew, these tenders increased in volume and value and local merchants were energetic in meeting them. The Fairfields, Cartwrights, Macaulays, and Marklands had all established warehouses at Kingston to facilitate their growing trade. They were well prepared to satisfy the military's appetite for supplies. Cattle, oxen, shoes, boots, teas, wine, liquor, candles, soap, tobacco, flour, pork, and beef were acquired by them from Europe, eastern British North America, and the United States. Even during the hottest years of the war, the Fairfields continued to trade with their American connections across the St Lawrence. Commodity prices were lower on the other side of the "line" and Canadian profits were thus guaranteed to be higher. That patriotism and good business acumen ensured financial success for the merchants is evidenced by the advances of at least one of them. Richard Cartwright did not let his wartime duties as the militia officer in command of the Midland District interfere with his commercial interests; by 1815, he owned a sawmill, a fulling mill, distillery, tavern, grist mill, shop, storehouse, warehouse, and some 28,632 acres of land throughout the province, including town lots in both Kingston and York.[14]

The community at large also benefited from the extensive military activity during the War of 1812-1814. While the naval shipyard's complement of shipwrights, sailmakers, blacksmiths, storekeepers, and labourers constituted a modest establishment of 131 men, many others were hired as day labourers from the town and still others were involved in providing materials and services. It has been estimated that the naval establishment alone spent £47,327 in 1814, while a contemporary estimate of overall military expenditures in the community was much higher. Writing in 1818 Francis Hall estimated that the commissariat paid out £1,000 per day during the war years, that the navy yard employed 1,200 labourers, and that the naval establishment cost £25,000 per annum "in defence of a country, one half of which is little better than a barren waste of snows, and the other, a wild forest, scarcely intersected by a thread of population."[15]

If the surrounding countryside did not seem to show much benefit, the town itself reflected the impact of the revenue generated by military expenditures. At the outbreak of the war Kingston had been a village of some thousand people occupying a mere 150 houses and served by two churches, a school, a court house and jail, a few shops and a market, three hotels, and more taverns and unlicensed groggeries than it needed. The "Freemasons," "Old King's Head," "Rob Roy," "Bottle and Glass," and many others profited from the arrival of four thousand thirsty soldiers and five hundred equally thirsty sailors. Servicing the various needs of this friendly and lucrative invasion brought an economic windfall for the resident population in general and for certain professions in particular. Moreover, apart from the demand for labour, supplies, and services, there was also a demand for accommodation for military personnel and camp followers. The town was bursting at its seams. Accordingly, house construction boomed, with some hundred new houses being built between 1812 and 1816, and a further 150 between 1817 and 1820 in a community still flush with war-time profits. Writing in 1821 James Strachan recognized all this and noted, "Kingston looks well as you approach it from the water. The war was of much use to it, not only more than doubling the population, but likewise distributing among its inhabitants large sums of money. The number of houses built, and well built since the war, is very honourable to the taste and enterprise of the people."[16]

The war, therefore, was indeed critical to Kingston's development and gave it a momentum that was to last for a generation. Military, commercial, and administrative functions became centered on Kingston and were to become vital agents in the future destiny of the town.[17]

FORTRESS KINGSTON

With the termination of the War of 1812-1814 a recession set in at Kingston. The garrison was reduced, falling to a complement of 1,583 men in 1815, and by 1817 there were fewer than one thousand left in the town. Only 478 military personnel remained in Kingston by 1824. The departure of several regiments meant not only a loss of a colourful, if sometimes cantankerous, dimension of the social life of the community but also the loss of some three thousand consumers. The military establishment had looked to Kingston and its district for the provision of its victuals and general supplies. The sale of beef, flour, cordwood, candles, fodder, straw, and even water had stimulated the commercial enterprise of the local merchants, retailers, and farmers. The more informal though no less important needs of the soldiers had also been accommodated. Many of the military had been billetted throughout the town, while the hostelries, taverns, and unlicensed grog-houses provided entertainment for officers and men.

The signing of the Treaty of Ghent on Christmas Eve, 1814, marked the end of the War of 1812-1814. Fortunately for Kingston, however, the advent of peace by no means removed the fear of future conflicts. The events of the recent war had highlighted the vulnerability of the communications between Upper and Lower Canada and the weakness of the military establishment in British North America. Moreover, while the Rush-Bagot Treaty of 1817 had virtually demilitarized the lakes, it did not signal an end to military competition on the Canadian-American frontier. Indeed, its effect was to direct new efforts to better prepare defences against possible land attacks. Two major initiatives were embarked upon to remedy these deficiencies, and both of them were to have a profound impact upon Kingston.[18]

If Kingston itself had not experienced any significant military activity during the war, communities along the St Lawrence below Kingston had not been so fortunate. Both sides had forayed across the river into each others' territory, and it was clear that in time of war, communication along this, the principal artery of commerce, was easily interrupted. From the British perspective, the basic strategic point was that the United States controlled the south bank of the St Lawrence from Lake Ontario eastward to St Regis, a little south and east of Cornwall. The military significance of this was obvious: the route to the interior from the Atlantic seaboard could be interrupted along the international section of the St Lawrence whenever the Americans chose to do so. Initially, the Duke of Wellington, Britain's presiding military genius, and master general of Ordnance, proposed to ensure a protected corridor from Montreal to Lake Ontario by positioning a 5,000-man army corps in the Rideau region to repel any future thrust by the Americans across the St Lawrence. This proved to be unrealistic, although the location of loyal and reliable British settlers at Richmond, Perth, and Lanark was accomplished.

Rideau Canal locks under construction at Lower Brewer's (also called Washburn), by Thomas Burrowes. (AO)

In 1825, the commission charged with the task of examining the defences of British North America reported back to Wellington. Chaired by Major-General James Carmichael Smyth, the committee recommended the construction of an alternative waterway connection between the Great Lakes and the seaboard as a key feature of their comprehensive plan for the defence of British North America. Attention was directed to the traditional route followed by the Indians and fur-traders in their travels into the interior. The major alternative to the St Lawrence was the Ottawa River, and several of the Ottawa's southern tributaries offered possible lines of communication into peninsula Ontario. While suited to movement by canoe and batteaux, these routes were generally inadequate for development to accommodate heavier traffic. The Madawaska toward Lake Simcoe, the Mississippi toward Napanee, the Rideau toward Gananoque, and the South Nation toward Johnstown were all advocated at various times; but all were found to be unsuitable because of inadequate depth, problems of construction, or the strategic vulnerability of the southern terminus.

One route, however, did meet all requirements. Colonel John By proposed that a waterway be constructed from the Ottawa River, along its tributary, the Rideau, to link with the interior lakes, and thence down the Great Cataraqui River to Lake Ontario at Kingston. Locks were to be constructed to overcome rapids and falls; dams were required to flood shallow lakes and divert the drainage to ensure sufficient water for navigation; blockhouses would guarantee the military security of the system, which would be anchored on the strengthened fortifications at Kingston. The actual execution of these projects required considerable ingenuity, funds, and effort. The Rideau Waterway was to be more than a canal. The experience of British "navvies" in constructing the necessary dams and locks allowed its completion. Reliance upon the new technology of steam navigation, in an area where towing or sailing was difficult at best, made the operation of the system possible. Commenced in 1826, the works were completed by May 1832. Starting at Kingston Mills, fourteen locks lifted vessels the 163 feet from Lake Ontario to the highpoint – or summit – at Upper Rideau Lake. From there, thirty-three locks dropped 271 feet to the Ottawa River at Bytown, named after the architect of the Rideau. From Bytown, soon to be renamed Ottawa, it was easy to navigate the Ottawa River to Montreal. Thus, Montreal and Lake Ontario were connected by an all-British route, secure from any threat of American interdiction.

Constructing the Rideau system was not inexpensive. The preliminary estimate of £169,000 in 1827 was woefully inadequate, being increased to £693,449 in 1830 – while the actual final accounting reported an expenditure of some £822,804. Such a cost overrun was in no way excessive even for By's day, but he was pilloried for it anyway. Nor was the project without considerable human cost. Suffice it to say that there were some 1,316 men working along the canal between Kingston and Newboro, and in 1830 alone some five hundred died in that pestilential section of lakes and swamps. But with its completion the Rideau Canal served to emphasize the strategic significance of Kingston in the military affairs of the province.

The second major initiative was the strengthening of the fortifications at Kingston itself.[19] The original defences of the town had been bolstered considerably during the War of 1812-1814, but it was clear that Kingston's importance as a communications and military centre necessitated further Imperial expenditures. The decision to make Kingston the Lake Ontario terminus of the Rideau Canal ensured that such expenditures would be forthcoming, and during the 1820s the British authorized the enhancing of the defences there.

There then ensued a series of investigations, reports, deferred decisions, and (ultimately) actions that resulted in a significant – if substantially less than originally intended – contribution to the townscape of Kingston. Moreover, the period 1815-1845 has been described as being one of "stasis and neglect" in terms of ordnance and military technology in general.[20] Predictably, therefore, those military works that were carried out reflected a strategic, tactical, and logistic mind-set more attuned to the past Napoleonic Wars than to the future threats they were designed to counter.

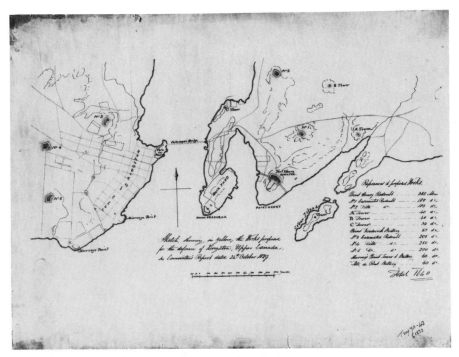

Proposals for improved defence at Kingston, 1829. (NA)

Nevertheless, reconsideration of Kingston's defences was initiated in 1825 when Wellington dispatched a commission of engineers under Major-General James Carmichael Smyth, of the Royal Engineers, to review the defences of British North America. Apart from recommending the construction of the Rideau Canal, Smyth's committee also advocated concentrations of military resources and the strengthening of the defence works at Halifax, Montreal, and Kingston, and along the upper Great Lakes frontier. The specific recommendations for Kingston were in response to the threat of naval attack from the American station at Sacket's Harbor. Apart from the construction of a "keep and rallying point" in the centre of the town of Kingston, their principal recommendations were intended to defend Navy Bay. Fort Henry and the batteries at Point Frederick and Mississauga Point were to be improved, and three towers were to be constructed at Cedar Island, Snake Island, and in advance of Fort Henry – all at a cost of £201,718; the Vauban-style fortress at Fort Henry alone amounted to £171,000.

These works were approved by Wellington in March 1826, but in February 1827 Lieutenant-Colonel Wright, the commanding Royal Engineer in Upper Canada, argued for an additional two towers in advance of Point Frederick to supplement the defences of the dockyard. Opposed by Smyth, Wright's recommendation was

Fort Henry guarding the entrance to the Rideau Canal, by Lieut.-Col. H.F. Ainslie, 1839. (NA)

eventually approved in October 1827 – priority being given to Fort Henry and to the towers at Cedar Island and Snake Island – only to be held up by budgetary considerations. In the summer of 1828, following this set-back, His Excellency Lieutenant General Sir James Kempt CCB, presided over a Canadian sub-committee ordered to reconsider Kingston's defences. They reported to a new commission headed by Major General Sir Alexander Bryce. New plans were in the air.

In 1828 Lieutenant-Colonels Fanshawe and Lewis prepared a different concept of fortifications overlooking Kingston and the naval dockyard. Directed to bring in a recommendation within a budget of £186,087, the original plans for Fort Henry were reduced to a large casemated redoubt that would accommodate 350 men. With this as the central strong-point, it was also proposed that another five redoubts, garrisoned by a total of 980 men, be constructed to the north and west of Kingston. These would be integrated with five Martello towers and a battery at Tête-du-Pont that would be manned by a force of some 210 men. In this way, they intended that the town, the harbour, and the naval base be protected by an arc of fortifications extending from Cedar Island to Murney Point, as well as providing for landward defences. Had it been constructed, this grand military design would have made Kingston the most heavily fortified centre in British North America. At an estimated cost of over a quarter of a million pounds sterling, it would also have been among the most expensive of Imperial defences to date. However, the Imperial government again baulked at the budget of £273,000.

In January a short-term and piecemeal compromise was reached. While the concept of redoubts and towers was approved in principle, the final outcome was the construction of only one of the redoubts, Fort Henry. Quarrying the stone for construction had commenced as early as 1828, but three years later Kingstonians were cynical at the lack of progress. The *Chronicle* complained that "the long projected works at Kingston are slumbering like the stone which covers so many acres on the government quarries at Point Henry in a state of such torpidity" and recommended "a public sale of the thousands of pounds worth which are carved and squared and numbered so mechanically."[21]

Under the direction of Sir Richard Bonnycastle of the Royal Engineers, actual construction proceeded in 1832, and by 1836 the redoubt, advanced battery, and east and west ditches had been completed, at a cost of £81,587.[22]

Within a decade of the completion of Fort Henry, there were doubts as to its effectiveness. In 1841 a military survey of the fortifications and defence of the frontier argued:

Our chance of acquiring and retaining naval ascendancy upon Lake Ontario in War depends upon the security of Kingston and its Harbour.

There is no protection to either at present. Fort Henry however good in itself as a detached work is inadequate to this purpose.

Kingston is a place of the greatest importance to us and should be protected by a system of good permanent works.[23]

Another report later in the same year, with the benefit of hindsight, referred to the original plans of the 1820s as "well calculated to accomplish the defence of the Town, Harbour, Dock Yard and arsenal." This assessment regretted the "system of defence" could not be realized because "the necessary sites were not immediately purchased."[24]

The major problem concerned the extensive defence works proposed to the west of the Cataraqui River. Some 1,958 acres were needed, and the military estimated that this would cost £97,848 – at £50 per acre. But this was too sanguine. The Reverend William Herchmer owned 200 acres of the land required for Redoubts 4 and 5, and both his initial price of £600 per acre and the subsequent compromise of £500 per acre were too rich for the parsimonious Ordnance purse. In the face of such hard bargaining, the 1841 planners had to settle for something less grand, and recommended that "field defences contingent upon circumstances be substituted" for the earlier proposal of six redoubts.[25]

One interesting compromise proposal advanced in 1843 by N. Holloway of the Royal Engineers was that St Mark's, the new stone church to be constructed at Barriefield, be so designed that in times of attack it could serve as a defensive point in lieu of Redoubt 2 that had been planned for the location. While this proposal was as imaginative as it was irreverent – and not without precedent elsewhere – it appears that it did not meet with military favour. With deteriorating Anglo-American relations making hostilities at least probable, the British experts recommended that additional defences "be constructed forthwith."[26]

Accordingly, an advanced battery overlooking the harbour was added to Fort Henry in 1842, while the Oregon Crisis of the mid-1840s resulted in the appropriation of monies to enhance the defences around the town and harbour. Earlier military recommendations were dusted off. Between 1846 and 1848 Martello towers were constructed on Murney's Point (Murray Redoubt), the Market Shoal (Victoria Tower), Point Frederick (Fort Frederick Tower), and Cedar Island (Cathcart Redoubt), together with additional work on existing fortifications. For a decade these elements stood as mere monuments to military architecture as they were not fully armed until 1863.

If the period after the War of 1812-1814 saw increased military expenditures on Kingston's fortifications, the naval establishment experienced considerable retrenchment. The war had developed Kingston's Point Frederick and Navy Bay into the premier naval base on the Great Lakes. Its yards had geared up to peak production by the close of hostilities; but with the signing of the Treaty of Ghent the ships were taken off the lakes, their crews were paid off, and further construction was halted. The experience of the war had demonstrated to both the British and the Americans that dominance of the lakes required considerable investment in ship-building and support facilities, and that demilitarization of the lakes was the preferred route to resolving their disputes in the region.

The ensuing Rush-Bagot Treaty guaranteed demilitarization and laid the basis for the eventual dismantling of Kingston's naval establishment. Moreover, there had been continuous concern over the vulnerability of the Point Frederick naval base. Such was the concern that in 1828 Commodore Barrie and Colonel Wright had surveyed the Bay of Quinte for alternative locations, and having considered several to be superior to Point Frederick, recommended

making the Entrance to the Canal at Kingston Mills the principal Depot for the Naval Stores, provided the ground be capable of being thoroughly fortified, being free from any apprehension of nautical Attack, to which Kingston Dockyard is subject, as well during the absence of the Fleet, or in case that even meeting with adversity of any sort, and being also far more subject to land Attack than the Inland Position of Kingston Mills.[27]

Land was aquired at Kingston Mills and a naval reserve surveyed there, but with the decision to fortify Kingston and its harbour, the emphasis shifted away from

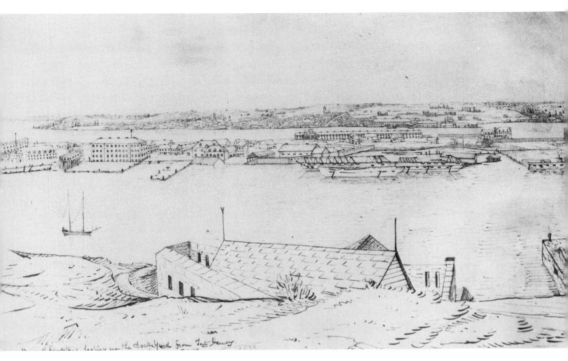

View of Point Frederick and Kingston, by Lieut. E.C. Frome, 1833. (QU Agnes Etherington Art Centre)

naval toward military defences. The fleet was laid up in the nineteenth-century version of "mothballs," and visitors of the period frequently commented on the sight of the hulks moored in Navy Bay and the incomplete hulls on the stocks on Point Frederick. Some monies were expended in the construction of storehouses, wharves, and walls around the yards; but in 1832, several of the vessels and much equipment were auctioned off, the hulk of the once-splendid *St Lawrence* being purchased for a mere £25.

In 1834, the naval yard was closed and its personnel paid off. The Kingston *Spectator* bemoaned the loss:

The Navy Point ... has the appearance of something like a deserted town. It presents a strange contrast to the life and vitality it exhibited a few years ago. Nearly all the houses are unoccupied, the Yard closed, and the guard withdrawn. ... Nothing is more missed than the regularness of the Dockyard Bell; it was as good as a town clock to the inhabitants.[28]

The Rebellion of 1837-1838, the Oregon Crisis of the 1840s, and the Fenian troubles of the 1860s resulted in brief and limited periods of revitalization, but Kingston's days as the centre of the British naval presence on the Great Lakes were ended.

THE MILITARY PRESENCE IN KINGSTON

Between 1820 and 1870, Kingston continued to be very much a military town. Even though not all the grandiose plans of the 1820s were implemented, and even though the naval base was inactive, the investment in Kingston's defences during the 1830s and 1840s reinforced the "citadel" character of Kingston. Only Halifax and Quebec City could claim to possess equally visible and dominant military presences. Indeed, this was not lost on the neighbouring American communities to the south. The construction activity in the 1840s must have appeared to them as threateningly bellicose, and certainly it prompted comment in Watertown, New York:

Great Britain is carefully fostering her resources, pouring in a class of superior emigrants, strengthening the military positions, and in every respect putting the country in such a condition that in case of war, we will find there formidable antagonists.[29]

The same report raised the spectre of the aftermath of a future British invasion that had "destroyed our farm houses and barns, laid in ashes our fair towns and villages, destroyed our crops, and drove off our flocks and herds."

In Kingston, however, the military prospect augured growth and prosperity. Throughout this period, a garrison of approximately a thousand men looked to the townspeople of Kingston for the satisfaction of its various wants. In 1841, for example, the complement of soldiers and officers in Kingston consisted of two field officers, thirty officers, ten staff sergeants, and 1,190 non-commissioned officers and men.[30] In that year, some £21,571 in pay and allowances was dispensed to this establishment, much of which eventually trickled down to the local economy.[31] Moreover, the daily issue of provisions for each rank consisted of a pound of bread or biscuit, a pound of fresh meat, and half a pint of peas. There was an allowance of sixteen cubic feet of firewood for cooking for every twelve men, while another forty-eight cubic feet were allocated for heating the barracks. Officers' horses were issued nine pounds of oats, draught horses fourteen pounds of bran, oxen sixteen pounds of hay and six pounds of straw, and artillery horses required ten pounds of oats, twelve pounds of hay, and eight pounds of straw.[32] It may be estimated that during the 1830s, some 2,000 cords of wood, 1,600 barrels of flour, 36,000 pounds of straw, and 4,500 pounds of candles were purchased annually from local suppliers – while still other suppliers were hired to provide water, laundry services, and general repairs. The call for tenders for the provision of water to the Fort reveals that no less than five hundred gallons a day were required throughout the year.[33]

By 1845, the military were spending some $20,000 to $24,000 a month in the community. This was obviously a benefit to Kingston's economy, but there were negative effects as well. Certainly, the considerable demand for craftsmen and the wages paid them were considered to be inflationary. The flurry of construction activity in 1846 was particularly disruptive and occasioned much comment:

With the certainty of an increase of wages from the number of men required and the rapidity with which the work is to be done with the chance of War, prudent persons have calculated on a contingency of at least 25 per cent over the ordinary wages and costs of materials. ... However, this may be these works will cause a circulation during the next year of some 60 to 70,000 pounds, so that somebody will benefit by the expenditure.[34]

As construction proceeded, these fears were realized and the *Daily British Whig* lamented that "there is a great scarcity in Kingston of tradesmen, labourers and farm servants. Not a carpenter, or bricklayer can be had for love or money ... the Government works absorb all the labourers."[35]

The social impact was equally mixed. The Kingston Histrionic Society opened its 1844 season with productions of the patriotic *The Youthful Queen* and the more prosaic *The Rent Day*. The audience included His Excellency The Governor-General, and the entertainment benefited from the presence of the band of the 14th Regiment in the orchestra. Concerts, cricket matches, skating parties, picnics, and soirées all reflected the presence of the military who were closely integrated into the Kingston social scene.

But the forays of the other ranks into the streets of Kingston were not viewed so favourably. Maintaining harmonious relations between the garrison and its host-community taxed the military and municipal authorities alike. As early as 1820 Commander Barrie recommended the construction of a stone wall around the naval establishment at Point Frederick. His concern was a double-barrelled one: not only "intended for defence as well as to enclose the Naval Hospital & confine the artificers belonging to the Dock Yard Establishment within bounds," the wall was also for the protection of his command from an invasion of "Houses (Chanties) many of these are occupied by people in no way attached to the services – for the most part a very disorderly set – some keeping Boarding & Lodging Houses in the present acceptance of the term."[36] With the burgeoning of the garrison in the 1830s these problems worsened, and in 1840 the Kingston *Chronicle* complained that "Disguise it as we may, the streets of Kingston are night and day swarming with Drunkards and prostitutes, and never since we have been residents of the Town have we seen so much vice as now prevails, and which seems to be daily increasing."[37] The greatest abuse was thought to be the large number of licensed and, worse, unlicensed drinking houses. In Barriefield alone, proximity to the military and naval establishments ensured the success of no fewer than nine public houses engaged in the "sale of liquors to soldiers and sailors who are led to the greatest of all crimes, desertion, through intoxication."[38]

Given the severity of the contemporary response to desertion, one wonders why any soldier would contemplate it – even when intoxicated! One visitor to Kingston during wartime described the execution of one poor miscreant on the common outside the town. He further recorded the prevailing practice of inducing Indians to

Tête-du-Pont Barracks and Front (Ontario) Street, by Maj.-Gen. James Pattison Cockburn, 1830. (QUA)

intercept deserters in the woods by rewards for their apprehension, dead or alive. He witnessed them bringing back some members of the Glengarry Regiment who had failed to elude them – one body hanging on a pole – and holding aloft the head of one of De Watteville's Regiment to serve as a discouragement of the "pernicious effects of desertion in time of war."[39]

There were other social impacts of the carousing. In March 1846, the worst case of violence between the military and the local populace took place, and one provincial surveyor visiting the city was confined to his room by the "horrible affrays and much bloodshed" in street fighting between "the soldiers and a lot of rapscallions among the civilians." With his "chain-man" wounded and he himself fearing that "several lives have been lost," we can sympathize with his further lament "I am getting homesick and sick of Kingston."[40] No doubt others in the community found Kingston's first-hand experience with the troops of the Empire to be a mixed blessing, however remunerative it may have been.

By mid-century the continued contribution of the military to the economy and society of Kingston was beginning to be questioned. The considerable construction activity of the 1830s and 1840s was not to be repeated. The closing of the naval dockyards in the 1830s was a portent of things to come, as was the departure of the garrison for the Crimean War in 1854. While the complement of soldiers based at Kingston returned to an average of 629 officers and men throughout the period 1854-1865, it was evident that the city could not count on its military function continuing much longer.

Concern over this problem had been expressed on previous occasions by several interested parties in Kingston. Writing in 1856, C.W. Cooper, for example, in a prize-winning essay, advanced a critique of the mixed blessings of the military presence. Cooper was generally critical of the town's dependence upon this external source of revenue:

Kingston has always been a military station, and ... in the construction of military works, the maintenance of a dock yard, and of troops, and the public and private expenditure of officers and men, much money has been laid out which was not earned or created there; that is, such money was not, save to a limited extent, paid for [by] the products of the soil, or produced by manufactures, or the increased value of materials in return for the labor and skill bestowed upon them.[41]

He went on to complain about the "transient" benefits of this relationship and the consequent dependency "on these external sources of wealth." Cooper preferred the use of the "legitimate resources of the country," and deplored the employment of people in "unproductive, not to say demoralizing" tasks. The result was "a great increase of small inns, taverns and groggeries." In conclusion, Cooper argued that "one thousand pounds expended in the macadamization of a road, is equal in general benefit to many thousands of casual outlay occasioned by the troops and officers in garrison."[42]

Others disagreed, however, and vexed themselves over the departure of the military, worrying that "The military spent £100,000 a year in the city, and the loss has to be made good, but how?"[43]

On 3 October 1870 the last noon gun was fired by Imperial forces at Fort Henry,[44] and the city was forced to look elsewhere for its main revenues.

FOUR

Loyal in Rebellion

THE THREAT

Upper Canada was shaken to its roots by the cataclysmic events that occurred between 1836 and 1840. Every facet of provincial life, including the province's very existence, was affected. Kingston had little influence over these events, but the events profoundly influenced the city.

The arrival in Toronto of the new lieutenant-governor, Sir Francis Bond Head, in January 1836, was seen by many as auspicious. He was to pursue a policy of conciliation and bring calm to a turbulent colony. Such was not the outcome. In a show of unprecedented independence Head broke the Family Compact's stranglehold on the Executive Council by appointing Reformers to that august body. But Head was a hopeless conciliator, and was soon at loggerheads with the Reform-dominated Assembly that had been elected in 1834. In a deepening political and economic crisis, Head dissolved the Assembly and gave personal leadership to Tory forces in the ensuing campaign. This was Upper Canada's first overt "loyalty" election, and Head and the Tories won a sweeping victory. Christopher Hagerman, a pillar of the Compact, was acclaimed in Kingston.

Electoral success did not solve Head's problems, and embittered and extremist Reformers took over the opposition forces. William Lyon Mackenzie rose to an undisputed leadership that ended in tragedy when he led his men into a hopeless and foolish rebellion that culminated in a decisive engagement properly described by Gerald Craig as "tragicomedy," on 5 December 1837.[1] Mackenzie "had no broad following," and the rising was easily suppressed by Upper Canadians within the context of their own constitution and their own institutions.[2]

Concomitant with Upper Canada's political crisis were other movements well-designed to have a profound impact on conservative Kingstonians. Rebellion anywhere was abhorrent to them, and internal violence was combined with a vastly more serious and protracted movement in Lower Canada that extended well into 1838 and involved the ever-distrusted French Canadians.

Even more threatening to a Loyalist town was the internationalization of the Canadian rebellion movements. Mackenzie and other Patriot leaders fled to the

United States after the December fiasco. On 15 December Mackenzie and his cohorts occupied Navy Island, Canadian territory in the Niagara River. There they established a "provisional government" and pledged to conquer Upper Canada. Navy Island was to be provisioned by an American ship, the *Caroline*. A.B. Corey described how Colonel Allan MacNab, an Upper Canadian militia leader and Compact stalwart, took steps to prevent this necessary logistical support by attacking the supply ship on 29 December:

he commissioned Commander Andrew Drew, R.N., to command a nocturnal expedition to destroy the *Caroline*. Drew's force of seven boats and fifty men set out that evening for Navy Island where they expected to find the *Caroline* moored for the night. Not finding the ship there, they continued across the river to Schlosser in New York State where they discovered the *Caroline* made fast to a dock. In addition to the crew there were on board some twenty passengers who had been unable to secure accommodations at the single small tavern in the village. Nothing daunted, since his instructions authorized him to destroy the ship wherever he found it, Drew led his men aboard. In the general melee which followed, one man, Amos Durfee, was killed and several were wounded. The ship was set on fire and towed out into the current of the Niagara River where it sank before it reached the Falls.[3]

The result was a raging fury to the south of the border, and a major crisis in Canadian-American relations: as Corey explained, "war between Great Britain and the United States was universally expected."[4]

Canadian *émigrés* alone could not mount and sustain an assault on British power in North America. They needed American help, and were quick to get it. The American border country, suffering the results of the economic panic of 1836 and inflamed by the sinking of the *Caroline*, was quick to respond. And why not? All that Mackenzie and his people were doing was attempting to repeat the success of the American Revolution. Canadians, it was widely believed across the line, were oppressed by the British and anxious to shed their colonial yoke. All they needed was some help.

Assistance came quickly. During 1838 and 1839 at least five secret societies dedicated to Canadian liberation were organized in the United States. The first was the Canadian Refugee Relief Association; it was "bent upon embroiling the United States and Great Britain in war."[5] The most famous and effective such society was the Hunters' Lodges. They required members to take an oath that illustrates the nature of the organization and makes crystal-clear why it was so abhorrent to loyal Kingstonians:

I swear to do my utmost to promote Republican Institutions and ideas throughout the world – to cherish them, to defend them; and especially to devote myself to the propagation, protection, and defence of these institutions in North America. I pledge my life, my property, and my sacred honor [*sic*] to the Association; I bind myself to its interests,

and I promise, until death, that I will attack, combat, and help to destroy, by all means
that my superior may think proper, every power, or authority, of Royal origin, upon this
continent; and especially never to rest till all tyrants of Britain cease to have any dominion or footing whatever in North America. I further solemnly swear to obey the orders
delivered to me by my superior, and never to disclose any such order, or orders, except
to a brother "Hunter" of the same degree. So help me God.[6]

These secret societies were not mere social clubs for men who wanted to play at being
soldiers. Men were armed and drilled; invasion plans were formulated and occasionally executed. American authorities were maddeningly slow to intervene and
enforce neutrality in the border areas.

An early invasion plan, devised before the spread of secret societies, was directed
at Kingston:

Of the three proposed advances against the Canadas, that against Kingston was the only
one which started on February 22 [1838]. Throughout the previous week Mackenzie
directed preparations from Watertown, New York, some twenty-five miles from the
border. Food and arms were moved to the mouth of French Creek which flows into the
St. Lawrence opposite Gananoque, sixteen miles east of Kingston. Here the Patriots
gathered, some three to five hundred in number, on the afternoon of the twenty-second,
while people from miles around came to witness the invasion. Under the leadership of
Van Rensselaer, the force occupied Hickory Island within Canadian jurisdiction.[7]

Van Rensselaer did not have enough volunteers to proceed, however, and withdrew
to American territory.

The strength of the secret societies became evident in the spring of 1838. On 28
or 29 May 1838, the Canadian Refugee Relief Association stranded and burned the
steamliner *Sir Robert Peel* (largely owned by Brockville magnates) in American waters
near Clayton. This was no doubt to avenge the sinking of the *Caroline*. Further incursions followed rapidly. Between two and four hundred men occupied Navy Island
and Chippewa in June. They won a brief skirmish at Short Hills, but on 23 June
1838 the invaders were soundly defeated by a combined force of British regulars and
Canadian militia, some thirty-one being taken prisoner.[8] The most famous incident
of all occurred in November 1838, when troops of Hunters crossed the St Lawrence
in order to capture Fort Wellington at Prescott. The mission was not a success, but
then a force led by Nils von Schoultz landed at Windmill Point, downstream from
Prescott, their original objective, and occupied the thick-walled mill. It was only
with substantial difficulty and significant losses that the regulars and militia crushed
the Patriots and took most of them prisoners. The victory at Windmill Point did
not end the military phase of the border crisis. On 4 December 1838 some two hun-

dred filibusters invaded Windsor. They were repulsed, with twenty-five killed and forty-four taken prisoner.

Mackenzie and his allies were not able to muster enough power to conquer Upper Canada, but they had enough to make 1838 a year of fear and terror, and the diplomatic crisis continued into 1840 and 1841. Kingston was a conservative town that supported the Family Compact. Rebellion and invasion strengthened its loyalty and support for the constitution that had not only weathered but suppressed risings, invasion, and treason. Now, however, that system of government was under even more serious assault, and this from an inexplicable quarter.

The rebellions of 1837-1838, especially the more sustained rising in Lower Canada, brought Canadian problems to the centre of attention in British governing circles. There was obviously a problem in the Canadas, and the British government determined to analyze and solve it. In 1838 it appointed John George Lambton, earl of Durham, as governor-in-chief of British North America and high commissioner "for the adjustment of certain important questions depending in the said Provinces of *Lower* and *Upper Canada* respecting the form and future government of the said Provinces. ..."9

Durham was a known radical, and his enquiry was regarded with considerable trepidation among conservatives. His overall stay in the Canadas was not long, and his visit to Upper Canada lasted only a few days. Early in 1839 the famous report was published. It constituted a full-scale assault on the Upper Canadian *status quo*. Lord Durham recommended the legislative union of Upper and Lower Canada. This would bring Upper Canadians into intimate proximity with French Canadians. He recommended further that the principle of responsible government be accepted, and that it become the governing principle in a new constitutional settlement. Conservatives were aghast at what they regarded as a major concession to treason. Perhaps worse was Durham's frontal assault on the Family Compact and a system of government that had proved its worth in suppressing rebellion and invasion. He dismissed the Compact out of hand and gave comfort to its opponents:

A monopoly of power so extensive and so lasting could not fail, in process of time, to excite envy, create dissatisfaction, and ultimately provoke attack; and an opposition consequently grew up in the Assembly which assailed the ruling party, by appealing to popular principles of government, by denouncing the alleged jobbing and profusion of the official body, and by instituting inquiries into abuses, for the purpose of promoting reform, and especially economy. 10

Not all of Durham's recommendations were accepted, but the crucial recommendation that the Canadas be united became Imperial policy.

Durham's successor, Charles Poulett Thomson, soon to be made Lord Sydenham, arrived in Canada in October 1839 to implement union.

KINGSTON FIGHTS BACK

Kingston was not central to the cataclysmic events of 1836-1841, but it was nonetheless intimately involved in them. Christopher Alexander Hagerman, for example, was a major Family Compact figure, and on 23 March 1837 he became attorney-general of Upper Canada. He held that crucial post during the rebellion and filibustering periods. Hagerman left the Executive Council on 15 February 1840 to accept a place on the court of king's bench, where he remained until he died.[11] Hagerman's departure from politics symbolizes the demise of the Family Compact, which never recovered from the blows delivered by Head, Durham, and Sydenham. Kingston was, however, able to enter the post-Compact age under new leaders who were able to adjust to the reality of the era of the union.

And, of course, Kingston, as a primary target for the Patriots, was central to the military situation in the period 1837-1839. The garrison, substantially smaller than had been the case during the War of 1812-1814, had for the most part been sent by Lieutenant-Governor Sir Francis Bond Head to Lower Canada. Kingston was responsible for its own defence during these exciting years.

Threats to Kingston's world confirmed Kingstonians in their loyalty. An editorial in the *Chronicle* made this abundantly clear in a first-rate summary statement:

We say to the Americans we have been in daily intercourse with you, we have had large commercial transactions with you, we have even entwined ourselves with you by numerous family connexions, even by the nearest and dearest ties of relationship; we have witnessed with pleasure your prosperity; we have sympathized with you in adversity; but we never asked your aid, we never wished your help, to detach us from the mother country, to take from us the British Constitution, and to institute for it a republic; we tell you, and we say it advisedly, that nine-tenths of our population prefer the form of government we have to yours; we tell you that we are not an ill-governed or oppressed people, we are almost wholly free from taxation, we enjoy full, free and perfect liberty.[12]

This was no mere newspaper talk. When the Lower Canadian situation became frightening in the fall of 1837, Kingstonians gathered in a public meeting and resolved that "We cannot any longer defer the declaration of our determination to support with our lives and fortunes the supremacy of the British Constitution and the just dependence of the Canadas upon the British Crown."[13]

When rebellion erupted in the Toronto district, Kingston found itself stripped of regular troops. Kingston was left in the care of the local militia units and, in Donald Creighton's words, the populace

rushed together, in a great spontaneous movement, to improvise their own defence. ... The town was divided into wards for protective purposes; the townsmen were hurriedly enrolled and armed; and all night long, stout patrols, each headed by a magistrate, tramped through the echoing streets.[14]

Fort Henry was manned by a company of volunteer artillery and over five hundred citizens were armed. Major Richard Bonnycastle was appointed lieutenant-colonel of the militia, and he later recalled that

it being judged expedient and most urgent that Kingston, the key of the Province and the Depot of Ordnance Stores should be placed in such a position as to ensure its safe keeping against the designs of the disaffected and the Banditti from the United States, I was ordered to place the Fort Batteries and Town in an immediate State of Defence and to Garrison them with Militia.[15]

Particular attention was directed to the defence of the Rideau Canal, the vulnerability of which was very much on the minds of the Kingston garrison during the months of insecurity. The locks and dams were particularly susceptible to attack and destruction, and the threat posed by American irregulars like the Hunters' Lodges was sufficient to require action to ensure that this strategic line of transportation was not interrupted. Additional guard-houses were constructed at Jones Falls, the crucial water-control point at Whitefish Dam, and several other lock stations. The local militia manned these defences until September 1838, when a detachment of the 71st Regiment relieved them. Moreover, on learning of Mackenzie's revolt to the west, Kingston's leaders sent aid against him: "Arms, ammunition, and a couple of field pieces – all watched over by a strong, volunteer guard – were despatched back to Toronto by the *Traveller*."[16] The Upper Canadian rebellion movement was suppressed by the end of the year, but the threat from the south was a more protracted problem.

In February 1838, as noted briefly before this, the Patriots centred on Watertown, New York, determined to conquer Kingston, and some three to four hundred of these hopeful conquerors did manage to occupy Hickory Island. Militia units from the adjoining counties of Hastings, Lennox and Addington, Prince Edward, and Leeds joined the three companies of Frontenac militiamen. By February 1838, Bonnycastle was in command of three troops of dragoons, five companies of artillery, a considerable if variegated body of infantry, together with a band of Mohawk Indian warriors. Bonnycastle, while not omitting to refer to his own services, credited this force of some 1,300 officers and men with preventing

the Plan of the Conspirators on the 22nd. February, 1838, of attacking this Place from the States and the Interior simultaneously from taking place, as the pirate force assembled at Hickory Island was dispersed and I intercepted part of the Rebel Force at Napanee and some Prisoners and Arms were taken from both.[17]

The most serious threat to Kingston, however, came in November. The Hunters' Lodges, visible and noisy, were prepared for a major incursion. The garrison was back from Lower Canada, but the militiamen were still filled with martial enthusiasm and were quick to organize. As Creighton notes, "On November 1 ... the Kingstonians assembled in public meetings, divided the town into five wards for protective purposes and re-established the night watch which had been formed just nearly a year before."[18] More was to come: "The second regiment of the Frontenac Militia was called out; the volunteer company of artillery was stationed at Fort Henry; over 500 citizens were armed; and at night the civic guard perambulated the town and cavalry patrols trotted through the silent streets."[19]

The big event of November, as noted before, was an abortive invasion of eastern Ontario. The grandiose plans were bungled, and a small invasion led by Nils von Schoultz was crushed, this time by regular troops under Colonel Dundas. The battle had been bloody, with "About sixty of all ranks ... wounded, and sixteen killed ...," and this before the mill was stormed.[20] A sensation of the Windmill incident was the mutilation, allegedly by Patriots, of the corpse of a British regular, Lieutenant Johnston. Loyal Kingstonians were aghast, and tantalizingly horrified.[21]

It is somewhat paradoxical, and even symbolic, that despite these fervent military preparations and movements, the only contact Kingston had with the enemy and the conflict was the vicarious one of confining prisoners and trying traitors. The weapons were law-books, the champions were lawyers, the battlefield the military courts, and the strains and horrors of these difficult years were manifested in legal cases. Most of them involved the rising star of Kingston politics, John A. Macdonald. The first trial occurred during the summer of 1838. Eight men, all from surrounding districts, had been charged with treason. They were almost certainly guilty, although their offences, which dated from February, involved little more than hare-brained plots against public order. Their manifest guilt was forgiven in Justice McLean's court – no doubt because of their inherent harmlessness. John A. Macdonald had won an early, if hardly typical, acquittal.

Then came a genuine *cause célèbre* that tested the extent to which the town and its institutions were able to maintain impartiality. Late on 29 July 1838, fifteen prisoners of state, including the notorious John Montgomery, escaped from Fort Henry and fled to safety across the border. It was clear after a quick investigation that escape was possible only by the assistance of one or more of the custodians. In a display of panicked judgment, Colonel Henry Dundas arrested and confined the jailer himself, John Ashley, to jail. Unfortunately for Dundas, the arrest was irregular because no warrant was obtained for several hours after the event. Even worse, there was not a shred of evidence against Ashley, who after eight hours was released.

John Ashley was a thoroughly respectable man who lived in a community that esteemed respectability. He was properly furious, and sued Dundas for £1,000. He retained John A. Macdonald and Henry Smith Jr as his attorneys. Dundas retained Christopher Hagerman. It was, of course, a spectacular trial, involving as it did several of Kingston's leading citizens. It also symbolized "the tension between civil and military authority in Kingston. ..."[22] Ashley won his case, and was awarded £200.

An early photograph of a young John A. Macdonald. (Orlo and Meridon Miller)

The community was clearly divided over this clash between civil and military power. The *Upper Canada Herald*, which held the jurors who made the award "as men who understand the rights of British subjects, and have the spirit to maintain those rights," commented:

A few persons affect to be surprised at this verdict, and utter lamentable outcries against the Jury for giving it. ... If [Colonel Dundas's] suspicions had been certainties still he would have had no right to interfere. It was for the civil power, not the military commandant, to arrest and deal with the offender. ... In this case, Colonel Dundas allowed his zeal to outrun his discretion, and he must pay the penalty of his error. It will never be allowed in this country that a man shall be arrested and imprisoned all day by a military commandant on suspicion, and then marched between a guard of soldiers from Fort Henry to Kingston gaol as if he had been some notorious criminal. [23]

The most spectacular legal event of the season, however, arose out of the Battle of the Windmill. The captured Patriots were put on display in Prescott (where they had planned a massacre of leading Tories), and then transferred to Kingston by boat. A prisoner later described the scene:

It was about midnight when we arrived at Kingston. We were tied together in couples, von Schoultz at the head, a rope passing between us. ... In this condition, with a line of soldiers on each side, we were marched to Fort Henry, about one mile distant from the landing, the band playing "Yankee Doodle." During this march we were subjected to the foulest abuse from the spectators, pelted with clubs, and spit upon with impunity. Our heroic leader was struck with a stroke on the hip, which caused lameness from which he never recovered. [24]

Von Schoultz, the "heroic leader," was in actual fact an unstable philanderer who was also a very foolish soldier of fortune. Nonetheless, he looked and acted like a brave and noble man while his badly-deluded colleagues, many of them little more than children, were terrified of the death by hanging that they quickly learned was the fate of aliens taken in arms upon Canadian soil. Under the law, such persons were court-martialled without benefit of legal representation. Many were spared death, but eleven were hanged, including von Schoultz, who was given the dubious privilege of a private execution. Daniel Heustis, one of the prisoners who was spared, later described the grisly scene:

After his condemnation, von Schoultz was removed from Fort Henry to the jail in the village of Kingston, and we never saw him again. The last parting scene, in which he bid us all farewell, filled every heart with grief. He spoke a kind word to each one and exhorted us all to die like men. His bearing, in this hour of severe trial, as it had ever been, was manly and noble. On the 6th, 3 days after the sham trial, the death-warrant

was read to him, and on the 8th he suffered a martyr's death on the scaffold. During his
short imprisonment, he won the esteem of all who had come in contact with him. The
officers of the 83rd Regiment, in particular, who had witnessed his heroism on the field
of battle, sought his acquaintance, and became deeply interested in his fate. They im-
plored Sir George Arthur [lieutenant-governor of Upper Canada, and major general
commanding the forces therein] to spare his life, but that bloody tyrant turned a deaf
ear to every supplication in behalf of the victim he had determined to sacrifice. When
the hour of execution arrived, von Schoultz shook hands with those around him, and
every eye was suffused with tears. He was prepared to die; in his last moments he
betrayed no unmanly weakness; he marched with a firm and fearless step to the gallows,
where his virtuous and patriotic life was brought to a premature close.[25]

Poor von Schoultz. He left behind a wife and family in Europe, and at least one
fiancée in the United States, and it was all for nothing. In one of his last letters he
acknowledged the fact that Canadians did not require liberation:

My last wish to the Americans is that they may not think of avenging my death. Let no
further blood be shed; and believe me, from what I have seen, that all the stories that
were told about the sufferings of the Canadian people were untrue.[26]

Ten additional executions were spaced throughout December 1838 and January and
February 1839.[27] They served to mark the breaking of the rebellion locally and
underscore Kingston's continued commitment to Loyalism and the Crown.

FIVE

Capital of Canada

LORD SYDENHAM'S CHOICE

Rebels, battles, patriots, and trials convulsed Kingston in 1837 and 1838. In 1839, attention was refocused, this time on the future, and it was indeed exciting to contemplate what might be in store for the old Loyalist capital.

Durham's mission to Canada ended in crisis when the governor-general was censured by Imperial authorities for his decision to use Bermuda as a dumping-ground for exiled Lower Canadian rebels. His *Report* was nonetheless written, and his successor, Charles Poulett Thomson – soon to be Lord Sydenham – was instructed to implement some of his recommendations. Lord Durham's key recommendation, the granting of responsible government, was rejected. The union of the Canadas, however, was accepted. Durham's solution to the French problem was also accepted: the French Canadians were to be anglicized. Union and anglicization were very serious matters that contained profoundly important implications for Kingston.

British Imperial policy during the 1830s was complicated. Responsible government was not conceded. At the same time local constitutions were not to be interfered with lightly. Thomson was thus instructed to secure Canadian approval for an Act of Union that would encompass the desired policy. This was easy in the case of Lower Canada. Its constitution *had* been interfered with. Indeed it had collapsed during the Rebellion of 1837-1838. Lower Canada's supreme legislative body was an appointive Special Council. Its members had been hand-picked by Durham and posed no threat to the union scheme.[1] Upper Canada's constitution, however, had not collapsed. In fact, Upper Canadians had crushed their little rebellion and fended off most of the border raids without benefit of Imperial troops, who had rather been sent to assist the authorities in Lower Canada.

In a word, Upper Canada's conservative leaders were bullish, and were not about to give easy agreement to a new constitution that would end their province's autonomy. Many factors came into play on this issue. Francophobia influenced many, as did a more general fear of merging Upper Canada with a substantially more populous Lower Canada. But some key Upper Canadians, including many Kingstonians, favoured a reconstitution of the political and economic unity of the St Lawrence.[2] Conservative leaders – and the conservatives were clearly in the ascendant after their crushing victory over the rebels – were also susceptible to British pressure. They were men of self-conscious loyalty. Resisting the pressures, threats, and blandishments of the Imperial government would not be easy. Upper Canada was almost certain to come around, but at a price.

The legislative leaders negotiated. They failed to get everything that they desired, but they got a lot. Upper Canada's heavy debt would be assumed by the Union government, which meant that much of it would be paid by French Canada. The Union would be an anglicizing unit, with English the only official language. Numbers and justice notwithstanding, each section of the new Union would have an identical number of members in the elected Assembly. And the capital of the Union would be located in the old province of Upper Canada.

This last condition was logical within the framework of Sydenham's overall policy mandate. If the French Canadians were to be anglicized, it would make no sense to locate the seat of government in Quebec City or Montreal. An Anglophone community in Upper Canada would clearly win that prize, and so Sydenham agreed.

The location of the seat of government could be nothing but divisive: several Upper Canadian communities vied for the honour. Sydenham had no desire to have his work sidetracked by the capital question. Publicly the issue was left open. Hence, Section XXX of the Act of Union that was passed on 23 July 1840 stated simply: "it shall be lawful for the Governor of the Province of Canada for the time being to fix such place or places within any part of the Province of Canada, and such times for holding the first and every other session of the Legislative Council and Assembly of the said Province as he may think fit. ..."[3] The fat was in the fire.

For Kingston it was a welcome opportunity. The town had always wanted to be capital, and on more than one occasion had confidently anticipated the honour. The Reverend John Stuart expected as much on 1 October 1785: "Cataraqui will certainly be the Capital of all the new Settlements."[4] And why not? Kingston was Ontario's oldest settlement and continued as the province's key naval and military town until well into the nineteenth century. It was loyal and prosperous, and was for many years the largest town in Upper Canada. But the capital had not come.

Simcoe preferred more western sites: Newark (later Niagara-on-the-Lake), London, or York (Toronto). Lieutenant-Governor Francis Gore was twice instructed to deal with the capital question. When he first arrived in 1806 he was to examine the feasibility of transferring the capital to Kingston. York's reaction was predictably strong, and York remained the seat of government. The general progress of the War of 1812-1814, and the capture of York in 1813 in particular, made the vulnerability of the capital there crystal-clear. Gore, back in the province after an absence of four years, was ordered to remedy the problem by moving the capital to Kingston. Again York campaigned vigorously to retain its dignity, and again it won. The tone of the campaign is illustrated by Sir F.P. Robinson's comment to J.B. Robinson: "tho' York is at present not tenable against an enemy, yet that it might be made so, and at no very great expense. The removal of the Seat of Government will be the ruin of the whole Bay of Quinte, and the vast sums expended by the Navy and Army, will serve to enrich the people in and near to Kingston only."[5]

There was another flurry in the mid-1820s after Sir James Carmichael Smyth's *Report to His Grace the Duke of Wellington ... Relative to His Majesty's North American Provinces* was published. Smyth was firm in his view that York was the wrong choice:

Kingston appears to us to be the natural Capital, in a Military point of view, and being the point where most important of the proposed Canals will meet, it's [*sic*] commercial importance must proportionally increase. If Kingston could be made the Seat of Government, the Civil Military and Naval Authorities would be more collected, and as appears to us, with the happiest effects to His Majesty's Service.[6]

Smyth's report did not result in the removal of the capital from York, but the issue persisted. In 1830 two votes in the Assembly affirmed the wisdom of removing the capital to a "place of security," which was the current euphemism for Kingston.[7] No action was taken. Yet another discussion in 1834 was fruitless.[8]

The Union gave Kingston its chance. Anglicization, a key Imperial policy, was unlikely to be facilitated by locating the capital in Lower Canada. Toronto was too far west to function as a capital for the new Union. By process of elimination Kingston became the obvious choice. Sydenham had given a discreet commitment that Ontario would have the honour, and Kingston was the most likely spot in central Canada. All of these arguments came together in a lengthy letter that Sydenham penned to Lord Russell on 22 May 1840.[9] Bytown was dismissed out of hand as a "very small place" that "would require such vast increase of buildings, and is altogether so remote from thickly settled Districts. ..." Toronto and Quebec City "are unfortunately, utterly unfit from their position and other circumstances for being made the permanent seat of Government. ..." These cities were at the extremities of the vast new colony, which would stretch from Gaspé in the east to what is now Thunder Bay in the west. Quebec was "surrounded by a French population," and Toronto was too much the town of the Family Compact. Montreal, of course, was a large and sophisticated city. It was also central. Unfortunately, it included too many Francophones to meet the needs of anglicization.

As Sydenham put it, the need was to have the capital in an English-speaking town:

To bring the French members to the middle of English population would instil English ideas into their minds, destroy the immediate influence upon their actions of the host of little Lawyers, Notaries & Doctors – the pest of Lower Canada ... and shew them the advantages of practical improvements & the working of English habits.

Lord Sydenham brought capital status to Kingston. (QUA)

Kingston, by this process of logic, was ideally suited to host the government. Kingston was "defensible and may be rendered still more so." Geography, argued Sydenham, favoured Kingston, which "is more central to the whole Province."

Perhaps more important to Sydenham's thinking was his view of the Union, which was heavily dependent on the wealth and prosperity of Upper Canada:

I am strongly of [the] opinion that the most important portion of the Canadas is the Upper Province. The fertility of its soil – the character of its people, the nature of Settlement, the direction which it has taken Westward – the Capabilities for improvement, the room afforded for Emigration, make Upper Canada even now an object demanding the utmost care & attention from the Government, and will render it if properly governed hereafter the source of our wealth & greatness on this Continent.

Lower Canada, on the other hand, consisted "Of a vast body of French Canadian Peasantry cultivating in the most barbarous way a soil of far less fertility. ..." The government, argued Sydenham, should be placed "as far as possible in a situation to superintend & give close attention to the affairs of that which demands it most, namely Upper Canada. ..." Kingston had plenty of Crown land that could be used for public purposes.

Taking everything into consideration, Sydenham gave "the preference decidedly to Kingston. ..." Lord Russell approved the choice in a despatch dated 22 June 1840.[10] Sydenham's choice was clear enough, but he had no intention of making any early announcement. The location of the capital was a powerful bargaining tool, and he intended to use it to the fullest.

Kingston expected the capital, and wanted the honour. The years 1839, 1840, and 1841 were exciting and tense as the city reacted to every rumour. As early as 1839 land prices "started to rise sharply," as Kingstonians began to speculate on coming up in the world.[11] Visits to the city of senior public servants sparked rounds of rumours, but Sydenham did nothing to verify or deny them. In the fall of 1840 Sydenham purchased the bulk of Lot 23 from the Reverend William Macaulay Herchmer through the Ordnance. As the master general of Ordnance put it, this magnificent property was "contiguous [sic] to the sites of certain intended works which might prove advantageous to the public service."[12] Reverend Herchmer, "a shrewd bargainer," sold his property for £25,000 and retained twelve and a half acres as a family reserve.[13]

In the midst of all this rumour and activity Sydenham, not usually regarded as naïve, wrote blithely to Lord Russell: "Hitherto not a soul suspects my intention of holding the Parlt. at Kingston and making it the seat of Govt. – on the contrary I have purposely discouraged the idea, in order to pick up for the Province the land which was necessary for Public buildings &c, in which I have just succeeded to my heart's content."[14]

By a proclamation of 5 February 1841, the Province of Canada was to come into legal existence on 10 February. The *Upper Canada Herald* proclaimed even better news to Kingstonians on 2 February 1841: "We are happy to be able to inform our readers that the secret is at last out. Kingston is to be the Seat of Government."[15] A few days later the *Chronicle and Gazette* crowed to a vanquished Toronto, "the Public Records will now be placed in a situation equally secure from foreign invasion on the one hand and from internal insurrection on the other."[16] Poor Toronto. It had hosted both rebels and raiders. It *deserved* to lose its epic struggle with its rival at the other end of the lake!

Kingston's rivals gave no easy acquiescence to the governor-general's decision. Sydenham "expected that there would be a breeze at Toronto about the Seat of Government," and he was not disappointed.[17] "The good people of Toronto without distinction of party," we are told, "have been astounded at the intelligence that the first meeting of the United Legislature is to be held at Kingston."[18] Most Lower Canadian opinion was opposed to anything connected with the Union, and could hardly be expected to endorse the choice of Kingston, which *Le Canadien* dismissed as "a town without local colour, without character."[19] Some Montreal opinion disdained the whole debate from a lofty height: "Notes of wailing and wrath have already reached us from Toronto upon the selection of Kingston for the first Session of the Legislature," noted the *Morning Courier*. "As for Montreal, we hear not her lament upon the subject. The independent citizens feel that they are to acquire greatness without artificial aids, by the advantage of position and their own energies."[20] The issue was not by any means closed, but Kingstonians were jubilant over their victory. The town was about to enter its most exciting period. It had been given the most spectacular "artificial aid" in its history.

KINGSTON TRIUMPHANT

The province of Canada came into existence on 10 February 1841. Kingston became the capital of an immense and important colony. The other major cities were Quebec, Montreal, Toronto, and Hamilton. Lower Canada, now called Canada East, was largely French-Canadian and contained some 650,000 souls. Canada West, the old Upper Canada, was much smaller and almost exclusively Anglophone. It boasted a mere 450,000 people. The two sections, however, had equal representation in the parliament that would meet in Kingston in June. It is doubtful that the Union was genuinely popular anywhere but in small and exclusive commercial circles.

The new capital was one of the oldest settlements in Canada West. But Kingston had been incorporated as a town only in 1838, four years after Toronto had become a city, and did not itself attain that status until 1846. It was small, with only some 3,000 inhabitants in 1841, and was not very extensive. The ancillary settlements remained miniscule. Portsmouth dated from the 1830s and emerged only because of the establishment there of the provincial penitentiary and the presence of good docking facilities. The Garden Island community was still in embryo, and Barriefield Village included only a handful of houses huddled behind Fort Henry.

Kingston was nonetheless an important place. Its Loyalist antecedents and leadership gave it self-confidence. Its Imperial past and pretentions lent it a sense of destiny not shared by many other emerging towns. The transshipment function provided prosperity and a mercantile élite. Effective public men with good Compact connections had kept the town in the forefront of provincial politics. Kingston's élite

Harriet Dobbs Cartwright, wife of an assistant minister at St George's, was a gifted artist and left valuable commentaries on nineteenth-century Kingston. (QUA)

was not as sophisticated as its leaders might have believed, but there was no hesitancy about assuming the role of capital. Kingstonians were confident that they possessed the facilities, the amenities, and the society required of the capital of an enormous territory with a brilliant future.

By virtue of its status, Kingston hosted some of the great public figures of the Union, and provided the arena for a number of political events of far-ranging importance. Fascinating as these men and events are, they belong more to the history of Canada than to the history of Kingston. There were, however, spin-offs that had profound implications for the town during the capital period and over the long run.

It would of course be a gross distortion of social reality not to recognize the impact on a town of the size and nature of Kingston of the arrival, as a resident, of a man as important as the governor-general of Canada, Baron Sydenham of Kent (in England) and Toronto (in Canada).

Sydenham took up residence in Kingston on Friday, 28 May 1841.[21] His arrival in town was a gala event that was marked with appropriate ceremony and festivity. The association between Sydenham and Kingston was, however, complicated. It is perhaps best described as bitter-sweet. Sydenham stood for everything the community wanted, but he was at the same time above and removed from the town. Moreover, he was highly critical of Kingston and disliked his capital intensely. His first attendance at holy worship was profoundly symbolic.

He attended St George's Anglican Church on Sunday, 30 May. Here he listened to an interminable sermon by Robert Cartwright, the assistant minister. Cartwright, son of old Richard Cartwright, was a popular clergyman, but his sermons – even in this great age of lengthy sermons – were inordinately dull. Sydenham was furious and vowed never to enter St George's again. With one fateful exception, he kept his word.

Cartwright's wife later described the incident to her parents. "Since the arrival of the Governor we have only once been favoured with his presence at the church," she reported, and went on to comment on Sydenham's choleric response to her husband's sermon:

Robert preached on the occasion and although the subject was on the Holy Spirit's influence, was of a general nature, and nothing in it ... could be deemed personal to anyone in particular. Yet it certainly was a sermon of so plain and searching a character, and delivered with so much of solemn earnestness, that it was well calculated to leave the impression, that the minister who delivered it was one who would never condescend to modify or conceal the truth or dress it up to suit fastidious ears. Whether it was the sermon or the manner he [Sydenham] disliked, I know not, but he said he would never enter the Kingston church again and he has kept his word. As he wishes to save appearances however, and is never at a loss for ways and means, he has prevailed on a neighbouring clergyman to whom he took a fancy [Agar Adamson], to make other arrangements for his own duty and to attend at Government House for the morning service.

All logic indicated that the governor-general would become at once the pillar and the idol of Kingston society. But such was not the case for Mrs Cartwright: "In all likelihood," she continued, "he will leave this place in September – I hope the turn of affairs will bring men to the helm of more principle and integrity. ..."[22]

Others, even more direct, regarded Sydenham as "lax in his morality,"[23] and John Richardson was appalled:

His Lordship, with all his activity and energy of mind, was a sensualist, and his sacrifices to Venus were scarcely less copious than those rendered to Bacchus. It was well known that his establishment at one time acknowledged the sway of at least one mistress. ... His Lordship, moreover, paid great court to several Canadian ladies, both in Toronto and Montreal. Married as well as unmarried – French and English – in turn, excited his homage. ... At the table, Lord Sydenham is said to have indulged, and fed the gout, by which he had been so long and painfully afflicted, with every viand the most calculated to ensure its continuance ... turtle or mock-turtle soup ... porter ... champagne.

A portion of the will that Sydenham made the day before his death indicates that the critics and gossips were at least partially correct: "I give and bequeath unto my Housekeeper Amy Washer and to the child with which she is now big or of which she has lately been delivered, an annuity of £200 for their joint lives and the life of the survivor of them, and I request my aforesaid brother George, to act as the guardian of such child."[24]

Sydenham was Kingston's most important resident, but other important men flooded into the little city that was now the centre of Canada in a very real way. As the governor-general explained, "Here everything centres in the Government. The most trifling affairs are a matter of reference from all parts of the country, and the most constant and immediate reference is daily required to the Public Departments and the Documents preserved in them."[25]

One of the more important of the newcomers was Kingston's own sitting member. The local political situation was most interesting. Christopher Hagerman, a veteran legislator and supporter of the old Compact, had been acclaimed in 1836. He typified Kingston's past, but not its future. Hagerman, a staunch defender of Anglican privilege – especially its exclusive access to the province's Clergy Reserves – had alienated the rising and dynamic Scots Presbyterian community in Kingston.

Kingston was no less conservative in 1841 than it had been in 1820, when it gained status as a separate constituency, and first sent Hagerman to York. But its conservatism was changing. Anglicans, Loyalists, and Compact men were no longer dominant. The Scots Presbyterians, many of them men who arrived some time after the Loyalists, and almost all supporters of the established Church of Scotland, were the ascendant faction. They were making their way in business, the professions, and politics. They chaffed under the leadership of Compact Anglicans like Hagerman who, in 1837, had beaten back Presbyterian claims to share Clergy Reserve revenues – claims that were theoretically valid, since the Church of Scotland, like the Church of England, was established in the United Kingdom.[26]

By 1841 Hagerman was safely on the bench, and the election for Kingston could proceed without his candidacy. There were two candidates, Anthony Manahan and John Richardson Forsyth. Neither represented the tradition of Hagerman and the Compact. Manahan was a good Conservative, and had been elected to the

Assembly for Hastings in 1836. However, Manahan was an Irish Roman Catholic, hardly a Compact type. Forsyth for his part possessed impeccable family connections, but adhered to and defended the Church of Scotland. Surprisingly enough, Manahan won the election, if only by a narrow margin.[27]

Manahan's tenure as MP for Kingston was short. The problem involved Sydenham and political management. The governor-general acted as his own prime minister, and took a substantial hand in the general election of 1841. Sydenham's choice for provincial secretary, the senior minister, was a recent immigrant from England, Samuel Bealey Harrison.[28] The appointment was made on 13 February 1841, but getting Harrison elected to the Assembly was a different matter. He ran in Hamilton against Sir Allan MacNab, and was badly beaten. Harrison was then parachuted into Kent County, where he was again devastated. Sydenham was a persistent man, however. He offered Anthony Manahan the lucrative position of collector of customs in Toronto; Manahan accepted – which action forced Manahan to resign as member for Kingston. And Harrison was then duly returned by acclamation in his place. Kingston, the capital of Canada, suddenly found itself represented by Sydenham's most important minister and the government leader in the Assembly.

Harrison was a quiet, unassuming man who maintained a low public profile until he resigned office in 1843. He was nonetheless a central figure in the administration of Lord Sydenham. As a moderate with close ties to the Reformers, he represented a break with Kingston's Tory tradition. However, Harrison represented no break whatever with another Kingston tradition that has become almost instinctual: like Kingston members before him, and many since, he was at the centre of political power. This helps explain why Kingston has usually been a city of much more political importance than its size or wealth warrant.

Two neighbouring constituencies were represented by important Kingstonians. John Solomon Cartwright, Richard Cartwright's son, was member for Lennox and Addington. Cartwright, a lawyer and the president of the Commercial Bank, was a man of aristocratic tastes and attainments. He opposed the Union and was one of the leaders of the Compact remnant. Cartwright was sufficiently intransigent in his principles to reject an offer of the important post of solicitor-general in 1842.

Henry Smith Jr represented Frontenac County. Smith was the son of the notorious founding warden of the provincial penitentiary at Portsmouth. He was a lawyer and an associate of John A. Macdonald. Although destined to remain in politics until his premature death in 1868, Henry Smith (Sir Henry after 1860) was an unsavoury individual with a strong predilection for political intrigue and leisurely hunting expeditions in northern parts of the county. He was solicitor-general for Canada West from 1854 to 1858, and the speaker of the Union parliament from 1858 to 1861. After a dramatic factional break with John A. Macdonald, Smith went into political eclipse until 1867, when he had been sufficiently rehabilitated to warrant election to the parliament of Ontario.

Cartwright and Smith were established Kingstonians who had the luxury of sitting in a parliament that met in their home town. Sydenham and Harrison were new and very prominent citizens who now made Kingston their home. But they were only two of many who swelled the size of the little city to some six thousand souls. The new Assembly included eighty-four members, who came in all political shapes and sizes. Robert Baldwin, the leader of the hard-line Responsible Government men, was there, as was his overly pragmatic lieutenant, Francis Hincks. Hincks, known as "The Hyena" for his venality, was nevertheless the Reformers' contact man with the French Canadians, and an architect of Canada's first truly bi-racial political movement. John Sandfield Macdonald, the only man to serve in all eight Union parliaments, represented Glengarry. He was a prickly individualist, then in his Tory phase. Sandfield was destined to serve as premier of Canada from 1862 to 1864 and as first premier of Ontario from 1867 to 1871.

John Solomon Cartwright was by no means the only member who had supported the old Family Compact. Others were present, and their fates and dispositions illustrated the fact that Compact Toryism was a spent option. William Henry Draper represented Russell. He had been a Compact man, but was now a moderate – a Sydenhamite. "Sweet William," as he was called, was to succeed Harrison as the senior executive councillor. W.H. Merritt was there, too. He had been responsible for the construction of the Welland Canal. His Compact associations were intimate. He was now a moderate Reformer. Sir Allan MacNab sat for Hamilton. He was no friend of the governor-general and stood for the values of the old Tories. But not even MacNab was willing to devote an excessive share of his life to a lost cause. Quickly he found that entrepreneurial activity eroded his pre-Union position. By the 1850s he was perfectly willing to cooperate with both Reformers and French Canadians.

French-Canadian politicians joined the little community at the mouth of the Cataraqui. French was spoken volubly in the streets of Kingston during these years. The powerful Louis-Hippolyte LaFontaine was not successful in the election of 1841, but he quickly secured the unlikely seat of Fourth York in the Toronto district and became the single most important opposition leader in the Assembly. A.N. Morin sat for Nicolet. His career was long and distinguished; he ultimately took LaFontaine's bloc of *bleus* into alliance with Allan MacNab and John A. Macdonald. Étienne Parent represented a distinguished variant of French-Canadian nationalism. He edited *Le Canadien* and was a leading intellectual force in French Canada.

"Père Parent," as he was called, was "a prototype and an example" whose "thought dominated the first half of the French Canadian 19th century."[29] He had been imprisoned during the uprising of 1838, an experience that cost him most of his hearing. Parent found his deafness incompatible with his parliamentary duties. Consequently he left politics in 1842 to become clerk of the Executive Council. Parent, an architect of modern French-Canadian nationalism, never became a Kingstonian. But he lived in Kingston for a time and brought an exotic intellectualism to the city.

Politicians abounded in the Kingston of the early 1840s. One of the most colourful was Hamilton Hartley Killaly, who represented London and was an avid fisherman. The Reverend Agar Adamson, rector on Amherst Island and Sydenham's "personal chaplain," was a fishing companion.[30] Adamson wrote *Salmon Fishing in Canada*, in which he described Killaly during his Kingston days:

He was the most expensively and the worst dressed man on the wide continent of North America. ... I have seen him at one time promenading a populous city in a dirty, powder-smeared and blood-stained shooting coat, while his nether man was encased in black dress pantaloons, silk stockings and highly varnished french-leather dancing pumps. ... It was a complete puzzle to his acquaintances where he obtained all the old hats he wore. ... Though his head was white, and his face purple – like a red cabbage in snow – he was, as Nathaniel Hawthorne says, "a wonderful specimen of wintergreen. ..." His voice and laugh ... came strutting out of his lungs, like the crow of a cock. ... His temper was uncertain as the wind towards his subordinates, sometimes familiar as a playfellow, at others as injurious, overbearing and unreasoning as a Turk. He was more cautious, however, with his superiors, and with those whose opinions might affect his interests.[31]

Killaly cut a considerable figure in Kingston, and clearly meant it when he said, "I care not what the world says."[32]

Killaly provided Kingston with far more than colour; he became chairman of the Board of Works on 29 December 1841 and acted in that capacity before his appointment was made official.[33] He was in charge of what was later called the Department of Public Works and was thus responsible for the housekeeping aspects of government. In this capacity he had a major impact on the development of Kingston.

The first requirement was suitable housing for the governor-general. Alwington House, Kingston's finest mansion, was rented for Sydenham. It was built in 1834 for Charles William Grant, hereditary baron de Longueuil, and occupied a magnificent waterfront site east of the penitentiary. Alwington House was renovated and enlarged, and turned into a very appropriate vice-regal residence.

John Counter, the mayor and moving force in the Marine Railway Company, rented the firm's accommodation to the government for office spaces. The new and as-yet-unused general hospital was also rented, and was turned into a parliament that Sydenham thought quite lavish. "I think we shall do very well at Kingston," he explained to Lord John Russell:

I have really a very fair house for the Assembly and Council to meet in and the accommodation would be thought magnificent by us Members of the English House of Commons. But the fellows in these Colonies have been spoiled by all sorts of luxuries, large arm chairs, desks with stationery before each man, & heaven knows what, so I suppose they will complain.[34]

Alwington House, official residence of the first governors-general of the United Province of Canada 1841–1844. Destroyed by fire in 1958. (QUA)

Local entrepreneurs exploited the capital situation, and some made a permanent mark on the city. Charles Hales, for example, who had built Bellevue House (where John A. Macdonald lived from 1848 to 1849) before the Union, now built five connected stone cottages on King Street West in 1841. Hales's concern was to rent them in the booming house market occasioned by the arrival of the capital. It seems almost three thousand newcomers descended on Kingston in 1841, putting an inordinate pressure on Kingston's hotel and housing markets. Hales's judgment was correct, no doubt aided by a perfect location: the cottages overlooked the lake and were almost exactly halfway between the temporary parliament buildings and Alwington House. (Four of the cottages survive. They are located behind a limestone wall and constitute one of the most beautiful residential sites in Kingston.)

Summerhill was built for Archdeacon George Okill Stuart between 1836 and 1839.

It was an enormous residence, called "Stuart's Folly" or "The Archdeacon's Great Castle."[35] A Torontonian named Botsford rented it from Stuart, renamed it the Sydenham Inn, and ran it as a residence for politicians and officials.[36] It had such a convenient location, within sight of parliament, that the government rented it within a year and used it as government offices.[37] All over Kingston houses were divided into smaller units, and additions were attached to dozens of buildings. The British American Hotel (a landmark until it burned in 1963) added twenty-four rooms.[38]

Some government actions had a permanent, if unanticipated, effect on the city. The beautiful property purchased from the estate of Captain Henry Murney as a site for regular parliament buildings was never used for that purpose. It survives, however, as Kingston's City Park, a haven of peace and beauty in the heart of the modern city.

Perhaps the most important permanent effect the capital had on Kingston was purely fortuitous. The government architect in Killaly's Public Works Department was an Ulster Irishman named George Browne.[39] When Killaly began the work of equipping Kingston to be the capital, Browne was immediately and heavily involved. His official work was perhaps not very important; he supervised the renovations required to house Sydenham and the government officials who moved to town. Much more important were his private works as an "architect, measurer, and landscape gardener."[40] During his three years in Kingston Browne was responsible for the construction of several buildings that made him a leading nineteenth-century architect, and that have ever since played a major role in defining Kingston's streetscapes. Fortunately, most of Browne's work survives.

One of his most distinctive designs was the round-corner commercial structure. He built three such buildings: Mowat's Round Corner Building (since demolished), Wilson's Buildings (now a beautifully-restored office for the Victoria and Grey Trust Company), and the Commercial Mart (now the large and very cluttered S&R Department Store). Browne also designed town houses, his "finest" according to J.D. Stewart, being the manse at St Andrew's Presbyterian Church.[41] This superb limestone house, with its beautiful doorway, still delights the eye of those who walk in the central part of downtown Kingston. More impressive and famous is Rockwood Villa, which Browne built in 1841 for the Tory lawyer and politician John Solomon Cartwright. Rockwood, now on the grounds of the Kingston Psychiatric Hospital, was a country house, and is the best surviving example of the elegance and charm that the Kingston élite sought in such homes during the 1840s. Rockwood was constructed amid spacious grounds overlooking Lake Ontario, a situation that added to its claim to be a "gem of architecture" in the "Tuscan mode."[42]

Browne's greatest achievement, which remains Kingston's most impressive building, is city hall, built in 1843-1844. A contemporary, W.H. Smith, described it as "the finest and most substantial building in Canada."[43] A leading military figure in Kingston commented: "The Town Hall is probably the finest edifice of the kind

George Browne, Kingston's greatest architect during its time as capital, designer of city hall. (QUA)

on the continent of American, and cost £30,000, containing two splendid rooms of vast size, Post-office, Custom-house, Commercial Newsroom, shops, and a complete Market Place, with Mayor's Court and Police-office, and a lofty cupola, commanding a view of immense extent."[44]

SHADOWS

It would be misleading to leave the impression that possession of the seat of government was an undiluted blessing for Kingston. It was not. There were major problems related to the inability of a little city to accommodate a vast increase in population and the desire to make as much windfall profit as possible.

Sir Richard Bonnycastle explained that this problem was harmful to the city. "The presence of Government at Kingston," he wrote at the end of the 1840s,

> gave an unnatural stimulus to speculation among a population very far from wealthy; and buildings of the most frail construction were run up in hundreds, for the sake of the rent which they yielded temporarily. The plan upon which these houses were erected was that of mortgage; thus almost all are now in possession of one person who became suddenly possessed of the requisite means by the sale of a large tract required for military purposes [probably Herchmer]. But this species of property seldom does the owner good in his lifetime; and, if he does reclaim it, there is no tenant to be had now; so that the building decays, and in a very short time becomes an incumbrance. Mortgages only thrive where the demand is superior and certain to the investment; and then, if all goes smoothly, mortgager and mortgagee may benefit; but where a mechanic or a storekeeper, with little or no capital, undertakes to run up an extensive range of houses to meet an equivocal demand, the result is obvious. If the houses he builds are of stone or brick, and well finished, the man who loans the money is the gainer; if they are of wood, indifferently constructed and of green materials, both must suffer. So it is a speculation, and, like all speculations, a good deal of repudiation mixes up with it.[45]

But in 1841 the focus of attention was not yet on problems associated with the *loss* of the seat of government. The town was optimistic and filled with bustle. Construction boomed; inns and taverns received more business than they could handle. The presence of government produced all sorts of unanticipated spin-offs. There was, for example, a boom in the publishing trade; almost half of all titles published in Kingston before Confederation (1867) appeared between 1841 and 1844. Most were government publications.[46]

Personalities continued to provide most excitement. On 4 September 1841, Sydenham fell from his horse. He was alone when his accident occurred, because he had "called upon a lady in Kingston, to whom, as rumour said, he was much attached." His dalliance "proved so entertaining that it was protracted beyond ordinary length. Suddenly remembering that he had a dinner that evening, he abruptly took his leave and rode off at a gallop for Alwington House. In the hurry his horse stumbled and fell with him, causing injuries. ..."[47] The Toronto *Patriot*, not wishing to miss a chance to malign its arch-rival, commented, "Kingston is about the worst place in the world for such an accident as a fall from a horse, as there is little earth or vegetation to break the force of contact with the hard ground."[48]

Sydenham's accident was not regarded as serious, but he contracted lockjaw and died on 19 September. Thus ended in tragedy a brilliant and constructive career. The governor-general's funeral was held on 24 September 1841. Lord Sydenham had vowed that "he would never enter the Kingston church again,"[49] but to this day he occupies a tomb in St George's Cathedral.

Sir Charles Bagot, second governor-general resident in Kingston. Like Sydenham, he died in Alwington House. (QUA)

Sydenham had achieved Union and established Kingston as the capital. To the aristocratic Englishman Charles Grenville he might well have been "the greatest coxcomb I ever saw and the vainest dog,"[50] but his achievement was great. Economic confidence was returning to the Canadas; the public service had been thoroughly reformed and streamlined; representative government, with an embryonic cabinet system, was established. Sydenham, in short, had restored confidence in the régime and established a system that was compatible with responsible government and, to some, even looked like it.

There were also problems. Government that was in theory not responsible, but in practice required to be popular and representative, could be maintained only by a political management that was adroit and endless. Sydenham maintained his system during his brief tenure as governor-general. Even he, however, could not have kept the system functioning much longer. This was especially true given his determination to keep legitimate representatives of the French Canadians out of power.

This was the key problem that confronted Sydenham's successor Sir Charles Bagot. Bagot was the second governor-general to live in Alwington House. He arrived in Kingston on 10 January 1842 and governed Canada for little more than a year. All the while his health declined and he suffered.

During these months Kingston hosted some the most exciting political developments in Canadian history. Sir Charles quickly became aware of the weaknesses of the political position bequeathed him by Sydenham. His ultimate solution involved one of the key decisions in Canadian history. Bagot resolved that the policy of anglicization espoused by Durham and Sydenham had failed. The French Canadians, he concluded, *had* to be admitted to power.

Louis LaFontaine, leader of the French-Canadian bloc, would not agree to serve Bagot until two concessions were made. First, LaFontaine would enter government only with Robert Baldwin and other leaders of the bi-racial Reform movement. Second, any new administration would have to be conducted along the lines of responsible government. A certain amount of camouflage was used, but in essence LaFontaine won his points. He and Baldwin joined the Executive Council in September 1842. Kingston was thus the site of what was in fact, if not in name, the first responsible government in British North America, or in the British Empire, for that matter.

Bagot's innovations were ill-received by Imperial authorities, and his declining health made it impossible for him to continue as governor-general. He died in Alwington House, on 18 May 1843. Within twenty months and a few days more, two major governors-general had died in what seemed to be an ill-fated capital.

Bagot's successor, Sir Charles Theophilus Metcalfe, had arrived several weeks before Bagot's death. Kingstonians gave Sir Charles a wildly enthusiastic welcome on the afternoon of 29 March 1843. A newspaper correspondent described the scene:

He came from the American side, in a close-bodied sleigh drawn by four greys. He was received, on arriving at the foot of Arthur-street [*sic*] (Ives' Wharf), by an immense con-course of people. The military escort was composed of a detachment of the Incorporated Lancers, and the guard of honour from the 23rd Regiment. Notwithstanding the repeated disappointments as to the time of the arrival, the male population of the place turned out *en masse* to greet Sir Charles, which they did with great enthusiasm. The various branches of the Fire Department, the Mechanics' Institution, and the National Societies, turned out with their banners, which, with many sleighs decorated with flags, made quite a show. The streets from Daley's Hotel to the Governor's residence were lined by the military. ... Sir Charles Metcalfe is a thorough-looking Englishman, with a jolly visage. He looks older than he really is, but this may proceed from the fatigues of his very rough journey.[51]

Metcalfe held office for two unhappy and difficult years. Bagot's constitutional innovations had been poorly received by Downing Street. Metcalfe's job was to hold the line; responsible government was not to be accepted as the operating principle of the Canadian constitution. The result was bitter acrimony that was intensified by the nasty and divisive election of 1844. Metcalfe and his Tory supporters won that election, but only barely. Metcalfe's chief minister, "Sweet William" Draper, was unable to provide either effective or creative government for Canada.

More tragic was Metcalfe's personal situation. He may have impressed local newspapermen as "a thorough-looking Englishman, with a jolly visage,"[52] but he was a very sick man when he arrived in North America. Sir Charles suffered from cancer of the cheek: he had brought his own death with him. By 1844, the situation was hopeless, as Metcalfe himself acknowledged:

It is now left very much to nature. ... It has been nearly stationary, neither better nor worse, for nearly three months; but it got rapidly worse while the nitric acid and arsenic mixture was applied. The doctors have recommended my return to England, and I would gladly adopt that remedy if I could with propriety do so, but public duty puts that out of the question, and no personal consideration would induce me to quit my post at present.[53]

The ravages of the disease were horrible. Metcalfe described his state at the end of 1844. "The disease," he wrote to J.R. Martin,

remains uneradicated, and has spread to the eye and taken away its sight. This at least is my opinion, although I am bound to hesitate in entertaining it, as I am not sure that Pollock is satisfied of the extension of the actual disease to the eye, but if it be not the disease which has produced the blindness it must be the remedy. I am inclined, however, to believe that it is in reality the disease – both from appearances and from the continued pain. The complaint appears to me to have taken possession of the whole of that side of the face, although the surface is not so much ulcerated as it has heretofore been. I feel pain and tenderness in the head, above the eye and down the right side of the face as far as the chin: the cheek towards the nose and mouth being permanently swelled. I cannot open my mouth to its usual width, and have difficulty in inserting and masticating pieces of food. After all that has been done in vain, I am disposed to believe that a perfect cure is hopeless. ... Having no hope of a cure, my chief anxiety now regards my remaining eye, which sympathises so much with the other that I am not without fear of total blindness. ...[54]

The wretched man finally accepted the advice of his doctors and resigned his post.

Sir Charles Metcalfe, Baron Metcalfe of Fern Hill, third and final governor-general to rule from Kingston. He was fatally ill when he left the city in 1844. (QUA)

He returned to England in December 1845, and died in September 1846. Sir Charles Metcalfe was the third and last governor-general of Canada to live at Government House, Kingston.

SIX

Crisis

PORTENTS OF DISASTER

The capital period was one of glitter, excitement, and economic optimism. But the reality was somewhat grim. The presence of the seat of government was a chimera. Those with power and influence never took the aspirations of Kingston seriously: the seat of government would remain for only a brief, transitional period. All the while, Kingston's tenuous status as a metropolis of any economic importance continued to undergo rapid erosion.

Kingston was just not up to its status as capital. It was too small and primitive to provide the amenities demanded by politicians, who were in some cases sophisticated and travelled. Kingston was too British for the French Canadians and too conservative for Reformers of either culture. Sydenham made Kingston the capital, and defended his choice. But he had found the town trying. In June 1841 Baron Sydenham of Kent and Toronto complained to Lord Russell, "I am ready to hang myself half a dozen times a day. ... I long for September, beyond which I will not stay if they were to make me Duke of Canada and Prince of Regiopolis, as this place is called."[1]

Bagot had been in Kingston for exactly one week when he rendered judgment. The town, he reported to Colonial Secretary Stanley, is "small and poor, and the Country around is unproductive." It lacks "accommodation for the Members of the Legislature when the Session is in progress." Further, argued Sir Charles, the place was indefensible: "Situated on the border of the Lake to which it is perfectly open – within twelve miles of the American shore and within fifteen miles of their principal naval Station on Lake Ontario [Sacket's Harbor], it is evident that its security must depend on the enemy never being able, even for a few hours to obtain the superiority on this end of the Lake." Bagot's ultimate argument was political. Kingston, reported the governor-general, was "unacceptable to the great body of people."[2]

It was unavoidable, then, that the question would quickly be reopened. More correctly, however, it might be said the seat-of-government issue was never closed. The announcement of Kingston's good fortune came in any case on 6 February 1841.[3]

Assaults on the decision were immediate and sustained. Lieutenant-Governor Sir George Arthur reported dissatisfaction in Toronto and assured Sydenham that "Toronto will be a Hotbed of dissatisfaction for some time to come."[4] The Toronto *Examiner* snapped, "The good people of Toronto without distinction of party, have been astounded at the intelligence that the first meeting of the United Legislature is to be held at Kingston."[5]

Reaction from Lower Canada was slower to come and somewhat muted, no doubt because French Canadians were under no illusions that the capital would not be in the Upper Province. *Le Canadien*, however, found Kingston to be "a town without a distinctive face, without character." And further, "the water above all is almost undrinkable."[6] A short while later, the touring novelist and lecturer Charles Dickens passed his famous and oft-quoted judgment on Kingston

which is now the seat of government in Canada ... a very poor town, rendered still poorer in the appearance of its market-place by the ravages of a recent fire. Indeed, it may be said of Kingston, that one half of it appears to be burnt down, and the other half not to be built up. The Government House is neither elegant nor commodious, yet it is almost the only house of any importance in the neighbourhood.[7]

The issue could not be kept out of the political arena, if indeed it had ever left it. Kingston never received any firm assurances that its status was safe. This unpleasant fact of life was underscored by Sydenham as early as June 1841. He replied to an address from a group of Kingstonians with a statement that included the phrase "*Should* Kingston become the permanent Seat of Government. ..."[8] That single word "should" was fateful.

The first session of the first parliament of the Province of Canada met in the converted hospital on 14 June 1841. The seat-of-government question quickly became an issue, although initially in a somewhat muted manner. In August, a representative for York County moved that Sydenham be asked to provide information concerning the permanent location of the capital and the status of Kingston. The matter did not come to a vote, but several members participated in the debate, and only the member for Kingston considered the issue settled. Two weeks later the first real blow fell. A group of Torontonians petitioned the house "to cause the Parliament of Canada to meet alternately at Toronto and Quebec. ..."[9] The petition went to a committee, which reported on 1 September 1841. The committee endorsed the alternating system because, it argued, "such a measure would not only be acceptable to the great body of the inhabitants of Canada, but would, at the same time result in a great saving of expenditures to the public. ..."[10] On 16 September the essence of the Toronto petition and the committee report received the support of the Assembly as an address to Queen Victoria.[11] The address concluded,

Wherefore we most earnestly entreat that Your Majesty, in the exercise of Your Royal prerogative, will be pleased to order that the Parliament of Canada, hereafter, assemble alternately at *Quebec* and *Toronto*, the respective capitals of the late Province of *Upper* and *Lower* Canada, or should such prayer be thought unadvisable, and any other measure be adopted, that adequate and just renumeration [*sic*] be granted for the loss sustained by the inhabitants of *Toronto* and *Quebec*.[12]

Sir Richard Jackson, administrator of the Province of Canada, and Lord Stanley, the British colonial secretary, resisted a quick removal of the seat of government from Kingston; but the writing was on the wall. Fewer than eight months earlier, Kingstonians had learned of their good fortune. Now the Assembly had pronounced against the city. It goes without saying that the city fathers were worried men.

WHY WAS CITY HALL BUILT?

A little over a year later the Assembly debated the issue again, and resolved that "the building in which the Legislative Assembly is now held ... does not afford sufficient accommodation and the locality of Kingston is not central to the majority of the population, and is badly provided with accommodation for the residence of members, particularly during the winter. ..."[13] The vote was held on 5 October 1842.

All was not lost. Opponents of Kingston were not agreed on an alternative capital, and Kingstonians, both within and without the Assembly, defended their town. The most spectacular such attempt came in October 1843, when the city fathers offered to give the province the lavish municipal building then under construction.[14] This was a generous if somewhat desperate offer, and it was not inappropriate. The city hall was large enough and grand enough to serve as the province's legislature. It also came equipped with two rooms, at opposite ends of the second floor, that would be large enough to give very nice accommodation to a bicameral parliament.

The offer, combined with the scale of the city hall and its eminent suitability as a legislative building, has caused some scholars to debate whether or not Kingston's city hall was conceived and built as a desperate attempt to bribe the province into retaining Kingston as the seat of government. Donald Creighton argued this point. The city fathers, he says,

had realized for some time that their rapidly growing capital was badly in need of a new town hall and new market buildings; and they were aware also – and the thought hovered always at the back of their speculations – that the provincial legislature, completely ignoring the need of permanent provision, still occupied its avowedly temporary quarters, the four-storey limestone building which had been erected as a hospital. Contemplating these two necessities, the town council reached an audacious and grandiose decision. It would build an elegant, spacious, and splendid town hall ... [with] chambers, fit, perhaps, for the deliberations of still greater and more august assemblies.[15]

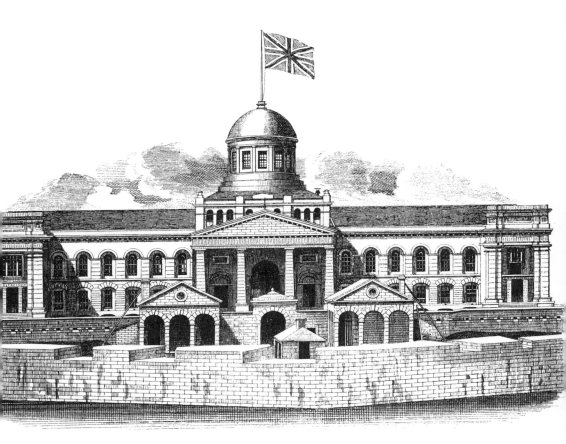

City hall, with the grimly picturesque market battery in the foreground. (QUA)

Historians of city hall take grave exception to this interpretation. J.D. Stewart, for example, counters: "Perhaps the most persistent myth of all is that the Kingston City Hall was originally designed as the Parliament Buildings for the Province of Canada. Local tradition clings firmly to this idea. ..."[16]According to Stewart and others, the genesis of the city hall can be traced to the great fire that devastated the downtown waterfront section, including the market area, in the early hours of Saturday, 18 April 1840 – the fire that, incidentally, initiated developments that were to make Kingston into the "Limestone City" thereafter.[17]

The devastation of that Easter weekend wrecked the market, which was of substantial economic importance to Kingston. It is not surprising that civic boosters like John Counter, who became mayor in April 1841, had called for a new market house immediately after the fire of 1840.[18] It would have been surprising had such demands not been made. That does not, of course, lead in any logical manner to the magnificent building that was ultimately constructed.

John Counter, mayor of Kingston 1841, 1842, 1843, 1846, 1850, 1852, 1853, and 1855. Counter played a crucial role in the political decision to build city hall against all odds. (QUA)

Resolving this conflict of interpretation is difficult. Mayor Counter and other local worthies were hardly likely to give public (or possibly even private) utterance to a resolve to undertake an inordinately expensive municipal work for purposes of bribery. The evidence does suggest, however, that the genesis of city hall was murky at best.

The first problem relates to timing. The Assembly indicated its initial desire to move the capital away from Kingston on 16 September 1841. The Assembly specifically repudiated Kingston on 5 October 1842. These were public declarations that were never countered with a single parliamentary endorsation of the wisdom of using Kingston as the seat of government. No city father who was even vaguely responsible or peripherally aware could have misunderstood the importance of these Assembly resolutions. There was, however, more. The member for Kingston, S.B. Harrison, who was also a powerful minister, made clear to Mayor Counter during the early summer of 1842 that dissatisfaction with Kingston was acute. Harrison's particular concern was the prevalence of "drunkenness and crime."[19] In reply Counter admitted that the problem was severe and asked that the common council be permitted to control the licensing of taverns. The mayor noted that Kingston and the nearby settled areas included between 8,000 and 9,000 people and 136 licensed taverns.[20] Kingston was a "boom town" in more ways than one. Accommodation also remained a critical problem. Between 1840 and 1842 the number of houses doubled to nine hundred. Many of these were flimsy and inadequate structures, and not surprisingly there were "many dissatisfied temporary residents."[21]

In spite of these pressing problems and clear indications that Kingston would not retain the seat of government for long, council pressed on. It accepted George Browne's grand plan for the building, and it sent Mayor Counter to London to borrow the money needed for construction. There was no confusion in council's mind concerning the relationship between the municipal building and the location of the capital: Counter "also carried an address to the Queen on the progress of Kingston and its need to be assured that the capital would stay in Kingston."[22] The mayor did not leave for London until late November 1842. The Assembly's dissatisfaction with Kingston had been public knowledge for over fourteen months, and its reiterated desire to remove the capital to another location had been known for over a month.

Nonetheless, Counter forged ahead. He spent several months in England, returning to Canada with Governor-General Metcalf on 29 March 1843.[23] Shortly after his return home, Counter reported to Council. He had "negotiated a loan of £20,000 through the London Stock Bank at a rate of 6% and an agreement that the Commercial Bank of the Midland District in Kingston would guarantee the interest."[24] What Counter did not bring back, however, was any intimation whatever that Kingston would remain the capital. The fact that he travelled home with Metcalfe and his party makes even clearer the point that he had made no progress whatever on the issue of retaining the seat of government at Kingston. It is inconceivable that the capital question could have been avoided on the long sea voyage; it is equally inconceivable that Counter could have arrived at his first council meeting under any illusion whatsoever concerning the most important single problem facing his city. Yet he persisted. Without the retention of the capital, the construction of city hall was civic madness, a madcap financial adventure that had devastating and long-term results.

The cornerstone of the building was laid on 5 June 1843. In October of the same year the council offered the yet-to-be-completed building to the province in a last desperate attempt to postpone the inevitable. Margaret Angus describes this famous offer: "Frantically the town fathers attempted to end such talk [of moving the capital] by offering *the free use of the City Buildings and Market House now in the course of erection for the meetings of the Legislature for any period that they may be required.*"[25] The use of the phrase "such talk" is revealing. It was not of course "talk" at all. The policy of the Assembly had been public knowledge for over three months before the first tenders arrived in January 1843 and for some five months before Counter reported to council that he had secured the £20,000 loan.[26]

The evidence concerning the genesis of the city hall is by no means satisfactory, but two probable alternative explanations stand out.

The first possibility is that Mayor Counter and his colleagues were fully aware that there was very little chance that Kingston could remain the seat of government – even over the short run. The petition that Counter took with him to London in November 1842 is sufficient evidence of this. Accordingly, Kingston's leaders made a desperate and very expensive gamble with municipal funds. The central thrust of this initiative was the proposed city hall, a building so large that it has been argued that at that time probably no other building in British North America rivalled it in size.[27] Thus, the assumption might have been that they could use the building as a bribe. Or else that the very existence of such an enormously costly government-related structure would bring sufficient pressure on Canadian or British officials to reverse their decision and save Kingston's status.

The second possibility is that Mayor Counter and his colleagues were unaware of the tenuousness of Kingston's hold on the seat of government. Further, that, in good faith, they resolved to erect a building large and impressive enough to serve as the seat of municipal government and as a market place for the town that was now the capital of a huge and expanding colonial state.

In short, one can opt either for the first alternative, which was irresponsible and dishonest, or for the second alternative, which could be described as stupid.

That the decision to proceed with the construction of city hall was irresponsible is illustrated by the subsequent history of the building and its impact on municipal finances. Kingston had no need for anything nearly as large or as elaborate as the city hall and market building, and when the edifice was completed in November 1844, the main concern was finding tenants who could occupy the substantial amounts of vacant space.[28]

Pewter medallion commemorating the laying of the foundation stone of city hall, 1843. (City of Kingston)

The council was both generous and innovative in its long struggle to fill its building. The south wing of the main floor was taken over by the Board of Trade; another portion of the same wing was occupied by the Custom House. The Post Office rented part of the north wing, and in 1850 the Bank of British North America began a seventy-four-year tenancy in the basement. Space was found for a drygoods merchant, a saloon, the Mechanics' Institute, the Orange Order, and the Masons. The council originally met in the great hall in the north wing, now known as Memorial Hall, but quickly gave up grandeur for the informal comfort of the mayor's large office. Memorial Hall, known in the nineteenth century as the town hall or city hall, was widely used as a place for public entertainments and meetings.

Perhaps the most revealing use of the building was authorized by the city shortly after city hall was built. Rooms in the basement, on the Ontario Street side, were rented to welfare recipients as living quarters. The experiment was unsuccessful and the city ordered its wards out on 1 May 1848. The eviction was about as successful as the initial policy. "Seven years later," Margaret Angus noted, "city officials were still trying to persuade Mrs. Shanahan and her children to move out."[29]

There was substantial movement into and out of the building during the nineteenth century. Several church congregations, for example, met in the building at various times. It seems clear that the council had no use for the space it had provided, and was required to resort to some extreme measures to see that such space was profitably occupied. It is also clear that the use made of the building had little to do with the structure's functional design. The intentions of Counter and his colleagues cannot be discerned by studying the building's design. A study of its use adds weight to the suggestion that the entire project was informed with irresponsibility.

The great wing that ran from the main building to King Street was designed as a public market known, according to nineteenth-century usage, as the "market shambles." Its use also suggests that irresponsibility shaped the design and scope of the structure. It was of course used by butchers, greengrocers, and hucksters; but when the wing burned in 1865 "there was little pressure to rebuild the entire wing" because there had been "a gradual shift of shop keepers to larger quarters elsewhere in the city and, as health regulations were imposed, fewer butchers rented the stalls."[30] A very much smaller wing, which still stands, was regarded as quite sufficient. In short, the market wing, like city hall, was vastly grander than necessary and never given thorough use.

City hall and its market wing were by mid-nineteenth-century standards extremely costly. The final bill came to over £28,000.[31] Some £20,000 of this had been borrowed in London. The interest on the "English debt," as it was called, was guaranteed by the Commercial Bank of the Midland District, which was a very flourishing enterprise during the 1840s. The assumption of this debt was appropriate, but only provided that the seat of government remained in Kingston. Duncan McDowall explains:

Civic taxes being calculated on the assessed value of city property, it was assumed that, as the capital of the province, city property would continue to command high values and the city coffers would therefore continue to enjoy a high tax return. Thus the English loan would be speedily amortized. Unfortunately there was no leeway in this financial scheme for the unexpected. In 1843, just as George Browne's masterful architectural work was nearing completion in the Market Square, Kingstonians were served with the unpalatable news that the seat of government was to be moved. ... [T]his development immediately caused the value of city property to plummet, thereby drastically diminishing the city's tax return and consequently its ability to liquidate the debts contracted during its tenure as provincial capital.[32]

City hall, designed and executed 1843–1844 by George Browne, remains one of Kingston's finest buildings. It was renovated and restored in the 1960s. Photo taken in 1970s. (QUA)

Of course, the city fathers were perfectly aware of the connection between the city's ability to pay the debt and the city's retention of the seat of government. The removal of the capital was not "unexpected" in any way. The decision to proceed with the construction of the municipal building was an incredible and irresponsible gamble for which the city paid dearly. As McDowall explained, the English debt "was largely beyond [the city's] means to make good. ..."[33] No amount of the principal was retired, and interest charges accumulated; in fact the city's financial position deteriorated further when Kingston borrowed £7,000 from the Commercial

Restored Council Chamber in city hall. (QUA)

Bank to pay construction costs. By the mid-1840s Kingston's debt stood at £31,222, and the city's financial position was in a "state of near hopelessness."[34]

The citizenry realized that their affairs had been bungled. As the Kingston *Argus* explained, "It is quite evident that the Corporation cannot safely be trusted – Their conduct during the past four years fully warrants the assertion. Therefore the people must attend to their own interests, and see that they are not humbugged or swindled out of their money."[35]

In 1849 the city reached an agreement with the Commercial Bank for repayment

Memorial Hall honours the many Kingstonians who died in the First World War. It was restored in the 1960s. (QUA)

of the £7,000 loan, but this solved very little. The city was not even paying the *interest* on the English debt, and by 1850 Kingston's indebtedness had soared to £42,127.[36] The problem was finally brought under control in 1852, when Counter secured a provincial statute that enabled the city to borrow £75,000. The debts were consolidated, and the remaining funds used for civic improvements. Orderly repayment was made possible, and Kingston's finances stabilized.[37]

Of course, other, less heroic remedies had been sought. In 1844 Mayor James Sampson, assisted by Counter, asked the province to bail out the town. They ap-

Restored alcove in city
hall. (QUA)

proached Governor-General Metcalfe and asked that the government guarantee
repayment of the English loan. They also asked that Kingston be given the fine tract
of land that Sydenham had once purchased for parliament buildings. Both requests
were denied, although the land was released in 1852 for use as a park and eventually
given to the city in 1865.[38]

Kingston's city hall stands as one of Canada's finest surviving pre-Confederation
buildings. Beautifully restored during the 1960s, it is the most impressive structure
in Kingston and dominates the city's downtown. Our twentieth-century good
fortune should not, however, confuse our understanding of the past. Mayor Counter
and his fellow-civic-boosters did not plan city hall as a twentieth-century tourist
attraction. They ostensibly planned it as the headquarters of municipal government in the capital of Canada. It was financed on the assumption that the prosperity
that came with the seat of government would continue. But it was built after
Canada's legislature had made it abundantly clear to any but the most obtuse

political observer that the seat of government was to be moved.

There is no doubt that Counter and his colleagues linked the capital question and the city-hall question. In the period 1842-1843 they tried to obtain a guarantee that the capital would remain in Kingston. In 1844 they tried to saddle the province with the chaos of Kingston's finances. It is also clear that the design of the building made no sense should the structure be used exclusively for municipal purposes. They had no use for much of its space, and within a short time council did not even meet in the room designed for them; furthermore, they seemed not to care much for the building that is now the city's pride. In 1850 the *Whig* described city hall as "shamefully dirty."[39] In 1854 a committee of council referred to the building's "very soiled and unsightly appearance."[40] And, of course, the building was offered to the province if the capital remained in Kingston.

It is difficult not to conclude that Mayor Counter and other politicians believed that by proceeding with construction in 1843 it would be possible to induce the government of Canada to change its mind and let Kingston retain its honour as the capital of Canada.

DISASTER

The attempted "bribe" of October 1843 came to nothing: the basic decision had been made. Robert Baldwin and Louis LaFontaine had entered Bagot's Executive Council in September 1842. They dominated the government and owed no allegiance to Sydenham and his policies. Their opposition to Kingston was profound. Baldwin dismissed the city as an "Orange Hole,"[41] and LaFontaine was as uncomfortable in the uncompromisingly Anglophone capital as were other Francophone politicians.

Baldwin's appointment as attorney-general for Canada West occasioned a by-election in Hastings, which he lost. The result led a number of Kingstonians to commit a particularly imprudent gaffe. Sir Joseph Pope tells the story:

In October, 1842, Mr. Robert Baldwin, who had vacated his seat on being appointed Attorney General for Upper Canada, was defeated in Hastings by Edmund Murney. When the news reached Kingston, where Parliament was sitting, it caused much excitement. The populace, among whom Mr. [John A.] Macdonald was prominent, had a great jubilation, their shouts of triumph reaching the ears of the legislators. This so irritated Mr. La Fontaine, who was leading the House at the time, that he vehemently declared that he would have the Government removed from among such a turbulent lot. He carried out his threat, and this is how the seat of government came to be transferred from Kingston to Montreal.[42]

Like many other historians, Pope exaggerated Kingston's hold on the seat of government. LaFontaine was not swayed by public displays. The Tory mob no doubt firmed up his resolve, however, and made it somewhat pleasant to dash the hopes of Kingstonians.

The Assembly resolution of 5 October 1842 had pronounced Kingston unacceptable. On 16 March 1843 the Executive Council formally recommended that the capital be removed to Montreal. Samuel Bealey Harrison, the MP for Kingston and still a member of the Executive Council, promptly informed Metcalfe that "he has not concurred in the Minute of Council. ..."[43] In September of the same year he resigned from his ministry because of his opposition to the relocation of the capital.

The truth began to filter into the consciousness of Kingstonians during 1843, and the reaction was bitter. The Kingston *Herald* declared "that to remove the Seat of Government from Kingston would be a breach of faith on the part of the Government with the people of Kingston and to remove it from Kingston to Montreal would be a breach of faith with the people of Upper Canada. ..."[44]

The mood became even more bitter when Baldwin took the matter to the Assembly and moved that "it is the opinion of this House, that it is expedient that the Seat of Her Majesty's Provincial Government for this Province should be at the City of *Montreal*."[45] Baldwin's motion carried on 3 November 1843. London confirmed the decision before the end of the year.[46]

Reaction from Kingstonians and other residents of the district was predictably severe. Some 30,000 signatures were affixed to a petition and presented to Lord Stanley, but "they had not the slightest effect. ..."[47] For the *News*, "it would certainly have been much better that the Seat of Government had never been fixed here, if it is now to be removed, as a large amount of capital which would have been, in all probability, applied to more useful purposes, has been applied to that of erecting buildings which for some time may be tenantless."[48] In a remarkably revealing passage, the *Herald* whined that the "whole of the front building, termed the City Hall, forming by far the largest and most expensive part of the whole, is altogether useless and unnecessary."[49] For the *Chronicle and Gazette* it was an awesome calamity:

The dread news has fallen upon the good people of Kingston like one of those sudden convulsions of nature, which all regard as possible, yet few look for as probable. Had an earthquake laid down the fairest portion of Kingston, the population being preserved from destruction, we do not believe that the injury would be less to the sufferers, while they would have the consoling satisfaction of public sympathy, if not pucuniary [*sic*] relief. Kingston must descend from metropolitan rank to the condition of a second rate provincial town.[50]

A stunned population watched some 1,700 people leave all at once.[51] Is it any wonder that James Hopkirk suggested that "two thirds of [the people of Kingston] will be ruined"?[52] In June 1844, the *Herald* reported that "most of the Government Offices have moved ... to Montreal and the remainder will soon follow."[53]

The departure of Governor-General Metcalfe on 21 June 1844 symbolized the termination of Kingston's age of greatness. "The inhabitants did not muster strong-ly," reported the *British Whig*,

and of those present a general air of gloom and discontent was on each countenance. Shortly after twelve o'clock a salute of nineteen guns commenced firing, and His Excellency moved towards the steamer, accompanied by his guests. During his progress to the Ottawa and Rideau Wharf, no cheer greeted his ear, no single hat was lifted to do him reverence – he passed to his boat amid the most profound and ominous silence. ... Thus did the Governor General leave Kingston, the chosen capital of Canada ... and with him departed the pledged faith of the Imperial Government. [54]

Alexander Scougall set the prevailing gloom to verse:

> Thus now I wander on Ontario's shore,
> Where Kingston, sheltered from the tempest's roar,
> Spreads its fair front expansive to the view,
> With cots and villas where the pine wood grew,
> With wharfs and mansions springing up anon,
> 'Midst varied comforts for the busy throng;
> And see! the spacious pile no rival knows,
> This vast stone-mart, which amply, nobly shows,
> A spirit and an enterprise, unspared
> Since Kingston the capital was declared,
> Since Sydenham's promises and Stanley's pen
> Proclaimed it so to every citizen,
> And caused them with an outlay large and free,
> Extend its bounds with rich rapidity. [55]

In subsequent years there was sporadic talk among Kingstonians concerning the possibility of bringing the capital back, but it was never in the cards. John A. Macdonald, by now attorney-general, Canada West, admitted as much in 1856. The capital question, in process of reaching its permanent solution, was again convulsing the politics of the Union. John A. confided to his mother: "We are now discussing the question of the seat of Government. ... I am afraid that we have no chance for Kingston. We will however make a fight for it." [56]

The loss of the capital was a grievous blow to Kingston, occasioning fear and in-security, and requiring a careful retrenchment if the town's prosperity were to be preserved. Max Magill explained the situation nicely:

When the capital was transferred to Montreal in 1844 Kingston businessmen realized that the future of the city depended on its success in meeting the competition of Toronto for the commercial leadership of Canada West. In spite of some disadvantages it must have seemed that its chances in this competition were good. It was still an important lake port, with a flourishing local trade and growing industries and, above all, as the headquarters of the Commercial Bank it was the financial centre of a region extending eastward from the vicinity of Port Hope to the old boundary with Lower Canada. [57]

Point Frederick and Kingston from Fort Henry, by the famous English illustrator William Henry Bartlett, 1840. (QUA)

SEVEN

From Village to City

During the early years of the nineteenth century a procession of emigrants, travellers, and military men passed through Kingston, and their literary descriptions are reinforced by the artistic renderings of James Pattison Cockburn, Harriet Dobbs Cartwright, Edward Charles Frome, and others. Their views reveal a bucolic townscape, empty of people, and devoid of any signs of the hustle and bustle of town life. Streets are wide but unpaved; the buildings are a mixture of styles, scales, and materials, but with wooden structures predominating. Of the public buildings, the most prominent are St George's Church and the military establishments.

The more detailed, if more romantic, works of William Henry Bartlett transmute Fort Henry into a Gibraltar and the Kingston waterfront into a Mediterranean or Caribbean fishing village. But as a symbolic expression of the dominance of the "Citadel" in the contemporary townscape, of the garrison in town life, they are appropriate. Similarly, Bartlett's view of Kingston from Fort Henry Heights – a perspective favoured by so many other visiting artists – is another artistic statement of the essence of Kingston's social and physical fabric at mid-century. The military dominate the foreground, the reduced naval yards lie behind, while the townscape of Kingston itself is characterized by a skyline accented with church towers and spires, a waterfront skirted with wharves and warehouses, and a forest of ships' masts and spars in the harbour. Even if an over-imaginative rendering, Bartlett's view again underscores how Kingston was constituted, if not how it actually appeared, at this period in its history.

But what of the people in these pictures? What was the quality of their life in Kingston during this period? Artistic two-dimensional views give no impression of how the community administered it affairs, what its social structure was, and what the daily and seasonal regimen of town life in a developing society was. The sounds, smells, and rhythms of life, together with the personalities and action groups throughout the population, are essential dimensions of the experience of the people living in communities like Kingston at this time.

View of Kingston's King Street *c.* 1834, by Harriet Dobbs Cartwright. (NA)

GOVERNING A GROWING TOWN

The system of government, administration, and management of urban affairs by means of the courts of the quarter sessions started to break down with the strains imposed by the War of 1812-1814. Indeed, it was an awareness of the need to improve the material and social circumstances of everyday life in Kingston that produced pressures for a more representative, responsible, and efficient form of municipal government. Crises like the cholera outbreaks underscored the absence of basic services and conveniences that, if not preventing such epidemics, would have better equipped the community to respond effectively to them. Concern over the policing of public nuisances, crime, and civil disorder, and the general need for an improvement of public utilities – all argued for innovations in urban government. The pressure for reform was therefore motivated both by the esoteric argument for participatory democracy and by a pragmatic concern for the more effective regulation of the affairs of a growing town. The absence of minimal facilities and civic agencies, together with a concern for the aesthetics of the townscape, motivated a letter to the editor of the *Gazette* as early as 1815. Noting the town's centrality and prosperity, the writer advocated that Kingston's "inhabitants should adopt some plan of improving and embellishing of it." The letter reads as a litany of deficiencies:

The streets require very great repairs, as in the rainy season, it is scarcely possible to move about without being in mud to the ankles; from their breadth they will admit of very wide foot paths on either side. ... The next thing required in my opinion would be lamps to light the streets in the dark of the moon. ... By way of embellishing the town ... there might trees be [*sic*] planted on both sides; it would have a fine effect, and be a very great ornament. ... They should also be kept free from lumber of every description; nothing can be more offensive to the eye than piles of wood, piles of staves, of casks and of filth; which at present is the case more or less in most of the streets. And among the many wants of this town, and certainly not the least, is an engine with the necessary pipes, and a certain number of Buckets for the preservation of property.[1]

A particular concern for some were the "frequent assaults, batteries, and affrays which occur in the streets." During the consideration of the causes of such disturbances, several factors were advanced, ranging from the "peculiarity of the native temperament, or the education of the inhabitants, to the variety of their national characters, the intermixture of military and naval residents of the lower class, the neglect of informing and prosecuting officers, and to the laxness or want of energy of the magistrates."[2] These were thought to be but symptoms of the main cause – an absence of appropriate municipal government – and it was urged that "the legislature must furnish the town with a code of laws, forming a complete police for its internal Government, and commissioners with sufficient authority to enforce them by fine or otherwise."[3]

The result was the passage of the Kingston Police Act in 1816. The town was to continue to be regulated by the magistrates in the quarter sessions, and the justices of the peace now had authority to levy taxes, although they could collect no more than £100 in any one year. Their concerns were quite comprehensive. "Police Rules and Regulations" published in the Kingston *Gazette* in September of that year identified their program of reform. Streets were to be turnpiked and footpaths provided; no firewood, empty casks, cases, boxes, rubbish, filth, timber, or stones were to be left out in the streets; casks and carriages were to be arranged along the sides of the streets, and the running of horses in the streets was prohibited; fire was to be prevented by the provision of ladders and buckets and the prohibition of chimneys of wood or clay; hogs running loose were to be impounded; slaughtering was prohibited in the town and the market house was to be kept clean.

Regulating and policing the sanitary arrangements of the town were particularly pressing in an age when concepts of disease were still rudimentary and medical treatment wanting. Complaints were to be expected. The heat of August produced a protest against the stench emanating from the market place and the concern that the "health of individuals and families residing therein, is endangered, and their comfort wholly destroyed."[4] The magistrates were urged to correct this. Such arrangements served to improve conditions in Kingston in its formative years and became the model for other towns in the province.

While the authority of the quarter sessions was strengthened by the Police Act that, among other things, permitted justices to effect many much-needed reforms, the magistrature was clearly woefully unrepresentative and undemocratic. A visitor to Kingston in 1832 chanced upon the spectacle of the officers of the court and was unimpressed:

Justice appeared to be distributed and the representatives of the law to be attired in the same plain and simple manner as in the States. We saw the Sheriff dressed in plain clothes, but with a cocked-hat, queue, and sword, walking through the streets to the court house, with a judge, undistinguished by dress, upon either side of him. [5]

Apart from the absence of pomp and circumstance, there was also much local dissatisfaction with the actual operation of the system throughout the 1830s. A letter to the editor of the *British Whig* in 1835 referred to the people of Kingston as being "so supine and indolent of disposition that they present not the spirit to help themselves," and went to on to complain that

Kingston is I believe the only place of any size or importance in this province that does not elect its own magistrates and what is the consequence? It is the only place in the province which is falling to decay. The one may possibly not be the cause of the other but in connection with other causes it has an evident tendency to prevent emigrants from making Kingston their home. They hear everywhere that Kingston is a "tory-hole" that it is governed by one or two families who have intermarried and that its inhabitants have not the chance of rising to office by either industry or talent and as all men have more or less ambition they pass our town in search of places less aristocratic. All this may please and gratify those gentlemen of fortune who delight in calling Kingston a charming country residence but on the suffering merchant, shopkeeper and mechanic it has a contrary effect. [6]

Some favoured incorporation and an elective system. Others, however, were opposed, probably because of a fear of increased taxation. The parties favouring municipal reform prevailed, and in 1838 Kingston was finally incorporated as a town, with a mayor and an elected corporation of aldermen and councillors. It had been preceeded in this by Brockville (1832) and Hamilton (1833), and by Belleville, Cornwall, Prescott, and Port Hope (all in 1834) – and even by little Cobourg and Picton (both 1837). Kingston's arch-rival, Toronto, had been elevated to city status as early as 1834.

On incorporation, the "Commonality of the Town of Kingston" was divided into four wards, each of which elected on a rotating system an alderman and a common councillor, for terms of four years. The chief magistrate of the town was the mayor, who was selected by council from townsmen who possessed the vote. The franchise was restricted to men with property assessed at £10. The council could levy taxes, appoint officials, and manage the general affairs of the town. All of this was carried out under the watchful supervision of the provincial administration. The new representative municipal government meant taxes as well as votes, and, as it would soon appear, it meant acrimony as well as democracy.

While no longer a mere police town, Kingston's first attempt at popular representation and participation did not sit well with the people. Opinion was sharply divided on incorporation, and that division persisted. There were several petitions to the government asking for the repeal of the 1838 Act of Incorporation. Opponents of incorporation pointed to an inefficient council, street violence, corruption in municipal politics, misuse of public funds, and embarrassments concerning the activities of senior town officials. The first mayor, Thomas Kirkpatrick, had been forced to resign because he lived outside the town in contravention of the 1838 Act, and N. Dawe, clerk of the council, was widely regarded as a drunkard. The 1840s were characterized by much discontent with the new system as it came to be practised, and in 1846 the *Argus* trumpeted against

the gross neglect and incompetency which have always marked their [town council] proceedings. Dissatisfaction of the public with the management of that body has loudly been expressed ... enough has been ascertained to demonstrate the absolute necessity of an instant and thorough reform in the management of our civic affairs.[7]

The *Argus* summed up much of Kingston's anti-incorporation sentiment when it advised voters during the municipal elections of 1846:

In the election of municipal officers, care should be taken that the intelligence, the integrity and the education of the candidates, places them beyond the sphere of being made actors in ruining the credit of the Town. ... The electors will find it to conduce to their own welfare to raise the standard of qualification much higher than it has yet been raised.[8]

Complaints and dissatisfaction such as this had a champion in John A. Macdonald, a former alderman and Kingston's member in the Union parliament since 1844. Change was strenuously pressed at a public meeting in March 1846, and a month later, Macdonald moved to incorporate Kingston as a city in an attempt to remedy a number of specific and vexing problems. He wanted to curtail Kingston's contributions to the Midland District, which – at £1,000 a year – were extortionately high. Macdonald believed that the size of the town's council should be expanded and its inflexible quorum rule changed in order to expedite business. There was also a strong desire to abolish the system of rotating elections, whereby one quarter of the council was elected annually. The March meeting had agreed unanimously to the annual election of the entire council. There was also an increasing demand for a more equitable system of assessing property.

In most particulars, John A. obtained what he and Kingstonians wanted with the passage of his bill in 1846. An annually-elected and bigger council was provided. Kingston's five historic wards – Sydenham, Ontario, St Lawrence, Cataraqui, and Frontenac – were established. Each ward elected two aldermen and two councillors. The council selected the mayor as before, but now the chief magistrate must have been elected to council. Kingston's contribution to the Midland District was limited to £300 per year, and even that sum was to be paid only until Kingston provided facilities for its own criminals.

But the 1846 incorporation did not include all of Macdonald's recommendations. Kingston opinion, for example, was heavily in favour of reducing the £10 voting qualification. Macdonald attempted to get it reduced to £7 10s, but the "House would not listen to the proposed reduction – not one member could be found in favour of the change."[9] Kingston's new adventure in city government was neither protracted nor particularly successful. Elections were held for the new twenty-man council. The only striking thing about the results was the strength of the Irish, who captured most of the seats. The veteran politician John Counter was narrowly elected first mayor of the city of Kingston.

The early years of new municipal government were fractious ones, however, and such was public disquiet that the *Argus* recommended "council to advertise for some person to teach them to address one another with becoming courtesy – a schoolmaster is very much needed among them."[10] The city was governed under the terms of the 1846 statute for less than four years, and the experiment was not particularly successful. The problems faced by the incoming council were considerable. City finances were in disarray, with a £3,000 deficit resulting from earlier mismanagement and the on-going "English debt" of £20,000 incurred by previous council's grandiose expectations for the city buildings. The interest on the municipal debt was a healthy 9 per cent per annum, and by late 1849 the accumulated debt amounted to £40,500. The 1846 incorporation did nothing to improve the quality of municipal leadership, and the new corporation lacked either the will or the financial acumen to deal effectively with the debt problem. Also, the maintenance of the material and social fabric of the city required that streets be drained, gas lighting and clean water be provided, liquor licences be regulated, and poverty relieved.

And then there were the suburbs. By 1848, while Kingston had a population of 8,362, a further 3,656 persons were to be found in such "outer suburbs" as "Stuartsville," "Williamsville," "Chathamville," "Charlesville," "Picardville," and "Orchardville."[11] Property in the suburb of the "French Village" (Picardville) elicited the comment that it was not "the most favourable [location] to catch the fancy of a respectable purchaser."[12] Farther out in the "exurbs" along the shores of Little Cataraqui Creek, the 1851 census enumerator was prompted to moralize on the living conditions of another community there:

a race of Muskrats have settled near the borders of this stream and like many of the people of this Township notwithstanding the many improvements in the arts of civilization continue their ancient mode of building and erect inumerable mud cabins having nothing more in view than their own comfort to which they are well adapted.[13]

Moreover, there were other other concerns:

The number of Bachelors in this locality occupying land and trying to live without the aid of the fair sex is alarming; if something is not done soon to prevent it, our asylums will be filled with inmates and the country become depopulated.[14]

The most vexatious problem, however, was "Lot 24," or Stuartsville, as it was more commonly called. This was a parcel of land west of both the town limits of 1838 and the city limits of 1846, land that by 1848 was home to some 2,286 persons. Originally owned by the Reverend John Stuart, Lot 24 was "developed" by his son, Archdeacon George Okill Stuart. Stuartsville did not enjoy a high reputation among Kingstonians. It was considered unsanitary, crowded, "copiously dotted with hog-pens and slaughter houses and consequent accumulations of feculent matter," and "chiefly inhabited by working classes."[15] Other complaints were the distress, poverty, and alleged drinking habits of the population who were served by the excessive number of Stuartsville taverns. Stuartsville was referred to variously as a "crying evil," an "overgrown and populous suburb," and a "millstone around the neck of Kingston." It was argued that "Kingston, call it what you will, never can be anything more than a miserable village while Lot No. 24 operates against it like its nightmare."[16] At best, it was viewed as a working-class suburb; at worst, as Arch-deacon Stuart's slum.

Kingston's politicians wanted to annex the area in order to enhance the city's tax base; the Midland District, of course, took the opposite stand. The issue reverberated through Kingston and Midland politics for years. The people of Stuartsville seem to have been strongly opposed to annexation. This was logical enough. They were, after all, primarily "mechanics and labouring men who were at first mainly induced to settle there in order that with some inconvenience they might escape the Police Tax at that not a heavy burthen."[17] The politics of municipal annexation were as personal and complicated in 1849 as they are today. Satellite communities were anxious to retain their individuality and low taxes; urban areas regarded them as parasitic users of services at somebody else's expense.

The opportunity for major and long-term change in Kingston's municipal government came with the rise to power of the Reform alliance of Robert Baldwin and Louis LaFontaine in 1848. Responsible government was at last implemented. The Reformers then moved to make some social changes that they had long ad-vocated. Central to Baldwin's thinking was sweeping reform of Ontario's system of local government. Baldwin's scheme was of a province-wide dimension, and ap-plied to Kingston as much as to other urban centres. Baldwin's Municipal Act (1849), which became effective on 1 January 1850, incorporated some key general principles. Larger towns like Hamilton, Toronto, and Kingston were granted the powers of

Land sale by H. Bartliff, auctioneer and broker, advertised in 1850. (QUA)

counties, while retaining their city status. For Kingston, the Act delineated the main features of municipal government that were to function there for the next century. It also represented the culmination of a movement toward local self-government initiated by the legislation of 1838 and 1846; it replaced the last vestiges of centralized administrative control. The efforts of Richard Cartwright, John A. Macdonald, and John Counter were at last rewarded.

The Municipal Act of 1849 also solved some problems that were peculiar to Kingston. Municipalities were empowered to create "outer wards" of adjacent lands, and when such wards became as populous and wealthy as the least-populous and least-wealthy of the original wards, cities were required to annex them. [18] Accordingly, on 1 January 1850, Kingston exercised its powers, and Lot 24 and other "suburbs" were annexed. Organized into two additional wards, Rideau and Victoria, the ex-villages increased the total number of wards to seven. The three remaining suburban outliers to the newly-established town limits were: the pleasant and almost inaccessible village-cum-company-town of Garden Island; Portsmouth, to the west of Kingston, which retained its autonomy until it was annexed by the city in 1952; and Barriefield, a residential suburb located across the Cataraqui River to the east in Pittsburgh township.

THE MARKET

The quality of urban life is very much influenced by the absence or presence of services and facilities. The move toward municipal organization provided mechanisms for the better organization and management of the growing community.

Much attention was given to the important institution of the town market place. In many ways, this daily market was the very pulse of the little community, isolated as it was on the developing frontier. Originally established in 1801, the market square was not formally designated as such until 1811. New butchers' stalls were added in 1819, and it was anticipated that such was the demand that they would be

productive of a considerable revenue applicable only to public purposes – this revenue so judiciously obtained by parcelling out and leasing a certain portion of the Market ground, when added to the funds at the disposal of the magistrates, will be amply sufficient to pave all the side paths in a few years as well as to make other necessary improvements in the town. [19]

In theory, the regulated market place was the only location in the city for the sale of produce with specified hours of operation, close monitoring of weights and measures, and, to some degree, control over the quality of produce displayed for sale. Some avoided these controls by offering

their produce in the public streets and yards of the city. This they do to the great injury of the public. The public or a large majority of the inhabitants of the Town, resort to the

Market Square in order to find such things as they need, but they frequently stand with pain and see the very things they most needed purchased before their eyes by retailers and hucksters in the open streets. Not only are the public generally thus injured but also the Collector of Tolls, for in this manner is he deprived of about one fourth of the Tolls he ought to receive.[20]

Moreover, alternative retailing systems were taking their place in the urban scene. Thus, several stores had located themselves along the adjoining streets, and the buyers of farmer's produce could also avail themselves of the products of the linen and woollen draper, saddlery and hardware store, bakeries, watch and clock repairers, dry-goods merchants, a chemist and apothecary, and even a "tobacco factory."

Several factors interfered with the efficient supply of produce to the local populace. Perhaps the most common complaint was about "forestalling," by which practice speculators intervened between consumers and farmers and raised the prices of essential commodities. It was claimed that "when a waggon from the county, loaded with vegitables [sic] butter, eggs, etc. arrives in sight of the Market it is immediately met by a swarm of forestallers."[21] By buying cheap and selling dear, such speculators displeased both farmers and townspeople. The complaints continued through the 1820s, and in 1827 "Plain Truth" wrote to the editor of the *Chronicle* to complain that the market was not fulfilling its original function and that higher prices were the result of "middlemen" intervening between the townspeople and the farmers. More specifically, he complained that "forestallers (who are ever on the watch) buy from the farmers at an under value, before they reach the market place, and again sell out to the consumer and housekeeper at any advanced profits. Such are at present the facts and consequent loss to both the consumer and farmer."[22] Forestalling such as this prevented public access to the producers and allowed retailers to control prices by buying up available produce.

The logistics of maintaining an adequate supply of produce in a town like Kingston were problematic enough without their being further endangered by manipulation of scarce commodities. It is no wonder, therefore, that a common complaint of the day was that "we are sorry to say that everything edible in Kingston Market continues uncommonly dear and scarce."[23] One farmer complained that Kingston merchants would not pay cash for produce and he was reduced to peddling his produce from door to door. Citizens agreed that merchants were the problem, arguing, for example, that the "Kingston market is anything but well supplied. Eggs, beef, mutton, veal etc. in great demand and the Butchers and Bakers are raising their prices and playing the tyrant so spiritedly that unless the farmer interferes, the case is hopeless."[24]

Communications were vital to supplying the town's needs. The onset of winter offered an alternative to the somewhat dubious road system, as is seen in several contemporary reports. The winter of 1831 was "early and delightful," the "snow is solid and substantial, and the sleighing consequently universal," and the market, accordingly, displayed "an abundance of those 'creative comforts' so indespensable in a season of keen appetitical requirements."[25] A decade later, the same image is given of a vital market extending its influence out to a considerable region, when communications were favourable:

[The] market for the last few days has been well supplied, the roads being excellent – enabling our farmers living at a distance, to visit us with their well laden
sleighs. ... A few sleighs have arrived from Jefferson County [New York], with Pork,
Mutton Hams, and c. [*sic*] but not in sufficient number to affect our market in the least.
We presume the principal object of their visit is to procure a few yards of Broodscloth
[*sic*] at a cheap rate.[26]

The failure to sustain adequate supplies of food was laid squarely at the feet of the magistrates:

It is surprising that in the year 1823, the Market of this town should remain without any
regulations. To protect the fair dealer, and detect the fraudulent one, is the object of all
established regulations for markets and without them it is impossible that those who
have the supply in their hands can meet with that encouragement which alone secures
competition. ... At a time when our town is becoming daily more extensive by substantial and handsome buildings our market remains in the same confused state that we
may suppose it to have been in fifty years ago. How creditable to our magistrates.[27]

Municipal authorities were obliged to establish a better regulated system that would, ideally, satisfy the interests of both producers and consumers, and at least monitor the activities of retailers. Accordingly, in 1847, an Act was passed to "Regulate the Public Market in the City of Kingston." The market square was reaffirmed as the sole location in the city for the sale "in the open air" of "corn, grain, flour, meal, bran, fruit, vegetables, eggs, butter, cheese, lard, poultry, game, farmstock, and other animals whether live or dead, shell or other fish, hay, fodder, boards, scant-ling, staves, shingles, lath, fuel, or other woods, coal or lime."[28]

The comprehensiveness of this list underscores the extent and complexity of the market's contribution to the community. Previously, while produce had been sold at the market square, a wood, hay, and cattle market had been located in the vicinity of Place d'Armes, and a fish market was comprised of boats "ranged on the Beach at the foot of Brock Street."[29] Indeed, the marketing of fish required special con-sideration, and it was noted that

fresh fish brought to market in boats may be sold by the owner of such boats on the
beach nearest to the fish house; that salted fish may be sold at all seasons in the
hucksters stall, and that fresh fish may be exposed for sale in the Market Square from
the 20th day of December, to the 20th day of March.[30]

Busy market in the late nineteenth century. (QUA)

Once marketing was centralized, the past abuses could be curtailed, the quality
of the produce controlled, and fair dealing ensured. This was the system that was
to continue for much of the nineteenth century, until new modes of transport and
increased demand were to generate new forms of retail organization.

HEALTH

The 1830s also saw some improvements in urban facilities, like the paving of
sidewalks, the construction of a sewer along Store Street (Princess Street), and the
general draining of the streets. Nonetheless, "abominable nuisances" continued,
like the running of swine throughout the streets, and the dumping of waste and
debris in public thoroughfares. Visitors to Kingston complained of "the endless out-

door squabbles of its pigs and dogs, both of which domestic animals infest the streets in shoals." In fairness, it should be pointed out that the same commentator reported that Toronto differed only in that "there dogs and cows, in lieu of dogs and pigs, are seen in daily contest."[31] The vicinity of the market was particularly noisome as

The walls are covered with stove pipes, stoves, old boxes, stinking mackerel, and all manner of trumpery, and in consequence of the crowd around the auctioneer, people are actually obliged to go out into the street in the mud, in order to get to the market where, again, they stand a fair chance of being covered with mud, and upset by some old horse mounted by an awkward boy displaying him to the greatest advantage.[32]

This rather acerbic description and complaint fill out our image of the townscape of the day. Others were more concerned with the sanitation than with the aesthetics, complaining of "the practice of filling our streets with dead animals and other filth, calculated to produce putrification and disease."[33]

The visitations of cholera, typhus, and other diseases cannot be disassociated from the general neglect of municipal hygiene and public health. In the 1830s, cholera was the most feared and most deadly of the diseases ravaging the western world. *Cholera morbus*, or Asian cholera, spread out from Southeast Asia to China and Japan in 1822, appeared in Moscow in 1825, and in October 1831 the port of Sunderland reported the first case in England.[34] Kingston awaited the arrival of the 1832 immigrant season with considerable alarm, prompting one local scribe to pen a most dismal poem:

From the south to the north
  hath the cholera come,
He came like a despot king.
He hath swept the earth with conqueror's step
And the air with spirits wing.

We shut him out with a girdle of ships,
And a guarded quarantine;
What ho! now which of your watchers slept?
The Cholera's past your line!

There's a curse of the blessed sun and air,
What will we do for breath?
For breath, which was once but a word for life,
Is now but a word for death.

The months pass on, and the circle spreads
And the time is drawing nigh
When each street may have a darkened house,
Or a coffin passing by.

Our lot is cast upon evil days,
And the world's winter-time;
The earth is old, and worn with years
Of want, of woe, and of crime.

Then out of the folly of ancient time –
The folly which wished you mirth;
Look round on the anguish,
  look round on the vice,
Then dare to be glad upon earth![35]

Apart from the questionable literary merit of such creations, the gloomy sentiments and forebodings did nothing to relieve the considerable fears of the population awaiting the arrival of the disease. On 26 April 1832, Lieutenant-

Governor Sir John Colborne issued a proclamation that while invoking intervention from on high, must have done little to allay the fears of Kingston's citizens:

KNOW YE, that taking into our most serious consideration the dangers threatened by the
progress of a very grievous disease, with which it has pleased Almighty God, in the
dispensations of His providence, to visit several parts of our Dominions, We have
resolved, and by the advice of our Executive Council for our Province of Upper
Canada, do hereby command, that a day of Public Fasting, Humiliation and Prayer, be
observed throughout our said Province, on Wednesday, the Sixteenth of May next, so
that all our people therein may humble themselves before Almighty God, and in the
most devout and solemn manner send up their Prayers and Supplications to the Divine
Majesty, for averting the heavy judgements which our manifold provocations have most
justly deserved. ...[36]

Others preferred more practical preparations. Noting that three recent cholera
deaths in Belfast were of "decided drunkards,"[37] the town mounted an attack on its
many taverns; groups of men were hired to clean the streets of manure and filth;
private homes were inspected to discover unhealthy privies, fouled wells, and rotting
piles of garbage.[38]

Dependent only upon an inadequate one-storey hospital, located in Number 2
Blockhouse at the junction of King and West streets, treatment of the sick relied
heavily upon the services of the military establishment. Army and navy doctors
attended the sick lying in the encampment hastily erected on the waterfront, and
their sterling services were much appreciated by the sorely-taxed community:

They have left no portion of the town unvisited, and have removed every particle of filth
that could possibly create or cherish this dreadful disorder; still, much remains to be
done by the inhabitants themselves, and every facility should be afforded the
magistrates to carry their benevolent intentions into effect. Their subsequent resolutions
will be obeyed, we trust, with alacrity; and it is most consoling to the public to think
that a town is supplied with a corps of medical gentlemen as distinguished by humanity
and disinterestedness, as they are by professional skill and experience; and who appear
to have abandoned every other consideration on the present occasion, to the purposes of
general utility.[39]

On 3 June 1832, the sailing ship *Carricks* arrived at Grosse Isle, at Quebec City,
having lost forty-two passengers to the disease. By 9 June the disease had appeared
in Montreal, spread to Prescott by 15 June, and on 17 June Kingston experienced
its first death from cholera.[40] The onset of "this dreadful calamity" prompted the
formation of a Board of Health that immediately attempted to provide moral, if
not medical, support in the face of "the unnecessary alarm which prevails throughout the country":

[A]lthough a very few cases of Cholera had appeared in this Town, the Committee considered it a duty, which they owe to the Public, to state, that several of the cases which have appeared, have been brought by steam and other Boats – that only a very few deaths have occurred, and that no death has occurred, where proper medical, and other attention has been early, and promptly applied; that several have been discharged cured; and that this Committee possesses the fullest evidence, that the Town at the moment is in other respects unusually healthy.[41]

One contemporary observer, a military man, has left us his account of the community's response to the epidemic:

The appearance of Kingston during the epidemic was most melancholy. No business was done, for the country people kept aloof from the infected town. The yellow flag was hoisted near the market place on the beach, and intercourse with the Steamers put under Quarantine regulations. The conduct of the inhabitants was admirable, and reflected great credit on this good little town.[42]

Kingston was visited by the cholera again in 1833, but the outbreak in 1834 was even more severe. Initially, reports suggested that the feared disease was limited to the immigrants in Montreal, and there was thought to be little "cause of alarm, as the disorder, if it be the cholera, has not spread in the rapid manner it did in 1832."[43] By August, however, the worst fears of some were realized and even the losses of 1832 were surpassed.

The responses were varied. The citizenry were urged to effect a "cheerful fortitude," as "it is folly to fear, because fear only hastens the calamity it seeks to avoid."[44] Following the precedent of 1832, 13 August was declared a day of penance and prayer, and of "seeking to the Lord" instead of "to the physician."[45] Others turned to remedies like the anti-cholera pills prescribed by Surgeon Adamson, late of the Bengal Army[46]; some advocated the consumption of "anti-cholera tinctures" consisting of brandy, cinnamon, cloves, nutmegs, and cayenne pepper, the "patient retiring to bed, bottles of hot water are applied to his feet, heated plates to the abdomen, with warm covering, a profuse perspiration comes almost immediately, and relief follows."[47] For others, the secret was to avoid fish, fruit, vegetables, purgatives – and hopefully most of the putative cures being bandied about![48] The list of substances prescribed for consumption or application was impressive: calomel, mercurous chloride, opium, castor oil, laudanum, bleeding by leeches, sulphate of quinine, and various emetics. Saline fluids were injected into the veins of some poor unfortunates: Kingston's most famous doctor, James Sampson, tried this treatment on no fewer than twenty patients – without a single success.[49] More prosaically, temporary hospitals were also built, and sanitation regulations enforced.

But despite these initiatives, some four hundred deaths occurred out of a population of only five thousand, and a visitor to the town immediately after the epidemic had broken out remarked: "everything wears a very melancholy aspect, so sombre indeed was the appearance of that town that it was an absolute relief to one's spirit to leave it. I was particularly struck by the number of persons who were mourning; nearly every third person I met was habited in black."[50] Such was the severity of the 1834 cholera outbreak, that "awful visitation of Providence," that it was reported to have caused the death of one in every sixteen persons in the town and contributed to an additional loss through migration. Later years were to prove to be equally trying, and disease and sickness were to be all too prevalent a feature of life in Kingston in the mid-nineteenth century.

The year 1847 surpassed even 1834 in the virulence of the outbreak of disease. Again associated with the through-traffic of immigrants, typhus fever replaced cholera as the killer this time. Over half of the 100,000 or so immigrants to Canada moved west into Upper Canada. Virtually all of these passed through Kingston via the Rideau or St Lawrence routes, and the community's facilities were greatly pressed by the need to accommodate, albeit briefly, some 2,500 transients a week. Though they were confined to the wharfs and dockside, the treatment of the destitute immigrants aroused the concern of at least one Kingstonian:

The wharf being generally covered with steamboat firewood, many immigrants already feverish, are obliged to be all day on this wood, under a burning sun; and those of them who are too frail to climb have to creep along on the very edge of the dock, at the risk of falling over and drowning. They are moreover, under the necessity of remaining encased in the filth in which they are coated when they arrive, and the exposure of persons of such of them that attempt to get free of this crust is sometimes very indecent. By drinking the stagnant water in the slip (there being none else to which they can have acess [sic] in the neighbourhood) they are compelled to consume their own — and other matter with which this water is impregnated.[51]

The first deaths occurred on 13 June, and by early July the relief afforded by the Hotel Dieu and Female Benevolent Society was overwhelmed by the flow of sick from "all the lodging houses in the city and its neighbourhood to the extent of several miles."[52] Public anxiety increased as the epidemic swept through the community, and by August there was a fear that "the evil we deplore is not, alas, at its height. The malignant month of September has yet to come and pass away; and how many of us will be alive at its termination is a problem that will not take longer than six weeks in solving. ..."[53]

The Kingston Board of Health attempted to relieve the pressure by construction of emigrant sheds at Emily and King, which themselves were soon overflowing and the subject of complaint. Indeed, the mayor, emigrant agent, and two members of the Board of Health were charged with obstructing the highway with the emigrant facilities, with constructing "privies" that necessitated the Baroness de Rottenburg "keeping a scent bottle in close contiguity with her nostrils," and with "filling the sheds with diseased sick, and other immigrants and dead bodies, to the common nuisance of all." This complaint continued:

Throughout the summer hundreds and thousands of emigrants had passed through the town and immense numbers had been congregated in and around the sheds. During the warm weather the stench which had pervaded that part of the town had been intolerable. As evening closed in during the sultry summer days, the air was charged with a heavy mephitic vapour, and insufferable odour proceeding from these sheds. The board walk leading along King Street was covered with the foulest filth and vermin, and no lady could pass there without the danger of contamination. The foulest smells pervaded the air and the most indecent exposure of their persons by the emigrants, male and female, close to the board walk, and under the eyes and noses of the passersby, were things of every-day occurrence. Not a single Policeman was set to keep guard over them. The Boardwalk is covered with people, whose garments were probably infected; and the whole front of the Artillery parade ground along the boardwalk was covered with an unbroken line of professional beggars.[54]

While these offending sheds were later moved to the foot of Albert Street, others attempted to have the facilities moved away to the dockyard at Point Frederick, to the outlying Molson's Wharf – or even to have a quarantine station established on Garden Island.[55]

By the end of 1847, St Mary's Cathedral alone had recorded 1,515 deaths between June and December, whereas only 64 had occurred in the whole of 1846.[56] No fewer than 1,200 immigrants were interred in an unmarked common grave. Often, surviving widows and orphans were left destitute, and assistance was provided by such groups as the Distressed Scotch and Irish Fund, the Cedar Island Relief Fund, the Dorcas Society, the St Patrick Society, and the newly-established House of Industry.[57]

Ironically, the aftermath of the 1847 epidemic and social unrest was the establishment of several charitable and tax-supported institutions that, while founded to cater to the needs of the transient poor, grew into valued organizations serving Kingston.

UTILITIES

It is not surprising that, in the face of these annual ravages, some saw a need to correct Kingston's more obvious deficiencies in sanitary arrangements. The threat of a renewed spread of cholera in 1848 prompted one inhabitant to advocate the formation of a town "health police," as it was complained that "some persons may be of the opinion that wherever filth has been permitted to accumulate the approaching snows of winter will cover and render it innocuous."[58] Others addressed the equally vexatious problem of the provision of a healthy water supply. As early as 1836 it was argued that a water-supply system based upon "steam propulsion" and movement by hydraulic means was preferable to damming the Cataraqui Creek to provide a fresh-water reservoir. The proposal to lift water by means of a steam pump was advanced again in 1839, it being noted that

Although at first sight it may appear an undertaking of great magnitude and of very great uncertainty, yet I am convinced that the difference between a certain and a constant supply of fresh and soft water from the lake and the hard water from the wells, which, independent of its hardness, from the constant filtration of filth of the town, will in course of time become unpalatable, together with the uncertainty of the carters' supply.[59]

By such technological innovations, the water supply would therefore be soft, more reliable, a preventative against fires in a town "built mainly of wood," but most importantly, *clean*. It was again reported in 1841 that "complaints against the Water in this place have been very loud and frequent during the past summer."[60] Apart from the wells that were in danger of pollution, town dwellers obtained their water from carters who drew their supply from Lake Ontario, a source "considered as pure and palatable a drink as any in the world, but unfortunately in the Harbour of Kingston, not being within reach of the current, and subject to be mixed up with the filth of the Town, it is rendered unfit for use."[61]

The remedy sought was the establishment of a municipally-controlled system. Some would not wait, however, and embarked on their own projects. A steam pump had already been constructed at the west end of the town, and this pumped over a hundred gallons a minute into a cistern to supply the carters. The intake was sixteen feet deep in the main lake current and allowed "every family in Town, to have the use of pure and clean Water."[62] Thomas Kirkpatrick installed his own pump in his own house, 467 feet from the lake and 41 feet above it. Complete with filtering system, a metal pipe conveyed the water from the lake to a cistern at the top of his dwelling.

Such arrangements were much envied by those forced to rely on less wholesome Lake Ontario water, especially when "the hot summer months return, and on looking around on the Bay of Kingston [they] find it covered with a verdant green coat."[63] While Kirkpatrick led the way for improved supply for the élite of the town, the general populace still relied on its wells and dubious lake water. The remedy – public access to water piped from a reliable source – was delayed by the problem of excavating the limestone underlying the town; but it was argued that even the provision of additional reservoirs of pumped water would be beneficial since it would decrease the carters' charge by three to four pence a puncheon (roughly sixty-six gallons).

Substantive progress came with the incorporation of Kingston in 1846. The city now had the right to "erect, preserve and regulate Public Cisterns, Reservoirs or other conveniences for the supply of good and wholesome water or for the ex-

Thomas Kirkpatrick, first mayor of the town of Kingston, 1838. He served again in 1847. From 1867 to 1870, he was Conservative MP for Frontenac. (QUA)

tinguishment of fires, and to make reasonable charge for the use thereof, and to prevent the waste and fouling of public water." In 1847 a private company was organized for the purposes of supplying Kingston with water, but it was not until 30 May 1849 that the Bill for the Incorporation of the City of Kingston Water Works

Kingston still a town of wood, by Lieut. E.C. Frome, *c*. 1833. The Great Fire would make it "The Limestone City." (QU Agnes Etherington Art Centre)

Company received final approval.[64] Later in that year, city council agreed to subscribe for $1,000 of stock in return for the provision of "a fountain in the Market Square and the City Buildings with water, and also a sufficient number of Hydrants to serve for the extinguishment of Fires, Public Baths for the Use of the Poor, and watering of the Streets, and the thickly settled parts of the City. ..."[65] Others were considering even grander schemes and called for the erection of a steam engine to pump water "to a reservoir at the summit level of the town, there to be distributed through every street to every house."[66]

Prosaic though it may be, the history of sewers and water mains is important to the quality of life of nineteenth-century urban dwellers. The initial provision of water mains, public faucets, and the first twenty hydrants improved Kingston's sanitation and provided a degree of protection from the hazard of fire. Frequent fires had occurred before the disastrous conflagration of 17 April 1840. This disaster in the commercial and social centre of the town destroyed forty buildings, left forty-five families homeless, and resulted in an estimated loss of £70,000-worth of property.[67] As in many early-nineteenth-century Canadian cities, most of Kingston's buildings were constructed of wood; and in the weeks following the fire, both the *Herald* and the *Chronicle* used their pages to campaign against "wooden buildings" in the "heart of the Town."[68] Along with Dr Barker's *British Whig*, these papers debated the causes of the fire. Some focused attention on the damage caused by the associated explosion of a store of gunpowder during the blaze. Shortly after the disaster, Barker pontificated,

Although the 'Upper Canada Herald' attempts to gainsay the statements of the 'Chronicle', as well as our own, that the market block was set on fire by the explosion of the gunpowder in Mr. Fraser's store, the fact remains the same, nevertheless. A few sparks of fire had probably alighted on the roofs of some houses, which careful attention would have prevented from bursting into flames; but immediately after the explosion the whole block was on fire at once, and so paralysed were the exertions of the inhabitants by the fearfullness of the shock, that the fire gained head amazingly – so fast, indeed, that the tenants of the houses in the next block had hardly time to save themselves, letting alone their effects and furniture. ... Mr. Fraser has lost by this fire the fruits of a long course of industry, and in his general life is trustworthy, and unassuming; yet as the gunpowder improperly stored in his warehouse ... was the chief cause of ruining above 50 families, he cannot take it ill if his conduct is made the subject of public and personal animadversion.[69]

The fire made it clear that corrective action was needed. That action came in 1847 with the passage of "An Act to prevent Wooden Buildings being erected in the thickly-built parts of the City of Kingston, and for the further prevention of fires." John Spurr was correct when he concluded that the "night of the fire" – more than any other agency or institution – explains how Kingston came to be the "Limestone City."

The efforts of the Kingston Water Works Company to provide a reliable water supply were also effective in protecting the city, although the system was limited in coverage and city council was in conflict with the company over the need for extra hydrants and cheaper water. Further criticism arose from the discovery that the company's main intake, which extended only 150 feet offshore, was drawing in raw sewage.[70] The agitation came to a head in 1886, when the system failed to prevent the destruction of the Queen Street Methodist Church. In October 1886 the committee charged with investigating the state of Kingston's water system concluded that

after many months consideration and investigation of the matters referred to them, after repeated interviews and attempts to negotiate with the KWC and after obtaining the assistance of experts have unanimously arrived at the conclusion that the only way to secure a Satisfactory Water Supply for the City and meet the requirements of the Fire

Underwriters Association, the demands of the people and the reasonable wants of the Corporation at a reasonable price is to acquire the present plant, property and franchise of the Company, and when acquired proceed to make such improvements as will then appear necessary.[71]

A by-law to raise $120,000 to effect this purchase was put to the vote on 10 August 1887, and on 1 October of that year the city became the owner and manager of its own municipal water supply. By this action, the city fathers not only moved toward ensuring a greater security from fire and disease but also took another step – albeit a small one – towards a concept of municipal government that provided a fuller range of services for the people.

LAW, ORDER, AND CIVILITY

If in some ways Kingston was beginning to exhibit some of the social and cultural amenities befitting one of the premier cities of Upper Canada, there were also distressing signs of social unrest and civil ills. "Disguise it as we may," complained a correspondent in 1840, "the streets of Kingston are night and day swarming with drunkards and prostitutes, and never since we have been residents in the Town have we seen so much vice as now prevails, and which seems to be daily increasing."[72]

If the poor had always been with Kingstonians, so – almost always – had members of the oldest profession. As early as 1818 the town magistrates convicted both Mary Flake and another worthy, Alice Brydon, of "keeping a house of ill fame."[73] But the magistrates were not the only guardians of public morality. In 1835, incensed that both single and married men had been lured to "a noted ladies' house" located in the "French Village" by "handsome circulars," the editor of the *British Whig* threatened to "publish a list of the local notables who attended."[74]

The "intemperance," "prostitution," and "pauperism" that incurred the wrath of many Kingstonians in the 1830s and 1840s were often attributed by them to the excessive number of taverns and unlicensed drinking houses throughout the town. "Picardville" (or "French Village," as it was sometimes called), "Stuartsville" (or Lot 24), the village of Barriefield, several districts to the northwest of Division Street, and the whole waterfront strip, were well served with taverns and drinking houses. Indeed, one editorial compared Kingston with the St-Roch Ward of Quebec City, to the disadvantage of the "conservative capital of Upper Canada." St-Roch had a mere fourteen taverns serving a population of 10,850 in 1842; but in Kingston, with a total population of about 5,000 in the same year, "every street swarms with taverns and drinking shops" and eleven such establishments were to be found on Quarry (Wellington) Street alone. The report went on to note,

Quarry Street is not singular in the possession of this disproportionate number of taverns; for a traveller would in fact, after walking through the Town, be led almost irresistibly to the conclusion, that one of the great staple trades of the place, was that of retailing drams, so large is the proportion of taverns in every quarter of the Town to the number of houses occupied for other purposes.[75]

The reasons advanced included the laxity of the magistrates, a "want of zeal" on the part of the clergy, the general "intemperate habits of the population," and "some cause, peculiar to the locality." This led the good editor to conclude that it was "the scarcity and dearness of house room, and ... the consequent deprivation of those sources of social comfort and domestic enjoyment, which are so effective, wherever they exist, in staying the progress of vice and overcoming habits of intemperance and brutish sensuality."[76] The remedy, therefore, was the construction of more homes and the propagation of family life. More prosaically, the call for a public meeting to debate the establishment of a gas company to provide street lighting was motivated not only by a desire for "public convenience and economy" but also by a conviction that "experience had fully proved in the mother country, [that] there was a diminished amount of crime."[77] Sir Francis Bond Head was petitioned that "intemperance and pauperism are great and growing evils in this province calling loud for legislative aid"; it was advocated that a tax of 100 per cent be imposed on spirits, the revenue being directed to the erection of "houses of industry" in each district.[78]

Others turned to the make-up of the population for an indication of the cause of various social abuses. Certainly, the military posed a problem: "Town-Crown" frictions of the nineteenth century were to be echoed later in the "Town-Gown" stresses of the twentieth. But not all the violence should be attributed to brawling soldiers.

At first sight, Kingston's ethnic structure may appear to have been quite unified. While over half of Kingston's 11,585 people in 1851 were foreign-born, over a third had been born in Ireland, and some 16 per cent hailed from England, Scotland, or Wales. Less than 5 per cent of the total population were from outside the British Isles, and of these the largest group was from the United States. Not surprisingly, therefore, the social fabric was enlivened by the St George, St Patrick, and St Andrew societies, which were supported by their respective ethnic communities – English, Irish, and Scottish.

By mid-century, however, the St Andrew society was concerned about the apathy exhibited by its members, and hoped that "there will be a proper display" on the occasion of the annual parade on 30 November.[79] No fears were ever entertained that there would be lack of support from the fractious Irish community for the institutions perpetuating *their* ethnic distinctiveness. Conflicts between the Orange and Green factions were as vexatious in Kingston as elsewhere in Canada in the mid-nineteenth century. Celebrations of the "Glorious Twelfth" in 1843 turned into an anti-Catholic riot, complete with "drunken assaults, wanton destruction of property, sacrilege and murder."[80]

Seventeen years later, the visit by His Royal Highness The Prince of Wales in

September 1860 precipitated the construction of an Orange Order archway over the planned route and the promised attendance of some "fifteen thousand loyal Orangemen ... in full regalia, and with flags, banners, and music."[81] The Orange Order may have been legal in Canada, but it was not so in Britain. The Prince's advisers concluded that his passage under the arch would constitute an improper recognition of the Order. The intransigent Orangemen refused to remove the arch; the Prince, to the excruciating disappointment of Kingstonians, refused to land and continued to sail westward. Orangemen in Kingston were enraged to the point that John A. Macdonald, then attorney-general, had to tour the province in order to satisfy Orangemen that neither he nor his government was in any way responsible for the activities of the Prince of Wales.

Ethnic conflicts were not peculiar to Kingston, but in a small community of some 13,000 people they often became personalized and extremely bitter. Indeed, many of the town's numerous fires were thought to be due to an incendiarism that was on at least one occasion motivated by hatreds rooted in Protestant and Catholic factionalism. On 27 September the *Daily British Whig* reported four fires over the previous two days, three of which were due to arson; three years later, local newspapers claimed that "Incendiarism is certainly the most prominent offence against the laws of public safety in vogue at present. ..."[82] Between 12 October and 4 December 1858, there were seven fires, and all were attributed to arson.[83]

Furthermore, the problem of factional arson was rendered worse by conflict between factional *fire-companies*, culminating in the murder of one of their members, George Bowen, when "a parcel of loafers and lookers-on attacked the firemen of No. 2 Engine and Hose Company" while they were attending a fire at Archdeacon Stuart's stable.[84] Demonstrating more optimism than objectivity, the local press attempted to look elsewhere for the underlying roots of these confrontations, arguing that

these Incendiary Fires are the acts of boys, not men. Green and Orange Factionists may quarrel among themselves, and, in moments of passion, do each other mischief; but that any class of Irishmen could wantonly, and in cold blood, burn down each other's dwellings, is more than we can believe.[85]

These were violent years in the streets of Kingston. A solution was sought in 1841 with "An Act to establish a Police Force ... for the preservation of good order and public morals."[86] Accordingly, city council appointed a chief of police, head constable, and police constables. Though completely untrained, these servants of the public were required to collect taxes and market tolls, fight fires, serve as court officers, maintain law and order, and monitor the general behaviour of the public. Their job was an unenviable one. An account of an incident in 1855 serves to illustrate the duty they were often called upon to perform:

An improved fire protection service. (Kingston Fire Department Museum)

a large number of sailors and dock workers assailed the police and overpowered them and rescued McNiven (the prisoner) in a state of nudity. During the action, which lasted for some time, the police were brutally treated. Constable Beattie was knocked down by a stone which broke his jaw and left him minus six teeth. The High Bailiff arrived at the crisis, and rallying the police force, and aided by some of our citizens, immediately charged into the rebels, and after some hard fighting, succeeded in rescuing McNiven, besides taking two prisoners.[87]

The report of the committee on police of that year complained that "the citizens of Kingston have been kept in an almost constant state of alarm in consequence of the numerous acts of incendiarism and robbery. ..."[88] The list of violent incidents in Kingston reported by the Prescott *Telegraph* – even when inter-urban bias and rivalry is allowed for – presents an image more in keeping with that of an American wild-west frontier town:

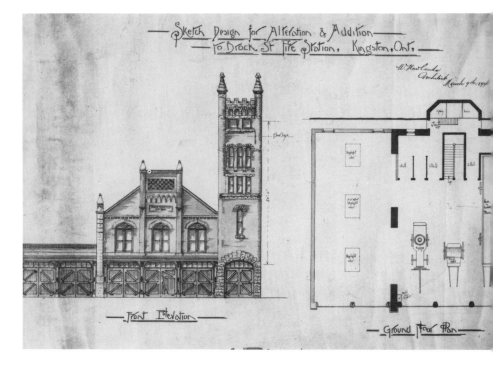

Design for the new Brock Street fire station, by William Newlands, 1894. (Kingston Fire Department Museum)

Society in Kingston, from all we can learn, must be in a deplorable state. We are informed that scarcely a night passes without a number of pistols or gunshots being heard in the public streets. During the late election it was dangerous for a person to be out after nightfall. It seems that a bad feeling has existed for some time among firemen which has sometimes led to open breaches of the peace ... it is said that many parties go armed with pistols or dirks.[89]

Some relief was afforded by the passage of the 1858 Act Respecting the Municipal Institutions of Upper Canada, which allowed for the establishment of municipal boards of commissioners of police.[90] Kingston immediately availed itself of this opportunity, appointed its own commissioners, and increased its police force from six to twenty constables.

Morale was raised by the provision of "blue uniform-frock coats with silver buttons for ordinary wear and grey military great coats for cold weather."[91] With improved drill, more specialized duties, and an increasing sense of professionalism, the Kingston police force was better able to address the considerable challenges posed by mid-nineteenth-century street life.

Despite the apparent frequency of riots and affrays during this period of Kingston's development, there were attempts to provide some degree of urbanity for the population. For example, it was announced in 1849 that the Misses White "were to open a boarding and day school for young ladies where they could be instructed in language, writing, arithmetic and needlework, with additional training available in the harp, guitar and pianoforte."[92] A petition from the shop clerks of Kingston to the Board of Trade requested that stores be required to close at 7 pm, as they did in Montreal and Toronto.[93] They complained of the "serious inconvenience under which we labor, for want of a little relaxation from business in order to devote it to our mental improvement."

A more formal and accessible system of public education was needed, however, and in the face of opposition from those confronting increased property taxes, city council established the Kingston Board of Common School (Primary School) Trustees in 1850. The Board's initial concern was the acquisition of school sites, buildings, books, and apparatus. By 1859 they could report seven school buildings equipped and staffed with sixteen teachers serving Kingston's children. Nor were the needs of Kingston's young adults ignored by the Board. In 1865 the Wellington Street School was "placed at the disposal of the young men of the City, who may desire to attend Night School during the coming winter. ..."[94]

The provincial Department of Education's guidelines for 1877 suggested that the curriculum was moving beyond the traditional "Three Rs," with courses in bookkeeping, geography, history, drawing, vocal music, and hygiene, with domestic economy for girls and drill and callisthenics for boys. Discipline, or "inflicting punishment," was monitored, although Inspector Kidd's report on one incident raises more questions about the prevailing system than it answers:

After the strictest investigation I have not been able to find any boy who has had a slate thrown at or broken across his head by his teacher. ... Nor is there any evidence to show that a boy has been shut up in a cupboard by his teacher in any one of our schools during the present year. The little girl referred to does not appear to know much about the matter, but she denies that she was ever severely beaten by her teacher.

I am constantly urging our teachers to exercise the utmost caution when inflicting punishment, and to use no weapons but those that are permitted by the regulations.[95]

The amalgamation of Kingston's Board of Public Schools with the high school board to form the Board of Education in 1897 allowed Kingston's educational system to attain a new level of maturity, sophistication, and public service.

HELPING THE NEEDY

The poor, the halt, and the lame were another social irritant in mid-nineteenth-century Kingston, and the community offered but few facilities to alleviate their distress. Often confused with vagrants, the poor were jailed or driven away, while the sick, insane, widowed, orphaned, and handicapped fared little better. Irritation and moral indignation were often more to the fore than Christian charity. One good citizen complained of the begging and urged that "the constant wail of 'Please help the blind!'" in the streets of Kingston "should not be allowed to become a public annoyance."[96] Increasingly, residents wanted municipal authorities to control "begging about our streets, and from door to door," arguing that it "destroys every feeling of self respect in the poor body who resorts to the practice, and it of course induces habits of indolence, lying, dishonesty and vagrancy."[97] The prospect in 1847 of a "House of Industry" supported by local taxes certainly appealed to at least one Kingstonian, who thought it would be "worth a handsome sum to each housekeeper to be relieved of the annoyance which a pretty strong regiment of street-beggars has for some time occasioned."[98] With such expressions of concern, city council in January 1848 passed a by-law "to restrain and punish Drunkards, Mendicants and Street Beggars" that empowered the general citizenry with the right to arrest offenders on sight "without any warrant for that person." [99]

Ultimately, it was the transient needy rather than the resident needy who served as a catalyst for the development of a minimal system of social services in nineteenth-century Kingston. Immigrants were particularly associated with poverty, and it is difficult to imagine the problem they posed for the community during these years. A.B. Hawkes, "Chief Emigrant Agent" for Upper Canada, initiated an investigation of the towns above Montreal prior to the 1832 immigration season

for the purpose of ascertaining to what extent the Emigrant and Sanitary Societies established at these ports are prepared to render assistance to Emigrants; and also to collect information from the principal Merchants in Montreal, as to the number of Emigrants that may be expected in the ships consigned to their charge, so that His Excellency may be enabled to decide upon the extent of the arrangements required for the current year.[100]

Not all the immigrants were indigent. In 1838 Captain Jones's *William IV* brought 150 Mormons to Kingston, mostly from Prescott and Brockville – complete with forty horses and twenty wagons "to aid them in their journey to the wilderness."[101] In 1840, however, Kingston's facilities were strained by the arrival of some *twelve thousand* immigrants. While most of these were heading further west and only stayed briefly, 3,000 disembarked to settle in the district, 1,200 moved directly from Kingston to the United States, while a further 1,300 entered Kingston from the United States, "including 50 run away slaves."[102] This was very much the pattern

RULES FOR INMATES.

1. Every Applicant for Admission to the House of Industry must present a Ticket of Admission from at least one Director of the Institution.

2. All Applicants must disclose all the particulars concerning themselves required by the Institution for entry in the Admission Book kept by the Superintendent.

3. All Inmates who are able shall rise at the ringing of the bell at six o'clock, during the months of May, June, July, August and September, and at seven o'clock during the remainder of the year.

4. No Inmate shall be allowed to sit down to meals without appearing clean and properly washed.

5. No profane or immoral language or conduct shall be permitted in the Institution. No smoking allowed in the dormitories and no spirituous liquors allowed on the premises, without permission from a Medical Officer being given in writing.

6. The Inmates who are able may attend their several places of worship on Sundays but shall return to the house immediately after service, unless permission to the contrary has been obtained from the Superintendent.

7. All Inmates are required to attend Divine Service when held in the house, unless excused by the Superintendent.

8. Persons supported in this Institution shall perform any work they are required to do by the Superintendent or Committee.

9. No Inmate shall leave the Institution expecting to return without permission of the Superintendent.

10. Any Inmate found in a state of intoxication shall be immediately reported by the Superintendent to the weekly Committee.

11. Any Inmate violating any of the above rules, for the first offence, shall be reported in writing by the Superintendent to the weekly Committee, and for the second offence, shall be subject to dismissal by the Superintendent, who shall report his action.

Persons who are Ineligible for Admission
TO THIS INSTITUTION.

1. Any former Inmate who has been dismissed from the Institution for bad conduct, unless the Directors are satisfied as to a reformation in character.

2. Persons who are depraved in their morals and whose general character is bad.

3. All persons with contagious disorders or who require constant medical treatment.

The tone and reality of the House of Industry are made clear by its *Rules for Inmates*. (QUA)

for a period during which immigrants were conveyed by water transport along the Rideau and St Lawrence routes. It reached a peak in the 1847 "Famine Migration," when most of the 40,000 or so immigrants to Canada West in that year passed through Kingston, a town of a mere 7,000 inhabitants. These immigrants were particularly needy, and Kingston's facilities were greatly overburdened. Clearly, new initiatives were required.

As had happened earlier, community charity took over where provincial and municipal authorities failed. In 1820 a sense of social responsibility had prompted the establishment of the Female Benevolent Society of Kingston to attend to the needs of the poor. And again in 1847 the local élite took the lead, when Mrs Robert Cartwright (who had once discreetly arraigned Lord Sydenham for his irreligion) argued for the establishment of "a House of Industry, as the most effectual means of according relief to the many destitute persons arising from the famine in Ireland."[103]

Neither the problem nor such prominent advocates of remedies could be ignored, and on 13 May 1850 Kingston's House of Industry was established on Upper Princess Street. In 1852, it was moved to 303-305 Earl Street. The House of Industry was organized on the same basis as an English workhouse, offering shelter and sustenance to such needy people as the elderly, widowed, orphaned, and the unemployed. These favoured ones were the "deserving poor." No relief whatever was afforded the ranks of the "undeserving poor," which included the able-bodied, or those with family support, or "women depraved in their morals."[104]

In the first few months of its operation, the House of Industry admitted 183 of the deserving poor, of whom 174 were Irish.[105] True to its name, the House encouraged inmates to be industrious. Those who were not employed throughout the community were required to occupy themselves at the institution in painting, breaking stones (into gravel), cleaning, or gardening. It is clear that the governance of the institution was exacting, if not draconian.

Rations were abundant, if uninspired, and consisted of a daily allocation of a half-pound of bread, a pound of potatoes, a quarter-pound of beef or mutton, and some tea, sugar, milk, molasses, oatmeal, salt, and pepper. Bad behaviour could result in discharge, and several inmates were sent on their way for various infractions. For example, a Mrs Quiveir who, on 18 April 1860, having been "permitted along with others to go out for St. Patrick's Day," returned "on the Sabbath evening, almost perfectly naked, having sold her clothes ... being in a state of intoxication and in short, in appearance and in every other way a perfect disgrace to the institution."[106] Despite such public displays, the city gradually increased its support of the institution by providing a new building on Montreal Street in 1872, and by 1882 the city was contributing $1,500 a year to its operation.

Throughout this period, other philanthropic, charitable, and Christian agencies came into being. The ever-busy Female Benevolent Society also established an Orphans' Home and Widows' Friend Society, opening an orphanage and school on Earl Street in 1857. (It was moved to the corner of University and Union in 1862.) The Sisters of Providence of St Vincent de Paul had arrived in Kingston in 1847 to help the Irish immigrants. In 1861, they established the House of Providence, at Montreal and Ordnance streets, to care for the sick, orphans, and female convicts, and to tend the prison chapel. Similarly, the nuns from the Notre-Dame Convent of Montreal settled in Kingston in 1841 to provide a Catholic education for young girls in a boarding school that was located initially near the market square, later on in Earl Street, and finally in the Bishop's House at Bagot and Johnson. And finally, again in the troubled year of 1847, the Religious Hospitallers, or Sisters of the Hotel Dieu, were brought to Kingston from Montreal by Bishop Horan, to care for the immigrant sick and orphaned. The Sisters, too, were to become an important social agency and, eventually, a medical facility serving the community as a whole as "The Religious Hospitallers of St Joseph of the Hotel Dieu of Kingston."

AN EMERGING COMMUNITY

The years between 1820 and 1880 were portentous ones for Kingston. It had developed from a large village into a small city, and size notwithstanding, it had for a brief period occupied a position of considerable prominence in the affairs of the colony. As capital, centre of commerce, and citadel it ranked among the major outposts of Empire to many mid-century soldiers, administrators, and merchants.

And even in the subsequent years of decline, as it failed to keep up with the growth experienced by the emerging metropolitan centres to east and west, it had an internal social dynamic of its own. To be sure, many visitors continued to find it parochial and isolated. But while not pretending to be cosmopolitan in its diversity, Kingston possessed a social regimen that reflected the military presence – with regattas, cricket, and support for a meeting "for the purpose of getting up Olympic Games in Kingston, this season, at which those fond of manly amusements are requested to attend."[107] The predominantly British background of Kingston's population ensured the visibility and vitality of the societies of St George, St Andrew, and St Patrick, together with Hibernian and Orange lodges. The refined interests of the populace were accommodated by the theatricals of the Theatre Royal, while the Mechanics' Institute stimulated the minds of the more intellectual citizens of the town, starting with its artisans. Indeed, for some, there may have been an *excess* of educational opportunities, and "No Humbug" complained to the *Chronicle and News* of the deception and fraud of some of those claiming to be "Professors" throughout the town:

Time was when the title PROFESSOR implied character, learning and attainments, in those who bore it; but now the name stinks in the nostril – for it argues little less than quackery, ignorance, and impudence. We have Professors – heaven save the mark – of Dancing, Hair Cutting, Necromancy & 'Mesmerism', & it is impossible to say to what lower depth the title may still sink or what greater degree of charlatancy it may yet cloak, if it be not soon reclaimed from the clutches of its purloiners.[108]

More importantly, this was the period when Kingston came to grips with the administrative structures necessary to ensure an adequate quality of life for its citizens. Sanitation, education, police, and social agencies may be mundane concerns, but they were of considerable importance to the people of the day and did much to energize the movement toward more efficient municipal government.

PART TWO

ADJUSTMENTS

Kingston's waterfront from the recently-constructed Cataraqui Bridge, 1830, by Maj.-Gen. James Pattison Cockburn. (Royal Ontario Museum)

EIGHT

Entrepot of the Great Lakes

Kingston had entered the nineteenth century as the leading settlement in Upper Canada, with important military, commercial, and trade functions. York, while the capital of the province, was still second to Kingston in importance. The decades following the Treaty of Ghent witnessed Kingston's further rise. The events of the War of 1812-1814 had acted as a catalyst for the development of the town's dominant enterprises, and Kingston emerged from the conflict with certain dimensions of its function clearly established.

Contemporary estimates of Kingston's population in the early 1820s ranged from John Howison's inflated 5,000, through Phillip Stansbury's more modest 4,000, to Edward Allen Talbot's more realistic 2,336. But if the clerk of the peace's returns corroborated Talbot's estimate, all would have agreed with Stansbury that, in appearance, the community reminded him of a "large European village" rather than a town.[1] Others commented in a similar vein.

John Howison visited Kingston in the 1820s and painted a choleric picture:

The plan of the town is elegant and extensive, but not yet nearly realized. ... There is nothing the least interesting, or remarkable in either the streets or buildings of this place. The better class of people, most of whom are in the mercantile line, live in good style, but are not very hospitable; and there appears to be little polish among them, and not much social communication.[2]

Talbot presents a similar description of the fabric of this, the largest community in Upper Canada in 1821:

The streets are laid out with considerable regularity; but the houses, like almost all others in the Canadas, are very irregularly built. In consequence of the neglected condition of the roads in this as well as in every other part of the Province, it is scarcely possible in wet weather to walk out without sticking fast in the mire. The public buildings of Kingston are of such inferior description as scarcely to be worth notice.[3]

To be sure, visitors continued to see Kingston as merely a "large English village"[4] in ensuing decades, although population figures confirmed the community's dominance in the emerging settlement hierarchy. In the 1820s Kingston experienced a population increase of some 91 per cent and, by 1831, with 3,587 inhabitants, it stood above York (2,800), London (2,416), Hamilton (2,013), and Brockville (1,130).

Indeed, the decades up to the 1830s may be said to be the only period of Kingston's *uncontested* dominance in economic, military, and social affairs of the province – if not in political matters. Writing in 1831, Joseph Bouchette could report:

The town has attained considerable importance within the last twenty years: wharfs have been constructed, and many spacious workhouses erected, that are usually filled with merchandise: in fact it is now become the main entrepot between Montreal and all the settlements along the lakes to the westward.[5]

By 1830 the wharves were full, the military expenditures were flowing into local coffers, and all the signs for continued commerce, and political and social advancement, were propitious. Moreover, with such signs of vitality and such evidence of material advancement, it was thought by some, especially Kingstonians, to be both natural and just that Kingston should become the political as well as the economic metropolis of the United Canadas. The establishment of the capital at Kingston in 1841 marked the realization of these aspirations, and in many ways constituted the apogee of Kingston's fortunes as the dominant urban centre of the province.

These were to be Kingston's best years. But they were not appreciated by all. Probably influenced by the noise and disarray occasioned by the construction activity during this "boom-town" period, one visitor was moved to poesy, albeit somewhat jaundiced and punny poesy. Certainly his work "First Impressions of Regiopolis," penned in March 1842, was not flattering:

> Capital city! young metropolis
> Of this wide wooden land, thy rugged way
> A medley strange presents, a queer display
> Thy thorofare O Regiopolis!
> Elderly females, dogs and horned cattle,
> And swine for filthy offals "doing battle",
> And men on crutches scramble to and fro,
> "Go it ye cripples!" Hark the cry of "fire!"
> The quarrier's warning cry before a "blow";
> Down down the miners on their faces go,
> Like hawks "upon their quarry stooping" low,
> Bang! there it goes – "like bricks" the folks retire;
> I'm blowed if I don't run! Upon my soul
> Kingston thou art indeed a blasted hole![6]

Adjusting to the loss of certain functions would soon cause even more disruption in the affairs of the town, and the evident decline in the place did not go unnoticed. One contemporary visitor was struck

by the peculiar sombre hue which everything around him seems to wear. It is impossible to divest the mind of a feeling that the inhabitants have put their city into half mourning; and it is a long time before the eye becomes familiar with this appearance, which is due to the bluish limestone, of which it is built.[7]

Another visitor in the 1850s declared that "since the removal of the seat of government from the place, it has a deserted look," claiming further that

The impression is not pleasant on landing at Kingston: it is an uncomfortable-looking place, and the public buildings are out of proportion to the size of the town; some of the streets are drearily wide, and rank grass grows on their sides.[8]

But if all else failed, Kingston was still at mid-century a thriving port serving provincial commerce and providing a vital function for Kingstonians themselves. As late as 1841 Sir Richard Bonnycastle was as sanguine, if as unrealistic, as ever about Kingston's role in national and, indeed, continental commerce:

When the St. Lawrence Canal is completed, the Welland Canal made fully available for steamers, the railroads finished to connect Huron and Ontario and Erie, and the Rideau in full operation, Kingston will no doubt become a great city, as the trade of all the surrounding countries, from the Atlantic to Superior, from Hudson's Bay to the farthest southern extremity of the States, will centre on its magnificent roadstead.[9]

However, Bonnycastle's hyperbole notwithstanding, Kingston's role as a commercial centre was to prove quite vulnerable.

MERCANTILE KINGSTON

The commerce and expenditures associated with the War of 1812-1814 had benefited shipping and mercantile activities at Kingston, and as the settlement and economic development of the province continued apace, Kingston's function as a port was advanced. Its traditional significance as a point of transshipment from lake to river vessels was complemented by the construction of the Rideau Canal and the introduction of steam navigation – which, initially, furthered the fortunes of the port at Kingston.

Commerce and lake shipping bulked large in the economy of Kingston during the first half of the nineteenth century, and the community's "boosters" looked to the future with confidence. The determining factor in the development of Ontario's

Calvin Company workers navigated timber rafts some 350 miles to Quebec City. Sometimes including up to 165,000 cubic feet of pine and oak, the rafts could range to a half-mile in length. (QUA)

pre-Confederation economy was the production, trade, and movement of the major staple crop, wheat. Since 1825 British markets allowed the entry of Canadian flour without tariff, and the processing of American grain into Canadian flour occasioned a significant burgeoning of the grain-and-flour trade. Kingston shared in this wheat economy, but not to the same degree as Toronto, Hamilton, and London to the west. If politics augmented the volume of flow of grain, geography dictated the direction of flow along the Great Lakes and St Lawrence, and transshipment at the junction of the two systems. British North America may be compared to a funnel, with the cone covering the drainage basin of the Great Lakes and Kingston located at the neck of the funnel, where it joins the "tube" of the St Lawrence. Through this tube flowed not only the grain and flour of Upper Canada but also much of that produced in the interior of the United States. Moreover, the St Lawrence islands, shoals, and rapids posed a problem for navigation by sail.

Given this combination of economics, politics, and geography, Kingston was located strategically athwart the west-east transport route at the point where Lake

Ontario entered the St Lawrence River. Rafts, batteaux, and, at a later date, some steamers were able to negotiate these hazardous and restricted waters when moving downstream; but much of the traffic of staple commodities out of the province was transshipped at Kingston. Wheat, flour, meat, and potash were unloaded at Kingston and stored there to await vessels for the St Lawrence run. Timber brought in from the Great Lakes and Kingston's immediate hinterland was marshalled in the waters off Garden Island (two miles south of Kingston) to be assembled into river rafts that were initially self-propelled (by sails and poles) and in later years towed by steam-tugs.

Gananoque, Brockville, and, in particular, Prescott also participated in the business of forwarding and were competitors for Kingston's title as the chief point for this "break-in-bulk" function, with all its associated processing and mercantile activities. Thus, in noting that a lake schooner loaded with some two hundred barrels of potash had gone aground on a shoal between Kingston and Prescott, the *Chronicle and Gazette* felt obliged to admonish the captain and remind others that "were Kingston the universal place of transshipment for Montreal, as nature in fact designed it to be, how many schooner shipwrecks would be avoided, and how much valuable property would be saved."[10] Clearly, therefore, Kingston depended much upon the transshipment role, as did the prosperity of Kingston's businessmen and workers. The port's economy was extremely vulnerable to changes in trading patterns and volumes, and also to any innovation in transportation technology that would reduce the need for transshipment.

Another of Kingston's most serious deficiencies as a port, one that was to become increasingly apparent as the volume and scale of shipping increased, was the nature of the harbour itself. Kingston simply did not have the "magnificent roadstead" ascribed to it by Richard Bonnycastle. Moreover, what potential there was for developing an effective port facility had been neglected. The French settlement had focused on the little bay behind the spit protruding into the sheltered waters of the Cataraqui River where it entered Lake Ontario – the "cannotage." With the shift of the British base from Carleton Island to Kingston, the bay lying between Point Frederick and Point Henry had been appropriated for the naval harbour, and its shoreline was developed for purely naval and military purposes. While the first merchants and forwarders to establish themselves at the townsite used the old French harbour and constructed their wharves and warehouses there, later arrivals located along the more open lake frontage that lay before the town. This waterfront was somewhat sheltered from the prevailing southwesterly winds that swept across the approaches to Kingston from the open lake, and while the harbour was able to accommodate the shipping in early years, subsequent developments were to underscore the deficiencies of the location.

As shipping increased in size and draught, shoals offshore proved to be a problem. They should have been removed and breakwaters constructed. By 1836 the need for the protection of shipping and provision of more extensive wharfage became

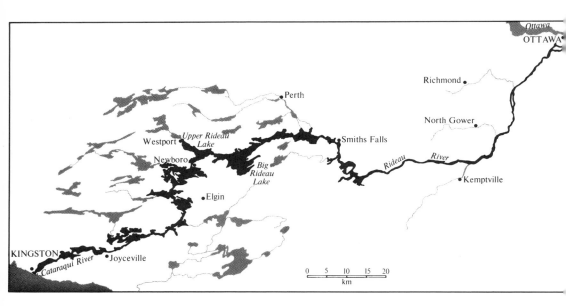

The Rideau Canal system has been in use since 1832. Though designed as a military facility, it came to serve as an important commercial link with Kingston's back country.

an issue of some concern. A letter to the *Chronicle and Gazette* in that year argued,
somewhat defensively, that "recent gales and the damage done to the vessels, have
clearly shewn that our harbour, however well protected by nature, and we contend
that few are more so, would still require some improvement to render it secure,
especially during the prevalence of heavy southerly gales."[11] The letter proposed
that Kingston be made the "best harbour in the Province" by the construction of
a 1,400-foot-long breakwater at Mississauga Point to shelter some fifty vessels.

Also, military priorities required communication between military establishments at Kingston and those across the Cataraqui River at Point Frederick and
Point Henry; the construction of the Cataraqui Bridge allowed this, but it also closed
off the extensive inner harbour at the mouth of the Great Cataraqui. Shifting port
activities to either the Little Cataraqui or the Great Cataraqui River would have
provided Kingston with better harbours. Certainly, without considerable improvements, the actual waterfront chosen for development was inadequate for future
developments in shipping.

A NEW COMMERCIAL ROUTE

With the opening of the Rideau Canal in 1832, Kingston's commercial advancement seemed assured. Despite the primarily military rationale for its construction,

the Rideau Waterway also afforded a much less hazardous, albeit more time-consuming, route to Montreal. Appropriate for a region that in 1816 had launched the first steamer to operate on the Great Lakes, the SS *Frontenac*, the Rideau route was from the outset designed for steam navigation. Indeed, had Colonel By's original plan been implemented – with locks 150 feet long, 50 feet wide, and 10 feet in draught – it would have constituted the first Great Lakes-Atlantic seaway for the steam vessels of the day. However, military parsimony and conservatism required a compromise, and the Rideau was restricted to smaller steam vessels and tugs.

But even this was to Kingston's advantage. Instead of by-passing Kingston and moving directly into the system from Lake Ontario, as By had intended, lakers were required to transfer their cargoes and passengers to the Rideau Canal carriers at Kingston. No wonder some looked to the future with assurance:

But our day is coming. In the course of the next season the opening of the Rideau Canal, that great and glorious Byway will at once place us on an eminence far above any of our sister towns. It being now ascertained beyond a doubt, that the transmission of goods and produce will be exclusively by this route; the transshipment which must necessarily take place at Kingston will benefit the town beyond the most sanguine expectations of its inhabitants.[12]

New initiatives were prompted by the promise of the new route, including the formation of a local "Steam Navigation Forwarding Company," a development that elicited some considerable surprise:

Our good Town has not hitherto been remarkable for the enterprise of its inhabitants, and we therefore, hail with pleasure any indication of the dawning of a new day upon us in this respect. The Canal will be completed in the course of next summer and no doubt is entertained but the greater portion of travelling and transmission of goods will be by this route.[13]

Indeed, not only were the estimates of traffic to be borne by the Rideau Canal, and thus of traffic passing through Kingston, quite promising, but also they were often exceeded. Colonel By had predicted some 8,000 passengers a year. While actual returns record a mere 2,097 in the best year, 1844, they do not include the thousands of immigrants who entered the province as "deck cargoes" on the steamers and barges.

Given the experience of some of the passengers in these early days of traffic, one wonders why anyone would hazard traversing Kingston's back country. Certainly, they would have been dissuaded from travelling the route if they had encountered the *canard* of Montreal origin that warned travellers that along one section of the route, "a large scoop or shovel is placed into the hands of each passenger, who will be compelled to enter the water and make a way through the soft mud for the steamboat to pass, the passage filling up as the vessel passes."[14] But the actual experiences of travellers could be just as shocking as these fictitious claims. Thus, the diary of one worthy, John Treffry, documents the ordeal of an unfortunate, if ingenious, party of travellers:

The first adventure occurred when the steamer sprang a leak and it became necessary to borrow a pump from a barge in tow to keep the water under control. Two days later the engine broke down and the captain took one of the Durham boats, which the steamer was also towing and started for Kingston to secure assistance. Meantime those on board the steamer ran short of provisions and had to make good the deficiency by fishing. They even tried to capture a deer which appeared on the bank but failed in the attempt. The situation was not made brighter when the cook mutinied. Finally the captain returned with help and provisions and the "Enterprise" was able to reach Kingston by May 13, seven days after leaving Bytown.[15]

In terms of cargo, By's estimate of 20,000 tons of general merchandise per annum was exceeded by 1844, and as early as 1841 practically all of the goods entering Upper Canada from the east did so via the Rideau. Agricultural produce continued to favour the shorter St Lawrence route, however, and wheat, flour, and cattle were not commodities prominent in the Rideau traffic. The one commodity that By did not provide estimates for – lumber products – subsequently proved to be one of the most significant items of trade, with 400,000 feet of oak in 1835, 1,400,000 feet of pine in 1840, and over 4,000,000 feet of boards and planks in 1843. By 1850, 293 lock-fills of lumber were recorded as having moved south for Kingston along the Rideau in barges and rafts.[16]

From 1833 to 1848, the Rideau contributed a new component to Kingston's shipping activities. At first there were insufficient steamers and barges to ply the locks and lakes between Kingston and Bytown. But by 1848 the monthly average of vessels passing through the Kingston section amounted to seventy-five steamers and 195 barges. There was also a considerable volume of rafting traffic. Unfortunately, there was a strong directional bias in this traffic. A contemporary account describes the logistics of the new patterns of movement made possible by integrating the Rideau into the Laurentian system:

The Company's barges are now fitted up with masts and sails in order to proceed by the St. Lawrence to Montreal which it is said they can do in two days, while they return by the Rideau Canal in tow of steam boats in four days, making the trip from Kingston to Montreal and back in six days.[17]

In June 1842, while 280 barges passed *up* through the Narrows *en route* for Kingston, none passed *down*; in June 1846, 115 steamers passed up through the Jones Falls locks to Kingston, but only 22 moved down.[18] This was an ominous portent

The Rideau system was a reliable mode of passenger transportation before road and rail links were established with Ottawa. (QUA)

of traffic preferences. While the locks were safer, it did require nve days to negotiate them – as opposed to two or three days running the rapids of the St Lawrence, as many rafts, batteaux, and steamers elected to do.

CHALLENGES TO THE SYSTEM

Politics and technology were to strike a blow against this flourishing trade, however. In 1846, Britain opted for free trade by repealing the infamous Corn (Wheat) Laws. With this abolition of British preferential treatment of Canadian wheat and flour, and with the repeal of the Navigation Laws in 1849, the rationale for using the St Lawrence route was undermined. The Erie Canal–New York route held a competitive edge, and of course, the diminution of the Laurentian flow undercut Kingston's traffic.

If shifting economic policy in Britain occasioned a decrease in the flow of grain along the St Lawrence, technology allowed the grain that did move by that route to by-pass Kingston. The need for transshipment from lake to river transport had already been challenged by steam navigation, which allowed lakers to negotiate at least the upper reaches of the St Lawrence as far as Gananoque, Brockville, Cornwall, and Prescott before transshipment. Some even risked running the rapids. But with the completion of the St Lawrence canals, they could now also navigate *up* the river. As early as 1834, the vulnerability of Kingston's dominance as a point of transshipment had been appreciated:

If the trade by this canal [Rideau] is encouraged, nearly the whole benefits of it must inevitably be centred in Kingston: if the trade by the St. Lawrence should be preferred, and be made to predominate, Kingston has then a dozen rivals to participate in the gains, some of whom are very likely to surpass her in commercial importance.[19]

The prospect canals gave of by-passing the St Lawrence rapids was even more ominous for Kingston forwarding interests, prompting W.H. Smith's pessimistic prognosis:

What effect the opening of the St. Lawrence Canals and the enlarging of the locks of the Welland Canal, will have upon it [Kingston's transshipment] remains to be seen. Hitherto, all the up and down freight has been transshipped at Kingston, to either larger or smaller vessels according as it has been going up or down; in carrying which a fleet of about two hundred barges and schooners, of from sixty to two hundred and fifty tons burthen, has been employed. As soon as the improvements in canals are completed, large vessels will be enabled to run direct from Montreal to Toronto and Hamilton, thus avoiding Kingston altogether.[20]

By mid-century, developments in river improvements and steam navigation favoured the St Lawrence over the Rideau, both developments serving to encourage through-traffic and diminish Kingston's transshipment role. The canalization of the rapids in 1848 meant that even up-traffic could be accommodated by the St Lawrence, and passengers, merchandise, and other traffic dropped off considerably, leaving the Rideau as a secondary tap-line serving Kingston and Bytown's respective hinterlands.

If the St Lawrence canals allowed more traffic to by-pass Kingston's wharves, the new technology of railways was to serve as a major competitor for several categories of cargoes that had formerly moved by water. Railroad fever first hit Kingston in the 1830s, with news of the advent of rail to the south, in New York State. Local enthusiasm for railways was unbounded. Railroads could do almost anything. During the first flush of enthusiasm for the new technology, progressive people looked to the new rail connections for substantial improvements in the quality of life of town dwellers:

It is said that even new milk, as well as fruit, vegetables etc. are brought some 50 or 100 miles to supply large Cities, who before the construction of railroads were obliged to use an adulterated article at an exorbitant price, and are now supplied pure and abundant at half the cost of a bad commodity.[21]

Imagine, editorialized the *Chronicle and Gazette*, the value a line adds to

every farm on the route by making a farm forty miles from Toronto, or Belleville, or Kingston as close ... as one within five miles of these places. The advantages it holds out in a Military point of view, by enabling a General to make ten thousand men do the duty of seventy thousand. ... These are all topics and arguments which we hope yet to be able to press warmly upon our readers of every class and shade of politics. Let every one think of the Railroad, speak of the Railroad, and all who can write of the Railroad. Agitate! Agitate! Agitate![22]

And agitate they did. Numerous railroad schemes were mooted over the next three decades. The first wave of speculation and fantasy turned to Kingston's two traditional vectors of communication: a line to the south to connect with the United States system and its ports; an east-west route to compete with or complement the established water routes to the seaboard at Montreal. Initially not seen as a threat to Kingston's commercial ventures, rail was welcomed as yet another portent of progress and future greatness. There were some, however, who recognized the threat posed to shipping interests and, thus, to Kingston. Even so, the general sentiment continued to be, as the *Chronicle and Gazette* put it, "let us make rail roads and the rail roads will make us."[23]

The first railway scheme was conceived to forge a link with the expanding United States railroad system and to replace Montreal by New York as the seaboard outport. Even during the first half of the century, when the St Lawrence River trade dominated Kingston's commerce, the port had maintained regular connections across Lake Ontario with Cape Vincent, Sacket's Harbor, Oswego, and Rochester. Indeed, such was the connection with these ports that the Niagara *Gleaner* had reported in 1825 that "half the beef, butter, cheese, potatoes, oats, whiskey, (and often the flour) consumed in that town [Kingston] comes from the United States."[24] In 1837 the directors of the Watertown & Cape Vincent Railroad visited Kingston to attract Canadian investors.[25] They explicitly declared that their strategy was to capture the Great Lakes trade for New York, with Kingston as one of the main links.[26] Here was not a project that extended Kingston's trading hinterland; here was a project rather to make Kingston tributary to New York. Predictably, subsequent promotional literature claimed that there would be some benefits accruing to the city – benefits that would do much to redress recent misfortunes that had befallen Kingston:

Kingston has ceased to be the seat of Government. In all probability, had this Road been in operation, she would have avoided this misfortune – for, certainly, it is most disasterous to her prosperity. But the evil is done, and her businessmen are anxious to remedy it. The building of this road will counterbalance the loss they have experienced.[27]

Local opinion also favoured this lynch-pin role in a Canadian-American rail network:

The simple fact is that the completion of the Rome and Cape Vincent Railway is a matter of vital importance to Kingston. ... Kingston must gain by the advantage of a direct railway connection with New York. It is idle to dispute this point. In the spring, fall and winter season, such a communication will be of immense convenience not only to this city, but to the country for eighty or ninety miles on either side of it.[28]

In such a scheme, Kingston would become a major point of transshipment between the Great Lakes water transport from the west and the rail communications to New York to the south.

Some Kingstonian investors could not wait for American rail to come to Kingston and took steps to move south to meet it! In 1835, Kingston's potential as the junction point for Canadian and American rail networks prompted the formulation of a plan for a canal link across Wolfe Island. In that year it was reported that brush was being cut along the route of the "Long Island Canal."[29] Two years later, the proposal for the canal link with Cape Vincent, with specially-constructed steamers plying the shorter route, was still being touted as a possibility.[30] But it was not until 1845, with the formation of the Wolfe Island, Kingston & Toronto Railway Company, that the concept came nearer to reality – the "Toronto" portion of the scheme being mere promotional window-dressing. The Wolfe Island portion was the problem. The bridging of the two channels separating Wolfe Island from the Canadian and American shores proved to be insuperable at the time, and the WIK&TR never got off the ground – or rather, never crossed the water. The scheme was revived in the 1850s, although the new formulation was again for a canal across the island, rather than track. Rail was expected to reach Chaumont in the fall of 1851, and there was much enthusiasm in Kingston for the Wolfe Island Canal and its system of steamships towing barges carrying freight-cars.[31] Construction of the canal commenced in 1852, with the contract being awarded to Joseph Milner of Kingston.[32] The following year saw the construction of the *John Counter*, a "railway steamer" of 200-foot length and 34-foot beam.[33] While the Wolfe Island Canal was eventually completed, it failed to serve its intended role. Deepened from four-foot to seven-foot draught in the period 1868-1870, it had fallen into disuse by 1892.

Interest in the Watertown & Cape Vincent Railroad continued to run high, however, and by March 1848, twenty Kingstonians had invested $20,000 in the venture. For these investors, those who opposed the innovations were a "few old fashioned folk," and they looked to the railways to "alter the entire state of our social condition." They tried to appease the shipping and forwarding fraternity by promising that "however their individual interests may for the moment appear to suffer, that they know the injury will be only temporary, and that new channels will be opened to their enterprize and capital."[34] For these optimists, rail and water together comprised an opportunity to bolster Kingston's economic fortunes.

If the canal-rail link across Wolfe Island to the United States was at best tenuous and at worst quite impractical, rail communications along the Toronto-Montreal corridor were much more tangible. The connection between Toronto and Montreal by means of the Grand Trunk Railway was completed in 1856. Kingston's reaction to the railway had been mixed. Boosterish interests had viewed the approach of rail optimistically, and the ground-breaking ceremony for the depot had been marked by the quaffing of a half-dozen kegs of ale and the consumption of copious quantities of bread and beef at a reception that most of the "local gentry" attended.[35] And on Monday, 27 October 1856, it was reported that

the usually quiet citizens of this usually quiet City of Kingston were on the qui vive for the events of the "opening day" of the Grand Trunk Railroad. ... all seemed bent upon having a sight of the Toronto and Montreal trains – the train from the capital of Lower Canada and the train from the capital of Upper Canada – meeting at Kingston as the centre of the *United Canada*.[36]

Modern travellers will not be surprised to learn that this initiation of Kingston's rail service was marked by *both* trains arriving late, although forgiving Kingstonians commented that this was but "a slight delay, indeed, for a first passenger train."[37] Even though late, the delivery by 3 pm that day of the Montreal and Toronto newspapers was recognized as "one of the many advantages which we must derive from the completion of our main line of railway communications."[38]

Despite such euphoria over the revolution in communications, the first tracks by-passed the city and the first station was located some three miles to the east of the downtown area. Originally, Thomas Keefer's report on the Montreal and Kingston route to be followed by the Grand Trunk stated that "In view of the large amount of business to be anticipated in connection with the Lake, the Terminus at Kingston is scarcely less important than that at Montreal."[39] Keefer considered two possible sites on Kingston's waterfront. The outer-harbour terminus was not favoured because of the grade and because it was "somewhat exposed to the effect

Waterfront terminus for the Grand Trunk Railway. (QUA)

of Lake storms." The preferred site was the inner harbour, although Keefer expressed a concern that was to be echoed fifty years later:

It is hardly probable that the city of Kingston will continue to cut off so fine a portion of her harbour by maintaining the Cataraqui Bridge in its present injurious site; but as there must be at all events a new "draw" [bridge] which will pass the largest class of Steamer the Cataraqui terminus should be selected.[40]

That neither of these options was realized, however, was not due to the deficiencies of their sites or acute lobbying by mercantile interests. It was avarice rather than business sense that kept rail out of Kingston: local speculators drove up the price of land required by the railroad. But within a year of the arrival of the railway at the suburban depot, steps were being taken to acquire a branch-line to downtown Kingston. Construction was commenced in March 1858 following the purchase of various wharves and the Phillips Brewery, the demolition of several houses obstructing the proposed right of way, and the infilling of the water space between the fish market and Scobell's Wharf.[41] The route followed the west bank of the Cataraqui River, and much concern was expressed over the health threat posed by the stagnant water trapped behind the railway embankments that had been constructed along the shore.[42] But by 1859 the GTR had entered the city proper and established its sidings and downtown station along the waterfront.

The import of this new transport development was not lost upon Kingstonians. From the outset, those representing shipping interests complained of the threat of competition and the decline in lake-borne traffic. The railway provided an all-year-round alternative to water transportation, especially for passengers and high-value freight. Three years before the entry of the Grand Trunk into Kingston, the Royal Mail Line could advertise the comforts and efficiencies of its passenger service:

The Steamers of this line have been built expressly, and with greatest care, for Lake and River Navigation; the River Steamers with a Draft of Water, rendering the greatest security in descending the rapids; while the Lake Steamers are large, staunch, and commodious, with powerful engines; securing to travellers the greatest safety and comfort in all weathers. They are filed [sic] with Saloons and State rooms elegantly furnished, and in point of speed unsurpassed.[43]

But the eventual completion of the Toronto-Montreal line through Kingston occasioned several letters to the editor and articles complaining of the impact on Kingston's shipping activities, and subsequent years were to see these fears realized. As early as 1859, the GTR had a virtual monopoly of the passenger traffic along the Montreal-Toronto corridor, having acquired control of the Royal Mail steamers.[44]

STORMY WATERS

With the prospect of these several new commercial and technological developments looming on the horizon, Kingston's port activities during the 1840s continued to prosper. At the close of the previous decade, there was much confidence over Kingston's continued commercial vitality:

The increasing trade and general prosperity of our good old town are the subject of general remark. The appearance of our harbour is highly gratifying, and presents more substantial symptoms of heavy and extensive business than any other inland port within the range of our acquaintance, on either side of the line.[45]

The 1840 season opened with ten schooners from the "upper lake" arriving in Portsmouth with cargoes of staves, timber, flour, and provisions.[46] On one day in July, no fewer than thirty-three schooners loaded with wheat and flour "from the west" were tied up along Kingston's wharves.[47] Such was the volume of that season's traffic that it elicited comment from across "the line," the New York *Chronicle* reporting that

We now hear from an Oswego correspondant of the 1st June that the wharves of Kingston are loaded with Western produce, and for want of boats it will take four weeks and upwards to clear off what has accumulated in store and under sheds put up temporarily.[48]

The Kingston waterfront must have been alive with activity and confidence. There was also understandable pride as the "fast sailing bark William Salthome" cleared the Custom House for Sydney, New South Wales, with a cargo of flour, pork, and fish. "This we understand," reported the local observer, "is the first merchant vessel which has sailed from this port with a cargo for that distant part of the world."[49] As preferential trade arrangements were crumbling, and as railways pushed into Kingston's commercial empire, the barometer of local commercial prosperity appeared to be rising. In March 1844, the *Chronicle* reported that there were "upwards of 300 men at present employed in erecting piers, wharves and warehouses in the Kingston Harbour."[50] And in the following year it was reported that "The quantity of wheat and flour received in Kingston since the opening of navigation has been immense and has exceeded that of the previous year by nearly one third."[51] As late as 1848, the harbour-master reported on the number of sailing vessels arriving in Kingston during the 1848 navigation season between 5 April and 22 December: 166 vessels of under fifty tons; 162 vessels between fifty and one hundred tons; and 183 of over 150 tons. This total of 511 sailing vessels was matched by approximately the same number of steamship arrivals.[52]

It is difficult to recapture the bustling image of this port in these halcyon days of the early 1840s. Cockburn's and Bartlett's impressions of the waterfront give some indication; but an even more emotive picture of the daily routine of port activity is provided by the editor of one of the local newspapers:

The greatest activity now prevails in all matters connected with the Steam Boat and the Forwarding Trade here. Every morning is ushered in by the arrival of one of our splendid Mail Packets from Toronto, about 6 o'clock, with passengers and laden with the valuable produce of the West. At 7, one of the Montreal line leaves for that City – either the *Canada*, the *Gildersleeve*, or the *Highlander*. Every wharf during the day exhibits the greatest bustle in loading barges, and the smaller class of steam boats, for the same destination – whilst arrivals are almost hourly taking place of those vessels, loaded with newly imported goods on their return by the Rideau Canal. At about 3 o'clock in the afternoon one of the upwards river line arrives from Montreal bringing the Mail. At 4, two of the fine class of American steam boats call at Greer's Wharf, one on its way up from Ogdensburg for Lewiston and intermediate ports, and the other on her downward trip on the same line. At 6 the steam boats leave for the several ports on the Bay of Quinte between Kingston and the River Trent – and at 7 the Mail steamer leaves for Toronto. There is besides a small steamer plying regularly three times a day between Kingston and Wolfe Island, touching at Garden Island. All these, with the beautiful class of sailing vessels which frequent this port presents a most interesting scene, and this is of a daily occurrence.[53]

During the 1840s, therefore, Kingston's port function continued to flourish, with three major components: the linear traffic to it and through it from the Upper Lakes to Montreal, via the St Lawrence; the trans-lake traffic to the adjacent American ports and the local trade servicing the local communities throughout eastern Ontario; and the circular traffic of the integrated Rideau Canal-Ottawa River-St Lawrence system, with steamers and barges moving up the Ottawa-Rideau and down the St Lawrence to Montreal.

Indeed, there appeared to be but little change in the amplitude, direction, and content of water-borne trade and commerce into the 1850s. It was reported in 1851 that Kingston imported some $743,232 worth of merchandise from the United States, amounting to 9.3 per cent of the total Canadian trade of $8 million in that year – which made Kingston the fifth-largest importer after Toronto, St John, Hamilton, and Montreal. Moreover, the same report recorded that Kingston's exports to the United States amounted to $421,016, or 8 per cent of the total of $2.3 million, and Kingston was second only to St John in Canadian exports south.[54] This component of Kingston's port function – the north-south interaction across Lake Ontario – was not affected by the developments along the St Lawrence. And even the transshipment of grain along the St Lawrence continued, if on a reduced scale: the award of a government contract to the Calvin Company of Garden Island to provide tug service on the upper St Lawrence encouraged some shippers to revert to the use of barges and transshipment at Kingston. Certainly, the completion in 1853 of a grain elevator at the foot of Queen Street was a signal demonstration of continued faith in this activity. Capable of handling 3,000 bushels an hour, and of storing 80,000 bushels, this elevator allowed the firm of Walker and Berry to ship some 600,000 bushels a year from Kingston.[55] Finally, it has been estimated that of Kingston's 3,424 employees in 1852, 191 were engaged in such water-transport occupations as sailmaker, ship-builder, and warehouseman, and this figure does not include the labourers and carpenters, many of whom may also have been employed in the shipyards of the port.[56]

But active as it may have been, Kingston's port trade declined between 1850 and 1880. Initially, tonnages of arrivals and departures continued to be high, as Kingston remained a port of call even though fewer cargoes were transshipped. Thus, total

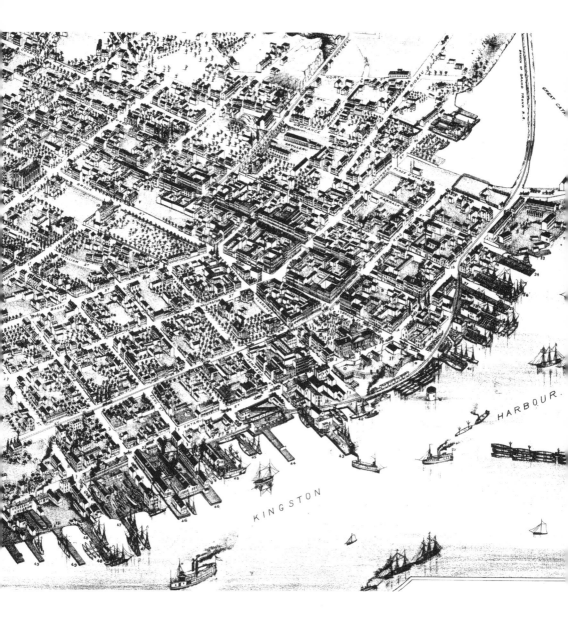

A bird's-eye view of Kingston's waterfront and downtown by H. Brosius, 1875. (QUA)

arrivals and departures peaked in 1856 with 983,032 tons (2,743 vessels), but declined to a low of 420,427 tons (2,928 vessels) in 1875. The values of imports and exports are another indicator of port trade, and as the following table shows, Kingston failed to show the growth experienced by two of its major competitors, Toronto and Hamilton[57]:

		1860	1870	1880
Kingston	Exports	$423,598	$527,519	$729,279
	Imports	$2,016,976	$5,441,554	$897,173
	Total	$2,440,574	$5,969,073	$1,626,452
Toronto	Exports	$1,786,773	$2,039,215	$3,448,138
	Imports	$4,048,458	$7,268,015	$12,192,942
	Total	$5,835,231	$9,307,230	$15,681,079
Hamilton	Exports	$1,353,948	$826,936	$1,218,781
	Imports	$2,376,804	$3,662,550	$3,507,418
	Total	$3,730,752	$4,489,486	$4,726,199

While serving to demonstrate that Kingston continued to participate in lake and river commerce during this period, these figures do reveal the demise of Kingston's claim to be the main "entrepot" of the Great Lakes.

THE NEED FOR ADJUSTMENT

The three decades following the War of 1812-1814 witnessed considerable advancement of the economy and influence of "Loyalist Kingston," although certain developments were destined to serve the city ill over the next period. The loss of the significant military presence was a major blow to the economic fortunes of the city. Kingston's experience as the centre of political affairs was short-lived, and the psychological impact of the loss of the capital was another severe shock to the community's aspirations. (Indeed, both of these developments have mesmerized and preoccupied later historians as much as they stunned the city and the leaders of the day.) But the two losses did serve to underscore the more fundamental reasons for Kingston's failure to maintain its prominence. The shift in demographic and economic influence to the western regions of the province, and transportation developments that facilitated through-traffic, served to erode the port's specialized commercial function and port activities. All this had been foreseen by one J.R. Godley, who argued that Toronto or Hamilton were "much better places than Kingston," and went on to provide a critical evaluation of the town's economic fortunes:

If the seat of government be removed to Montreal, and the St. Lawrence canal completed, both of which are likely to take place soon, the forced and rapid progress which Kingston has lately been making, will be stopped at once; sea-going vessels will then run direct to the lakes, without the necessity of transshipment, and having no important "back country" to depend upon, it will be left almost entirely on one side by the great commercial stream.[58]

Godley's predictions were realized, and population figures serve as indicators of Kingston's relative decline and of greater vitality elsewhere. As early as the period 1829-1835, while Kingston itself continued to maintain the lead, the Midland District in which it was located fared less well. Its population increased a mere 11 per cent in the face of a massive 128 per cent in the Home District surrounding York. This boded ill for the future, and some Kingstonians feared their town would become "a 'deserted village,' notwithstanding the many advantages it possesses; while the forests of the West produce new [towns] daily like mushrooms."[59]

Such regional variations in growth had to be reflected in the urban hierarchy. By mid-century, Toronto's population of 30,775 marked its urban dominance in the province, while Kingston (11,697) had fallen to third place behind Hamilton (14,112). Kingston's preeminence was gone. A moderate increase of some 19 per cent in the fifties to 13,743 was followed by a dramatic decrease of 10 per cent in the sixties, which left Kingston with a population of 12,407. By 1881, the modern urban hierarchy was established: Toronto (86,415), Hamilton (35,961), Ottawa (27,412), London (19,746), Kingston (14,091). And more significantly, the accelerating rates of growth of her competitors were underscored by Kingston's decelerating growth interspersed with periods of absolute decline of population.

Politicians and businessmen – the two roles were often combined in the small group of interrelated individuals who made up Kingston's social and economic élite – were to search desperately for alternative activities that would restore Kingston as a major centre. At various times, they launched new initiatives in the development of its back country and aggressively pursued innovative developments in the technology of transport. They never ceased in attempts to advance transshipment and associated endeavours by attempting to enhance harbour facilities for its role as a transshipment centre. As that cause became patently hopeless, Kingston's leaders became obsessed with industrial growth and development. This obsession came to be the diagnostic mark of Kingston's civic leadership in the late nineteenth century, albeit often accompanied by lethargy and the lack of entrepreneurial vigour. Indeed, this faith in the credo of "growth" – a growth so often associated with misplaced, misdirected, and inappropriate ventures – explains much about subsequent policies pursued by Kingston's leadership up to the very present.

Building a timber raft at the foot of Garden Island. (QUA)

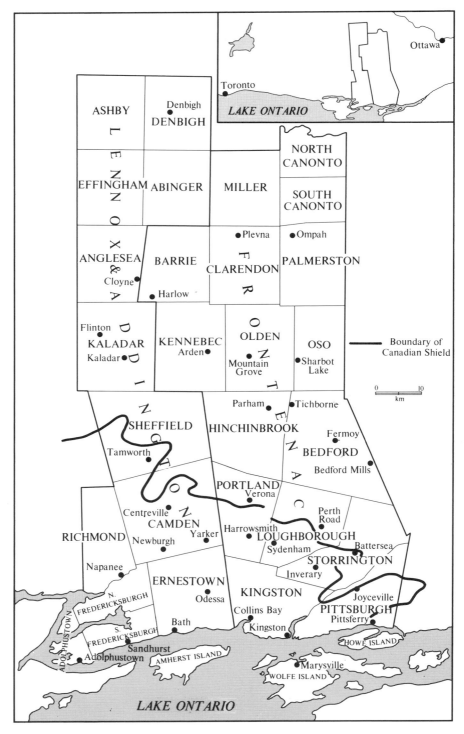

Kingston's back country.

NINE

The Search for a
"Populous Back Country"

As early as mid-century, some had recognized that Kingston's old economic strategy was dead and that alternatives to commerce and shipping must be found. Kingston could no longer consider that Ontario and upper New York State were tributary to it. The city needed new hinterlands with good transportation links to replace the diminished water-borne traffic. If the east-west traffic along the Great Lakes-St Lawrence axis was no longer viable, then perhaps there were possibilities for developing a new hinterland in Kingston's own back country to the north. For these initiatives, significant investment in, and development of, new lines of communication was required to tap more of the surrounding region.

KINGSTON LOOKS NORTH

Writing in 1822, the radical Scottish statistician Robert Gourlay had observed that "Kingston is subject to one local disadvantage, the want of a populous back country."[1] The dramatic growth of Toronto, Hamilton, and London was attributed to their productive and populous hinterlands, and Kingstonians increasingly looked inland in search of similar possibilities for development.

But unlike the hinterlands of Toronto, Hamilton, or London, Kingston's back country was not well endowed with land conducive to agricultural production, especially not land amenable to the dominant staple, winter wheat. To be sure, the southern strip of lands fronting the Bay of Quinte possessed much cultivable acreage with tractable soils – even if it was interspersed with sections of limestone pavement – and a level topography that was only occasionally poorly drained. But the second range of townships was more rugged, consisting of the badly-drained lands and rock outcrops of the contact zone with the Canadian Shield. Alex Aitken attempted to survey these lands in the rear of Pittsburgh Township in 1792, but abandoned his task: "I would be putting Government to a useless expense to Survey lands that will never be settled."[2] Samuel Wilmot's survey of Portland Township in 1808 reported that the land "cannot settle being either Swamps or Rocks [and] in many places there is nothing growing except small Ironwoods and Elm Timber with Juniper Berries."[3] Clearly, Kingston's agricultural hinterland was limited by the presence of the Pre-Cambrian Shield, which gave the "Limestone City" a back country of granite. The responses were imaginative but often deluded.

For some Kingstonians, obstacles other than the local ecology had to be overcome if their district were to experience a progressive policy of developing the hinterland. According to one report,

We have been ingeniously discovering a hundred reasons for the unprosperous state of things under which we suffer – there is a want of fertile land – a want of water – a want of capital but the real want, the want of enterprise has been little thought of.[4]

Accordingly, the Midland District Land Company was formed in 1835 to stimulate the settlement of an area north of Kingston; and it did so by promoting a more sanguine view of the agricultural potential of the interior lands:

But let emigrants go equal distances from Kingston for good lands as they do there [Toronto], and they shall find such as would surprise them. Let them pass the gloomy woods of Portland, and open their eyes on the fine lands in Hinchinbrooke, Holden [sic] etc not forgetting many parts of Loughborough, with their small crystal lakes of countless numbers, their rivers and rivulets, and springs, not of muddy and stagnant waters, but clear as Ferintosh, and all abounding with fish. The very sight of the timber itself, without putting a spade in the ground is sufficient to convince any judge of the fertility of the soil.[5]

The allusion to Ferintosh is an interesting one. As a reference to a barony in Scotland, it was perhaps meant to invoke an image of a certain topography and serve as a familiar allusion for at least some of the settlers; as a contemporary term for Scotch whiskey, it may have served both as an inducement and an essential prerequisite for settling these rugged lands!

Despite this optimistic rhetoric, surveys of the northernmost townships of Kingston's back country reported that the lands there were generally "uneven and much broken by rocky hills and swamps," but the same surveys went on to claim that there were also "cultivable and fertile tracts of land."[6] It was noted that where settlement had been attempted, crops of wheat, oats, corn, potatoes, and turnips were being produced, although generally the land was "better adapted for grazing and pasture than other kinds of farming."[7] Also favouring such pastoral enterprises were the ubiquitous natural meadows of "Beaver Hay" associated with the lakes and swamps of the Shield country, and it was anticipated that "A large portion of this tract will no doubt be purchased for the meadow alone."[8] Kingstonians looking to the rear for a new future welcomed such views, arguing that "Kingston, being one of the foremost markets in the province, such a tract of land would be of great value if it were brought under cultivation."9 Another commentary referred to the opening up of this "splendid back country" that would bring "increased wealth and importance to this city and the extent of the country intervening."10

In advancing such pro-agrarian views, some Kingstonians were also advocating an anti-lumbering perspective. Some thought that the provision of roads and settlers in a region where lumbering companies provided both markets for supplies and employment opportunities for settlers could be the basis for a successful new initiative in settlement promotion. Unfortunately, the interests of the farmer and the logger were often more antithetical than symbiotic.

The lumberman's view of the pioneer as parasite and predator was advanced in a letter to the Bobcaygeon *Independent*:

A fictitious settlement follows the lumberman: he is followed by parasites, plunderers and blackmailers who dog his footsteps and victimize him at each turn; and then, when the lumberman's work is done and he leaves for new localities, this much boasted pioneer of civilization, this industrious settler, this stalwart and hardy frontiersman with the glittering axe, throws up the lot on which he has squatted, sacrifices all the improvements he has made on about an acre and a half of land and follows the lumberman to continue this predatory and plundering exercise. ... The story is told in scores of patches of clearing all through the province – the story of lumbermen robbed, of timber burnt, of law evaded.11

However, a scathing article in the *British Whig* advocated the farmer's position, drawing attention to the rigorous hardships faced by the settlers and the restrictive policies under which they struggled to survive.12 It argued that "Unless the settler in our northern townships is afforded some security for profitable employment in his location during the arduous labor of clearing the land, your petitioners think it little less than criminal to encourage him to settle on free grant land." The main recommendation was

to give equal rights to the colonist and the lumberman, as well as to compensate in some degree for the rigors of pioneer life in the backwoods, by making it the interest of those who may take up their abode there, to remain and found communities as intelligent and prosperous as those which throughout the front townships of Ontario have never known upon their farms the oppressive burden of the timber license.

But even with such special inducements, Kingston's back country simply was not conducive to settlement, and the schemes for establishing an agricultural population throughout the northern hinterland had failed. The harsh realities of farming in the Canadian Shield and the demise of the lumbering economy served to push these settlers out of the extensive tract of country lying between the Ottawa River and Lake Huron.

If pro-agrarian and anti-lumber, Kingstonians were always pro-commerce and, therefore, favoured any developments that ensured the movement of commodities from Kingston's back country to its wharves. The proponents of the agrarian model of hinterland development, and the advocates of resource development, while differing in their perceptions of the resource base to the north, were united in a strategy of development. Improved communications were clearly prerequisite to all forms of economic development in the region, and the second half of the nineteenth century witnessed several attempts to extend Kingston's influence throughout the rear townships.

ROADS AND SETTLEMENT

A detailed and evocative commentary on the road conditions prevailing in Kingston's back country is provided by A. Eliot, brigadier-major of the 68th Regiment, who in July 1824 had the temerity to travel crosscountry from Ottawa to Kingston. His comments on the Perth-to-Kingston section of his odyssey are telling statements of the conditions with which contemporary settlers and travellers had to contend.[13] The term "road" was clearly an optimistic expression: his report refers to the route being "a good deal intersected with swampy mudholes"; to another section as "requiring but little Logging, and would be an excellent Road if properly worked out." One section of corduroy road had its logs displaced, and Eliot warned that "although I had no difficulty in getting my horse through, I should think it must be impassable in the wet season"; other sections could not be "made out without a guide." Near the Narrows, another unpleasantness presented itself:

the Road has been opened thirty feet wide, but not being travelled on, the undergrowth has grown up to a great height, and not being shaded by large Trees is much worse than if it had not been touched; I got completely wet through from head to foot in a few Minutes and had I been merely passing along as a Traveller, should for comfort sake have carefully avoided the Road.

It must have been with some considerable relief that Eliot encountered the Kingston-Montreal road near Kingston Mills and was able to report that "From the place where the two Roads unite [it] is good, for about 7 Miles to the Town of Kingston."

Agitation for improved roads became a *leitmotif* of the 1830s. In 1835 the grand jury of the Midland District advocated the construction of roads to Hinchinbrooke, Kennebec, Kaladar, and Madoc, "the more effectually to arrive at some plan for opening the back Townships of this District."[14] In 1836, one James Cull was commissioned to macadamize the twenty-five miles of roadway linking Kingston and Napanee to extend Kingston's market area to the west. For Cull, the completion of such an all-weather road offered considerable promise to farmers and town dwellers:

CHECK GATE !

BEL LEVILLE & FRANKFORD ROAD.

RATE OF TOLLS.

For every Vehicle loaded or otherwise, drawn by
two horses or other beasts, - - - - - 1½d.

For each additional horse or other beast, - 1d.

For every Vehicle drawn by one horse or other beast, 1d.

For every Horse with or without rider, - - 1d.

For every head of Neat Cattle, - - - - ½d.

FOR EVERY SCORE OR LESS OF SHEEP OR SWINE, - 1D.

TOLLS TO BE PAID AT EACH TIME OF PASSING.

1856

Notices like this were to be found throughout the Kingston district. (QUA)

The farmers already see that the direct advantages will be equally great; that a journey to Kingston market and back may be made in one day which formerly required two – and that with half the wear and tear on the carriages and horses; they can in one day carry a double load, and that too at all periods of the year. ...[15]

More importantly, the Napanee road marked the advent of the joint-stock turnpike corporation as an institution for mounting new road construction, profits being derived from charges subsequently levied at toll gates. The new processes of road engineering that provided better travelling surfaces were not without cost, and the turnpike system of management offered a mechanism of recouping outlays and even making a profit. Complaints that "both the Loughborough and Portland Roads, in the fall and spring of the year, and even in mid-summer after heavy rains, are nearly impassable for carriage and weighty loads" required action.[16] By the 1850s, no fewer than six turnpike roads radiated out to the north and west of Kingston to localities such as Philipsville, Gananoque, Portland, Storrington, Pittsburgh, and Perth.[17]

Some wanted even more expanded connections. Arguing that "The extensive trade carried on at Toronto is maintained by the rich country in the rear of it," promoters claimed that a "well settled back country would greatly promote the prosperity of this City."[18] In 1844 John A. Macdonald made it clear that he wanted to "direct the attention of the Legislature to the settlement of the back townships of this district hitherto so utterly neglected and to press for the construction of the long projected plank road to Perth and the Ottawa and thus make Kingston the market for a large and fertile, though hitherto useless country."[19] On 5 May 1846, fifty petitions were submitted to the Executive Council for road improvements, one of which was advanced by John A. Macdonald and Benjamin Seymour, the member for Lennox and Addington, "relative to the construction of a road from Kingston to the Ottawa River." In acceding to this request, the commissioner of Crown Lands was directed to

Lay two ranges of Townships in the Midland district in rear of those already surveyed and that they be so placed as to front on a meandering road to be established between the new settlements of that District and the Ottawa. As an inducement to the Opening of that road, the Committee would recommend that one concession on each side of the road be surveyed into one hundred acre lots, one half of each to be granted free of expense for immediate and actual settlement on the Owen Sound principle.[20]

Macdonald also required action of the municipal authorities and, following a letter to the mayor advocating the formation of an immigrant aid society, the "Midland District Colonization and Emigration Society" was established on 7 July 1847. The following day, the society directed an address to the governor-general arguing that all emigrants necessarily stop for a longer or a shorter time at Kingston; and it is confidently believed, that if the waste lands of the Crown in the surveyed townships were placed at the disposal of the Colonization Society on such terms as would induce emigrants to settle ... the entire line from the St. Lawrence to the Ottawa would be easily settled. [21]

City council provided tangible evidence of its support of the policy of developing roads into Kingston's hinterland by purchasing £7,500 of stock in the Perth Road Company in 1852. [22] In the same year, the Kingston Board of Trade endorsed further developments, arguing "the great benefit which would flow from the opening of and settlement of the vast tract situated between the St. Lawrence and Ottawa."[23] With the passage of the Public Lands Act in 1853 and the passage of the Free Grant and Homesteads Act in 1868, the stimulation of agricultural settlement in the much-vaunted Ottawa-Huron tract to the rear of Kingston could proceed apace. The strategy was a clear one:

One or two roads connecting the lumbering districts on the Ottawa with the back settlements of the district on Lake Ontario, would be of great benefit to all parties; it would facilitate and cheapen the supplies to the lumbermen, and stimulate the farmer to raise larger crops, for which he would find a ready, home and cash market and employment for himself, and teams, in transportation, during the winter. ... These roads would open up that extensive region, called the "Huron and Ottawa Tract". ... which is known to contain a large amount of arable land and an almost unlimited supply of timber. ... there is no portion of Canada, perhaps of America, which can offer the same inducements to the industrious immigrants, if they could be transported to it. [24]

The optimism of the age was limitless, and it was claimed that the region was "capable of sustaining a population of EIGHT MILLIONS OF PEOPLE."[25] Assuming 100-acre lots (115,000 lots) and an average of five persons per family, 575,000 would have been a more reasonable figure. Whatever simple-minded comparisons with the population of New England or Ireland prompted this figure, the location of eight million people in a region of some eleven and a half million acres of Shield country was preposterous. [26]

Nevertheless, colonization roads were opened up, and the Frontenac Road promised to extend Kingston's hinterland some hundred miles to the north. The unrealistic expectations are well demonstrated by the predictions for one of Kingston's rear townships, Miller:

The facilities which will be afforded for transport by the Mississippi and Frontenac roads when completed, passing through a healthy section of country; the land tolerably good, building materials in abundance; a sufficient supply of water power for manufacturing purposes; a ready market for the surpluses produced of the settlers, and employment for themselves and teams during the winter months at the lumbering settlements; serve to render Miller and the adjacent townships as desirable a field for settlement, as this part of the country affords.[27]

Certainly, this optimism was shared by hundreds of settlers who moved north to settle along the Addington, Frontenac, and Lavant colonization roads. By 1862, 750 settlers had located along the Addington Road and had chopped, brushed, and cleared some 644 acres.[28] By 1864, it was reported that the "back townships of Miller and Palmerston are now filling up fast." It was also noted that many were "squatters" who were either delaying settlement until they had "practically tested the value of the lands they select" or were "from the United States [and had] come to Canada to escape the draft."[29]

Not all of the ramifications of an active pioneer frontier in the northern townships were of benefit to Kingston. In August 1881 the *British Whig* reported that Kingstonians could smell the smoke of forest fires burning to the north. By 1 September it was reported that "The fires are too numerous to count and they are to be found in all directions, causing a volume of smoke which has drifted to and hangs heavily over the city."[30] The report went on to say that the smoke was "so black as to obscure the sun" and that "Navigation has been considerably interfered with by the smoke, the density of which led to the detention of the steamers 'Margaret' and 'Spartan', Royal Mail Line, both bound down the river." The Montreal *Witness* reported on the catastrophe but added, "It is very hard for the Canadian to realize the state of things which is approaching, so long has it been our lot to contend with the forest that we look upon it rather as an enemy than as a friend."[31] But Kingstonians appreciated the consequences, noting, "The injury to the ground is bad enough, but the loss of woods is more serious, considering the present scarcity of fuel in some parts of the country."[32] By the end of September the fires had been burning for some six weeks. Clarendon and Miller were "swept over by the fiery scourge carrying destitution and loss," while Canonto was described as "a smouldering fire bed."[33] Attributed to pioneers clearing their lands, the fires of 1881 were an unwelcome symbol of the pioneers' battle with the forests to the north of Kingston.

All of this expansionist promotion of agricultural settlement of the back country was to no avail. A combination of misdirected agrarian optimism, urban boosterism, and entrepreneurial speculation introduced hundreds of pioneer settlers into country that was patently unsuited to commercial agriculture. By the 1880s, such interior townships as Sheffield, Hinchinbrook, and Bedford had seen their populations increase to 2,591, 1,322, and 2,019 respectively.[34] None of the dozen rear townships attained populations of more than 1,000 people, and all were to experience considerable out-migration over the ensuing decades. In 1901, the annual report of the commissioner of Crown Lands encapsulated the status of the Ottawa-Huron tract as a settlement field:

The public land in this region has been largely picked over. The remaining lots are rough and not much new settlement is now going on. The locations that take place there are caused mainly by the cancellation of old locations for non-performance of settlement conditions and their relocation to settlers in the vicinity, or the sons of settlers who have become old enough to take land and are desirous of settling down along side their parents, even if the land is rather rough and of inferior quality.[35]

The passage of the Algonquin National Park Act in 1893 and the Act to Establish Forest Reserves in 1898 had effectively withdrawn much of the area from settlement and reserved it as the domain of the lumberman, mineral explorer, and recreation-seeker. This was the destiny of much of Kingston's back country.[36]

RAILWAYS AND RESOURCES

If Kingston's road policy was closely associated with agricultural settlement, its subsequent rail policy was more concerned with resource-extraction. The city's original dalliances with railways had been with projects looking to the south. The enthusiasm for the east-west link provided by the Grand Trunk had been somewhat dampened by the perceived threat to shipping interests. But the several proposals mooted to extend Kingston's hinterland to the north were viewed with much favour. The urban and industrial growth of the late nineteenth century required lumber, wood pulp, and minerals that were abundant throughout Kingston's back country. Prior to the introduction of rail, timber literally flowed out of the area via the Mississippi and Madawaska – the two main tributaries of the Ottawa River – eventually moving to Montreal for shipment by water and rail to foreign metropolitan markets. Rail could do for Kingston what the drainage system had prevented: lumber, together with other Shield products, could move south to Kingston for forwarding.

Railways, therefore, like the colonization roads, were intended to play an important role in the opening up of the resources of the north, and in the period 1850-1900 some thirty-five "colonization railroads" were initiated, with the 1870s being the peak period of activity. Thus, in 1863, the Kingston Board of Trade supported the Kingston & Frontenac Railroad's plan to construct a wooden railway between Kingston and Knowlton Lake, and the following year it also backed the Kingston & Madoc Railroad Company, which proposed another wooden railway connecting the interior of Hastings County with Lake Ontario at Kingston.[37]

Of all these ventures, it was the Kingston & Pembroke Railway that received the most attention and generated the most enthusiasm and support, and that, in a modified form, was eventually realized. A rail connection with Pembroke made certain economic sense: this northern terminus on the Ottawa River was a centre of lumbering. Also, the proposed route crossed two tributaries of the Ottawa, the

Mississippi and Madawaska, both major west-east carriers of lumber. The Kingston & Pembroke Railway thus offered the promise of intercepting this traffic and diverting it to Kingston. Moreover, while the old river technology of floating lumber to Quebec was suited to the trans-Atlantic trade in squared lumber, rail better suited emerging new demands. The United States was an important market for sawn pine timbers, and such early railway ventures as the Brockville & Ottawa and the Port Hope & Lindsay companies had demonstrated that rail was well suited to such traffic. The railroad was also expected to open up some 195,000 acres for settlement, and to allow the movement of agricultural produce south to Kingston markets and the distribution of Kingston merchandise north throughout the back country.

Finally, an additional incentive became apparent after actual construction had got under way. Geological surveys of the area traversed by the Kingston & Pembroke reported several deposits of ores. In 1852, Alex Murray had reported on the presence of iron, galena, and plumbago in Bedford Township, and Henry Vennor's survey of the Ottawa-Huron tract corroborated the opinion that Kingston's hinterland was valuable mineral country.[38] Iron was mined at two locations in Bedford Township in the 1860s: at the Glendower Mine on Thirty Island Lake and at the Howse Mine. In both cases, operations were rendered difficult by isolation, ore being hauled some twenty-five miles to Kingston by wagon, and both mines were eventually forced to close because of prohibitive costs. Noting that the K&P would pass within three miles of the Glendower property, the *Canadian Illustrated News* predicted that the new transport facility would allow the mine to "resume operations and has given them prospects for a profitable future."[39] Further, all the other deposits of iron, galena, plumbago, phosphate, and mica would also become commercially viable and afford Kingston the prospect of becoming an important processing and manufacturing centre. Noting this considerable potential trade in lumber, agricultural products, and minerals, the Montreal *Herald* produced several editorials bemoaning Kingston's aggressive attempts to intercept Montreal's trade.[40] Such complaints serve to underscore the fact that Kingston's support of the Kingston & Pembroke was based on economic rationality rather than mere local boosterism.

Sponsorship of the proposed Kingston & Pembroke Railway was an important issue in the provincial election campaign of 1871. Whatever their partisan and ideological differences, local candidates vied with one another in their unstinting praise of the venture. In the Kingston constituency, John Breden had nailed his booster's colours to the mast with the declaration that his "politics were chiefly Railways, Railways." His official election platform was even more specific

I pledge myself to do all in my power to encourage and push forward that great enterprise, the Kingston and Pembroke Railway, the construction of which will not only be the means of developing the resources of the large territory lying north of Kingston, but will give a fresh impetus to the trade and industry of the city and surrounding countryside, – in fact, manufactures will spring up, commerce will revive, and a healthy tone prevail in all branches of trade.

The people of Kingston are entering upon a new era of progress. If they are only true to their best interests, discard faction and join in a united effort in the accomplishment of the great enterprise they have undertaken, prosperity will again return to them, and Kingston will rank ere long as one of the first cities of the Dominion.[41]

His opponent – and the ultimate victor – William Robinson, also campaigned on a platform of advancing the fortunes of Kingston, and his notice of candidacy assured the "Free and Independent Electors of Kingston" that

believing that a more liberal land and immigration policy, together with the removal of all useless restrictions upon our timber and mineral lands, must result in material benefits to our city, by filling up our sparsely settled back townships, I shall, if elected, urge upon the administration the adoption of such measures as may best conduce to this end.

I will support the Ministry on their railway policy. The Kingston and Pembroke Railway I will do all in my power to encourage and push forward, as in the successful completion of this and other like schemes, rests in a great measure the future prosperity of our city.[42]

The incumbent candidate for the adjacent rural constituency of Frontenac County was D.D. Calvin who, recognizing both the best interests of his constituents and the best interests of his own business affairs, took the opportunity to advance the previous government's progressive policies:

First – I am strongly in favour of encouraging a healthy immigration of the industrial classes into our splendid province. The extensive wild lands, with their vast amounts of mineral and timber resources, require not only to be developed to make the Province of Ontario one of the most desirable resorts for the redundant population of the old countries of Europe; and I do not know of any better plan to make these resources more readily available than by encouraging and aiding the construction of railways, gravel roads, and improving the inland navigation. ... I am in favour of offering large facilities to intending settlers who will occupy and render productive our present fertile territory, as yet almost wholly unoccupied.[43]

Perhaps it was Calvin's active role as one of the principal investors in the Kingston & Pembroke project that prevented him mentioning the railway by name. But, again, there can be no doubt of his opinion on the wisdom of such projects for the development of Kingston's hinterland.

Clearly, the Kingston & Pembroke Railway was regarded as an exciting new in-

Kingston & Pembroke section crew *c.* 1890. (QUA)

itiative in Kingston in 1871. Known locally as the "Kick and Push," it was incorporated on 14 April 1871. Given its rationale, it is not surprising that the Kingston
& Pembroke Railway was one of the first colonization railroads to receive a government subsidy under the terms of the provincial Railways Aid Act of 1870. This provincial legislation provided $112,000 for the first forty-five miles of construction:
$2,000 per mile for the first twenty miles of settled country; $2,650 per mile for fifteen
miles of thinly-settled country; $3,250 per mile for ten miles of unsettled country.[44]
Eventually, the province contributed over $350,000 to the "Kick and Push."

In addition, subsidies were received from municipalities along the proposed route. In all, some $600,000 was raised by various communities throughout Frontenac and Renfrew counties. Kingston, anticipating that the railway would "encourage the colonization and development of the resources of the Crown Land territory north of this city," voted a bonus of $300,000 and extended an interest-free loan of $5,000 to assist with the costs of survey.[45] This decision increased the city debt by some 200 per cent and committed one quarter of the municipal revenue to the venture.[46] Finally, another $180,000 of stock was subscribed by private shareholders, including some of Kingston's most prominent and politically-active citizens: C.F. Gildersleeve, Senator Alexander Campbell, George Kirkpatrick, MP, Richard Cartwright, MP, D.D. Calvin, MPP. But not all of the investors were Kingstonians, or even Canadians. Indeed, some $45,000 worth of shares were purchased from Watertown alone. For these investors, the Kingston & Pembroke was more than a mere extension of Kingston's hinterland, it was a tap-line for their *own* economic enterprises in the United States.

Construction began in 1872 and pushed north, linking Kingston with Harrowsmith, Verona, Tichborne, Oconto, and Sharbot Lake. In March the company applied for additional aid as a colonization railway to complete a further thirty miles to the Madawaska River. By 1881, sixty miles of track had been laid and trains were running as far north as the Mississippi River; but the additional forty-four miles to connect with the Canada Central at Renfrew, and thence over the CC tracks to Pembroke, were not completed until 1886.

But even before this completion, there were some early signs that the optimism of the backers was justified. As early as 1880 a revenue of $51,000 was generated – $12,726 for passengers and mail, and $38,277 for freight.[47] Thus, with the traffic flowing along the Kingston & Pembroke and the Grand Trunk, Kingston's aspirations to be a railroad centre, albeit a minor one, appeared to have been realized. Even without the construction of a link with the United States to the south, such an extension of the railway system into Kingston's hinterland was thought to be a major stimulus to its fortunes:

Not only will Kingston have an eastern outlet of inestimable value from a business point of view, but it will be a convenient and popular point at which Canadians and Americans can make railway connections with the capital and other points eastward for which they have [had] to go to points down the river heretofore. The outlook is better for Kingston. A place is generally prosperous when made a railway centre, and Kingston must be helped by every scheme which brings her into readier access with the country on all sides. The railway operations in this and the adjoining counties will, we hope, have the most satisfactory results.[48]

With these initiatives in place, the editor of the *British Whig* speculated with confidence on the success of the K&P and, in consequence, of Kingston:

In the comparatively long list of roads whose claims the Railway Committee of the Ontario Legislature has to consider, none is more deserving of attention than our own local line. It has admirably served the purpose of a colonization road and aided in the development of our natural resources, and its further extension would certainly extend its usefulness. [49]

There were high hopes for a burgeoning traffic in lumber products flowing south to Kingston. The Kingston & Pembroke intersected the west-east movement of lumber at the Mississippi River, and a mill was established there to process the lumber moving along the river and ready it for movement south by rail to Kingston's port. It was argued that not only did this occasion a shorter journey to ports and markets but also it ensured less damage to the lumber by avoiding rapids. After all, the Mississippi was prone to fluctuations in level; and it was also subject to obstruction by various logging interests who controlled the critical chutes around the rapids and, thus, the flow of lumber out of the region. The lumber companies' energetic cutting generated record lumber freight on the K&P in 1890, amounting to some 100,000 tons of the 150,000 total freight tons carried that year.

Their extensive overcutting also exhausted the resource, and both productivity and freight soon declined. By the late 1890s lumber freight had decreased to less than 30,000 tons a year. Indeed, J. Bauden, the K&P's receiver, noted the part that the railway had played in this process:

the falling-off of lumber freight is due to the decline of lumbering operations in this district. ... The construction of the railroad hastened the destruction of the forest, which had been going on previously. The "K. & P." runs through a poor agricultural district throughout 75 miles of its total length of 104 miles. The depressed condition of the farming interest, due in part to the causes mentioned above, also accounts for a considerable falling off in earnings of the railroad. [50]

Minerals were also expected to contribute to the traffic on the Kingston & Pembroke, thus stimulating the development of mineral processing and refining as well as manufacturing industries in Kingston. Several iron mines were located along the route of the railway and eventually three quarters of the stock of the company was held by New York interests, many of whom held stock in the Kingston and Pembroke Mining Company – a firm that operated several mines in the district. At the hamlet of Robertsville, 2,000 acres had been purchased by local interests and leased to the Mississippi Mining Company, which shipped ore to the Charlotte Iron Works near Rochester, any surplus being sold to Elmira and Pittsburgh companies. Other mines were located at Glendower, Lavant, Clyde Forks, and Wilbur – all connected to Kingston by the K&P. [51]

Mines were developed for the production of apatite, lead, feldspar, talc, graphite, and mica. Mica was particularly important, being produced at several sites that

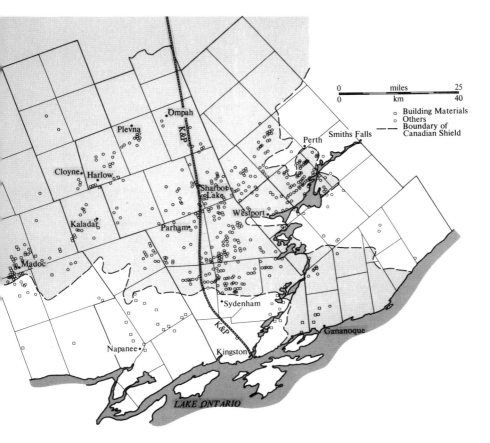

Mining and quarrying sites in the Kingston area.

were, because of the nature of the occurrence of the mineral, typically small-scale operations. The mined mica required trimming, cleaning, and "thumb splitting" into the plates used by industry; but much of this took place at the minehead, or at such local centres as Sydenham and Perth. Like other minerals. the mica moved by the Rideau Canal to Ottawa, or else by wagon, water, and branch railway lines to the Kingston & Pembroke, and then on to the Kingston waterfront. Here, forwarding agents like the James Richardson Company had diversified from grain into the transshipment of minerals to American or European markets. But the deposits of minerals throughout the southern Shield country behind Kingston were not extensive. With the depletion of the local high-grade reserves, and with the discovery of the extensive deposits of iron in Northern Ontario and large bodies of phosphates in Florida, mining activity in southeastern Ontario and, consequently, mineral traffic on the K&P diminished.

Rail connections with the interior had been completed, but the traffic was not sustained. The Ottawa-Huron tract did not turn into a populous back country, lumbering and mining were transient activities, and railways suffered accordingly.

CANALS

In the latter quarter of the nineteenth century, attention turned yet again to the old technology of canals for extending Kingston's sphere of influence to the north. While the primary rationale for the construction of the Rideau Canal had been military, its subsequent role in the regional economy was not unimportant. This was recognized by the Royal Commission of 1870, which was appointed to investigate the state of Canada's canals, including Eastern Ontario's Rideau. The work of the canal commission took place in 1871, and it solicited views from a wide variety of sectors of business and public opinion.

One of the questions posed by the commissioners was: "Is it your opinion that the business of this Canal is of sufficient importance to warrant any outlay for improvement?"[52] Benjamin Tett, MPP, and an influential entrepreneur, reminded the Commission that "The Canal passes through an old and well settled country, and supplies the cheapest mode of transport for merchandize" throughout the Rideau corridor.[53] J.D. Slater, superintending engineer, argued that the trade was "chiefly local," pointing out that "Ottawa and Kingston consumes [sic] in round numbers, 100,000 cords of wood annually, and of this quantity about a ⅓ [sic] is procured from the Rideau Canal; and were it not for this supply, the consumer would have to pay at least one dollar more per cord."[54] He also reported that "the principal tolls [were] collected on Salt, Wheat, Coal, Firewood, Floats, Traverses, Railroad ties, Shingles, Sawed Lumber, Saw-logs [and] Pork. ..."[55] John Chaffey, another backcountry entrepreneur from Newboro, also claimed that the Rideau was "indispensable to the country through which it runs," and he drew attention to the growing mineral traffic:

A Cleveland Company have made a contract for carrying through it 20,000 tons of Iron from Hull to Kingston, during 1871, and the tolls on that quantity will amount to $4,000. The trade of the Crosby Iron mines is increasing, and must increase to an unlimited extent.[56]

Another respondent reported that the opportunities for mineral production between Rideau Lake and Kingston were "varied and important, yielding iron, copper, lead, and phosphate of lime."[57] The Rideau was a very small cog in the national system. But in the light of this evidence, the commissioners recognized it as part of the national system, and wanted it maintained as a fully-functioning transportation unit. They concluded that it "be maintained as one of the public works of Canada." They also concluded that "as constructed it is quite sufficient for the wants of the trade, provided it is kept in good working order," and that "it requires no extension or enlargement."[58]

But not only did local opinion appreciate the existing good services of the Rideau, it also recognized the potential for enhancing its contribution to the development of Kingston's hinterland. As settlement and exploration progressed, the diverse resources of the Shield were becoming apparent. And the Rideau, by traversing Kingston's Shield country, provided a means for moving out resources from a region that was not suited to extensive road or rail systems. Accordingly, proposals were mooted for the extension of the region served by the Rideau.

One of these was the canalizing of the Gananoque River to Charleston Lake, and thence to the Rideau at Morton. When the Rideau Canal was constructed, several river systems were examined throughout the Rideau corridor, and a combination of economics and geography competed with numerous private interests to determine the best route. A variety of proposals designed to make the Gananoque River navigable from Morton to the St Lawrence had been considered in the past, but no concrete steps toward the realization of this end were taken before the 1880s. In 1883, a group from the region applied to make the St Lawrence-to-Morton section of the Gananoque navigable for steamboats at a cost of some $285,000.[59] Locks would be required at Lyndhurst, Charleston Lake, and Marble Rock, with bridges at several sites and dredging throughout.

In theory, the project was a viable one. The Gananoque River drained an area of three hundred square miles in the townships of South Crosby, Bastard, Leeds, Lansdowne, Yonge, and Kitley, most being well settled, with good farming country. The nearest railways were the Grand Trunk to the south and the Brockville & Ottawa to the east. Both lines, however, were fourteen miles from the centre of the Gananoque River's watershed. Because of the area's geography, it was doubtful if a railway would ever run through its centre: improving the navigation of the Gananoque and integrating it with the Rideau was the area's best possibilty for development.[60]

The proposal may have received initial government approval, but the necessary navigational improvements clashed with the established manufacturing interests of the Gananoque Water and Power Company. In 1885, after decades of discussion and lobbying, success seemed to be at hand. A sum of $20,000 was voted by parliament to improve the supply of water to the Rideau Canal and provide water to the Gananoque Water and Power Company.[61] By 1887 the dam at Charleston Lake was near completion, other dredging works had taken place, and some of the $20,000 allocation had been expended. But the major obstacle to the construction of the Gananoque branch was the problem of a guaranteed supply of water that would assure seasonal navigation on both the Rideau and the Gananoque. There was in many quarters a profound suspicion that there was simply not enough water for both purposes, and the project fizzled.

The Devil Lake Branch was another scheme for opening Kingston's back country. The promotional rhetoric was clear:

The ... improvements [to the system at Devil Lake] will open up a way for Barges to the head of Knowlton Lake giving the traffic of eighty-six miles of coast to the Rideau Canal, a largely increased water supply, both to the Canal and the Gananoque River, and, also make the Land-owners to cultivate their meadowlands and to work their mines besides enabling a large quantity of firewood now locked up to come to Kingston and thereby reducing the price of that commodity in the City.[62]

Many felt that the time was ripe for opening the Devil Lake watershed to development. A seventeen-mile-long navigable channel from Knowlton Lake to the Rideau would allow a steamer to travel to Kingston in four and a half hours. This could be an important economic development. It would permit the exploitation of some 125 square miles of timber that ran at thirty cords per acre, for a total of almost two and a half million cords of maple, beech, and assorted softwoods. Kingston would be a ready market for this wood.

But the main rationale for the Devil Lake branch was mineral development. Preliminary sightings of zinc, asbestos, and apatite had been reported close to the line of the proposed canal. Substantial quantities of feldspar were being mined at the Richardson Mine on Desert Lake, where an excavation of 200 feet by 150 feet by 40 feet was in the process of developing an estimated reserve of some 100,000 tons of the ore. The mine was worked with two steam drills and a steam hoist, with the product being carried out by horses and wagons to the lake. Here it was dumped into cars that were then ferried by tug and scow across Desert Lake to a tramway. The cars were then hauled by horses to the railway. This complicated and expensive route was in use for several years and did not prevent the mine-owners from realizing a profit. A second feldspar mine was also in operation nearby, with large untapped reserves of these crystalline minerals in the neighbourhood of Desert and Big Mud lakes.[63] Certainly, the region appeared best suited to mining and lumbering. Some optimists claimed it would be well suited to grazing and fruit-raising, and argued that the only impediment to the opening of Devil Lake country was the access problem.

In February 1883 a petition was filed with the Department of Railways and Canals requesting that improvements be made to the Devil Lake system. The proposed route to be rendered navigable from Knowlton Creek to the Rideau was seventeen miles long, with additional branch lines along the Otter Lake line and the Canoe Lake line. The project would be expensive, costing a total of $190,708 for the locks at Bedford Mills and Devil Lake, and for the dredging of Desert Creek, Mud Creek, and Knowlton Creek. Superintendent Wise submitted a detailed report expressing his doubts about the project. The two main problems were, not unexpectedly, the terrain and the cost. He noted that the 20,000 feet of channel to be deepened

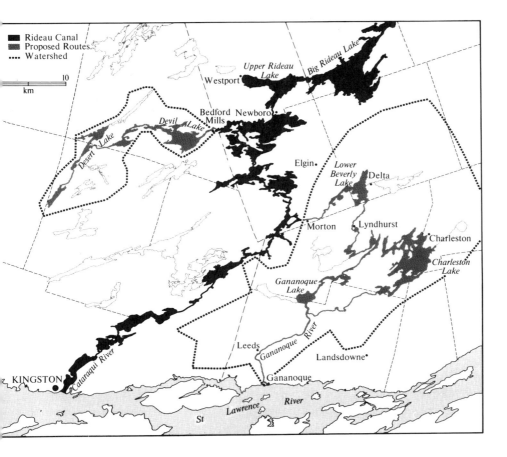

Proposed extensions of the Rideau system in the late nineteenth century.

was "hardly navigable for canoes at low water."[64] Wise agreed that if the Devil Lake region were opened, vast quantities of cordwood could be exploited, but he doubted the practicality of opening up such a bleak region: "what practical use of making a lock and passage in a country of that rocky description I fail to see."[65]

In the fall of 1903 the Devil Lake project emerged again, a major concern now being the $50,000 required to compensate the Tetts for losses to their considerable milling plant at the Bedford Mills lock-site. Kingstonians were irked at the lack of progress on these ventures because they were anxious to exploit the extensive mineral deposits of Frontenac County. In 1904, Kingston city council resolved to support the proposed extension of the Rideau to the Desert Lake country. Noting the "vast stores of mineral wealth which at present lie useless owing to the excessive cost of transportation," the resolution further argued that "the development of the mineral resources of this County is of the greatest importance to the City of Kingston."[66] Six years later, a similar proposal was submitted to the Department of Railways and Canals by Kingston's Board of Trade.[67] After 1910 the Devil Lake issue pretty much faded from view, but for a good thirty years the scheme had been a subject of substantial interest for both government and industry. The economic potential, and hence benefit, of the Devil Lake project was tied closely to the Frontenac County mining industry. Mining continued to be profitable for many years and could have yielded much more in the way of minerals, jobs, and multiplier effects had it been based on a substantially-improved transportation system.[68]

Both the Gananoque and Devil Lake schemes for expanding the Rideau waterway system serve to counter the image of the Rideau as redundant following the St Lawrence canal improvements. It played a vital role in Kingston's back country and was to continue to do so until well into the twentieth century.

REALITIES

While most of Kingston's rear townships experienced steady increases in population from 1861, they peaked in 1891 and declined thereafter. By 1881 some 800 farms with a total population of over 5,000 persons had been located north of Bedford and Hinchinbrook. This rural population was to peak in the early twentieth century, and while there were 935 farms in the northern townships in 1911, by 1941 only 616 producing farms remained. However, not only were Kingston's rear townships never to be fully settled but even the southern townships were beginning to lose population. Whereas in 1820 Kingston's immediate agricultural hinterland accommodated some 2,901 persons and approximately 500 farms, by 1881 Frontenac could boast of close to 4,000 farms and more than 26,000 rural dwellers. But many of these farmers and rural craftsmen were to fail in the ensuing generation. From the middle of the nineteenth century on, the lure of agricultural opportunities in the Canadian West, together with new opportunities in the cities emerging throughout North America, served to pull the rural population from Kingston's back country to farms in other rural areas or to industries in urban areas.[69]

And if agriculture failed, neither lumbering nor mining was to provide alternative systems to sustain a viable economic base throughout Kingston's back country. Some sections of the colonization roads were integrated into later road systems, but others soon became as neglected as many of the pioneer homesteads and logging shanties they were intended to sustain. Even the engine of the Industrial Age, railways, failed to develop Kingston's back country to the extent anticipated. Much of the traffic on the Kingston & Pembroke, either originating or terminating in Kingston, produced prosperity for neither Kingston nor the company's shareholders. In 1912 the "Kick and Push" was absorbed into the CPR. Kingston was left with a slender line of rail connecting it with such communities as Harrowsmith, Verona, Tichborne, Oconto, Sharbot Lake, Oso, Mississippi Station, Wilbur,

The "Iron Duke" (K&P no. 11), built by the Kingston Locomotive Company 1888. (QUA)

Calabogie, Opeongo, and Renfrew. The link was important to this corridor of settlement: produce was brought to Kingston's market, passengers moved easily between Kingston and the north, mail service was provided, and numerous men found employment. But the railways did not serve to develop Kingston's back country to the desired degree, because that corridor could not sustain substantial economic development nor provide a livelihood for a large population.

Walter Lewis concluded that the K&P was "a dismal failure."[70] Nonetheless, it did have a profound impact upon the city and its hinterland. For Kingston, the tracks, yards, and terminus in front of city hall became a bustling and vital section of the city's townscape. And for the settlements throughout the back country, the "Kick and Push" became an important part of community life and economy. The regular Kingston-to-Pembroke run continued until 1957, and the CPR maintained the tracks from Kingston to Tichborne until 1987, when they were torn up, leaving a right of way that remains as a visible part of the regional heritage to complement the rich folklore of experiences and memories:

> Listen to the jingle, the rumble and the roar,
> As she glides along the woodlands,
> By the lake and by the shore;
>
> Hear the mighty side-rods pounding,
> The lonesome whistle call:
> You're northward bound to Renfrew
> On the K and P Cannonball.[71]

Calvin Company scrip. Like many other operations, the company had a private money system. Scrip could be used to buy goods at the Calvin store on Garden Island. (John and Meg d'Esterre)

TEN

"Wake up Sleepy Hollow!"

THE FIRST "MANUFACTORIES"

If a famous critic of the industrial society of the day, Karl Marx, could exclaim, "religion is the opiate of the masses," he could also have argued that industry was the elixir of cities. Certainly, industry was thought to be the panacea for most of Kingston's economic and social ills.

Like other contemporary communities, Kingston already possessed a diverse, if modest, manufacturing sector. Prior to the industrialization of Canadian society and the concentration of industrial production in a few urban centres, communities like Kingston were characterized by many small-scale manufactories that used local raw materials and labour to produce various commodities for local consumption.

A survey of "Manufactures in Midland District for 1832" reported the "Number, name, situation and description of manufactories, Mills, Works etc. not including Grist and Saw Mills."[1] The preoccupation of this report was an inventory of the ways in which the new steam-technology had been applied to the manufacturing base. The list of "manufactures" comprised two air-furnaces in Adolphustown for casting "Plough Molds," a steam engine at Hallowell for "finishing machinery and fitting up Carding Machines," machinery for making "Hat Bodies" and "Wrapping and Press Paper" in Belleville, and eight "Carding and Fulling" machines throughout the district. There were two potteries in Kingston, a steam engine in Kingston "for driving a lathe for finishing Steam Machinery & other purposes," and one engine in each of the town and township of Kingston "for grinding grain and making whisky." It was also recorded that a "Steam Boat called the John By" of 120 tons "burthen" had been constructed in 1831, and that there were two schooners of seventy tons each "now on the Stocks." The return also commented that "Iron Ore is generally supposed to be abundant throughout the District and in the township of Marmora, the seat of the Iron Works, the supply is very Extensive from Beds of various qualities." And finally, a press had been established at Kingston to employ a local stone which "answers well for Lythography [sic]."

In this pre-industrial traditional society, most communities processed their own foodstuffs in their own flour and grist mills, and breweries and distilleries. Other small enterprises included tanneries, printing and publishing shops, cooperages, cabinet-makers, and pot- and pearl-asheries. Those domestic needs not satisfied by home skills were catered to by the bakers, tailors, dressmakers, boot-and-shoe makers, and the many other craftsmen to be found throughout the town. Some proto-industrial enterprises may be recognized in the shipyards, agricultural-implement factories, forges, and machine works. But most of these enterprises continued to be as small as they were diverse.

Apart from ubiquitous crafts and services, which were often individual or family operations, a few larger enterprises were developing by mid-century. In the 1850s, Kingston could boast of seven sawmills with thirty-three employees, two found-ries (thirty-two employees), two grist mills, a tannery, a distillery, and a brewery (fifty employees). By 1861 the list had diversified even further: six breweries, three foundries (145 employees), a steam-powered flour mill, two woollen mills, five soap-and-candle factories, four agricultural-implement shops, three carriage and wagon shops, three pot- and pearl-asheries, two shipyards, two sash-and-door mills, two sewing-machine factories, and two edged-tool factories.[2]

Other activities reflected Kingston's distinctive role in nineteenth-century Ontario. One was the presence of a significant concentration of publishing. Certainly, this activity had been much stimulated during Kingston's brief period as capital of the Province of Canada. A large number of government documents and general literary works were produced in Kingston at mid-century. Another distinctive activity was Kingston's penitentiary role, one that also stimulated its other specializations as convict labour was contracted out to the private sector. In 1857, contracts were awarded for labour in an axe and edged-tool establishment, an agricultural-implement works, a boot-and-shoe manufacturer, and a cabinet-and-furniture maker. Such a list constitutes a catalogue of traditional commercial and service activities, most of which were small and unsophisticated enterprises.

Not surprisingly, ship-building and ship-repair figured large in Kingston's economy. The *Kingston City Directory* for 1862-1863 predicted that "Kingston, at no distant day, promises to be an important manufacturing City. Already the trade of ship building has arrived at great proficiency."[3] Of the five hundred or so vessels registered at the port of Kingston in the second half of the nineteenth century, more than 90 per cent were built in in Kingston and its environs.[4] While the majority of these vessels were constructed in Kingston yards and adjacent bays, others came from sites on offshore islands, the interior lakes served by the Rideau Canal, and several locations throughout the Bay of Quinte and Prince Edward County. Indeed, more than fifty separate ship-building locations may be identified. During the early years, the industry was dominated by small enterprises and individual shipwrights like Beaupré, Jenkins, Cantin, Roney, and Robinson. Subsequently, these small-scale outfits (some of which were moved to where lumber, demand, and access

Morton's Distillery *c.* 1910, by Ella Frazer. (QUA)

allowed construction), were replaced by more specialized ship-building companies. Production came to be dominated by such enterprises as the Chaffeys of Bedford Mills, Samuel Knapp at Dog Lake, the Jarrells of Cranberry Lake, the Calvin Company of Garden Island, Power and Sons of Kingston, and the R. Davis Dry Dock Company. Moreover, there was a shift from enterprises producing the barges, scows, and sail vessels of the early period to the larger and more complex machine-works necessary for the production of steam-powered vessels in the later period. In 1871 some 147 men were variously employed in Kingston's shipyards, receiving approximately $51,000 in wages. By 1901, this figure had dropped to thirteen full-time employees and eighty-three part-time, with a mere $17,875 wage bill.[5]

In the midst of this essentially commercial economic structure, new ventures emerged that were to attain regional and even national significance. That they did so was due to the business acumen and initiative of such leading citizens as John Morton, Dileno Dexter Calvin, and James Richardson.

JOHN MORTON entered the brewing business in Kingston in 1831, operating on the waterfront to the west of the town. His business thrived, and he soon demonstrated his entrepreneurial skill by diversifying into a distillery, a lumberyard, a dockyard, and ship-building. More importantly, in 1855, he purchased the Ontario Foundry located at Mississauga Point on Kingston's waterfront and began to manufacture locomotives for the rapidly expanding Canadian railroad system. The early history of the firm is as murky as its achievements are impressive. How, when, or where Morton the miller-cum-machinist acquired his technological skills is unknown; but it is on record that in 1856 his Ontario Foundry delivered *five* locomotives to the Grand Trunk.[6] Two years later, a Kingston directory commented on the enterprise's production and on its contribution to the mechanization of the local milling industry:

The establishment under the superintendance of Mr. Francis Tutton is doing a rapidly increasing business; as it has already finished 12 locomotives and tenders which on trial are found to compare favourably with those imported from either England or the United States. Four others are now in a forward state. Three engines have been built here for Mr. Morton's saw mills at Trenton and four others for grist mills besides other business. The works employ 150 men from 5 shillings to 10 shillings per day; wages paid every Friday evening.[7]

By 1858 the foundry was Kingston's largest employer and demonstrated all the trappings of an emerging industrial enterprise, financed by commercial capital, in a mercantile city. The Kingston Directory for 1862-1863 reported further progress:

THE KINGSTON LOCOMOTIVE WORKS ... is one of the largest and most complete establishments in the Province. It comprises the Iron and Brass Foundry, the Finishing Shop, with the latest improved machinery, the Pattern Shop, the Boiler Shop, the Blacksmith Shop and Coppersmith Shop. They have built thirty complete locomotives, manufacturing everything pertaining to them except the axles and tyres, which were imported from England. They also do a large business in Boiler, Steamboat and Engine work. The number of hands employed vary from 50 to 150.[8]

But by 1864, Morton was bankrupt, and upon his death in that year control of the firm passed to the Montreal-based interests of the Canadian Engine and Machinery Company, the head offices being removed to that city. The Montreal régime lasted until 1878 when it was re-incorporated by federal charter as the Canadian Locomotive and Engine Company Limited. The head office was brought home to Kingston, but within two years the firm was again bankrupt. Despite its troubled finances and regular reorganizations, the works continued in Kingston in various forms following Morton's original initiative. He had provided the entrepreneurial leadership for the diversification of Kingston's economy, and had established one enterprise that was to serve the community well into the next century.

The *D.D. Calvin*, steam-powered vessel of the Calvin Company transshipping timber at Garden Island to be made into rafts. (QUA)

DILENO DEXTER CALVIN, another early entrepreneur, established himself on Garden Island, between Kingston and Wolfe Island, in 1836.[9] An American by birth and upbringing, Calvin operated a huge enterprise from his Garden Island base until his death in 1884. Ship-building, a salvage operation, freighting, and tug-boats were all part of his operation. He bought and sold commodities such as flour and salt, operated a freight business that moved rails along the Great Lakes, and opened a tug-boat service on the St Lawrence.

The heart of Calvin's business was his fleet of ships that collected oak and pine timber from whatever sources were profitable. The timbers or "sticks" were hauled to Garden Island for assembly into units called "drams," which were in turn assembled into rafts of up to half a mile in length. The rafts moved down the St Lawrence to the coves of Quebec City, some three hundred miles to the east, where

James Richardson and Sons Ltd. was the most important private enterprise in the history of Kingston. The basis of its success was the buying, selling, and transshipment of wheat. (QUA)

they were disassembled and transshipped for British markets. As the local forests became exhausted, Calvin collected lumber from the entire Great Lakes basin. Calvin's work was labour-intensive, and as many as seven hundred people lived in his island community, which was run along paternalistic and authoritarian lines. Unaffected by competition from railways and navigational improvements along the St Lawrence, Calvin's enterprise continued to thrive at Garden Island until the outbreak of the First World War in 1914.

JAMES RICHARDSON was one of Kingston's most remarkable business leaders.[10] His start was far from auspicious. He was born at Aughnacloy, County Tyrone, Ireland, in 1819. Shortly thereafter his mother died, and in 1823 his father Daniel moved with his small boy to Kingston. Then Daniel died; James was raised by an aunt, apprenticed to a tailor, and by 1844 had been sufficiently enterprising to acquire his own shop. Being a tailor did not exclude the young Richardson from broader commercial activities: bartering his services for farmers' grain introduced him to an activity that was to become of more importance to him later. By the 1850s such was his success that he was able to serve as a guarantor for the contractor who undertook the construction of Kingston's new Custom House. With the financial failure of that project, Richardson honoured his costly responsibility and completed the task, producing a building that remains as one of Kingston's finest public structures and the first of many gifts that succeeding generations of Richardsons have bestowed on Kingston (and Queen's University). Faced with major financial losses, Richardson abandoned tailoring for the forwarding trade, and the firm of James Richardson and Sons Ltd. dates from September 1857. It must be considered as the most successful enterprise in the business history of Kingston, and it remains the largest grain firm in the British Commonwealth.

James and his sons George and Henry built a well-integrated business during the closing decades of the century. Initially, they dealt with independent boat-owners who sought out and transported cargoes for the firm. These boats, known as Richardson's "mosquito fleet," transferred much grain directly from farm producers to purchasers. Later, Richardson built and operated his own vessels. The *Richardson* was the first. It was followed by numerous ships, including the *Ford River* and the *Queen of the Lakes*. Trade was by no means confined to the St Lawrence route. Much traffic was north-south, especially with Oswego. In 1868, the firm purchased waterfront land in the downtown district. The *Daily British Whig* described the plans for the site:

The old Commercial Wharf, so long the depot of the Royal Mail Line of steamers, having been purchased by Mr. James Richardson, that gentleman is putting it in a thorough state of repair, with a view to future occupation by the Kingston grain buyer. It has been greatly extended into the harbour, and will make one of the most commodious wharves in the town.[11]

This same waterfront property was to be used in subsequent years for the construction of a succession of ever-larger grain elevators.

The Richardsons did not limit themselves to grain alone. As we have seen before this, the Kingston & Pembroke Railway gave them access to the minerals to the north of Kingston, and the firm pursued an active forwarding business in coal, mica, feldspar, iron, and phosphates. James Richardson was imaginative, innovative, and expansionist. He was convinced of the potential of the prairie West and his agents followed the CPR into that new realm for development. In 1883 the firm exported the first prairie grain destined for offshore consumption, and increasingly the company emphasized the western trade in its operations. The Richardson firm became a crucial force in the evolution of the prairie economy and a central institution in Winnipeg. But the company's executive office remained in Kingston until 1923, and Winnipeg did not become the official headquarters for James Richardson and Sons until 1939.

These three entrepreneurs – Morton, Calvin, and Richardson – were symbolic of the transmutation being pursued by Kingston and the broader society of which it was part. The three managed the shift from traditional commercial trading roles to investment in various manufacturing and financial enterprises associated with the new industrial age. Moreover, they had been stimulated to invest in Kingston at the height of its commercial dominance in the mid-nineteenth century. If Kingston was to succeed in the latter half of that century, a fresh infusion of investment, vigour, and entrepreneurial ingenuity was required.

MUNICIPAL INITIATIVES

Apart from the efforts and speculative genius of a few, perhaps too few, enterprising individuals, the case for industrial diversification was also favoured in the 1880s by recent political developments. The general economic depression of the 1870s was followed by a decade dominated by the economic implications of Sir John A. Macdonald's "National Policy," which attempted to promote the Canadian economy by the imposition of substantial tariffs on foreign manufactured goods and the reduction of import duties on raw materials. Initiated by the budget of 14 March 1879, the protectionist "National Policy" served to stimulate investors in Kingston as elsewhere throughout Canada. [12]

Kingston's more local municipal agencies were not idle, either. The Board of Trade had been established in 1851. A group of city merchants, bankers, forwarders, and traders assembled to discuss the concept on 22 August of that year. Their intentions were quite explicitly formulated in their constitution: "the objects of the Board of Trade shall be to promote just and equitable principles in Trade, to correct abuses, and generally to protect the rights and advance the interests of the Mercantile Classes." [13]

In its first years, the Board was predictably preoccupied with enhancing commerce and trade, petitioning for the restriction of lake trade to Canadian carriers, for the removal of duties on imports and exports to further Kingston's port traffic, and for the encouragement of such navigational improvements as the St Lawrence Canals, the Welland Canal, and the Huron and Ontario Ship Canal. [14]

In the 1870s the Board became increasingly concerned with attracting manufacturing establishments to the city. As early as 1868 it was recorded in the *Annual Report* of the Board that

the subject of manufacturers should receive the attention of the businessmen of the city, as the establishment here of factories of various kinds would improve trade generally, and give employment to many of our citizens who are obliged to seek it elsewhere. [15]

Whereas Kingston's industries had numbered only twenty-seven in 1851, and forty-two in 1861, the 1871 Census enumerated no fewer than 156 enterprises. These employed some 1,279 workers, in a total work force of 3,379 persons; that is, 34 per cent of Kingston's workers were in the industrial sector. Moreover, the greater number of these establishments were quite small-scale, employing no more than five persons, and were modestly capitalized.[16] As late as 1871, therefore, Kingston had not managed to shed its dependency on shipping and commerce, despite its wooing of new "manufactories" and their engines and machinery. The Board of Trade lamented this state of affairs in its annual report for 1870:

It is to be regretted that there are so few manufactories in the City of Kingston, being from its central position a good distributing point for merchandise. There appears to be no well defined law by which the establishment of manufactories can be promoted. We are of the opinion that application might be made to the Legislature for power to assist such enterprises by giving permanency to a reduction of taxation.[17]

The spectacular level of support afforded the Kingston & Pembroke Railway established the precedent for "bonusing" and other inducements. For some, however, the money would have been better spent had it been directed to industrial enterprises, and William Brophy identified such ventures as "a sugar refinery which could be established for a grant of $20,000, woollen and cotton mills, a floating dock, and ... bringing the water from Kingston Mills to Bell's Island" as being preferable.[18] Certainly, this view was shared by other business interests, and in 1872 the Board of Trade presented various views to city council on the best means of nurturing industry. On 13 May of that year, the committee appointed by council to consider the Board's reports submitted its recommendations.[19] It was recognized that the city favoured the establishment of "various branches of manufactures" because of its lake, river, and rail communications, its "healthy location," and unlimited water supply for "manufactures worked by steam power." The report went on to advocate that "a large and suitable building [be] erected in some convenient locality where a powerful engine or engines could be placed with machinery therein suitable for various branches of manufacturing." They went even further by advocating that new businesses be exempt from taxation for five years, the only restrictions being that new enterprises not duplicate existing companies, and that they employ twenty-five hands or more. The committee baulked, however, at the granting of cash bonuses, low-interest loans, and city lots to "induce manufacturers to establish their businesses here," because of the "heavy and important engagements the City is now under." Clearly, the size of the Kingston & Pembroke bonus weighed mightily even on the optimistic boosters of the Board of Trade.

If bonusing was no longer in favour, other inducements were. Moreover, in March 1873, Kingston was allocated $25,000 from the province of Ontario's "Municipal Loan Fund."[20] The Canadian Engine and Machinery Company promptly applied for council's largesse to finance planned expansion of their Kingston facilities. The company was granted tax exemption for ten years, and a $5,000 bonus also received the support of the electorate.[21]

Even though the Canadian Engine and Machinery Company immediately encountered major financial problems, city council was besieged over the next twelve months by a series of other requests from industries willing to commit themselves to advancing prosperity in Kingston in return for appropriate municipal consideration. Thus, William Power requested tax exemptions for his shipyard and new dry dock[22]; two Brantford millers offered to construct a steam-powered flour mill employing twenty-five men, in return for $3,000[23]; the Weber Piano Company contemplated increasing its output from 350 pianos a year to 500, and asked for a ten-year tax exemption[24]; another request was for the grant of a city lot for the construction of a factory.

Over the ensuing five years, another dozen submissions were received by council, including a major proposal from the Kingston Iron and Steel Rolling Mills Company. Capitalized at $10,000, the company asked for a ten-year tax exemption and a $10,000 bonus. Predictably, the local newspapers trumpeted their support, urging Kingstonians to "Arise from your lethargy! Let us be not only the Limestone City of Canada but also the Iron City."[25] All the while the spectre of the K&P bonus still walked the streets of Kingston, and this, like other requests for municipal bonuses or stock subscriptions, was denied, council being prepared to grant only tax exemptions.

Clearly, Kingston's economic plight required that some action be taken to attract industry. While a regional administrative centre with commercial activities, nascent manufactories, and expectations of future growth, Kingston in 1880 was still only a modest town of some 14,000 inhabitants. As a market centre, it remained fundamentally dependent upon its own rural hinterland, which commenced within a mile of city hall. (Indeed, there were still twenty-four farm units within the city limits, producing hay, potatoes, and wheat – and with several head of horses, cows, sheep, and pigs). It was a city, therefore, whose council could be required to discuss the problems of cattle straying on the streets at the same meeting where they considered the need for tax relief for industries. To be sure, Kingston could boast of some 156 firms, with a total of 1,279 employees. These averaged less than ten hands per unit and $3,949 worth of products per unit annually. The average annual wage per worker was $280.[26] The civic leaders of the day understood the significance of these figures. "Truly Kingston needs to have manufactures beyond any other city in the Dominion," it was argued,

Her population is almost entirely dependent upon commerce and on a commerce restricted to six months of the year. Her trades and small manufactures are entirely local and similarly dependent on her commerce, so that the working man's wages of the six months are eaten up by the enforced idleness of winter. Besides this there is no employment for the working man's boys and girls to supplement his hardearned wages should he be laid aside through sickness or accident. ... See you to it Aldermen as citizens of Kingston; you will certainly create to some extent a pauper, or worse, a criminal population unless you make some inducement to manufacturers to establish themselves in your midst so as to make your city less dependent on your sole resources, your summer commerce and shipping trade.[27]

At the annual mayor's dinner in 1881 one speaker lamented that while "Manufact-ures were springing up in almost every city and town ... not a single new industry had been established in the city. What was the cause of this? Did the fault lie with the council or the people?"[28] He went on to identify the "bonus system" as a possible incentive for industry. The granting of "tax exemptions" was also "in accord with the economic needs of a city so well situated as Kingston undoubtedly is for manufacturing purposes." Without financial incentives Kingston would merit the accolade of "Sleepy Hollow." Between 1870 and 1901 council considered no fewer than thirty-one by-laws awarding bonuses, loans, or tax-exemptions in its endeavour to attract new enterprises.[29]

Certainly, there were signs that the 1880s were to be propitious years, and the decade opened with no fewer than five new industrial ventures that attracted some $500,000 in local investment. The Canadian Locomotive Company was re-organized, capitalized with an additional $200,000, and returned to its Kingston home. The Kingston Charcoal Works appeared to be the long-awaited means for Kingston to acquire the metallurgical industry promised by the minerals of Kingston & Pembroke country, and attracted $26,000 in local support. The Kingston Car Company raised $50,000 in its search for capital, while the Royal Knitting Company offered $100,000 in stock. Finally, the Kingston Cotton Mill moved between $150,000 and $250,000 of its stock.

Of these ventures, the Kingston Cotton Mill was the most exciting and attracted the support of such members of the local establishment as James Richardson, the Carruthers family, and B.M. Britton. Promising to employ some two hundred persons, with an annual wage roll of $45,000, and to invest in $140,000 worth of machinery, the company estimated it needed a capitalization of $250,000. In April 1881 the KCM approached Council for a bonus of $25,000.[30]

While subsequently reduced to a lesser amount and compensating tax exemp-tions, the proposal prompted considerable discussion. Those in favour argued that acquiescing to the request "may lead to the establishment of other industries, and if so, our city will take a new departure and will so grow that in a few years it will not be recognised by those who are now ready to speak of it as slow and finished and behind the times."[31] The editor of the *Daily News* echoed these sentiments, argu-ing that "Factories, like kindred birds, flock together, no capitalist being willing to commence business in a place which is commercially backward," and predicted that the cotton mill promised to be "the first step in Kingston's prosperity."[32] Despite these enthusiastic supporters, the electorate rejected the bonus in July 1881 and elicited the bitter and gloomy prediction that the rejection would "have a most chilling effect upon the present undertaking, and will certainly operate to prevent any further similar one."[33]

But if bonusing came into disfavour in the 1880s, Kingston's tax exemptions were considerable. By 1883 $1.5 million out of $5.5 million of assessed property was tax-exempt. But only $210,741 of this was due to industrial exemptions. By 1885 the industrial exemptions had been doubled, by extension to fourteen companies with a total assessment of $441,605 – accounting for a loss to taxation of $7,078. Some in the community expressed concern over "the alarming extent" of "municipal tax exemptions" and argued that if the system continued, "some of the best property in our cities and large towns will be relieved from taxation."[34] For "boosters," however, "the industries exempted are the strongest indicators of vitality Kingston has shown for many years. Their very presence has done more than any other thing to remove the reproach of deadness we have long meekly and justly borne."[35]

The 1880s, therefore, were witness to the addition of several new industrial establishments in Kingston's economy. The Kingston Cotton Mill eventually did come to town in 1882 and fulfilled its promises by employing some two hundred workers – including sixty children – in the processing of 115,000 pounds of cotton into 45,000 yards of grey sheeting and dyed goods per week.[36] Two hosiery factories, employing 161 workers between them, also located in the city during this period, while several lesser mills, forges, and works came into production.

The major development, however, was the reorganization and revitalization of the locomotive factory that had originated as Morton's Ontario Foundry. Between 1864 and 1878, it was called the Canadian Engine and Machinery Company; it was then reincorporated by federal charter as the Canadian Locomotive and Engine Company Ltd. In 1881, it was reorganized yet again by a group of Kingston businessmen-cum-politicians that included William Harty, George Kirkpatrick, Alexander Gunn, and Sir Richard Cartwright. Kirkpatrick became president, and held office for many years; but the moving spirit was William Harty, who became managing director of the company at the age of thirty-four.

Being both a Roman Catholic and a Liberal, Harty was hardly typical of the Kingston élite. After completing his education at Regiopolis, he had entered business in Kingston and become a director of the Kingston & Pembroke Railway. He won Kingston for the provincial Liberals in 1892 and served in the cabinet from 1894 to 1902. In the latter year he won Kingston for the federal Liberals in a by-election and held his seat until 1911. With such prominent and energetic Kingstonians as Harty on the board, and given Kingston's enthusiasm for industrial ventures, it is not surprising that there was a harmony of interest between the city and the locomotive company.

Granted tax exemptions, the company relocated its production of rolling stock for the Grand Trunk Railway from Grosse Pointe, Quebec, to Kingston; and the company reestablished itself as the largest industrial unit in the city. The company

BUILT BY

CANADIAN LOCOMOTIVE CO., LTD.
KINGSTON, ONT.

BEING ONE OF AN ORDER FOR SEVENTY-FIVE LOCOMOTIVES
FOR
INDIAN STATE RAILWAYS

The locomotive company, which has had several names over the years, was for long Kingston's largest employer. It went out of business in 1969. (QUA)

did very well under Harty's direction, but in 1887 it was sold to a Scottish firm, Dubs and Company, and its fortunes fluctuated in the 1890s. After at least one unsuccessful reorganization, the firm was eventually sold to William Harty and partners in 1901 and reorganized as the Canadian Locomotive Company.

As a senior Liberal in eastern Ontario, Harty was well able to take advantage of the massive expansion of railway mileage during the Laurier years. Railroads – at least some of them – and the Laurier government were in intimate alliance, and Harty was able to secure contracts for numerous locomotives for the Intercolonial and Great Northern Railroads. Harty remained in control of the Canadian Locomotive Company until 1911. His legacy to Kingston was a manufacturing firm that employed more hands than any other industry in the city and was strong enough to survive as a major employer "for another half-century in reasonable prosperity. ..."[37]

Another manufacturing innovation was anticipated to develop from the minerals to be brought to the city from Kingston's back country by the K&P. In 1881, it was claimed that one million tons of iron ore were shipped from Belleville and Kingston to Pennsylvania – but, enquired the Hamilton *Times* primly, "Where are the smelting furnaces?"[38] One attempt at remedying this deficiency was the Kingston Charcoal and Iron Company, which established charcoal kilns and furnaces for the smelting of local iron to the north of Kingston, at Sharbot Lake. Both fuel and ore were available locally, and it was argued that "from the superior quality of iron ore, resembling Swedish ore, in that portion of Ontario between Lake Ontario and the Ottawa river, and the abundant supply of wood, it is believed that by using the best processes a high standard of charcoal wrought iron can be produced at a reasonable cost."[39]

By the time the company was incorporated on 10 August 1881, $44,300 of the $50,000-worth of stock had been subscribed, and the company had acquired twenty acres of land for the works located alongside the K&P and a further 2,081 acres of forest at a cost of $2,492. Despite this initial activity, the venture did not materialize, and the ore continued to move out along the Kingston & Pembroke to Kingston's wharves for transshipment elsewhere. Another metallurgical venture was equally unsuccessful a few years later. In 1895 the American-financed Ontario Iron and Steel Company was lured to Kingston with a bonus of $250,000 in exchange for mortgage bonds, and a grant of $50,000 or free water for ten years. The company escalated its demands to a bounty of ten cents per ton of iron manufactured, and a free site. The city demurred and the company left for a site near the Welland Canal.[40]

Apart from the locomotive works, the cotton mills, and the hosiery factory, Kingston's manufacturing activities were still small-scale. The 1891 census reported 401 units employing a total of 2,671 workers, or an average of only 6.7 workers per unit. In all, $1,645,381 were invested in these plants ($4,103 per plant); they produced $3,113,573-worth of goods ($7,765 per plant), with a total payroll of $786,198 ($1,960 per plant, $294 per worker). A few new enterprises located in the city in the 1890s: F.G. Armstrong started selling farm equipment; Massey-Harris began to sell its products locally in 1893; and in 1895 the Crescent Wire and Iron Works commenced production. It has been argued that these developments "indicate that a healthy and active industrialization was taking place."[41] That the 1880s were prosperous years for Kingston is revealed in the increase in population from 14,091 in 1881 to 19,263 in 1891, a stunning and unprecedented 37-per-cent growth rate. Trends such as these prompted the *British Whig* headlines to declare "Kingston Going Up, Up." The evidence was to be found in the assessments, with "material increases in real estate, in personal property and in income."[42] Unfortunately, the following decade's indicators were not so propitious: the city experienced a 7-per-cent decrease in population.

Despite trend-setting initiatives in tax exemptions, bonusing, and other inducements, Kingston's success in industrializing was limited. What industry there was consisted largely of small-scale and traditional enterprises of the "old economy." These were not increasing at the rates of other industrializing metropolises, and Kingston was failing to attract the product-lines of the "new economy."

A PROGRESSIVE CITY

Considering Kingston's enthusiastic willingness to tinker with its municipal revenues to induce industrial investment, it is not surprising that certain groups in the city entertained a major revamping of the municipal tax system. The hot debate that ensued is informative because of the light it sheds on attitudes toward the prevailing system of urban management.[43]

The groundwork for discussion may have been prepared by the recent debate on bonusing and tax exemptions, but the immediate stimulus was the Single Tax Movement. Its advocate, Henry George, started with the premise that the "association of great poverty with great wealth is the great enigma of our time."[44] For George, access to land was the essential prerequisite for subsistence: he argued that "Land is the habitation of man, the storehouse on which he must draw for all his needs, the material to which his labour must be applied for the supply of all his desires."[45] Baulking at the obvious solution to the problem – expropriation and socialization of land – George advocated taxing profits accruing from land while maintaining individuals' proprietary rights to their lands. Picked up by many constituencies of diverse ideological perspectives, George's ideas were well received in the United States, and spread to Britain, Denmark, Germany, Australia, and New Zealand. In Canada, the Toronto Anti-Poverty Society was founded in 1871, with George's ideas central to their platform, and the Single Tax Movement became associated with tax reform in several municipalities from Halifax to Vancouver.

In Kingston, interest in the Single Tax Movement prompted much debate, meetings, letters to the editors of the local newspapers, and editorial comment from the Liberal *British Whig* and Tory *Daily News*. One R. Cartwright expressed himself as "a firm believer, and a careful student of George's works,"[46] while Alderman George Osborne advocated a Single Tax system for the city, consisting of a series of concentric tax-circles centred on city hall, the values decreasing out to the periphery.[47] Single Taxers like Osborne favoured such a system of land-based taxation (as opposed to the personality tax based on income and personal wealth) on ideological grounds. For others, the question was more pragmatic. Even those outside the Single Taxers' ideological camp favoured a reexamination of the prevailing municipal taxation system. The *British Whig* commented, "There are many in this city who do not know what the pith of 'Poverty and Progress' is, but who know that the system of taxation, now pursued by most municipalities, is wrong in principle and injurious in practice and in great need of remodelling and that right away."[48] Indeed, the *Whig* became the most powerful mouthpiece for the Single Tax Movement, but only as a means of effecting a review and possible reform of the existing taxation system.

Predictably the *Daily News* was opposed, arguing that Henry George exaggerated "the extent of the poverty and degradation of the lower orders."[49] The *News* further argued that anti-poverty societies prompted by George's ideas were "a curse to the country, for whatever influence they exert is in the direction of persuading the poor that their condition does not depend on their own exertions" and thus promoted "a dangerous discontent."[50] With such polarized views, the debate continued throughout the 1890s. But while it served to air the several constituencies' dissatisfaction with the prevailing social order and system of management, it had little influence on Kingston's municipal affairs.

Together with such cerebral exchanges over the theory and practice of Kingston's tax base and municipal revenues, the city continued to exhibit evidence of its municipal progress. A generation earlier the Montreal-Toronto-Buffalo telegraph line had been pushed through the region, and its arrival had caused quite a stir downstream from Kingston:

The people here [Edwardsburgh], the great majority of whom read but little and consequently are not over stocked with scientific knowledge have curious ideas of the telegraph. ... Some think that a letter will be put in the wire & pulled along with a string. Others think that the invention consists in applying some unknown power to the letter which makes it go without a string. Others who object to this theory will ask them how it will get past the top of the poles without being torn and how will it do in a heavy shower. Although they can thus silence others they allow that they themselves know no more about it than a cow does about fiddling. One old woman a neighbour of ours who has seen over fourscore winters believes that railways, steamboats and telegraphs are the inventions of the emissaries of his Satanic Majesty and are the means [of] bringing down famine on her native land. If they set up a pole at her door she is determined to set fire to it.[51]

The celebrated Canadian engineer and author Thomas Keefer, ever an advocate of technological change, commented in 1852 that "the Telegraph may be said to have superseded the Post Office."[52] However, Canadians still relied heavily on their reformed postal service. In 1874, free home-delivery of mail was first introduced in Montreal, and extended to Toronto, Quebec, Ottawa, Hamilton, Saint John, and Halifax in the following year. Not until 1 July 1882 was this service made available to Kingstonians; the district inspector then reported that as it was "being freely patronized by the public, a number of lock boxes and drawers have been given up."[53] Clearly, Canadian gladly availed themselves of this new and personalized service.

During this period there were even more revolutionary innovations in communications in the offing. In 1876 Alexander Graham Bell introduced the world to accessible electronic communications with his transmission of the first telephone message from Paris, Ontario, to Brantford. In 1879 the first telephone in Kingston was installed to connect Rockwood Mental Asylum with the superintendent's residence. The Bell Telephone Corporation was incorporated in 1880, with headquarters in Montreal, and by the following year a telephone system was in operation in Kingston. As early as 1883 Kingstonians could make a five-minute telephone call to Toronto for 50 cents and to Hamilton for 75 cents.[54] The Kingston telephone directory for that year lists no fewer than 107 subscribers. The figure tripled to 360 by 1891, and quadrupled to 1,328 by 1911. Bell executives originally feared that telephones would not be rapidly adopted in Kingston, but they soon concluded that the market here "had done well."[55] Initially, it was the business sector that adopted the innovation enthusiastically: less than a quarter of the 107 phones in 1883 were in homes. Not until 1911 did domestic phones dominate the Kingston system, although many of these were in the homes of members of the business community. That the spread of telephones was impressive was noted by a visitor to Canada in 1910:

the telephone [in Canada] is literally used for everything constantly and continually. ... the first operation you have to perform in arriving in a Canadian town is to ring up your friends on the telephone and let them know where you are. To omit this is unpardonable neglect.[56]

For those who could not afford home phones, public phones were provided, and by 1906 Kingston had three public pay-phones – all located in grocery stores. The first to adopt the new technology were government institutions like the hospitals, the penitentiary, and the military. Even the tradition-bound Rideau Canal system recognized the merits of the telephone:

In the spring time when the freshets are at their height the roads are almost impassable and should leaks break out it is advisable that the Lockmasters should have the means of communicating at once with the Head Office and also of warning each other at their respective stations.[57]

And as before, business leaders and professionals were also early leaders in the trend. Queen's University, however, held out until 1902, probably because of the charming idiosyncrasy of Principal Grant, who somehow managed to go through his life without ever using a telephone. Grant aside, Kingstonians were by the commencement of the twentieth century part of the expanding continental telephone communication system.

If telephones facilitated both long- and short-distance communications, Kingstonians also benefited by the close of the nineteenth century from a facility that allowed better movement around the city. As early as 1877 Kingston entered the age of street-railways and mass-transit systems, when J.L. Morrison incorporated the Kingston Street Railway Company.[58] This horse-powered street-railway system commenced operation on 15 June, and in the first four months of its operation it transported an astounding 155,870 passengers. Kingston's population of only some 13,000 people, and its limited sprawl, meant that it was still essentially a

An efficient electric street-railway served Kingston in the 1890s. (QUA)

pedestrian city, a place in which everywhere was always accessible to everyone on foot. Even so, the single-line track running from Alfred Street, along Princess, King, Barrie, Union, and Livingston streets, to its terminus at Pembroke and King, was clearly in demand. The run took about one hour from end to end, with several forty-passenger cars operating at twelve-minute intervals.

On 27 May 1893 this original system was electrified, although the legislation allowed for it to be powered by "electricity, ammonia, compressed air or by such other motive power as may hereafter be agreed upon."[59] On the occasion of its inaugural run on 23 September 1893, the *British Whig* was unstinting in its praise of this most recent example of municipal progress:

Credit must be given Mr. Folger and Mr. Carson for the improvement of Princess St. It has been changed from a by Street in a country village to a street that would do credit to a thriving metropolis. This transformation, great as it was, was accomplished in three weeks.[60]

Of some import for future developments, the company extended its line beyond the city limits to its recreational property, Lake Ontario Park. Power was purchased from the Kingston, Light, Heat & Power Company and several extensions of the service were made in subsequent years.

In 1905, following disputes with the city over a request to allow double-tracking, the street-railway company was bought out by a group of local citizens and reincorporated as the Kingston, Portsmouth & Cataraqui Street Railway. From the outset, the new company experienced problems. First, there were constant disputes with the city over the cost of power, the city having acquired the Kingston Light, Heat & Power Company in 1909. Second, the advent of the automobile required the paving of Kingston's streets, and the re-laying of the tracks cost the KP & CSR some $25,000. Finally, a fire in the company's car-barns on 1 March 1930 destroyed much equipment, and Mr Nickle, the president of the KP & CSR offered the company's assets to the city for $65,000. Following assessments of the viability of the operation, the city acquired the company for $23,000, including the outlying Lake Ontario Park. The latter property, while outside city limits, was to become a valuable asset for the city in its sponsorship of port developments in Little Cataraqui Bay. Coincidentally, the purchase marked the end of the street-railway, and the city entered the age of the automobile.

KINGSTON'S SECOND INDUSTRIAL REVOLUTION

Between 1901 and 1921 Kingston's population increased some 26 per cent, marking a major growth period for the city. But this increase was not associated with any major innovations or structural change in the economic base. The onset of the First World War stimulated the economies of other cities, but it did little to attract new industry to Kingston. (The only real prospect was a film company, Canadian National Features Ltd., which planned to locate in Kingston, using the fair grounds as a studio lot.)

But if no new industries located in Kingston, the war did serve to stimulate the output of those already established there, some being modified for wartime purposes. Kingston Shipyards, a firm controlled from Collingwood and associated with Canada Steamship Lines, built vessels for use in the North Atlantic. The Canadian Locomotive Company, reorganized yet again on the retirement of Harty in 1911, increased its capacity with the construction of new facilities and the expansion of production at a cost of $140,000. By 1917, it had a labour force of 1,500 men and a weekly wage bill of $27,000. In October 1917, the *Daily British Whig* reported that "The company has been of incalculable service during the war, producing 18 lb. shrapnel shells and building engines for the British and Russian governments, all of which have given unqualified satisfaction."[61] Whereas at the commencement of the war, the Dominion Textile Company mills had been working to only 70 per cent of capacity, the new demand ensured full production and an annual expenditure by the company of $100,000 "most of which is left in the city with employees and merchants."[62] New construction was undertaken by A. Davies Company, while the Hosiery Mill was "running night and day."[63] Indeed, the chief complaint was that "employers of labour have been feeling the scarcity of help."[64]

Despite the rhetoric of the boosterism of the 1880s and after, Kingston had always been less than aggressive in its search for new industries. In fact, in 1915, city council proposed the abolition of bonusing and moved away from granting tax exemptions. The only major new incentive offered during this period was recently-acquired electrical power. As early as January 1915, the Board of Trade declared that electrical power was "absolutely necessary to the industrial life and activity of the City," and the Civic Utilities Commission was encouraged to arrange for its introduction to Kingston.[65] In December 1916, a contract was signed between the city and the Hydro Electric Power Company of Ontario for the supply of power to the city. The mayor's inaugural address of 1917 referred to the purchase of the Seymour Power Company's rights to water power in eastern Ontario and anticipated that "the city will be able to induce manufacturers to locate here. With cheap power, rail and water connections, well staffed schools, colleges and the University, I think we can claim that Kingston should receive consideration from the manufacturer who is looking for a location."[66] The *Daily British Whig* bruited abroad that "Kingston Has Many Fine Factory Sites" and announced that there were fifty acres of first-class locations "along the waterfront and close to one or other of the railway lines." The paper also noted that "the city grants exceptionally favorable terms in the way of tax exemptions to manufacturers who think of settling in the neighbourhood."[67] Such policies did attract some interest. In April 1918, letters of enquiry were received from prospective industrialists from as far away as Chicago and New York.

It was recognized, however, that newspaper advertising was not enough. The city had an "Industries Committee" serving as part of the Board of Trade, and interest was expressed in appointing a professional industrial commissioner to further the city's policy of attracting industry. No action was taken until 1928, when the city promised a contribution of $4,500 as soon as "a Chamber of Commerce is formed in Kingston with a membership of 300 persons who have actually paid a membership fee of $15.00 each."[68] The newly-organized Chamber of Commerce quickly appointed a full-time manager whose duties included overseeing the city's active program of industrial inducements. In 1920 the city had spent $30,000 for industrial lands, and the incentives advanced in the spring of that year included free sites and exemptions from taxation "to concerns of sufficient magnitude."[69] An example of what the term "sufficient magnitude" implied was the offer of a $1,000 bonus for five years to Kingston Factories Ltd., providing that they employ seventy-five employees, "exclusive of office staff," with a monthly pay-roll of $3,000.[70] Small bonuses were again being mooted, but it was specified this time that they be tied to commitments to improvements.

THIRD ANNUAL OPEN AIR DEMONSTRATION
OF THE

KU KLUX KLAN
NEAR KINGSTON
ON

SUNDAY, JULY 29
2.30 and 7.30 p.m. Standard Time

ALL WHITE GENTILE PROTESTANTS ARE CORDIALLY
INVITED TO BE PRESENT.
GOOD SPEAKERS — MUSIC,
LUNCHES, TEA, COFFEE AND COLD SOFT DRINKS
AND ICE CREAM ON THE GROUNDS

"FOLLOW THE ARROW"

The Ku Klux Klan was active in Kingston in the 1920s. (Kingston *Whig-Standard*)

Another frequent dimension of the new industrial policy was the selling of Kingston's "image." The charge that the community was "stagnant" was met by its positive description as a town with a "conservative" investment climate, and possessing a community that believed in "solid," "steady" growth and "reliable" industries, rather than in boom-to-bust growth cycles.[71] (Indeed, so "steady" was the Kingston economy that six hundred persons were unemployed in 1920, although "every effort is being made to meet the situation."[72]) The rail and water transport facilities were also prominently highlighted, as were the schools and colleges and the general health of the city.

Even the city's freedom from strikes was blazoned abroad. That had not always been the case, however. On the 28 June 1906 Italian navvies working on the Grand Trunk track went on strike to raise their daily wage from $1.25 to $2.00.[73] Three of "Kingston's finest" faced a crowd of 150 strikers, and a sergeant of police was stabbed while attempting to arrest the ringleaders. Eventually, with the arrival of two companies of detectives from Montreal and the dispatch of soldiers from the Kingston Battery, the strikers' encampment was surrounded, twenty-one men arrested and the others dispersed. The tenor of public opinion is reflected in the newspaper references to "dagoes," "macaroni men," and the "white man's triumph."[74] Such sentiments coloured many Kingstonians' view of their community, prompting boosters

KKK klaverns used traditional American paraphernalia to terrorize their enemies. Hence the ridiculous pantomime of hoods, insignia, and burning crosses. (AO)

to trumpet the claim – albeit a claim of questionable relevance – that "We never have any trouble with the labour unions, and our mechanics and laborers are all Anglo-Saxon"[75] For some, however, the community was not Anglo-Saxon enough, and in July 1927 an estimated 25,000 people from eastern Ontario and New York State attended an open-air demonstration by the Ku Klux Klan at Bracken's Grove, one mile west of Kingston. The gathering was dominated by five fiery crosses as twenty-five candidates were inducted into the Klan by members of the order in full regalia. Subsequent years were to see return visits to the district by the KKK.[76]

Not even a purportedly docile and ethnically-monolithic labour force could attract industry to Kingston. The number of firms increased from forty-two in 1901 to sixty-one in 1931, but the number of those employed in manufacturing dropped to 1,269 in the latter year, some twenty-eight fewer than there were even in 1871. Despite the failure of these various attempts to attract industrial growth, Kingston gave some of its best lands to those enterprises that did respond. Kingston's waterfront was dedicated to industry and railway tracks, from Mississauga Point to the Cataraqui River, and from there along the shores of the inner harbour.

Clearly, the city fathers of the day concurred with the old nineteenth-century maxim "Where there's muck there's money." Kingston had muck, but little enough of the money.

AFTERMATH

The period 1860-1940 was an era of economic experimentation for Kingston. "Something old, something new, something borrowed, something blue" could be said to have been the town's motto. The late nineteenth century saw Kingston experiencing considerable structural change as the traditional mercantile activities associated with the handling, movement, and processing of staple products was increasingly accompanied by new industrial enterprises. Like other Canadian towns of this period, Kingston believed that attracting industrial units, generating electrical and steam power, and producing smoke and grime were welcome portents of material progress and economic growth – and pursued them aggressively with all the fervour and optimism so characteristic of the age.

Nonetheless, for the next half-century, Kingston's growth was slow when measured in terms of numbers of people and numbers of economic units. While the base population of 14,091 in 1881 had increased to 19,263 by 1891, the ensuing decade saw an attrition of 1,302 persons, constituting a 6.8-per-cent decline by 1901. The next two decades saw some growth, with the population increasing to over 20,000 by 1911, and to over 24,000 by 1921. A minor drop in the 1920s was followed by an increase in the thirties to 30,126. Overall, therefore, between 1881 and 1941, Kingston's population had increased from 14,091 to 30,126, a growth of only 114 per cent. By contrast, all of the major urban centres in Kingston's immediate Canadian and American zone of interaction had experienced uninterrupted and colossal growth. Thus, Ottawa had increased from 27,412 to 154,951 (465 per cent); Hamilton from 35,961 to 166,337 (363 per cent); while Toronto had grown from 86,415 to 667,457 (672 per cent). Kingston's annual growth rate of less than 2 per cent paled in comparison with Ottawa's 8 per cent, Hamilton's 6 per cent, and Toronto's explosive 11 per cent.[77]

By comparison, therefore, Kingston's growth was at best moderate, and underscored its failure to participate fully in the structural changes and economic growth experienced by other urban centres. To a correspondent of the Toronto *Globe*, Kingston in 1881 was "a drowsy antiquated place, the relic of a past when everybody was not all the time on a jump, but took life easily, a land where it is always afternoon, and people would sooner sit on the wharf and fish than engage in the eternal chase after the dollar."[78]

Kingston from city hall, late nineteenth century. (QUA)

As may be expected, Kingstonians did not appreciate such a condescending and patronizing tone from their arch-rival, and the Kingston *Whig's* response to the calumny was predictably boosterish:

Without claiming for Kingston that it is "a model of business activity and enterprise" it can be successfully maintained that there is as large a proportion of business ability and enterprise in it as in any place of its population in the country. The inception of new enterprises and the extension of old ones prove this, and go to disprove the charge of inanity which is so falsely, flippantly and frequently preferred against us. [79]

While recognizing the ancient rhetoric of the long-standing regional rivalry between the "Queen of the West" and the "Limestone Metropolis," one must note that the two views do represent the fundamental attitudes to Kingston's position in the 1880s.

Kingston no longer occupied a place of prominence in Ontario's urban hierarchy, and indeed experienced a period of economic stagnation that was to last until the beginning of the Second World War. Kingston's old transshipment strategy had failed, and while some industry was induced to locate here, it was not sufficient to transform the mercantile town into an industrial metropolis. For those advocating continued investments in transshipment, Kingston was to become Canada's Buffalo; for industrial promoters, it was to become Pittsburgh; but for many, it continued as "Sleepy Hollow."

Looking east down Princess Street *c.* 1890. (QUA)

The waterfront, turn of the century. (QUA)

ELEVEN

Revitalizing the Port

AN ACTIVE WATERFRONT

Despite Kingston's frenetic if ineffective search for other functions, the traditional activities associated with shipping continued. The mid-nineteenth century had delivered two major blows to Kingston's port. First, the improvement of the St Lawrence and Erie canal routes to Montreal and New York respectively had eroded Kingston's transshipment activities in the grain trade. Second, the advent and continued improvement of rail transport decreased Kingston's water-borne traffic in passengers, packages, and freight.

Despite these setbacks, Kingston continued to prosecute the transshipment trade and the economics were simple. By the 1880s, the draught of lake carriers had increased beyond the 9-foot-8-inch depth of the St Lawrence canals. Consequently, the 365 miles of lake, river, and canal navigation between Port Colborne and Montreal could be effected by one of three strategies in the 1880s – each of which involved transshipment at Kingston.[1] First, a seven-day trip by steamers that "lightened" 3,000 to 4,000 bushels at Kingston to allow them to pass through the St Lawrence locks, at an overall cost of 10.5 cents per bushel. Second, by sail to Kingston where the grain was transshipped to St Lawrence barges; this strategy also cost 10.5 cents per bushel, but took fifteen days. Third, by steam barges that transshipped to river barges at Kingston, the trip taking ten days and costing 7.0 cents per bushel. In support of this enterprise, Kingston's three forwarding companies – Montreal Transportation Company, Kingston and Montreal Forwarding Company, and St Lawrence and Chicago Forwarding Company – employed eighty barges with a total carrying capacity of 1.473 million bushels.[2] Allowing eight days to Montreal and back, this meant that Kingston's carriers could handle five million bushels a month during the navigation season. Manned by "French Canadian bargemen of most economical habits," these barges were operated uninsured as the forwarders "find it pays better to lose a barge occasionally than to pay the insurance premium demanded."[3]

Accordingly, the port continued to be active. Indeed, in 1880, a record 1,108,830 tons of shipping cleared the port, and while traffic dropped to a low of 702,772 tons in 1885, it continued at a general level of 800,000 tons per annum to 1894, when a new record of 1,377,777 tons was set. Certainly, by 1900, Kingston had been eclipsed in terms of its total values of imports and exports by Toronto's $41.3-million-worth of trade and Hamilton's $7.7-million-worth; but with its own $1.6 million, Kingston still maintained significant waterfront activity.[4]

Thus, the business directory for 1900 could report an impressive list of port and shipping activities: six marine-insurance firms, four wharfingers (wharf operators), two dry-dock repair companies, three forwarders, three ship-builders, ten steamship agencies, one yacht-fittings manufacturer, and several ships' chandlers.[5] Finally, it is not insignificant that the influential Dominion Marine Association was founded at Kingston in 1903 and recognized the city as its headquarters for much of the twentieth century.

Throughout the late nineteenth century, ship-building also continued its contribution to Kingston's waterfront economy, if at a slackened pace in comparison with earlier decades. Some forty-nine vessels were completed in the 1880s and another twenty-four in the 1890s. The opening of the Kingston Dry Dock at Mississauga Point on Kingston's Outer Harbour promised to further stimulate both ship-repair and ship-construction. On 19 June 1890, Sir John A. Macdonald marked the accomplishment of this project by "laying the first stone" – a somewhat confusing piece of naval parlance that refers to the ceremony of laying in place the last element of the masonry, the stone that ships entering the drydock first encountered.[6] When completed, this facility became an important adjunct to Kingston's port activity.[7]

Another substantial shipping function at Kingston was closely related to the limited grain-storage facilities of the Canadian grain trade. This was the wintering of ships. Frequently, as many as fifty ships would be moored along Kingston's wharfs, often with cargoes of western grain in their holds, waiting for the spring break-up and the move down the St Lawrence. This seasonal but nonetheless profitable activity was estimated to result in an average expenditure of $5,000 per boat. No wonder Kingstonians considered this activity to be one the town's biggest assets: "We all, directly or indirectly reap some benefit from this desirable class of work, and we hope that next year the number will be greatly increased."[8]

The presence of these vessels served as a visible indicator of Kingston's continued participation in transshipment, despite the mixed fortunes of the past half-century. Certainly, the greater portion of North American wheat now moved east via American rail and water routes; but Kingston still participated in handling that portion that moved along the St Lawrence. There were several reasons for this. As late as 1900, 864 of the total of 2,788 arrivals at Kingston were sailing vessels that had difficulty negotiating the narrow St Lawrence channel. Also, even though steam had been displacing sail since the early nineteenth century, large steam vessels found

Kingston dry dock in use. (QUA)

the shoals, islands, and narrow channel difficult to negotiate, and transshipment to river boats continued. Finally, and of most importance, until 1905 the St Lawrence canals had not been improved beyond their initial nine-foot draught, which, given the increased size of lakers, still necessitated transshipment to smaller canallers. Accordingly, in 1882 James Richardson constructed a new 60,000-bushel-capacity grain elevator on the Princess Street wharf, and when this "Richardson No. One" burned down in 1897, it was replaced by a 250,000-bushel-capacity unit that was ready for operation by the following year.

In 1899 the Montreal Transportation Company negotiated a municipal tax exemption and constructed an 800,000-bushel-capacity grain elevator. With these facilities in place, Kingston was able to participate in the increased traffic generated by the wheat boom of the Laurier period, to the extent that it continued to capture some of that portion of the grain moving east along the Great Lakes-St Lawrence system. That the Board of Trade thought their port facilities should command an even larger share of this traffic is implicit in their complaint against developments upstream:

> We see no necessity for spending public money in building large storage elevators at Port Colborne or any other port on the Great Lakes as there is no question but that the transhipment of grain from lake steamer to river barge should be done at the foot of lake navigation, and elevator and storage facilities for this work are already provided at the ports of Kingston and Prescott, situated at the foot of lake navigation.[9]

Unfortunately for Kingston's business community, the spokesmen of the Board of Trade were more sanguine than the facilities at Kingston merited. As the new century progressed, the increased traffic and the increased size of the lake carriers underscored the long-standing deficiencies of Kingston's harbour. Exposed to westerly gales, it was penalized by a difficult approach and a shallow harbour. Also, it suffered from an excess of enthusiastic, if unregulated private enterprise. A maze of wharves, railroad yards, and mixed industrial development stretched across Kingston's lakefront. In response to these problems, some thoughtful people directed their attention back to the area of eighteenth-century waterfront activity, the Inner Harbour of the Cataraqui River. This extensive area of sheltered anchorage and undeveloped waterfront had, to all intents and purposes, been severed from Lake Ontario in 1828 by the construction of the Cataraqui Bridge, which allowed the passage of Rideau Canal traffic but effectively obstructed larger vessels.

A further impetus to Kingston's search for alternative locations for an improved harbour was the proposed upgrading of the Great Lakes-St Lawrence navigation system. In 1913 the Senate of the United States unanimously approved a motion by the senator from Michigan

> Requesting the President to enter into negotiations with Great Britain with the view to securing an international agreement for the concurrent or co-operative improvement of navigation in the boundary waters of the United States and Canada, for the advancement of the commerce of the two countries.[10]

While the subsequent plans for a thirty-foot-deep navigational channel from lakehead to ocean progressed slowly, the plans for a refurbished canal at Welland were better received. With a proposed 859-foot-long, 80-foot-wide, and 30-foot-deep canal at Welland, and the existing 1,350-foot-long, 80-foot-wide, and 24.5-foot-deep canal at the American Sault, the concept of a "Seaway" was much advanced. But the 14-foot-deep St Lawrence canals still presented an obstacle to such through-traffic.[11]

With larger boats moving into the lower lakes via the new Welland Canal, the competition for the transshipment role was revitalized. Kingston's claim to becoming the "Foot of the Lakes Terminal" became one of the grandest concepts yet advanced by the struggling municipality, and one that was to preoccupy Kingstonians for most of the first quarter of the century. Once again, all the complex political, economic, and technological factors that affect transport questions came into play – not to mention the more emotional arguments of urban boosterism and inter-urban rivalry.

KINGSTON AS TERMINUS OF THE GREAT LAKES

In February 1911 Kingston's acting mayor, R.F. Elliot, explained the case to the minister of Public Works:

the port of Kingston, on account of its position and importance in the lake trade, and on account of the greater demands that will undoubtedly be made upon it in connection with the transhipment of grain if the Welland Canal is enlarged, is entitled to just as much consideration and assistance as have been given by the Dominion Government to the other important harbours on the Lakes in the interests of the trade of the country.[12]

Specifically, both a sheltered harbour and rail accommodation could be provided in the estuary of the Great Cataraqui River, behind the old Cataraqui Bridge. Elliot concluded that "having regard to the importance of Kingston as the harbour at which transshipment from lake to river barges will naturally take place to the greatest extent, steps should be taken to give the best facilities possible there for accommodation of this trade."

Certainly, Kingston had been neglected to this point. Between 1906 and 1910, the Department of Public Works had spent millions on harbour improvement at some seventeen locations, and while Port Arthur ($421,688), Toronto ($356,045), and Midland ($270,824) received the largest allocations, Kingston had received a mere $5,710, the smallest allocation of all. The annual meeting of the Dominion Marine Association also pressed Kingston's case, arguing that it was "a national undertaking." Their petition further claimed that such improvements to accommodate boats of "Welland size" were justified "in view of the increasing importance of the port of Kingston as a transshipping point in the carriage of grain cargoes from the west, and as a port of call and a port of repair for package and bulk freighters trading up and down the Lakes and St Lawrence."[13]

The city's plans were quite specific: dredge the inner harbour to a depth of twenty-two feet; use the resulting sludge to connect Belle's Island with the mainland; and replace the old Cataraqui Bridge with a new one at Belle's Island. All this, it was argued, "is necessary and in the interests of the Marine Transportation of Canada."[14]

By March 1912, S.J. Chapleau, district engineer of the Department of Public

Aerial view of the Inner and Outer harbours. (George Innes)

Works, reported on his estimates for the Kingston improvements, having consulted with the Dominion Marine Association, the Department of Militia and Defence, and the Kingston Board of Trade. The plan was not quite the same as the original Kingston scheme, but it was equally comprehensive and grandiose: the old Cataraqui Bridge was to be replaced by a rolling lift-bridge that was integrated into a combined roadway-wharf area ($230,000); the inner harbour would be dredged to a depth of twenty-two feet ($157,000); and transshipment facilities (including piers, freight-sheds, railway sidings, and a grain elevator with a storage capacity of one million bushels) would be constructed on reclaimed land at the south end of Belle's Island ($1,224,690). Together with other miscellaneous expenses, the total cost of the project would amount to $1,759,000 – the Department of Public Works' justification being that "while the total of the proposed improvements is large, yet it must be remembered that it embodies a very complete and comprehensive scheme, which should take care of any volume of shipping and transshipping that may be expected for a good many years to come."[15] Also, if commenced immediately, the improvements would be in place for the opening of the enlarged Welland Canal and the anticipated increased traffic flows into the lower Great Lakes. Accordingly, it was recommended that work commence on the first stage, the construction of the wharf-road-bridge connection and the dredging of an approach channel, twenty-two feet deep and 330 feet wide.

On 11 May 1911 the Cataraqui Bridge Company conveyed title to its now-dilapidated structure to the city of Kingston for $24,850, and the city then transferred the title to the Department of Public Works on 8 June 1912. Dredging proceeded in the following year, and in 1915 tenders were called for the construction of the bridge. The expenditures prompted a question on the floor of the House of Commons in April of that year, and it was argued by the government that "Kingston is a transshipping point of grain brought down the Great Lakes and owing to the enlargement of the Welland Canal the facilities there now are inadequate and this work is necessary in view of the change in conditions."[16]

The combined wharf-road-bridge was completed in 1917 and opened for traffic as the "La Salle Causeway." This 950 feet of wharfage and 1,700 feet of new roadway – with two bridge spans, incorporating a bascule lift-span over a twenty-two-foot-deep channel – constituted the first stage in the overall plan for the much grander concept of a Great Lakes Terminus. It appeared that Kingston was well on the way to realizing its objective of establishing itself as the major point of transshipment at the lower-lake end of the Great Lakes grain trade. Indeed, the Mayor's inaugural address on 10 January 1915 had referred to the possibility of extending the city's boundaries to the east into Pittsburgh Township by acquiring Barriefield Common. It was argued that with the construction of the La Salle Causeway, this would provide "the necessary dockage which we at present greatly lack and which we will need later on, when the deepening of the Welland Canal is completed."[17]

The implementation of the construction of the actual terminal facilities – docks, freight-sheds, grain elevator, railway yards – waited further allocations of funds. By 1919 Kingston's Board of Trade had appointed a special committee on "Harbour Improvements," and on 24 February that committee recommended the appointment of an engineer to cooperate with the Ministry of Public Works in the planning of a "modern marine terminal."[18]

The plan was becoming more elaborate by the day. In a letter to the local MP, W.F. Nickle, J.M. Campbell reported that the plan for Kingston's "Deep Water Terminal" included "not only the tracks necessary for handling grain from the proposed elevators but also the necessary yard and track lay-out for a coal handling plant with the object of making this terminal the distributing centre for the country

Cataraqui Bridge (the "Penny Bridge") separated the Inner from the Outer Harbour when built in 1828. Replaced by the La Salle Causeway in 1917. (QUA)

north and east of the city."[19] Nickle served his constituency well and duly transmitted these plans to the minister of Public Works, urging the appointment of a DPW engineer to oversee the project. By April, S.J. Chapleau had been assigned to the "proposed harbour and railway development at Kingston" and was instructed to "prepare a general plan showing a reasonable initial scheme of development to meet present requirements, which will at the same time permit of future gradual developments on well defined lines, should conditions of trade and Railway and water transportation render increased accommodation necessary."[20]

On 1 May 1919 the city attempted to take the initiative and requested that the Department of Public Works adopt the recommendations of Kingston's own harbour improvement committee for an expanded version of the original 1911 plan: the deep-water terminal was to be in the Inner Harbour; the terminal facility would include elevators and storage bins to accommodate five million bushels initially, with future expansion for forty million bushels; the basin would allow for the wintering of vessels with a further storage capacity of ten million bushels; the elevators would be designed to load and unload directly into both vessels and rail cars, with track sufficient for fifty cars at one loading; the railway yards would accommodate five hundred cars with a planned future capacity for 2,500 cars. An insight into the city fathers' image of their future city is provided by their preferred sites for these activities. If the Belle's Island site proved impractical, then the CPR frontage along the Cataraqui River could be used, while the Montreal Transportation Company site and the historic Tête-du-Pont Barracks were two other possibilities.[21]

Quite properly, Public Works did not accede to this request, arguing that the appointed engineers should "exercise their own judgement and submit it to the Department."[22] This they did on 21 January 1920, Chapleau reporting on the plan he had developed in cooperation with the city's representative, the up-and-coming C.D. Howe, and in consultation with the engineers of the Canadian National, Grand Trunk, and Canadian Pacific railways. Incorporating the work already completed in 1916, the main basin was to be behind the La Salle Causeway, and an approach channel three hundred feet wide and twenty-five feet deep was to be dredged to connect with Lake Ontario. The inner basin was to consist of a fifty-three-acre harbour dredged to a depth of twenty-five feet to accommodate 15,000-ton lakers – with an additional four acres to be dredged to a depth of sixteen feet for St Lawrence vessels of 2,000 tons. A pier would be constructed on the west of the basin to house the grain elevator, which would have a work capacity of 400,000 bushels (that is, it could unload four hundred cars in ten hours, and unload one boatload of 500,000 bushels in ten hours) and a storage annex for 2,800,000 bushels. Freight-sheds six hundred feet long and sixty feet wide would be located on wharves constructed adjacent to the former Belle's Island. Railway facilities were to be provided, together with generous provision for future harbour extension. The total cost for the dredging ($660,000), docks and revetments ($344,000), grain elevator ($1,249,000), freight and package sheds ($60,000), and trackage ($107,900) was $2,420,900. Between 1920 and 1922, $11,583 was spent on dredging: the approach channel was deepened to twenty-two feet and the inner basin to sixteen feet for some 1,200 feet behind the Causeway. But little else was ever done.[23]

In March 1923 J.M. Campbell of Kingston requested that the plans be brought to a meeting with the prime minister called for 15 March. The deputy minister of Public Works, J.B. Hunter, replied that he would "have the plans of the proposed harbour improvements at Kingston got out, dusted off and laid before the Minister" – his turn of phrase ("dusted off") perhaps serving as an indication of recent interest in the matter.[24] Another letter from Campbell in May requested news

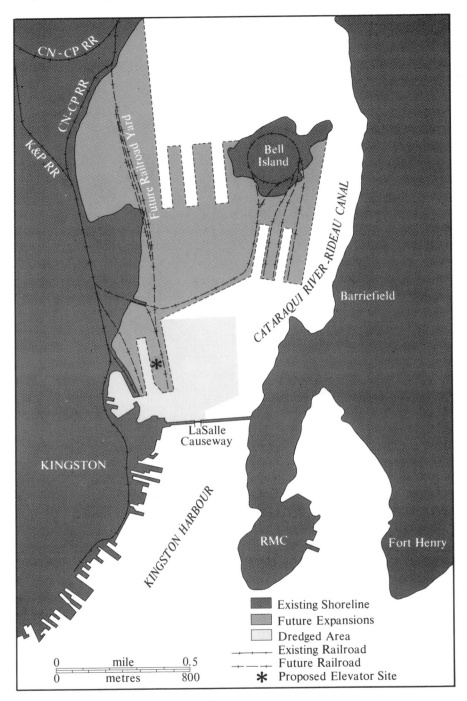

Proposed development of the Inner Harbour for Kingston as the foot-of-the-lakes shipping terminus.

of the Kingston scheme, adding "as we have another election coming on [it] may help us a little in that matter."[25]

Perhaps coincidentally, or perhaps because of such prompting, Public Works soon after contacted various interested parties, requesting their cooperation. Both the CNR and the CPR were queried on the impact of the opening of the Welland Canal on their respective operations. Noting that both Kingston and Prescott aspired to the position of "Foot-of-the-Lakes Terminal," the enquiry requested their "preference from the railway standpoint of the matter" since the "handling of grain from either Kingston or Prescott would not be economical if the necessity for supplementing the water service to a very great extent by rail handling was not provided for and to be depended upon. In this your company will be, I judge, very considerably interested."[26] The Dominion Marine Association was also requested to differentiate between the respective qualifications of Kingston and Prescott for terminal development:

It would naturally be supposed that the further down the cargoes could be taken without breaking bulk the more advantageous and economical it would be for shipment. The question resolves itself principally into a question of whether the factors claimed to exist in the St. Lawrence between Kingston and Prescott are so adverse as to militate against Prescott being considered as satisfactory a point for transshipment as Kingston.[27]

Of some significance to later developments, a letter requesting similar advice and cooperation was transmitted to the Department of Marine, an enquiry then redirected to the Department of Railways and Canals. A new actor was about to enter the scene.

The arguments advanced by the two principal contenders, Kingston and Prescott, were quite clear. Prescott's supporters argued that not only was Kingston an inferior port, one that required considerable expenditures to make it serviceable, but also that Prescott was some seventy miles closer to Montreal, "at the logical foot of the Great Lakes navigation, and that the expenditure required to bring the larger boats as far East as Prescott would be an inconsiderable amount as compared with that required at Kingston." Moreover, since Canada was "committed to the principle of a deep water route from the Great Lakes to the sea," the improvement of the Kingston-Prescott section would fit into the master plan for the Seaway.[28] Naturally, Kingston's strategy emphasized the support of the Dominion Marine Association, with its sixteen shipping companies, the excellent facilities promised by the Chapleau-Howe plan, and the strong ship-building and repair support facilities. The navigational problems of the St Lawrence River above Prescott were not overlooked, and it was reported that there had recently been seven sinkings and forty-one groundings in this narrow, foggy, and shoal-ridden channel.

But if Kingston's case was supported wholeheartedly by the Dominion Marine Association, that of Prescott was advocated by the Ogdensburg-based George Hall Company. Nine captains of Hall ships complied with their firm's promptings to write to Public Works to advance the superior attributes of Prescott, downplay the hazards of navigating the Kingston-Prescott stretch, and generally to denigrate Kingston's harbour. One of them, Captain J.E. Ouelette, attempted to move the issue from the realm of mere local rivalry and elevate it to a higher plane of patriotism. He charged Kingstonians with being "narrow minded, selfish and non-Canadian" and urged that the matter "is a national question and must be decided from a national point of view."[29]

The railroads' responses were less decisive. Indeed, the CPR thought that it "is largely a question for the ship owners to decide," arguing that "the railways will prefer to continue handling the bulk of the grain through the [Georgian] Bay ports, in order that the boats may be released more promptly for return movement to the Head of the Lakes."[30] The initial CNR opinion on the question was that "Prescott is the natural point," arguing further that this was sufficient reason to merit relocating their railway "terminal from Brockville to Prescott."[31] Another early response was that rail interests were generally opposed to both Kingston and Prescott, because the rail-haul would be too short, but that the CNR

should protect ourselves by the acquisition of sufficient land for terminal railway purposes. In this connection, I have had in mind, more particularly, the movement of grain for export during the winter season of navigation. This being so, Prescott would be a better place for us from a purely railway point of view as our road haulage would be less, and the water rates will, undoubtedly, be the same to both Kingston and Prescott. Therefore, the only other question to determine, as I can see it, is whether or not the terminal situation at Kingston will lend itself more advantageously to us, thereby offsetting the increased mileage vs. Prescott. Our rail rates from both Kingston and Prescott to, for instance, Portland will no doubt be the same.[32]

Predictably, the growing dispute spawned a committee to report back on the matter, with representatives from the various departments concerned with construction, freight, and economics. The first in-house report was noncommittal. It did, however, clarify the fundamental dimensions of any decision: in 1922, over 146 million bushels of grain were shipped from Montreal, which constituted 27.3 per cent of total American and Canadian shipments; actually, over 153 million bushels were received at Montreal, of which 74 million bushels arrived by rail and 79 million bushels by water. Of the 74 million bushels by rail, 36 million bushels were carried by the Canadian National, the balance by the Canadian Pacific. It was argued that for an all-water route – that is, from lakers to canallers – the 1922 Grain Elevator Committee report had found that either Kingston or Prescott would save a half-cent per bushel over Port Colborne. It was also argued, with some prescience, that since hydroelectric power and navigational considerations favoured the development of St Lawrence ship canals in the future, "Lake St. Francis, and for the Canadian National Railways, Coteau would be the end of Lake navigation and not Kingston or Prescott." However, in the interim, any choice between Kingston or Prescott for a water-to-rail terminus had to wait upon the resolution of several related questions: differentials in water-transport rates from lakehead to Kingston or Prescott; the canalization of the St Lawrence; and the proposed grade reduction and electrification of the Toronto-to-Montreal section of the Grand Trunk Railway line.[33]

But while these opinions were being developed and reported back to the Department of Public Works, there was increasing concern that Canadian ports would not be the main beneficiaries of Welland Canal improvements. More particularly, criticism was directed against the Department of Public Works's myopic focus on the Kingston-Prescott contest alone, with the momentum of past decisions apparently favouring Kingston. This concern was expressed most particularly by the Department of Railways and Canals, and its insistence on a more comprehensive analysis of the "terminal question" served to exacerbate relations between the two government departments.

In May 1926, Charles Dunning, minister of Railways and Canals, wrote to J.H. King, minister of Public Works, noting that

the approaching completion of the Welland Ship Canal will unsettle the present terminal and shipping arrangements in the lower lakes. ... After spending a hundred millions on this improved waterway we are naturally anxious to secure for Canadian ports and transportation interests as great a share as possible of the new movement which is in sight.[34]

His recommendation was that yet another committee be formed to study the terminal question – this time with representatives from Public Works, Railways and Canals, and the CNR. King's response was a polite rejection of the need for such a committee, noting that the situation was "well in hand." Moreover, his view on the matter was quite clear. Plans were already prepared for a major development scheme at Kingston, "of which a large part had already been built," and given the need for improvements of St Lawrence navigation in the international waters below Kingston, it was "impossible to consider Prescott as the lower terminal."[35]

Dunning's response quite as firmly reiterated the arguments of Railways and Canals for a study of the broader implications of the Welland Canal improvement "if Canada is to obtain the advantage." It would be regrettable, he argued, if the considerable expenditures were "merely to move the main transfer point for the grain traffic from Buffalo to Oswego," and since the distance from Kingston to Montreal is greater than that from Oswego to Albany, "Oswego is very much alive to the possibilities of the situation."[36] For Railways and Canals, it was imperative that the terminal question be considered in the context of continental-scale geography and economics. In considering the flows of grain to be anticipated, it was noted that the annual Canadian export of grain amounted to 300 million bushels, and that during the 1924-1926 navigational season it moved along the following routes: the all-water route to Montreal (38 per cent); the lake-and-rail route to Montreal (12 per cent); and the lake-and-rail route to American ports (50 per cent).

The dominance of Buffalo as the lower point of transshipment of grain was well established, and any Canadian port attempting to attract this trade would have to have facilities for winter storage in boats, and also be located closer to Atlantic ports. Even prior to the opening of the Welland, Buffalo was closer to New York than the Georgian Bay ports were to Montreal or Portland. With the Welland in operation, this advantage would move to other American ports further east, Oswego being ninety miles closer to New York, while the development of Albany on the Hudson would increase the American rail traffic even further. Implicit in this argument, therefore, was that the Welland improvements would have to be followed by St Lawrence improvements if Canada were to reap the full benefits. And that being the case, in considering interim lower-terminal arrangements, Railways and Canals favoured Prescott over Public Works's champion, Kingston.

The wrangle between the two ministries was resolved in September 1926 in a Privy Council order that basically accepted the telling arguments by the Department of Railways and Canals. A review committee was established along the lines recommended earlier and was instructed to report back to Railways and Canals on "the broad and general question as to the most advantageous site and most suitable development for the establishment of transshipping facilities to the end that Canada may obtain the advantage she has every reason to look forward to when the Welland Ship Canal work is finished."[37] By 15 October 1926, a committee had been struck; it consisted of S.J. Chapleau, representing Public Works, D.W. McLachlan for Railways and Canals, and R. Henry for the CNR. Interdepartmental conflict over areas of responsibility continued, however, and the original order in council was superceded by a later one of October 1926. Arguing that Public Works had the official federal mandate for construction and repair of Canadian harbours and piers, and for improving Canadian navigation, "it is deemed advisable to make the Department of Public Works, instead of the Department of Railways and Canals, the headquarters of the proposed board."[38]

Not surprisingly, little progress was made. As late as January 1927 Chapleau complained that there was much work to be done, but that he had been instructed by his department to do nothing, and that his "hands [were] tied as to proceeding further with the location of the terminal."[39] Much of that year found Chapleau listing for Cameron all the work yet to be done and complaining that "Cooperative progress along these lines is as you know at a standstill, as far as my connection with the Board is concerned."[40] Cameron passed this complaint on to his deputy minister:

KINGSTON THE TERMINAL
for Deep Water Navigation
through the New Welland Canal

S.S. GLENEAGLES		S.S. EDMONTON	
Length over all	596 feet	Length over all	250 feet
Breadth	60 "	Breadth	42.7 "
Depth	32 "	Depth	20.6 "
Carrying Capacity	12200 Tons	Carrying Capacity	2400 Tons

"THE LONG AND THE SHORT OF IT."

Kingston and the two systems of water transport, where lakers and canallers met. (NA)

"It is respectfully and strongly urged that a decision on the matter now under consideration as to the composition, duties etc. of the Board be clearly set out and the past uncertainties be eliminated."[41] That this view was shared by the deputy minister is evidenced by the pencilled comment "Minister, Please note the necessity of reaching some conclusion as to Board which is to make this investigation."

Clearly, a resolution of this impasse was urgently needed, and the outcome was a compromise: the Department of Public Works and the Department of Railways and Canals were to effect independent studies preparatory to a joint recommendation. A panel of Public Works engineers (consisting of Chapleau, Corriveau, and Coutlee) would consider the relative merits of Prescott and Kingston as terminal sites; Chapleau was also to produce an independent report on the need for channel improvements below Kingston as they related to the terminal question; for Railways and Canals, McLachlan and Henry would evaluate all possible sites for the proposed terminal. Neither side had budged an inch, and Kingston and Prescott – not to mention a whole array of less-probable contenders – awaited the outcome of the investigations.

THE LONG AND THE SHORT OF IT

It was in this atmosphere of interdepartmental conflict that the final decision was made. During the year of the board's delayed deliberations, newspapers commented on the possible outcome. In October 1926, the *Financial Post* reported that a prominent Buffalo "Shipping Man" – perhaps with the benefit of inside knowledge – considered the river route to Prescott too hazardous for big steamers and, despite improvements to Toronto's harbour, concluded that Kingston would be the principal beneficiary of the Welland improvements. He closed his case by arguing – with ominous prescience – that even "if the government doesn't provide dockage and elevator facilities there, the shippers themselves may be compelled to do so."[42] In January of the following year, however, the Ottawa *Citizen* championed Prescott as the terminal port because "After Canada has spent over a hundred million dollars on a new canal at Welland, it would be the blindest kind of parochialism to try to confine deep water navigation to Lake Ontario."[43] In April, the Toronto *Star* joined the fray, and after summarizing the essential arguments of the two main protagonists, Kingston and Prescott, as being the "long and the short of it," the *Star* concluded that "The decision whether elevators and transshipping facilities should be provided at one point or another, whatever it may be, should harmonize with the trend of the nation's navigation policies."[44] A month later, it announced that there was little doubt of the outcome in "well informed circles" and that "Almost certainly it will be Prescott and the chief reason is that it will shorten the rail haul to Montreal as well as to many Atlantic ports." The expenditures required for dredging the channel to Prescott constituted "the first step towards completing the greater St. Lawrence waterway."[45]

Towards the close of 1927, the three reports were ready for submission. Chapleau was the first to report, on 6 December 1927. Provided that the St Lawrence channel could be deepened to a depth of between twenty-five and thirty feet, he recommended Windmill Point, near Prescott, as the site of the terminal, at a cost of $4.9 million. The cost for developing Kingston's Inner Harbour site was prohibitive, at some $7.5 million.[46]

Next to report, on 21 December, was the McLachlan-Henry Board of Railways and Canals. Their "Report on Terminals for use with the Welland Ship Canal" considered

the most advantageous site and the most suitable development for the establishing of transhipping facilities below Lake Erie, so that the maximum advantage would be obtained by Canada, and Canadian transportation interests, of the improved transportation route which would be provided upon the completion of the Welland Ship canal.[47]

The report had taken several factors into account: the capital cost of the facilities; the reduction in transportation and winter storage costs; the reduction in navigational hazards; the costs of improving channels; the relative position of American and Canadian ports; the accessibility of ports to railway connections; bridge connections across the St Lawrence to American ports in winter; the accommodation for the winter storage of grain in boats. But the competition for the terminal facilities had been extended beyond the original choices of Kingston and Prescott. Cobourg, Port Hope, Deseronto, Bath, and Parrott Bay were all considered, and while some of these were favoured because of their suitability for harbour and elevator development, they were all rejected because of the extra distance of rail-haul required, or because of the extra distance of lake travel to which canallers would be subjected. The real choice lay between five locations: Collins Bay, Kingston, Sheriff Point (near Gananoque), Jones Creek, and Johnstown Bay (near Prescott). Two additional sites on Howe Island were also considered, but were rejected because of navigational or construction difficulties.

In considering these options, the report noted that the Collins Bay, Kingston, and Gananoque sites required no improvement of the St Lawrence channel, whereas the Jones Creek and Prescott sites were dependent upon significant expenditures before navigation by large steamers would be possible. Estimates were based upon the provision of similar facilities at all sites: a 1,200-foot-by-217-foot dock to accommodate two upper-lakes bulk freighters on one side, and four canal-size boats on the other; an elevator on the dock with a five-million-bushel capacity, allowing the unloading and loading at a rate of 75,000 bushels per hour; a 1.5-million-square-foot anchorage of twenty-three-foot draught to accommodate forty bulk freighters in winter; and connections with Canadian Pacific and Canadian National rail systems. The capital expenditures required at each of the five sites were estimated as follows:

	Terminal Works	Channel Works	Railway Works	Total Estimate
Collins Bay	$4,711,000	-	$1,395,000	$6,106,000
Kingston	$6,004,000	-	$1,582,000	$7,586,000
Gananoque	$5,224,000	$51,000	$1,282,000	$6,557,000
Jones Creek	$5,212,000	$2,314,000	$906,000	$8,432,000
Prescott	$5,378,000	$4,372,000	$316,000	$10,066,000

The committee's final report took the form of a double recommendation. If the St Lawrence channel improvements were to proceed without American cooperation, then Gananoque was recommended as the preferred site of the foot-of-the-lakes terminal. If, however, the United States were to agree to commence work on the channel in their waters east of Clayton, and were Canada to improve the Brockville Narrows, then Prescott was recommended as the transfer terminal. The committee was unambiguous in its conclusions that Collins Bay provided a site somewhat better than Kingston and, indeed, that "Kingston Harbour does not provide the best site for a transfer terminal under any conditions that can be foreseen."[48]

Finally, the last blow to Kingston's aspirations came on 3 January 1928, when the Corriveau-Chapleau-Coutlee board also entered a report favouring Prescott because of its excellent rail connections, its marine facilities "comparable to none outside of Kingston," and its proximity to Montreal. Moreover, noting the imminence of the St Lawrence Seaway, it was argued that Prescott terminal "would serve its purpose" in the anticipated fifteen-year interlude and that thereafter "it will continue as a valuable auxiliary."[49]

The official announcement of these committee findings on 6 June 1928 confirmed Prescott as the chosen site for the development of the terminus at the foot of the Great Lakes. An initial appropriation of $1.5 million was secured that year, tenders were awarded, and construction was commenced. After some two decades of rhetoric and intrigue, Prescott had won the competition between the "Long and the Short of It."

KINGSTON RESPONDS

Kingston had looked to 1928 with considerable optimism. The *Whig-Standard* cranked-up its boosterish campaign to new heights:

We are told by the best authorities that the next decade is to be Canada's. If Kingston does not share in this development to the greatest extent we will have no one to blame but ourselves. *Let us quit knocking and start boosting.* Let us forget the "five or six things wrong with Kingston" which some of us seem to delight to harp on, and talk about one hundred and one things that are right with Kingston. ... Our greatest trouble is that we do not make the most of our opportunities. Let everyone of us from the mayor-elect down to the humblest citizen endeavour to make 1928 a banner year for Kingston. Let us quit knocking and start boosting.[50]

Despite premonitions that Kingston's candidacy was being eclipsed by that of Prescott, the optimism had not waned three months later:

There seems to be no question but that Kingston is on the eve of greater prosperity than ever before enjoyed, and the Chamber of Commerce, properly organized and including everyone who has the city at heart, will be an essential part of the community. Kingston is riding on top of that prevailing wave of optimism which is sweeping Canada at the present time. If the Great Lakes Terminal is placed at Kingston, and there seems to be good reason for believing so, it will mean added prosperity.[51]

The announcement in favour of Prescott was a stunning blow to such aspirations. But as ever, Kingston's hopes died hard and the city had received strong support from influential allies. Thus, sharp on the heels of the announcement, the Department of Public Works received a communication from J.E. Ouelette, secretary of the Canadian Navigation Federation, reporting the resolution of a recent meeting of that organization to the effect that Kingston should be the terminal. Further: "If there were two elevators, one at Kingston and the other at Prescott, the Kingston Elevator would do all the business, or at least to its capacity because of the conditions which exist, and which will exist even under the new plans by the engineers."[52] Accordingly, Kingston's efforts switched from attracting government funds to attracting private financial support for their elevator complex.

On 8 March 1929, the *Whig-Standard* reported that W.H. Coverdale, president of Canada Steamship Lines, was prepared to back the scheme. Writing to Col. W.H. Craig, mayor of Kingston, Coverdale announced: "I am prepared to assume responsibility for the erection of a water transfer house, having a capacity of about 4,000,000 bushels of grain, at such time as the city of Kingston shall provide a suitable land site which should be served by an adequate water harbour for an operation of this character."[53] By "suitable" Coverdale meant a harbour outside of the Inner Harbour that he, too, rejected as being unsuitable. What was required was a harbour with a turning diameter of 1,200 feet, a 400-foot-wide approach, and a minimum depth of twenty-five feet. He warned, however, that these facilities "would be barely adequate for the largest size of Upper Lake bulk cargo carriers, and therefore, in my judgement, such boats will not avail of them, but will continue to serve Georgian Bay ports and other points west of the new Welland Canal."[54] Coverdale should have known. His Canada Steamship fleet included the *Lemoyne, Ashcroft, Gleneagles,* and *Stadacona,* all of which were over 600 feet in length, the giant *Lemoyne* being 633 feet long, 70 feet in beam, with a draught of some 32 feet.[55]

Noting that the enlarged Welland Canal was scheduled for completion by midsummer 1930, the city of Kingston and its harbour committee commenced their search for the appropriate site. The mayor felt sure that "the taxpayers of the city will support us in anything we find it necessary to do in order to acquire the necessary site."[56] C.D. Howe was commissioned to report on this matter and – busy as he was on the Prescott elevator – by 20 May 1929 he had examined five possible sites and rejected four of them. The Tête-du-Pont Barracks site would have to be purchased from the federal government at a cost of $350,000; the Kingston Yacht Club was available for appropriation, but it too was expensive at $250,000 for the waterfront, not to mention other costs for needed additional lands; the waterfront occupied by the Montreal Transportation Company until 1920 was not suitable for the anticipated use by upper lakers; and, despite earlier enthusiasms, the much-touted Inner Harbour was now rejected because of the cost of replacing the La Salle Causeway, which by this time had become a much-used traffic artery.[57] The site favoured by Howe was the Little Cataraqui Bay because

the location combines economy of protection and dredging, adequate space for navigation, adequate trackage possibilities, and anchorage for both shallow draught and deep draught boats, to an extent that we have been unable to find at any other site. The property required is owned by the Provincial Government and can be acquired at reasonable cost.[58]

All that was required at this site was a breakwater, some dredging, the acquisition of land, and a rail connection. The city fathers continued to dream of grand projects and were encouraged in this by the appearance of yet another possible development on the site.

In May 1929, Canadian Terminal System Ltd. offered to construct an elevator "with a minimum capacity of 2 million bushels to be completed in time to handle the 1930 crop providing of course that the necessary harbour facilities can be arranged for."[59] With this offer prompting them, the city fathers could argue to the Department of Public Works that the Little Cataraqui harbour "would be a public harbour capable of taking care of several developments rather than a private harbour for one development."[60] The city was encouraged by the announcement on 4 June of an initial allocation of $50,000 towards the anticipated total expenses of $320,000 for the improvement of the Little Cataraqui Bay harbour.[61] With Coverdale investing in the elevator and federal and provincial funding assisting harbour improvement, municipal support was sought for the provision of land to accommodate the proposed elevators and the CNR spur-line serving them. The cost of the spur-line from the CNR track to the elevator ($80,000) was put to the electorate on 2 December 1929.

The Kingston Chamber of Commerce pulled out all its rhetorical stops and urged the support of this project in a series of advertisements in the *Whig-Standard*:

When the hopes and ambitions of Kingstonians were depressed by the decision not to make Kingston the Great Lakes Terminal the real spirit, courage and determination of her people was asserted in no uncertain way. ... The Mayor and his colleagues among civic leaders welcomed the challenge. They tackled the job and won for Kingston. Pile drivers are hammering home the evidence out in Kingston's new deep water Harbor. A mammoth dredge and sand sucker is vomiting up the material from the bottom of the Harbor. People living along the new railroad right of way have sold or are considering proposals for sale of the needed property.[62]

With a total anticipated expenditure of $6 million, the $80,000 expense was advanced as a small issue, and the electorate was encouraged to be "unanimous now as we were when we decided to turn defeat into victory."[63] For Mayor Craig,

The elevator is the greatest thing that Kingston has succeeded in bringing here. ... It is the realization of an old dream in the old Board of Trade which was talked about for years and years. ... We will be establishing a big industrial area surrounding a deep water harbor and with railway facilities, all owned by the city, and future developments are most promising.[64]

By-law 45 was voted in by a sweeping majority on 2 December, and Kingston now had the resources to acquire land for railway connection and water lots 13, 14, and 15 in the First Concession of Kingston Township.

Other land that was needed was not forthcoming. The Little Cataraqui Bay site was located outside of the city boundaries, and the proposed development depended on acquisition of title to lands held by the Crown or private occupiers. Of particular importance was Lake Ontario Park – owned by the Kingston, Portsmouth, and Cataraqui Electric Railway Company – and lands held by the Cataraqui Golf and Country Club. On 18 August 1930, city council authorized the purchase of Lake Ontario Park for $17,000 and the submission of a by-law to raise $50,000 to purchase seventeen acres from the Cataraqui Golf and Country Club.[65] Four acres of this land was to be for the Canadian Terminal System elevator, the balance to be held for future elevator expansions and other industrial development. By-law 35 was carried easily on 1 December 1930, the voters clearly persuaded by the argument that without the acquisition of these properties "we will be unable to annex the land to the city and it will remain in the township and the township will collect all the taxes."[66] Annexation had to wait another two decades to be realized, but by the close of 1930, nothing stood in the way of the commercial-industrial development of Little Cataraqui Bay.

While the Canadian Terminal System elevator was never constructed, the Canada Steamship elevator was completed, on schedule, on 15 September 1930. The new facilities were equipped for a 2.5-million-bushel capacity, with an unloading

Coverdale elevator at Elevator Bay. (The authors)

capacity of 35,000 bushels per day, a 600-foot dock on the west side to accommodate two canallers, and a 700-foot dock on the east side for upper lakers. Ten days later, on 25 September, the Canadian Steamship Lines freighter *Kindersley* delivered the first cargo of 80,697 bushels of grain. Six days later, on 13 October 1920, the Paterson Steamship *Sarniadoc* delivered the first shipload of grain to the Prescott elevator. Ironically, because the Welland Canal was still not open, it was not until the fall of 1932 that the first upper laker entered the lower lakes. In that year, the *Lemoyne* carried a Richardson cargo of wheat, in a Coverdale bottom, to the new facility at Kingston that, in effect, became the eastern terminus for the Canada Steamship Lines' fleet, which carried almost 50 per cent of Canada's waterborne traffic in grain. No wonder that C.D. Howe predicted a rosy future for the Kingston elevator:

In my opinion the present lake carrier will always be the cheapest method of transportation for grain in the unrestricted channels of the Great Lakes, and that present types of river carriers or barges [are] the cheapest types in the restricted channels of the St. Lawrence river. This is being demonstrated by the grain elevators now in operation in Kingston and Prescott. In the first full season of operation for the two elevators,

Kingston has enjoyed an excellent transfer business, while no upper lake boat has ventured as far as Prescott. I believe Kingston will continue to be a transfer point for upper lake carriers after the St. Lawrence development is complete.[67]

From its opening in 1930 until 1955, the CSL elevator at Kingston consistently surpassed its larger rival at Prescott in its handling of grain. The prospects for Kingston's revitalized transshipment function looked bright:

From the time that the flotilla of Count Frontenac, the French governor of Canada, entered the harbor at the point where lake Ontario meets the River St. Lawrence and the Great Cataraqui river, on the 12th of July 1673, Kingston has become a commercial port. It was chiefly because of its geographical position that the French built a fort here. It was by the river route the United Empire Loyalists came to this place, and it was on the Point Frederick shore of old Cataraqui that British warships were built in 1812-1814. From Kingston ships sailed in the early days with grain and other produce to New York state ports on Lake Ontario. Then the Rideau Canal added to Kingston's harbor traffic. All through the years Kingston was the foot of the lakes port from which grain was transshipped to Montreal. It was the location of various elevators, and now the Welland Canal enables the big upper lake ships to reach the foot of lake Ontario. Because of its valuable harbor facilities and because of its large drydock, it is the wintering place of more vessels than any other lake port gathers. Its marine traffic promises to be once again a most important factor in the development of Kingston.[68]

BY-PASSED AGAIN

But despite such early assurances of its success, Kingston did not become a favoured competitor for either the Georgian Bay ports or Prescott, let alone for Buffalo. And some knew this was to be. While Coverdale invested capital in this project, the Richardson company closed its forwarding operation at Kingston after a century of activity and moved to Winnipeg. The commencement of the family's grain-trade activities in Kingston in the 1850s had been a response to the town's inherent locational advantages at that time, situated as it was athwart the east-west movement of goods. The company's departure was a signal that those advantages were no longer operational, and with the subsequent opening of the St Lawrence Seaway and its accommodation of through-traffic from Lakehead to seaboard, the company's decision to leave Kingston was vindicated.

Shifts in the technology of shipping and canalization always influenced Kingston's fortunes as a point of transshipment. Any increases in the size of the carriers on the lakes beyond the capacity of the locks below Kingston favoured transshipment there. Any increases in the capacity of the locks at Welland and the Sault also favoured Kingston, by allowing larger vessels to penetrate the lower lakes. With the completion of the St Lawrence Seaway, Kingston's old commercial shipping function collapsed entirely. Initially, local opinion refused to accept the inevitable, and as late as 1955 the *Whig-Standard*, as boosterish as ever, advanced "many good reasons" why government should undertake the regeneration of Kingston's waterfront:

Kingston has excellent repair facilities, and excellent shipbuilding potentialities. It also stands at the very head of the St. Lawrence, and has been a natural trans-shipping point ever since Kingston became a city. It is true that the construction of the new canals [i.e. the St. Lawrence Seaway] will mean that lake boats now denied access to the sea and seaports will be able to go through. But the fact is that not many of the lake boats really want to get through. It would be much better for them to operate on the lakes as before, where they can operate more economically. ... [I]t is obvious that Kingston is soon going to generate enough tonnage to merit a good harbour.[69]

But this was not to be, and Kingston's port function was not at all revitalized by the opening of the St Lawrence Seaway. The statistics are telling:

	Kingston	Hamilton	Toronto
	Port Revenues: Kingston, Hamilton and Toronto[70]		
1940	$334,198	$16,376,893	$58,975,187
1950	$803,293	$46,893,679	$165,694,701
1960	$1,169,260	$82,306,157	$457,282,867

Simply put, Kingston's harbour function certainly increased by a factor of three over the period; but that of Hamilton grew some fivefold, while that of Toronto increased eightfold. Moreover, it was now quite clear that in terms of relative scale, Kingston's mere million dollars of port revenue was miniscule in comparison with the figures returned by Toronto and Hamilton. The figures on the collapse of tonnage are equally dramatic. By 1966, 762,598 tons of shipping entered Kingston harbour, 467,700 in 1970, and a mere 408,169 in 1976, in comparison, say, to Hamilton's thirteen million tons.

The days of shipping along the wharves of downtown Kingston were over. The ultimate impact of these developments was put nicely in a remark attributed to Clifford Curtis, a Queen's economist and mayor of Kingston during the 1950s. When asked about the potential impact of the St Lawrence Seaway on Kingston, he replied that the Seaway would permit much larger ships to by-pass the city than did already.[71]

Thirty years later, the collapse of Kingston's shipping was complete. The year 1987 marked the closure of several of Kingston's remaining shipping enterprises: the McAllister Towing and Salvage operation was the last relic of the old Outer Harbour, while the closure of both the Coverdale elevator and the Richardson dock signalled the demise of the last vestiges of Kingston's commercial shipping activities at Little Cataraqui – or Elevator Bay, as it had come to be known locally. On Saturday, 17 October 1987, the last vessel to use the facility – a 700-foot laker, the *Algo-Soo* – unloaded 11,000 tonnes of road salt there. The event did not go unnoticed and the *Whig-Standard* recorded the "End of an era."[72] Donald Chown, Kingston's harbourmaster, recognized that "One could get cloyingly sentimental about the fact that we're not a commercial port anymore," but went on to evaluate realistically the implications of the closure, commenting astutely

the definition of commercial, I think, is very much open to question. As far as bringing business into the city, I think that the number of pleasure boats ... we have come in here in the summer time probably drop more dollars in Kingston than a whole lot of bulk carriers would.[73]

Kingston did retain some docks in service: the Crawford dock at the foot of Brock Street; the La Salle Causeway; the old Canada Steam Ship Lines dock at the foot of Queen Street; the Imperial Oil dock in Anglin Bay. But the closure of the Richardson dock and the departure of the *Algo-Soo* symbolized the termination of Kingston's role as a port and of the conversion of the former commercial docking facilities to other land-uses.

PART THREE

DEFINITION

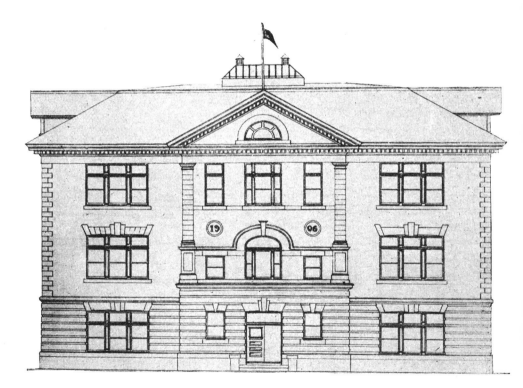

A medical building on Queen's lower campus; now Kathleen Ryan Hall, housing Queen's University Archives. (QUA)

TWELVE

An Institutional Town

THE AGE OF DEFINITION

Attempts to make Kingston a major manufacturing centre were unsuccessful. By the end of the century the city no longer occupied a place of importance in Ontario's urban hierarchy. Its old transshipment strategy had failed, and no new strategy had been found as a substitute. Some industry came, but not much in relative terms. As Marvin McInnis notes "at no time did Kingston have a significant industrial base." He comments further that the "leading concern in the history of Kingston in the later nineteenth century has to be its slow development relative to other urban centres in Canada."[1]

This view follows logically from a historical perspective that emphasizes economic development in particular and growth in general. But the history of Kingston's decline, which in some respects is a history of what the city did *not* become, does not explain the uniqueness of the city that *did* evolve from its nineteenth-century origins. The Kingston that emerged in the early twentieth century was not simply a second- or third-rate centre. It developed characteristics that make it unique among other Ontario and Canadian towns. These aspects of Kingston's development occurred simultaneously with the town's rise to economic primacy and then its decline to minor status. In fact, it might well be argued that they are much more important than economic development. After all, if Kingston's trading or industrial strategies had met with success, the town would have become a typical North American commercial and business centre. This did not happen, and Kingston became a unique community. Twentieth-century Kingston is a legacy of the second half of the nineteenth century, which might well be regarded as the town's age of definition.

The key to Kingston's uniqueness is its role as what Arthur Lower termed a "sub-capital."[2] The nature of the "sub-capital" function must be emphasized. All towns and cities possess important institutions that service local needs. These are operations like schools, health facilities, local jails, police departments, and municipal governments. "Sub-capital" functions are qualitatively different in that they transcend local needs and serve regional, provincial, or even national requirements in particular spheres of activity. Kingston acquired this status in a surprising variety of spheres, and this development took place, to a substantial extent, in ways that were at the time largely imperceptible to the citizens of the town.

Thus, early in its history, Kingston became an important centre for three of the major religions of nineteenth-century Ontario: Presbyterianism, Roman Catholicism, and Anglicanism. This is not to suggest that other religions were absent from Kingston. Certainly Methodists were active in Kingston and adjacent districts from the late eighteenth century and, according to the census of 1851, accounted for 10 per cent of the city's population. Baptists and Congregationalists were also present in nineteenth-century Kingston.

By the mid-nineteenth century, Kingston's place as an ecclesiastical sub-capital had been confirmed. Queen's and its leadership provided a focus for "Old Kirk" Presbyterians. The college provided intellectual and spiritual vitality for Canadian Presbyterians through its distinguished staff and large number of graduate clergymen. Roman Catholicism and Anglicanism of course evolved differently, in part because these faiths are episcopal in governance.

Furthermore, while Kingston lost its formal role as capital, it maintained its provincial and national influence by the active participation of several of its citizens as influential political figures. That they were not indifferent to the needs of their town is marked by the presence of institutions such as penitentiaries, the psychiatric hospital, and the Royal Military College. Certainly, it will be seen that there were rational geographic and economic locational factors operating in favour of such decisions; the fact that Kingston has always had active and influential political figures available to express its case forcefully has usually been more important.

ROMAN CATHOLICISM AND KINGSTON

The Roman Catholic Church was neither large nor prominent during the period of Loyalist settlement. Early Upper Canada's Catholics were primarily Highland Scots who were concentrated in the far-eastern part of the province, especially in Glengarry County. There were few Catholics in Kingston during the first years. Initially they conducted services at St George's Church. In 1808 St Joseph's, known as the "French Church" because of the language of many of its communicants, was built on the corner of Bagot and William streets. St Joseph's served the needs of Kingston's Catholics for a generation. With the major migrations of the mid-nineteenth century, however, there was a major infusion of Irish Catholics, and by 1851 they amounted to some 32 per cent of Kingston's population. Their spiritual needs were of increasing concern to the Canadian Roman Catholic establishment.

The spiritual leader of Upper Canada's Roman Catholic community was the Right Reverend Alexander Macdonell, a patriarchal and warlike Highlander who started his career as chaplain to the Glengarry Fencibles, a Catholic and Highland

Alexander Macdonell was appointed bishop of Regiopolis in 1826. Kingston was his diocesan seat, but he did not move there till 1834. Macdonell sat on the Upper Canadian Legislative Council 1831–1840. (QUA)

regiment in the British Army.[3] When the regiment disbanded in 1802, Macdonell worked to obtain land for his soldiers. He was successful, and led a substantial colony of Highlanders to eastern Ontario in 1804. Alexander Macdonell was the undisputed leader of Upper Canadian Catholicism after his arrival. He was able to obtain many advantages for his flock because of his high standing with the Family Compact that dominated the province until Upper Canada was fused with Lower Canada in 1841 to form the Province of Canada. Compact leaders admired Macdonell's uncompromising Toryism, anti-Americanism, and unabashed militarism. The War of 1812-1814 confirmed his standing with the Compact. His people, organized as the Glengarry Light Infantry, were quick to volunteer for service against the American enemy. Macdonell himself served as chaplain to his new regiment.

When Alexander Macdonell arrived in Canada, Pierre Denaut was bishop of Quebec. He was succeeded in 1806 by Joseph-Octave Plessis, a major figure in the history of French-Canadian Catholicism. These men faced a task that was all but insurmountable. They were, by virtue of their positions, national leaders of the French Canadians. At the same time their ecclesiastical burdens were impossible because their see included all of British North America. It is easy to understand why Plessis was anxious to divide his diocese – but division would be no simple task. The United Kingdom was still anti-Catholic in attitude and policy. The establishment of new North American bishoprics and the appointment of bishops required the approval of both Imperial authorities and the papacy. Delicate and possibly protracted negotiations would be required before Plessis's policy could be executed. These problems of diplomacy were exacerbated by the complexities of Napoleonic Europe. British attentions were hardly likely to focus on the problems of Roman Catholic ecclesiastical organization in British North America.

Nonetheless, Plessis proceeded. Shortly after his enthronement in 1806, he told Macdonell of his intentions. The first step would be the appointment of Macdonell as vicar-general of Upper Canada. That appointment came through in 1807, and Macdonell assumed responsibility for Catholic affairs in Upper Canada. In 1816 Macdonell was charged with the task of obtaining British approval for the division of the Diocese of Quebec. He succeeded: the diocese was split in 1817. In 1820 a further step was taken when Macdonell was appointed a vicar apostolic and made a suffragan to Plessis, with the title Bishop of Rhesina *in partibus infidelium*. In effect, Macdonell was bishop of Upper Canada, but he remained subordinate to Bishop Plessis.

As the 1820s progressed it became increasingly important to both colonial administrators and the church that Macdonell's position be regularized and strengthened. The concern was the influx of Irish Catholics, who were viewed as a yeasty group whose loyalty was questionable. Strong clerical leadership, provided by loyal and conservative priests led by Macdonell, would conduce to stability and social harmony. Finally, in 1826, he was made a bishop in ordinary, with the title Bishop of Regiopolis, a charming name meaning "Royal City" that – in a flight of philological fancy – amalgamated words from both Latin and Greek. Colonial officials were more than anxious to cooperate with the powerful prelate. Lieutenant-Governor Colborne wanted to extend formal recognition to Macdonell by appointing him to the Legislative Council. He argued that "Bishop Macdonell, lately nominated by the Pope, Bishop of Regiopolis, I am inclined to think, should be admitted to the Legislative Council. He has great influence in the Eastern part of this Province, and both he and his flock would be pleased with the compliment paid to him."[4] The bishop took his seat on the Council in 1831.

Macdonell's home had been with his people in Glengarry. That was convenient and sensible in 1804. It made no sense by the mid-1820s, when Catholics were dispersed throughout the province. Glengarry was insufficiently central; Kingston was selected as the diocesan seat for the Upper Canadian see, but Macdonell was reluctant to establish his permanent residence there. Political and ecclesiastical concerns kept him in Toronto much of the time, and he had major commitments throughout the province. In 1834, when he was seventy-two, he did move to Kingston. Kingston thus acquired a leader who, along with the Anglican John Strachan and the Methodist Egerton Ryerson, dominated the religious life of Upper Canada.

Alexander Macdonell was responsible for all of Upper Canada. As Ontario's Catholic population grew throughout the nineteenth century, his vast diocese was further divided into sees. However, Kingston remained an important diocese and was led by a number of men who were central figures in nineteenth-century Canadian Catholicism. Macdonell's more important successors were Rémigius Gaulin, Patrick Phelan, Edward John Horan, John O'Brien, and C.H. Gauthier (who served as archbishop from 1898 to 1910).

A diocese requires a cathedral. Macdonell turned his attention to that need but died in 1840 before work began. St Mary's was built by Bishop Gaulin, Macdonell's coadjutor and successor. The church was consecrated in October 1848. St Mary's, located on Johnson Street at Clergy, is a magnificent Gothic church that remains one of the distinctive features of Kingston's skyline. A massive structure, St Mary's is 210 feet long and eighty-eight feet wide, and is constructed out of limestone that was quarried on the site. In the late 1880s major additions were made, including a new front on Johnson Street and a grand tower of 200 feet. At the back of St Mary's is the Chapel of St James the Greater (Boanerges). It was added when Kingston was made an archdiocese.[5] Immediately west of the cathedral is a large and ornate house that was built as a bishop's residence in 1848. Macdonell himself lived in the first bishop's house on Johnson at Bagot. It was built about 1812 and owned by Macdonell as early as 1813. He left his house to the Sisters of Notre-Dame, who used it as an educational facility for girls. It is now integrated into the Kingston Public Library and preserved in part as a museum.

An institution of higher education for the Roman Catholics of this region was another brainchild of Macdonell's. From his earliest days in Upper Canada, Alexander Macdonell "stormed governmental portals for aid to establish Catholic schools. ..." He shared with Presbyterians, Methodists, Baptists, and others a very

The Hotel Dieu Hospital is the legacy of the Religious Hospitallers of St Joseph, who arrived in Kingston in 1847. Photo *c* 1912. (QUA)

strong opposition to the legally entrenched privileges of Anglicans, and especially to the "establishment of an exclusive Church of England university."[6] Of course, Macdonell wanted facilities within the province for the training of priests. It was this that led him to found a Roman Catholic seminary called "the College of Regiopolis."

His first task was to obtain an Act incorporating his seminary. This he did in 1836. He took advantage of his friendship with Sir Francis Bond Head and of the Tory sweep in the election of that year. Anthony Manahan, another friend and one of the members for Hastings, introduced the bill, which passed easily. Macdonell then donated some of his land at the site of the present Hotel Dieu Hospital for the original Regiopolis. He was able to scrape together enough money to commence construction, and laid the cornerstone in June 1839. The position of the college was very weak, however, because Macdonell had been unable to procure adequate funding for the institution within Canada. To remedy this, he left for Britain to raise money shortly after the cornerstone ceremony. Funds were not forthcoming, and the effort ended when the bishop died in Scotland on 14 January 1840.

Work on Regiopolis did proceed. The building, now the centre wing of the old part of today's Hotel Dieu Hospital, was completed, and it functioned as an arts college and seminary until 1869: "The general course of study ... embraced classics, mathematics, philosophy, and theology. The theological course extended over three years."[7] Regiopolis was revived in 1899 when the college's directors purchased the building (now the Empire Life Insurance Company) that had been the Commercial Bank of the Midland District. It was operated there as a boys' high school until 1914.[8]

Regiopolis College is now a coeducational high school that uses the name "Regiopolis-Notre Dame"; it continues to be a vital cultural centre for the Roman Catholic community of eastern Ontario. Regiolopolis-Notre Dame High School, together with the soaring spire of St Mary's, attest to the continued vigour of Catholicism in Kingston and mark the success of Macdonell's efforts to ensure it.

AN ANGLICAN DIOCESE

Anglicanism was for long the premier religion of Kingston. John Stuart, the founding rector, was the town's first clergyman. The first St George's Church was built in 1792 on the site of the present *Whig-Standard* building. In the beginning, Stuart was the only Anglican clergyman in the province, and is rightly regarded as the founder of Anglicanism in Ontario.

The fact that Kingston lost its role as the leader of Ontario's Anglicans is related to personality. John Stuart was a powerful figure within both Anglicanism and Kingston society. When he died in 1811 he was succeeded by his eldest son, George Okill Stuart, who was rector of Kingston until his death in 1862. He had been rector of York for a decade, but preferred Kingston, which was, after all, the centre of the faith in 1811. George Okill Stuart was succeeded at York by John Strachan.[9] These two men were in office during Upper Canada's considerable population expansion after the War of 1812-1814.

There was really no contest between John Strachan and George Okill Stuart. Strachan was doctrinaire, domineering, politically astute, and dedicated to the welfare of his church. He was also an educator who had trained a number of the leading members of the Family Compact. Stuart, on the other hand, was weak as a spiritual leader and far from dedicated to the work of the church. His interest was in developing the extensive properties his father had accumulated. As a real-estate operator he was an important man, but he had no interest in providing leadership to Ontario's Anglicans. Instead, he "made Kingston a bastion against expansion. In other words, the natural development centre was quiescent."[10] By the end of the War of 1812-1814, John Strachan was the recognized leader of Anglicanism in Ontario. He was also a major political force and one of the pivotal figures in the Family

Compact. Strachan's leadership was recognized in 1839, when he **was** made bishop of Toronto. His diocese included all of Ontario; George Okill Stuart remained archdeacon.

The Diocese of Toronto was too large for a single bishop. Strachan wanted division, and was able to create two new dioceses. Huron was established for the western portion of the province; Ontario was created for the area east of Belleville and north to the Ottawa River. This was an immense charge, and, in spite of old towns like Picton, Kingston, Brockville, and Prescott, it was very much a mission diocese. It was also a poor diocese, especially when compared with Huron and Toronto. Poverty impeded the collection of funds needed for the establishment of a new see, and it was not until 1861 that the clergy and laity of eastern Ontario met in Kingston to elect their first bishop. They chose John Travers Lewis, a young Irishman who was thirty-seven years old and who had been rector of St Peter's Church in Brockville. Though strongly opposed by St George's, Lewis was the overwhelmingly choice of the diocese.

Kingston was fortunate that Lewis made the initial decision to make Kingston his episcopal seat. The conflict between the bishop and his local vestry never abated. From 1870 until the late 1880s Lewis actually lived in Ottawa, which was perhaps a more logical centre for eastern Ontario Anglicanism. Save for the initial decision to make Kingston the diocesan seat, Lewis would almost certainly have located permanently in the national capital. He finally returned to Kingston, which became the centre of a diocese that grew rapidly, regardless of the hostility of St George's. When Lewis was elected in 1861, forty-one parishes cast votes. By the end of the century the Diocese of Ontario possessed 283 congregations. Lewis's leadership within Canadian Anglicanism was acknowledged in 1893 when he was made metropolitan of Canada. In 1894, he became archbishop. Lewis was still active as a senior Anglican figure when he died in 1901. John Travers Lewis restored to Kingston some of the importance and prestige within Canadian Anglicanism that the city had merited under the first Stuart. But he received little support or encouragement from a home congregation that had displayed an inability to influence the diocese in 1861 when it strove to block his election.

The Diocese of Ontario did not require a new cathedral; it had St George's. The original church had been replaced in 1825.That relatively simple, rectangular structure is the core of the architectural gem that evolved during the remainder of the century. In 1846 the nave was extended and the King Street portico added. Joseph Power, a local architect, added the dome in 1891. He also modified the Johnson Street portico. On New Year's morning, 1899, St George's suffered a disastrous fire. The interior was gutted; only the limestone walls remained. Power, who was intimately familiar with the structure, was able to recreate the church. By 1901, it had been rebuilt and completely refurbished.

St George's was influenced by two famous Anglican cathedrals: Holy Trinity in Quebec City and St Paul's in London, England. Built by a number of men over

St George's Church (later the Anglican Cathedral) as it appeared *c*. 1845. Artist unknown. (QUA)

St George's interior after the disastrous fire on New Year's Morning 1899. Rebuilt by 1901. (QUA)

a seventy-five-year period, the structure never lost its architectural integrity, and it has been claimed that "Each addition is so well proportioned that the Cathedral as we know it today, could well have been the result of a single design conceived at one time."[11] St George's is one of Canada's finest pre-Gothic churches and ranks as one of North America's most beautiful Christopher Wren-like structures. In some major respects, Kingston did little for the young Diocese of Ontario, but in St George's it supplied a superb cathedral that stands out even in a city of beautiful buildings.

FROM PRESBYTERIAN COLLEGE TO NATIONAL UNIVERSITY

An interesting bond exists between Kingston and higher education, which has produced yet another "sub-capital" function. Kingston is the site of several institutions of learning that have made a substantial impact on the character of the city. Primary among them is Queen's University, which was established during the 1840s by Kingston's burgeoning community of Scots Presbyterians. William Morris and John A. Macdonald were among the prominent Scots leaders who founded the university. [12]

"Queen's College at Kingston," as it was originally styled in its royal charter, began its crisis-ridden history when it opened its doors with fifteen students, a principal, and one professor on 7 March 1842. Its first home was a little house on Colborne Street that, with appropriate heritage designation, still stands. Queen's was a Scottish institution in most respects. It was a denominational college of the Presbyterian Church in Canada, in affiliation with the Church of Scotland. It retained that loyalty during the upheavals that were shortly to disrupt Presbyterianism both in Scotland and in Canada. The school was designed on the Scottish model. Its early principals were Scottish-trained Presbyterian clergymen; the faculty was recruited in Scotland. The college's primary purpose related to religion: it gave Canadian students an adequate background in arts to pursue theological training, and then provided that theological training.

Queen's was weak and halt at the beginning, and long after, but its mission was always grand. Ministers were to be produced not for Frontenac County, nor for eastern Ontario, nor even for all of Ontario. The field of service was to include the whole of British North America. During the college's early years, debate over the scope of Queen's mission was interminable, and there were regular suggestions that its activities – or, perhaps more accurately, its ambitions – suffer drastic curtailment. On more than one occasion the college came close to closing its doors for good. But the survivors won out, and they were the men who saw Queen's as having a great role in the nation. This became the single most important characteristic of the university – then and now. Queen's has maintained its national outlook and its assumption that its mission is national in scope.

The early years at Queen's have been well characterized by the official historian of the university, Hilda Neatby: "Queen's first decade had been one of experiments in survival. The second was marked by an expansion and an optimism which reflected the new prosperity and confidence in the province at large." [13] Perhaps the most significant event during these early years was the purchase of Summerhill in 1853 for £6,000. This gave Queen's its first permanent building and fixed its site at the location it has occupied, with endless expansion, ever since. Formerly the elegant home that Archdeacon George Okill Stuart built on family lands to the west of the town limits, Summerhill remains the major showpiece of the university; its east wing is the official residence of the principal. The cost of Summerhill was an enormous

This modest building on Colborne Street housed the first Queen's University in 1842. (QUA)

burden for the young and weak institution. It was paid for with the proceeds of a national fund-raising drive. This kind of activity has become another diagnostic mark of Queen's. National fund-raising activity has been built into the institution, and has provided the funds that have enabled Queen's to pursue her national mission.

Early relations between Queen's and Kingston were cordial. In many respects an offshoot of St Andrew's Presbyterian Church, the college was viewed not as something hostile to Kingston but as part of the community. Students and faculty were at some pains to integrate themselves into local society. Sunday schools, temperance societies, and churches in the area received valuable assistance from the undergraduates. Professors were quick to extend their services to the local citizenry. Extension work was an early feature of the college. Public lectures were also given: George Lawson, the college's leading scientist, lectured on "The Application of Chemistry to the Useful Arts of Life" as early as 1859-1860.[14]

William Snodgrass, the most important of the college's early leaders, was principal from 1864 to 1877. He did much to foster good town-gown relations, and understood the strength of the emerging bond. When Snodgrass launched the fundraising campaign of 1868-1869, he

displayed his shrewdness and common sense. He would begin immediately with an appeal to the City of Kingston to maintain its own university. Having made his home there now for four years, he knew not only the college staff and the circle of substantial citizens of St. Andrew's Church, but the town as a whole, and he confidently asked, not the church, but Kingston to set an example of generosity.[15]

By the time the books were closed, Kingstonians had responded generously and contributed some $15,000 to Principal Snodgrass's appeal. The early growth of the college in no way impaired this good rapport. Hilda Neatby makes this point in her discussion of the 1870s: "as the college grew the private relations between students and the people of Kingston grew ever closer and more cordial."[16]

This cordiality was a dramatic part of the development of Queen's during the long principalship of George Monro Grant, from 1877 to 1902. Principal Grant occupies a large place in the history of both Queen's and the nation. He ranks with such Kingstonians as Sir John A. Macdonald and Sir Richard Cartwright as a towering figure in late-nineteenth-century Canada. Grant is perceived, and correctly so, as a leading intellectual and moral leader. He is known as the principal who drove the roots of Queen's so firmly into the soil of Canada that the existence of the university as a vital and national institution was never again in doubt.

Grant accomplished these tasks with the impressive cooperation of the citizens of Kingston. This cooperation was displayed physically and permanently. Contributions from the town were responsible for the erection of the arts building (known now as the Old Arts Building or Theological Hall) in 1879. A local business leader, John Carruthers, provided over half of the money for a science building, which was named Carruthers Hall. In 1900 the city obtained approval from Kingstonians for a $50,000 gift to Queen's. The result was Kingston Hall, which now serves most of the needs of the French and foreign-language departments. According to the plans of Grant and his colleagues, Kingston Hall was to be twinned with a "Frontenac Hall." Unfortunately, the citizens of the country vetoed the proposed appropriation because of irritation with Grant's refusal to accept Prohibition. The building, with its fine auditorium for musical presentations, was built anyway, and paid for by students and friends of the university. Appropriately named Grant Hall, it stands today as one of the landmarks on the Queen's campus.

By the early years of the twentieth century, Queen's was an established university with a national reputation. Although small in student numbers, its strengths in arts and science, medicine, and theology were impressive. Its students, both men

Queen's students were a welcome if occasionally rambunctious element in Kingston's urban life. (QUA)

and women, were loyal to the university and had already established the famous transcontinental network of Queen's alumni that has been an abiding source of strength to the school. Leading faculty members like John Watson, W.L. Goodwin, Adam Shortt, James Cappon, and S.W. Dyde enjoyed national and international reputations. Physically, the university was still small, bounded by University Avenue, Union Street, Arch Street, and by Stuart Street to the south. Summerhill, the Old Arts Building, the Old Medical Building, Kingston Hall, and Grant Hall – all built of limestone – were there then and still dominate the southern part of the campus.

Town-gown relations were good, and Kingston was becoming known across the nation as the city of Queen's University. But there was occasional friction. In November 1913 Queen's 12-7 defeat of McGill in football was the occasion of a veritable street riot. The editor of the *Daily Standard* protested on behalf of Kingstonians:

But there is a limit to all things – a point when endurance and toleration cease to be virtues. That limit was reached Saturday night when a gang of student hoodlums or, if you please, hoodlum students, took possession of the principal business street of the city, terrorized many of the citizens, interfered seriously with business, and finally wound up a disgraceful night by proceeding wantonly and deliberately to destroy property. ... [The citizens of Kingston] and not the students of Queen's are the people who have made this city; they, and not the students of Queen's, are the people who have money and property interests at stake here; they, and not the students of Queen's, pay the taxes which go to support the police force of the city whose duty it is to preserve peace and order and protect property. ... When in short the people are terrorized and the students turn blackguards and ruffians, then it is surely time to call a halt and put an end to this defiance of the law. [17]

A broken arm, a bonfire on Clergy Street, a woman "frightened into unconsciousness," a stoning of the Grand Theatre, over $1,000 of lost trade – all served to fuel the ire of the citizenry. [18]

A week later, fearing that the students intended to "raise a riot or disturbance of the peace, which the civil authorities would be unable to cope with," and because "the merchants of the City of Kingston were frightened to open their places of business unless protection was assured," the mayor appealed to the commanding officer of the 3rd Division to "call out the Troops in aid of the Civil Power." [19] The threat was taken seriously, and the military stood by:

A detail of 40 Mounted Men armed with swords, and 40 Dismounted Men with rifles from the Duty Battery were ordered to hold themselves in readiness to turn out at a moments notice. Ammunition was drawn but not distributed. [20]

Despite these preparations, or perhaps because of them, the "anticipated riot did not occur and the City of Kingston was orderly and quiet as usual on Saturday night." [21]

Such disruptions were, fortunately, as sporadic as they were distasteful. They would continue throughout the ensuing century as an unfortunate accompaniment to the more welcome intellectual, social, and economic contributions of the university to the Kingston community.

PRISONS

Perhaps Kingston's best known "sub-capital" function is as a major prison centre: for generations of Toronto hoods, "going down east" has been synonymous with incarceration in Kingston Penitentiary or one of the other penal institutions that came to dot the area in the twentieth century. [22]

Early scenes at Kingston Penitentiary. (*Canadian Illustrated News,* NA)

The provincial penitentiary was a product of the early nineteenth century. Penal institutions that could reform criminals were in the air. There was little doubt that the Canadas would acquire such institutions. The nature and location of a central prison for Upper Canada, and after that for the Union, was quite another matter. Hugh Christopher Thomson and Kingston's Tory élite were responsible both for the institution's nature and for its location.

Hugh Thomson was born in Kingston in 1791. Of Loyalist stock, he was a member of a distinguished family that in the twentieth century was to produce Lord Thomson of Fleet.[23] He was a successful entrepreneur who became a leading influence in Kingston after the War of 1812-1814. In September 1819 he launched the *Upper Canada Herald*, which for a time had the largest circulation and influence of any journal published in the province. Thomson, although essentially a Tory, was an independent thinker with a substantial interest in social reform. He entered politics in 1824 as the member for Frontenac, and held his seat until his death ten years later. Thomson began to agitate for a provincial prison in 1826. The Assembly listened to him, and he was appointed chairman of a select committee "on the expediency of erecting a Penitentiary."[24]

The committee of three also included Christopher Hagerman, another Kingstonian. The report, published in 1831, argued for an institution that could

be a place which by every means not cruel and not affecting the health of the offender shall be rendered so irksome and so terrible that during his after life he may dread nothing so much as a repetition of the punishment, and, if possible, that he should prefer death to such a contingency. This can all be done by hard labour and privations and not only without expense to the province, but possibly bringing it a revenue.

Thomson concluded his report with a strong pitch on behalf of his town:

The town of Kingston and its vicinity present numerous advantages. It is well protected by an effective Garrison and extensive fortifications – the situation is healthy, and land can be purchased at a moderate price. In addition to these recommendations, the materials for building are abundant, and of the most substantial kind, and the inexhaustible Quarries of stone, which exist in every direction within the township of Kingston, will afford convicts that description of employment which has been found by actual experiment to [be] the most useful in Institutions such as your committee recommend.

Thomson's report was well received. He suggested that, if the Assembly decided not to proceed immediately, it appoint "commissioners to collect information ... and ... procure plans and estimates of the expense of the contemplated buildings."[25] The house acted on that suggestion. Two commissioners, with a budget of £100, were appointed "for the purpose of obtaining Plans and Estimates of a Penitentiary to be erected in this Province."[26] This time Thomson was joined by John Macaulay, a Tory insider and a fellow-Kingstonian. They visited prisons in the United States and collected what data they could on North American penitentiaries. Their report was completed in 1832. Thomson and Macaulay, for reasons of pragmatism and economy, recommended strongly in favour of the "Auburn System" of prison design and management, which they described with some care:

Absolute solitude during the night; joint labour during the day, but without any communication with each other by word or sign; meals taken at the same table, but so disposed as not to see the faces of those opposite to them; religious instruction on Sundays received in a body; and a Sunday School in the same manner, twice a day; both in Church and School the same prohibition of intercourse; a full diet of meat, bread and vegetables; comfortable bedding, in very narrow, but well aired, well warmed cells, and the utmost attention to cleanliness in every department of the prison. Visitors are admitted, but without permission to speak to the convicts, who on their discharge receive a sum not exceeding three dollars, without any relation to their earnings. Their work is uninterrupted during the day, except by their meals, and is generally contracted for by mechanics, who find the materials. This enumeration is not one of what is merely required, but of what is actually done. And the strictness with which these rules have been enforced is such, that it is asserted, that among thirty or forty working together for years in the same shop, no two of them know each other's names. Nothing (it is well said) can be more imposing than the view of a prison conducted on these principles.[27]

The recommendations of Thomson and Macaulay were accepted by the House, which voted £12,500 to get the provincial penitentiary into operation. Following the quasi-congressional system that characterized pre-responsible-government administration in Canada, the Assembly appointed three commissioners to supervise the work. The fact that all three were Kingstonians – Hugh Thomson, John Macaulay, and Henry Smith Sr – made it abundantly clear that Kingston had won and was to be the site of the new facility.

The commissioners, with Thomson taking the lead, worked quickly. In June 1832 they purchased a hundred acres at Hatter's Bay (Portsmouth), west of Kingston, for £1,000, and hired William Powers from Auburn, New York, to supervise the construction of the approved design. Political commissioners could not, of course, run the institution once it became operational. Its governance was determined by a provincial statute that was the brainchild of the omnipresent Hugh Christopher Thomson, who would have left the Legislative Assembly and been appointed first warden but for his premature death from consumption on 23 April 1834.

The remaining commissioners retained an intimate relationship with the penitentiary. Smith became the first warden; Macaulay served as president of the board of inspectors that assumed supervisory authority in 1835. Known as "KP" to generations of Kingstonians, the institution received its first prisoners – six of them – in June 1835. Physically, it was still a very limited facility: the object was to cut costs by having convicts complete the construction of their temporary home. Labour was part of both punishment and therapy. The convicts were supposed to make the prison pay, and in the process acquire a skill that could provide them with employment after release. Their labour was even to be sold to the private sector – a policy that raised fears of competition among the artisan community of Kingston.[28] In the years after 1835 the imposing edifice, designed by the local architect William Coverdale, gradually took shape. It still stands, between King Street West and the waterfront, across the little harbour that served as headquarters for the 1976 Sailing Olympics.

If institutional success is measured in growth, "KP" was very successful indeed, as the following end-of-year population figures indicate[29]:

1835	55	1840	153	1845	478
1836	81	1841	151	1846	480
1837	123	1842	164	1847	468
1838	154	1843	256	1848	454
1839	148	1844	384		

The vast majority of these convicts were men, but the penitentiary also held women prisoners who were kept in segregated quarters.

The role and nature of prisons remains controversial. Endless debates go on concerning the most efficacious manner of rehabilitating criminals. The founders of

Kingston Penitentiary did not favour twentieth-century approaches to confinement and rehabilitation, and we would have been very surprised if they did. They did, however, represent the state of the art of the second third of the nineteenth century, as is indicated in the description by Charles Dickens, who visited Kingston in 1842:

There is an admirable jail here, well and wisely governed, and excellently regulated, in every respect. The men were employed as shoemakers, ropemakers, blacksmiths, tailors, carpenters, and stonecutters; and in building a new prison, which was pretty far advanced towards completion. The female prisoners were occupied in needlework.[30]

Nonetheless, conditions in an early Canadian prison strike the twentieth-century reader as harsh and exotic. This is clear from the initial "RULES and REGULATIONS made by the Inspectors," which spell out the implications of the Auburn system: convicts, it is stated,

must not exchange looks, wink, laugh, nod, or gesticulate to each other, nor shall they make use of any signs, except such as are necessary to explain their wants to the waiters. They must approach their Keepers in the most respectful manner, and be brief in their communications. They are not to speak to, or address, their Keepers on any subject but such as relates to their work, duty, or wants.[31]

Harsh regulations required harsh discipline, which was normally corporal: "flogging with the cat-o'nine tails," "irons," "solitary confinement," "bread and water, instead of the regular rations," and "shutting up in a box." Such punishments were administered routinely: "the number of punishments rose from seven hundred and seventy in 1843, to two thousand one hundred and two in 1845, and from three thousand four hundred and forty-five in 1846, to six thousand and sixty-three in the year following; the same number of men being subject to discipline in the two latter years."[32]

Floggings were administered in front of the whole prison population, a situation that a committee of enquiry of 1848-1849 found intolerable:

To see crowds of full grown men, day after day, and year after year, stripped and lashed in the presence of four or five hundred persons, because they whispered to their neighbour, or lifted their eyes to the face of a passerby, or laughed at some passing occurrence, must have obliterated from the minds of the unhappy men all perception of moral guilt, and thoroughly brutalized their feelings.[33]

The regulations prohibited the flogging of women, but such sensibilities did not apply to male children. Peter Charboneau, who was incarcerated at Kingston when he was only ten, "was stripped to the shirt, and publicly lashed 37 times in eight and a half months."[34] Another child, Louis Beauché, "was flogged within three days of his arrival, and got 39 punishments with the lash in the first eleven months of his imprisonment."[35]

It should also be noted that the operations of the penitentiary were well-known to the larger community in Kingston and beyond. The public was welcome to visit the prison, provided the proper admission fees were paid ("Male adults... 1s. 3d. each [...] Females and children ... 7 ½d. each").[36] Public access appears to have been largely unrestricted, as is indicated by one of the recommendations of the 1848-1849 committee of enquiry: "The indiscriminate admission of visitors, for the purpose of indulging a prurient curiosity, we consider fraught with such evil, that we recommend its discontinuance."[37] Operators of boat tours of the Thousand Islands were known to take their customers through Kingston Penitentiary as part of their introduction to the area. Some of these tours came from as far away as Toronto.

The Provincial Penitentiary at Portsmouth became a large institution that has expanded into a network of penal institutions in the Kingston district. The prison has not received much attention from historians, and we know far too little about its nature, or about its influence on Kingston. But for all the years after 1835 it has been a brooding presence on the waterfront to the west of the old city. It is inconceivable that its harshness, brutality, physical violence, and endless repression failed to exert a profound influence on its thousands of convicts, hundreds of keepers, and endless numbers of family members of both convicts and keepers. That the prison fed substantial amounts of money into the local economy, and provided large numbers of jobs for Kingstonians, is obvious. What is less measurable, although perhaps more important, is the way in which this powerful and repressive institution moulded the "mind-set" of the nineteenth-century town.

THE ASYLUM

The penitentiary's presence generated a companion institution that has since developed into a second very large facility located in Portsmouth. Nineteenth-century prison authorities were not slow to detect the need for the classification and segregation of convicts. However, early prisons had precious little of either, and regular criminals and the insane were mixed together. Attempts were made to correct this situation within a generation of the founding of Kingston Penitentiary.

John Solomon Cartwright's magnificent country villa, Rockwood, occupied a prime waterfront setting to the west of the penitentiary. After Cartwright's death in 1845, his widow and her family left Rockwood for quarters in the town. For a brief period the house was rented by Dr J.P. Litchfield, who used it as a home for "well-to-do gentlemen of unsound mind."[38] Cartwright's estate sold the property to the government for £5,000 in 1856, so that it could be converted into a provincial asylum.

A complex of buildings grew up around Rockwood. Some were converted outbuildings; others were new structures built by the "guests" at the adjacent institution, the penitentiary. The first inmates were removed to Rockwood from the prison.

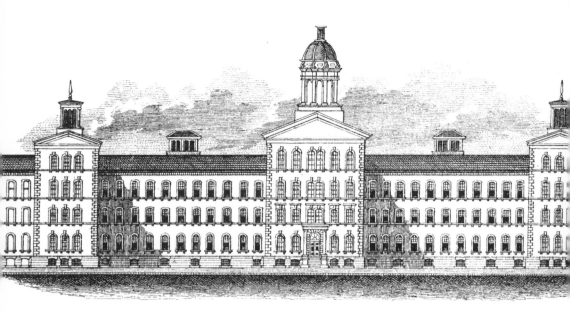

Precursor of the Kingston Psychiatric Hospital. (QUA)

A close association between prison and asylum was maintained until 1877, when the asylum was transferred from federal to provincial jurisdiction, and when medical rather than penal functions became its first concern.

The asylum, now the Kingston Psychiatric Hospital, also has long been part of the Kingston scene. Apart from its important medical role, it provides substantial amounts of employment for Kingstonians, and generates much income for the town. It, too, is one of Kingston's defining institutions.

THE PRESS, POLITICS, AND POLITICIANS

Great cathedrals, universities, prisons, asylums, and the military have done much to set Kingston apart from other Canadian towns. So have politics. During the initial period of settlement, Kingston was a major provincial centre. Toronto, as capital, was the centre of Family Compact strength, but Kingston held her place as a politically-powerful city throughout the nineteenth century and beyond.

Kingston's long-term political influence is a product of the combination of circumstances and personnel. Her early preeminence brought to the town men of wealth and talent. Many, like the Cartwrights, remained after metropolitan status eluded the city. The town's location was such that even in decline Kingston remained a regional centre and not just a county town. Sub-capital functions brought prestige, influence, and talent to Kingston. Anglican bishops do not seem to have been particularly active in politics, but Catholic leaders like Bishop Horan were extremely influential and their writ ran throughout eastern Ontario.[39]

Intellectually, Kingston has always been a lively place. H.P. Gundy notes: "Looking back, we see that in the early part of the last century, Kingston led the whole of Upper Canada. The first stable independent r wspaper, the first volumes of verse, the first novel, the first magazines were all pu shed in Kingston."[40] The town had to relinquish this pride of place to Toronto during the 1830s, but during the next generation she acquired two universities and, for a time, a Catholic seminary.

Kingston also maintained a lively and increasingly mature press. A number of very talented editors ran a series of justly famous newspapers. Stephen Miles began the tradition when he founded the Kingston *Gazette* in 1810. John Macaulay and J.A. Pringle turned the *Gazette* into the *Chronicle* in 1819, and later renamed it the *Chronicle and Gazette*. In the same year, Hugh C. Thomson began to publish the *Upper Canada Herald*, which was the best paper in Upper Canada until William Lyon Mackenzie launched the *Colonial Advocate* in 1824. Numerous other papers flourished on occasion. For a while after 1828 Thomas Dalton published *The Patriot*. Ogle R. Gowan's *Statesman* was transferred from Brockville to Kingston in the late 1830s and early 1840s. The *Argus*, a singularly nasty and eccentric tabloid, appeared from time to time after 1846. These early journalistic ventures faced unique marketing problems: "Those of our Subscribers who have been in the habit of sending Wood in payment of their subscriptions, will we hope, take advantage of the present state of the roads to keep us supplied."[41]

And, of course, at the very centre of Kingston's journalistic tradition is the English medical doctor Edward John Barker. A "cosmopolitan of cultural taste," Dr Barker was "a man who had a questing interest in human affairs, whether public or foreign. ..."[42] After serving as editor of the *Spectator*, he founded the *British Whig* in 1834. Barker was a very competent journalist. He was dedicated to his town and wrote well. Reporting in the *Whig* was good, and the attitudes represented by the paper appealed to the town. The paper's Toryism was moderate and flexible, like that of John A. Macdonald. The *Whig* became the dominant newspaper in Kingston.

During the nineteenth century, Kingston was usually a Tory town. That does not mean that its politics were either straightforward or unexciting. There was substantial division along economic and ethnic lines, but conflict was normally contained within the Conservative Party, which tended to be factionalized. Before the Union, Anglican Loyalists predominated. The Scottish middle class had become powerful by the mid-1840s. Communal tensions became acute during the 1850s, when Irish Catholics, who were a third of the population and normally voted *en bloc*, actively sought increased aid for separate schools, middle-class status, recognition in public life, and a fair share of patronage. They were confronted by a powerful local and provincial Orange Order that was well led and had become accepted as a part of Canadian life. Kingston, known as "the Derry of Canada," ranked with Toronto as one of the two major Orange centres in Ontario.[43] Even a politician as conciliatory towards Catholics as John A. Macdonald felt it prudent to be an Orangeman.

As Upper Canada came to the end of its constitutional career, Kingston was represented by Christopher Alexander Hagerman, the son of a United Empire Loyalist and a powerful local Tory. By the time Hagerman left politics for the bench in 1840, he was a veteran politician with a couple of decades experience in public life. Christopher Hagerman represented Kingston interests, but he was also very close to the Toronto-centered Family Compact. He has been described as "one of the pillars of the " 'Family compact,'"[44] and by 1840 was probably the most important Tory in the province. Hagerman's successor in the Kingston seat was Anthony Manahan, who became the town's first Union member in 1841. Manahan, a good-enough Tory, was both Irish and Roman Catholic – an unlikely combination in an elected Upper Canadian politician in the 1840s. Manahan had already served as a member for one of the Hastings ridings, and was the Assembly spokesman for Bishop Macdonell. His career as Kingston's spokesman lasted for only a few months. As noted earlier, he resigned his seat later in 1841 to make way for S.B. Harrison, Sydenham's principal minister, who had failed to secure election elsewhere. Harrison's political career was pretty well finished by 1844 when the Union's second election was held: he was not a candidate. John A. Macdonald, who was only twenty-nine, and who had been elected to city council the year before, won easy election in 1844. Macdonald lost Kingston in 1878 and represented other ridings until 1887, but he was the dominant figure in Union and federal politics from 1844 until his death in 1891.

In federal politics Kingstonians have veered towards a "ministerialist" position: that is, they have not normally elected members of the Opposition for long periods of time. The Kingston electorate tends to send government members to Ottawa. Hence, in a 1902 by-election, Kingston elected William Harty, an influential Liberal who had served in the provincial government. Harty never attained cabinet rank under Laurier, but he was assiduous in his cultivation of his town's interests until 1911, when he retired.

Kingston's political importance derived from far more than the presence of Sir John A. Macdonald in Ottawa. Other Kingstonians sought Union and federal office, either as representatives of other ridings or as members of the upper house. So prevalent was this pattern that it denuded provincial and municipal politics of ability, especially on the Conservative side. This was not always true, because Liberal politicians like William Harty and Charles Gildersleeve, who was elected mayor in 1879, sought opportunity where it could be found. However, throughout most of the period between 1840 and 1914, and long after, municipal politicians were undistinguished. Moreover, after 1867, members of the provincial parliament were normally as lackluster.

Christopher Alexander Hagerman. (QUA)

Sir Richard Cartwright. (QUA)   Sir Alexander Campbell. (QUA)

On the other hand, the roster of Kingstonians who joined the member for Kingston in the Union and federal capitals is unusually impressive. John Solomon Cartwright, a brilliant and aristocratic figure, won Lennox and Addington in 1841. He was a major Compact spokesman during the early 1840s. In the same election Henry Smith, a senior Kingston lawyer, was elected for Frontenac. Smith was a venal and unattractive member, but he held his seat until 1861. From 1854 to 1858 he was solicitor-general, Canada West, and he served as speaker from 1858 to 1861. Smith was knighted in 1860 and, as Sir Henry, sat in the first provincial parliament from 1867 to 1868. After Confederation Kingston was amazingly active in federal politics. Perhaps the city's greatest influence came after the general election of 1872, when no fewer than eight men who were either Kingstonians or closely connected with Kingston served in Canada's parliament. Their fellow-townsmen were fully apprised of the implications of this political success. After the election of one of these men, the *Daily News* crowed:

We heartily congratulate Mr. O'Reilly upon the result of the election. Apart from the gain to the Conservative party ... it is a gain to the city to have another of our talented sons in the great council of the Dominion, ready to throw in his influence for the city and this section of the country. Toronto has prospered in a great measure by the number of members which she has all over the county ready to stand up for her interests on all occasions, and thus adding to her strength.[45]

John A. Macdonald (Kingston), Richard Cartwright (Lennox), G.A. Kirkpatrick (Frontenac), James O'Reilly (South Renfrew), George Dormer (South Victoria), and Schuyler Shibley (Addington) sat in the House of Commons. Alexander Campbell and John Hamilton were senators. O'Reilly, Shibley, and Dormer had short, undistinguished careers as MPs. That cannot be said of the other five. John A. Macdonald's ministerial career spanned the years from 1847 to 1891. He was the key architect of Confederation and very likely Canada's greatest prime minister. In 1872 he was Conservative leader and prime minister. Campbell, also a Father of Confederation, was Conservative leader in the Senate and postmaster-general. Although he never sat in the House of Commons, Campbell was an important electoral and parliamentary manager, especially during the period of Macdonald's first Confederation régime, which lasted from 1867 to 1873. Sir Alexander, as he was after 1879, remained in the Senate until 1887, when he resigned to become lieutenant-governor of Ontario. For years after 1867 Macdonald and Campbell, two Kingstonians, ran the federal Conservative Party in Ontario and were major figures in the determination of Canadian public policy.

G.A. Kirkpatrick was never a cabinet minister, but he was a man of influence within his party. Possessing "large private means,"[46] he was able to take an independent line and, on occasion, criticized his own party. Kirkpatrick sat for Frontenac from 1870 to 1892. He was speaker of the House of Commons and succeeded Campbell as lieutenant-governor. Kirkpatrick was knighted in 1897. Shortly before he left the House of Commons, George Kirkpatrick expressed his loyalty to his city, regardless of the fact that he was elected by the people of the county. Kingston, he declared, was "the city whence I come, where I was born and brought up, and where I have lived all my life. It is therefore needless for me to say that I take a great interest in it."[47]

Richard Cartwright was another wealthy man who was free to indulge his passion for politics without concern for personal monetary advantage. Elected for Lennox and Addington as a Tory, as befitted a Cartwright, he had converted to the Liberal Party by the time he entered Alexander Mackenzie's Liberal government in 1873. Thereafter, his career was distinguished. He was minister of Finance from 1873 to 1878, and minister of Trade and Commerce from 1896 to 1911. Cartwright was Laurier's Ontario lieutenant for several years after 1887. Knighted in 1879, Sir Richard had an unusually long parliamentary career. He sat in either the House of Commons or the Senate from 1863 to 1912.

Cartwright's forty-nine years in parliament were actually exceeded by John Hamilton. Hamilton entered the Legislative Council of Upper Canada in 1831 and remained a councillor or senator until he died fifty-one years later. He was a major Kingston-based businessman who said little in public, but he well understood the Canadian political system and knew the location of the levers of authority.

These eight politicians typify the leadership of Kingston in the late nineteenth century. They were all from élite or middle-class backgrounds. Several were very well educated. By vocation three were businessmen-lawyers, two were businessmen, two were lawyers, and one was a businessman-farmer. Only O'Reilly and Dormer, the two Catholics in the group, were not heavily committed to business. The group's business interests were broad:

FINANCE   Macdonald, Campbell, Cartwright, Kirkpatrick, Hamilton.
TRANSPORT   Macdonald, Campbell, Cartwright, Kirkpatrick, O'Reilly, Shibley, Hamilton.
REAL ESTATE   Macdonald, Campbell, Cartwright, Shibley.
MINING   Campbell, Cartwright.
MANUFACTURING   Cartwright.
UTILITIES   Kirkpatrick.
AGRICULTURE   Shibley.

In short, this group represented Kingston's business and professional élite. But it represented more than that. These men all had deep roots in Kingston. They represented Queen's University, Presbyterianism, Anglicanism, Catholicism, and Methodism. They were socially well-connected and associated with prominent families and business interests throughout the province. The population of Kingston was only some 12,500 in 1872. It was a small city. But these federal politicians and a few allied provincial figures prolonged Kingston's role as a city of power and prestige during the years before the outbreak of the First World War.

A WHITE-COLLAR CITY

Kingston's institutional specialties have become more crucial to the economy than the industrial development the city leaders had sought in the nineteenth century. And while subsequent years contributed a degree of economic diversity, Kingston still remains an "institutional town" identified popularly with penitentiaries, the university, medical facilities, and the federal and provincial bureaucracies. All of these emphasize the importance of the institutional inheritance of the nineteenth century.

The persistence of this institutional base may run counter to the "progressive" programs of those continuing to favour industrial development. But the failure to industrialize is not without its benefits. As noted before, had Kingston's trading or industrial strategies met with success, the city could well have become another undistinguished North American industrial-metropolitan centre. In the place of railway tracks, smoke-stacks, and industrial plants, Kingston has been bequeathed the architecture, greenery, and open spaces of nineteenth-century institutions. They do much to define the ambiance and visual impression of the city.

Sir John A. Macdonald, elder statesman and Kingston's premier political leader. (NA)

Barriefield Camp during the Second World War. (Ross Hough)

THIRTEEN

Changing the Guard

A DOMINANT PRESENCE

While the Imperial garrison evacuated its fortifications at Kingston, Kingston continued to be a military town and the military continued as one of the key institutional bases of the economy and society. The Navy vacated Point Frederick, but it was soon replaced by Canada's Royal Military College. In 1871, Batteries A and B were formed as part of the Canadian School of Gunnery and, incidentally, as the first permanent units of the Canadian military forces. Battery A was located at Tête-du-Pont Barracks in Kingston, so initiating the traditional association of the city with the artillery in general and the Royal Canadian Horse Artillery in particular. Kingston became the "Gunners' Town."

Finally, Kingston continued to be considered as a fortified centre in any future conflict with the United States. The British had handed over their "Ordnance Lands" to the Dominion, but they specified that the properties were to be kept in good repair. Before the garrison left in 1870 there had been wars and rumours of war. The British and colonial governments fielded troops during the War of 1812-1814, the border problems that followed the Rebellion of 1837-1838, the New Brunswick-Maine border dispute that erupted into the Aroostook War in 1839, and the Fenian scares of the 1860s. The Oregon Crisis of the mid-1840s was thought by many to be a prelude to general war, as was the highly volatile situation created by the crisis in Anglo-American relations during the American Civil War.

Such tensions and crises did not end with the removal of the garrison and the attainment of Anglo-American détente through the Treaty of Washington of 1871. During the 1890s both the Venezuelan Crisis and the Alaska Boundary Dispute generated tensions of major proportions. Whenever such tensions were experienced, the well-tried and well-tested invasion plans of 1812 were dusted off and critiqued, and the fortifications of places like Quebec, Montreal, and Kingston were subjected to fresh scrutiny. The image and reality of Fortress Kingston was to continue until well into the twentieth century.

Tête-du-Pont Barracks during the years when it was associated with "The Gunners." (QUA)

ROYAL MILITARY COLLEGE

Regiopolis failed as an institution of post-secondary education. Nonetheless, Kingston did eventually acquire a second university. It was a product of one of the main continuities in the city's history: the military. It was appropriate that the military establishment should produce a college of national fame and importance, and in the process combine in one institution both higher education and military tradition. It can be argued that these two factors have had more influence than any other in determining the character of modern Kingston.

Of course, the garrison had always been part of Kingston, and had been important to the town. As R.A. Preston has pointed out, "It was not the rude illiterate soldiery who frequented the taverns around the Tête-du-Pont barracks who shaped Kingston. British officers and NCOs made the city what it was, and indeed still is."[1] Their influence maintained Kingston as a conservative and élitist society with strong cultural ties with Britain. The strength of the garrison, and its concomitant influence, varied during the first two generations of the nineteenth century. The War of 1812-1814 was a peak, and the construction of Fort Henry during the early 1830s was of profound symbolic significance. The presence of Fort Henry on the rise of ground on Point Henry and the Martello towers surrounding Kingston harbour were material statements of the military presence and permanent reminders of Kingston's place within the Empire. These structures helped make the military an omnipresent aspect of life in Kingston.

The withdrawal of Imperial troops created a "vacuum" in Kingston[2]; it also created a vacuum in what might euphemistically be called Canadian defence management. Until British garrisons left the soil of the newly-confederated Canada, the leadership of British regulars constituted the backbone of Canadian defence. There was of course a Canadian militia, and it had been active during the Fenian scares of the late 1860s. Unaided and unchanged, though, the militia could not replace the strength, expertise, and leadership that left with the British regulars. Political leaders concerned with defence matters were forced to consider this problem.

It would be an error to categorize military thinking along hard-and-fast political lines, but the Liberal and Conservative parties tended, on balance, to lean in different directions. The Conservatives were the party of the militia, perhaps because of the important role played by the militia in patronage politics. The Liberal Party, less astute about patronage matters, was nonetheless warm towards the militia. But Liberals also tended to favour some sort of permanent and professional military establishment, especially at the officer level. These differences did not divide the parties sharply; there was some division *within* each party. Also, the policy separation was not crucial: it was not an argument over a citizen army as opposed to a professional standing army. Virtually all political leaders favoured a militia-dominated defence system. The debate was rather over leadership and professionalization.

During the years immediately following the withdrawal of the British garrison, John A. Macdonald's government, which was running into very heavy weather, did little to fill the vacuum. A few steps were taken during those crisis-laden years of the early 1870s that affected Kingston: they were within the pattern of the Conservative Party's preference for a more or less unvarnished militia system. Tête-du-Pont Barracks was used by the militia during the early 1870s as a school to train artillery officers, and Point Frederick was used for militia summer camps. These were inefficient and makeshift responses to the removal of the officer-training component that left with the regulars. They brought little credit or comfort to Kingston.

The situation changed dramatically in November 1873, when the Liberal Party, led by Alexander Mackenzie, came to power. Mackenzie, who had lived in Kingston during the 1840s, was not successful as prime minister, but he was an Imperialist with a strong interest in the military in general and officer training in particular. Mackenzie accepted the need for a decent officer-training college in Canada, and agreed that it should be modelled on the American military academy at West Point. He accepted the West Point model because he concluded that it was the cheapest available system for officer training. In 1874 Mackenzie proposed that $50,000 be appropriated "to be applied to the establishment of a Military School of the character of the West Point Academy in the U.S."[3] Shortly before he left office in 1878, Mackenzie gave a lucid explanation of his decision in 1874:

> faith in voluntary organization was no doubt justified so far as the bravery of the men was concerned, but it was evident that without educated officers it would be impossible to place an Army Corps in the field for serious and continuous operations. This belief led me in 1874 to propose the establishment of a Military College modelled on existing similar institutions in England and the United States. ... The founding of the college was in fact laying the foundation of a future national military system, but a complete change could not be effected in a day or a year. ... We have, however, provided for the education of superior officers.[4]

This decision to found a major institution to train military officers was surprising. It probably stands as the most imaginative act of Alexander Mackenzie's government. However, there was no inevitability about its location in Kingston, which was after all the constituency of the disgraced and defeated Sir John A. Macdonald. Three cities competed for the college. Ottawa, as capital, was a logical site. Kingston and Quebec City were old garrison towns with extensive military traditions. What gave Kingston the edge was the pressure within Mackenzie's cabinet of a powerful and prestigious Kingstonian.

Richard Cartwright was a member of one of Kingston's oldest families. Rich and cultivated, Cartwright represented Loyalism and Toryism when he entered parliament as member for Lennox and Addington in 1863. After Confederation he became disenchanted with Macdonald and the Conservative Party, and took an increasingly independent line in the House of Commons. He was a bitter personal enemy of Sir John when the Pacific Scandal broke in 1873. Cartwright entered Mackenzie's government in November 1873, as minister of Finance. For the duration of the Liberal régime, he was one of its most powerful and senior ministers. Until the collapse of Sir Wilfrid Laurier's government in 1911, Sir Richard, as he was after 1879, remained a power in the Liberal Party.

Cartwright wanted to destroy John A. Macdonald as a public figure. The fact that Macdonald formed a new government in 1878, and held power until he died in 1891, should not obscure the precariousness of his position in the mid-1870s. He was in disgrace after the Pacific Scandal in 1873, and he faced a major drinking problem at the same time. Sir John was forced from office on 5 November 1873, and his party was badly beaten at the elections held in January 1874. Macdonald was particularly vulnerable in his home-base. He came within a hair of losing Kingston in 1874, and might well have lost had he not let it be known that he planned to retire and would not join the next Conservative government. In any event, his narrow victory was challenged, and he was unseated for electoral fraud. He won the ensuing by-election on 29 December 1874, by a paltry seventeen votes. Macdonald's position in Kingston was so weak that he was defeated in 1878 and did not regain his old riding until 1887. Cartwright wanted to erode Sir John's power-base by making it clear that Kingston would not suffer under a Liberal government. Kingston had enjoyed substantial benefits at Macdonald's hands; Cartwright would make clear the fact that patronage favours would continue *without* Sir John.

Cartwright used his influence in cabinet on behalf of Kingston, and inspired Michael Sullivan, the city's Conservative mayor, to hold a public meeting and petition the government to locate the military school in his city. In methodical fashion, Sullivan's petitioners detailed the advantages of Kingston. They described its "central location," "healthfulness," "moderate ... and orderly" population, "clean and elevated site," "facilities for aquatic and other sports," "military and naval buildings," "drill grounds," "rifle ranges," "religious facilities," and "genial and hospitable society." The "presence of Queen's College with its staff of learned professors, library, and scientific apparatus" was seen as complementary, not competitive. And, of course, the city's traditions were emphasized. Kingston, it was observed, was "not without historical fame in the annals of the country which would render it the more proper site for a military college." The local agitation was effective, as Mayor Sullivan reported to Cartwright: "For the short time at our disposal, I may say that the meeting called in connection with the matter by circular was highly influential."[5] The decision to locate the college in Kingston (or to be more precise, across the Cataraqui River in Pittsburgh Township) was known by November 1874. It might well have been timed to coincide with the December by-election that came close to terminating the political career of Sir John A. Macdonald.

A suitable founding commandant for what was soon to be called Royal Military College was not easy to find. It was agreed that he should be a professional officer in the British Army. After protracted negotiations, Major Edward Osborne Hewett, whose commission was in the Royal Engineers, finally accepted the post and sailed for Canada in September 1875. The organization of the college was completed quickly. Point Frederick, which was Crown property, was selected as the site for RMC. The "stone frigate" – a relic of the old naval station – was fitted out as the chief building, and the necessary staff was hired. RMC was not intended to be a large institution. Initially, the staff consisted of Major Hewett, three professors, an officer to command the cadets, and half a dozen people in junior positions.

Early and basic decisions were made concerning the instructional program. It was to be oriented towards engineering, and to be of a four-year duration. Students were to be admitted on the basis of competitive exams, and would be charged stiff fees: $200 for the first year and $150 per annum thereafter. The cadets were also required to supply their own uniforms, books, and miscellaneous equipment. The dress, described by the historian of RMC, was colourful:

Derived from the dress of the British army of the time, it consisted of a scarlet tunic and blue trousers with a scarlet side strip. The headdress was a four-inch shako with a gilt chain and gilt cap-plate with a sunburst with the words "Military College of Canada" around a crown. In winter cadets wore a grey greatcoat and a dark grey persian lamb cap with a side flap and scarlet top cloth.[6]

The early progress of RMC was far from easy as the Canada of the 1870s was neither united nor militaristic. Demand for places at RMC was limited. Only a few boys competed for places in the college's first class, and most of the competitors were from Ontario. College planning called for twenty-two cadets in the founding class; only eighteen were enrolled. This group, which acquired hallowed status in RMC's history as the "Old Eighteen," reported to the college on 1 June 1876. This was a thoroughly mixed group of cadets. Some were only fifteen years old, few had any real knowledge of military life, and academic backgrounds were not strong. Nonetheless, the life of the college had begun. Its military character was overwhelmingly evident at the outset: cadets were governed by the regulations in place for soldiers.

Commandant Hewett, who remained in office until 1886, was the major figure in the early history of the college. He must be given credit for some of the institution's initial successes. Hewett was largely responsible for a key characteristic of the college, one that perhaps explains its survival in a society that was largely unreceptive to military values: early graduates were well-suited to careers in the army or in civilian engineering. This point is amply demonstrated by the careers of cadets who graduated in the 1870s, 1880s, and 1890s. Many were highly successful in the British army, where RMC early acquired a reputation as a high-quality institution. The Canadian militia also obtained numerous first-rate officers from RMC. Many of these men distinguished themselves in the second Riel Rebellion, the Boer War, and the First World War. Civilian engineering throughout Canada was enriched by men trained at RMC.

Perhaps the gravest threat posed to the college during its early years was the return to power in 1878 of Sir John A. Macdonald. His government was hostile to the institution, which had been viewed as a Liberal patronage organization. Even as the college was opening, the Kingston *Daily News*, a Tory newspaper, charged that college supplies must be bought "from Grits so that the youth in training may neither eat bread made by Tory hands nor drink beer supplied by a Tory grocer."[7] Of course, Macdonald's Tories had no difficulty in turning RMC patronage opportunities to their own advantage. Once back in power they quickly made RMC a part of the Conservative machine. G.A. Kirkpatrick, a Kingstonian and MP for Frontenac, obtained a professorship for the Reverend K.L. Jones, whom he described as a member of "one of our oldest Conservative families."[8] Patronage abuse, endemic through the 1880s and 1890s, culminated with the appointment of Major-General D.R. Cameron as commandant in 1888. Cameron's chief qualification was his status

The Mackenzie Building at RMC, named for Alexander Mackenzie, prime minister of Canada 1873–1878. (QUA)

as Sir Charles Tupper's son-in-law. He was a poor commandant, and was dismissed when the Liberals returned to power in 1896. The increasing use of RMC for patronage weakened the institution in a variety of ways. Morale and quality suffered internally. Externally, the institution became increasingly controversial, as Liberal politicians assaulted patronage abuse.

Another problem that the Conservative revival in 1878 posed to the college was the lack of enthusiasm for RMC within the high command of the Conservative Party. It was regarded as a Liberal college, and it was not popular with the militia, which did not want officers thrust upon it from outside its own ranks. L.F.R. Masson, Macdonald's minister of Militia from 1878 to 1880, gave serious thought to closing RMC, which was probably saved only by virtue of its location in the prime minister's home-city. By the mid-1890s there was substantial support among both Liberals and Conservatives for closing the institution.

But Laurier's government did not close Royal Military College. Rather, it fired Major-General Cameron and installed Colonel Gerald Kitson in his place. Kitson can be seen as a second founder of RMC. He took over an embattled institution that was riddled with incompetence and plagued by low morale. He reorganized the college and dismissed a number of professors. The revived institution, strongly supported by active and influential alumni, entered a period of growth and health. Intellectual standards were strengthened and numbers increased. The fifty-seven cadets had become seventy-six in 1900 and 124 in 1912. There can be little doubt that the college was the preserve of the sons of English-Canadian businessmen and professionals. That no doubt helped to strengthen RMC during the years before 1914.

On the eve of the First World War, Royal Military College was a flourishing Canadian institution. It had been accepted because of its contribution to Canadian military, professional, and intellectual life. Earl Grey, the governor-general of Canada, expressed an increasingly common sentiment when he wrote the commandant in 1911 to apologize for his inability to pay the college a final, personal visit:

I do not think there is any institution in the whole of Canada in which I am more interested than I am in your college. I regard RMC as one of the formative influences for good on the national character. You turn out men who hit hard but hit fair, above the belt everytime, men who would rather lose a game playing fairly, than win an advantage by dishonourable means. ... I would wish that your yearly output, which I believe to be of such admirable quality, were double the quantity....[9]

By 1914, RMC had become an important and established national institution. For several decades it had been an integral part of society in Kingston. RMC could not replace the lost garrison, but it was able to perform some of the garrison's functions. It was a physical military presence in a prominent location on the east side of the harbour. Perhaps more important, it continued the British influence on Kingston. The commandant and his staff added a gloss of sophistication and exoticism to the small society of pre-1914 Kingston.

This is well-illustrated by Hewett and his activities. Commandant Hewett came from an established British military family. He was well educated and his engineering skills were notable. When Hewett arrived in Kingston with his large family, he decided not to occupy the commandant's house on Point Frederick. Instead, he took a house in town. He lived first in Bermingham House, one of the finest mansions in the district. In 1879, Hewett moved across the park to Edgewater, another very fine house, which he purchased. The Hewetts entertained a great deal and brought cadets, RMC staff, and local civilians into regular contact. This renewed the opportunity, long enjoyed by Kingstonians, of social intercourse with cultured and travelled Imperial officers (and their wives). These were men who knew the world of Imperial Britain, and had lived, served, and occasionally fought in Zululand, Afghanistan, South Africa, Ceylon, Bermuda, Egypt, and the Punjab.

And, of course, the cadets in their colourful uniforms added a romantic touch to Kingston that could not be rivalled by the dour Presbyterians of Queen's. Initially, contacts between Kingstonians and RMC cadets were severely limited. The cadets could visit the town "only when they could show a written invitation from a hostess."[10] Nonetheless, contacts proliferated and became pleasant additions to Kingston's social calendar. "Copper Sunday" dates from 1882. On that June day the gentlemen cadets paraded to their garrison church, St George's Cathedral. They presented to the church the large mass of pennies or coppers that they had collected for the occasion. From time to time they would disrupt the service by dropping their coppers on the floor during the Offertory, a prank enjoyed by all but the clergy and sidesmen.

It goes without saying that athletics constituted a major component in the education of a military officer. Cadets were routinely observed at play: track and field, tobogganing, canoeing, skating, sailing, tennis, football, and cricket were popular. As Earl Grey had underscored, the development of sportsmanship was an important nuance of RMC education, but these activities were more than part of a cadet's training. They were often social events and extended to involve townspeople. The evidence suggests that young ladies were often present to cheer on their favoured champions. Hockey occupies a special place in the tradition of the college. The origins of the game are obscure, but hockey might well be a version of British field hockey played on ice. Certainly, British officers probably developed the game while on garrison duty in Quebec or Ontario. Not surprisingly, hockey became popular at RMC very early in the history of the college. Indeed, according to a local legend that persists in spite of evidence to the contrary, the first organized hockey game was played on the ice of Kingston's harbour in 1888. The teams, so the legend goes, were drawn from RMC and Queen's.[11]

RMC's annual closing exercises in June have always involved many townspeople, and have included the most spectacular event in the college's social year: the June Ball. The *British Whig* was delighted with the public involvement in the college's first graduation festivities: "At night the commandant and staff entertained the ladies and gentlemen of the city and garrison in the educational block. Everyone present speaks with delight of the enjoyment and the courtesies extended by the hosts. A fine supper was spread and altogether the College surpassed itself in hospitality."[12] The Ball was a glamorous event that quickly became an entrenched part of the RMC cycle. It "made Kingston seem briefly to be the social metropolis of the Dominion."[13] One of the early balls has been carefully described. It "passed off as pleasantly as the warm weather would permit. ..," reported the *Whig*:

The heat was considerably mollified by the ingenuity of the cadets who had charge of the decorations. Adjoining the ballroom was the drawing room tastefully decorated with flags and bunting and decorated with military emblems. ... Just opposite the drawing room was a cool sitting room whose central attraction was a rockery covered with wild flowers and mosses and a huge block of ice whose grateful presence lent a delightful coolness to the air which was most acceptable. At the end of the ball a large Union Jack curtained off steps leading to a window through which many of the heated dancers retired to the roof of the portico to enjoy the beautiful view of the lighted city, the moonlight on the water, and the refreshing breeze which came down the lake.[14]

Royal Military College is a major Canadian institution: succeeding governors-general have taken a warm interest in the college, and have visited it often. It is because of RMC that Kingston receives more visits from governors-general than any other Canadian city save Quebec and Ottawa itself.

THE FIRST WORLD WAR: KINGSTON'S RESPONSE

Understandably, given Kingston's long association with the military, the events leading up to the First World War were followed with considerable interest. Indeed, for weeks before Britain's formal declaration of war on Germany on 4 August 1914, a combination of Imperial jingoism and paranoia had started to develop in Kingston.

Various articles in the 3 August edition of the *Daily Standard* reported that the Royal Canadian Horse Artillery batteries were at full strength, that British officers at RMC had been ordered home, and that two poor German employees at the Rockwood asylum had left for the United States for fear of imprisonment.[15] Germans and things German were suspect. Canadians might have been confident that the German threat would soon be ended by the onslaught of Allied troops, but in the interim they were convinced that the country was filled with spies and traitors. People of vaguely Teutonic origin were harassed, the Kingston *Standard* callously reporting that one Mr Timmerman, a Dutchman and "Kingston's capable and efficient Sanitary Inspector, is a worried man these days. He is kept busy denying he is German."[16] Another victim of war-time hysteria was Professor F.D. Willhoff, a Kingston resident and officer in the German reserve army. He fled to Watertown, New York, as

I have been put in the unfortunate position of living in a country which is at war with my native country. My actions have been suspected and criticized not only, but even my wife has not escaped unpleasantness. I wish to explain, although the reasons should be obvious to everybody, that I left Kingston on the morning war was declared between Great Britain and Germany, simply because in the opinion of myself not only, but of all my friends, whom I consulted, it was the wisest thing for me to do. Since then all kinds of more or less vicious rumours have been spread about me.[17]

Others were even less fortunate. On 12 August 1914 four Germans were arrested at Gananoque. They claimed, no doubt truthfully, that they had been fishing near Clayton, New York, and that their boat had drifted across the river into Canadian waters. Nevertheless, even though they were not kept captive for long, they were incarcerated in Fort Henry and thus initiated its use as an internment centre for spies, alleged spies, and prisoners of war. [18]

Declaring that Fort Henry could shelter "All Spies Found in Canada," the government then quickly fitted out the Fort to accommodate a hundred prisoners. "That the strength and security of Fort Henry is acknowledged by the government," reported the *Standard*, "is evident by the preparations which are being made to turn it into a military prison for the detention of all military prisoners in Canada."[19] Thirteen "spies" arrived toward the end of August. [20] The population of Fort Henry reached 180 by mid-September, and by April 1915 there were some four hundred detained there. The arrival of each new contingent came to be a public event attracting large crowds of Kingstonians.

Fear was also expressed that German agents could attack key facilities. Accordingly, the day war was declared, the commander of Kingston's Military District 3 attended to the security of Fort Henry, which was used as a storage depot for military supplies:

The guard at Fort Henry was doubled last night, thirteen men doing duty at the old fortification. ... [I]n this city, in one place or another, there are stored millions of rounds of ammunition, as well as thousands of tents, transport wagons, water carts, rifles and saddling, etc. for military purposes – in fact the entire equipment of the Third Division which extends as far west as Bowmanville and east to Coteau Junction. [21]

Additional troops were moved to the fort the next day:

A detachment of the Canadian Ordnance Stores Corps. occupy Fort Henry today. A considerable quantity of ammunition is stored at the Fort. ... While no definite information can be ascertained it is understood that there are over 100 tons of ammunition, cc sisting of shells etc. stored at the Fort in addition to coal, and equipment. ...[22]

Guards were also provided for the waterworks, water tower, drydock, bridges, wireless facilities, grain elevators, and the waterfront. Particular concern was expressed over the security of the water supply, the fear of poisoning being such that "there are some people who will not allow members of their household to drink the city water. ..."[23] The guards at these various facilities were as efficient as the community's fear was strong, much to the chagrin of one local journalist:

A Whig reporter, while making his rounds was stopped at the Kingston Shipbuilding Company gate. He was challenged with the sentence: "Where are you going?" The

Troops guard Kingston during the First World War. (Fort Henry)

reporter answered "Reporter." He was informed that this magic word had at present no charm on military men and that he would have to get a Pass from "the Major" before he could enter the gate.[24]

Obviously, some had complained of these overzealous guardians of the realm, and such complaints motivated one local patriot to rally to their defence. "I am surprised at some men and even women making unkind remarks about our local regiments," he wrote, and went on to charge that "This is treason."[25] Strange as it may now seem, precautions were even taken against the threat of air-attack! On 14 August 1914, the *Daily Standard* reported that military guards had been ordered to fire on aeroplanes and make an effort to "Bring Aviator to Earth," although it was conceded that the machine seen the previous evening was "Evidently Not German."[26]

As ever in garrison towns, business was good for the local men of commerce. The troops required large quantities of supplies and equipment, and Kingston's businessmen attempted to defend themselves from competition by enlisting political aid. Hence in 1915, W.F. Nickle, MP for Kingston, complained to the Militia Department:

W.J. Crothers has the contract for a supply of fodder to the Battery and heard a rumour the other day that hay was going to be shipped in from Val Cartier. Mr. Crothers has on hand the estimated supply of oats and hay. He feels aggrieved for fear it may be undelivered owing to the unexpected supply being sent in from Val Cartier. Do you think it quite fair to contractors to lessen the requirement under their contracts by using the Val Cartier supplies? Could they not be turned over and sold for other uses?[27]

Others needed protection as well. Moved by the prevailing mood of patriotism, Kingston merchants announced in a full-page advertisement their determination to control retail prices:

It will be understood that the prices may increase, but we, as LOYAL CANADIANS, promise to carry on our business with the least margin of Profit possible. ... We firmly believe that the merchant who attempts to take advantage of the public at a crisis such as this, is as much a traitor to his flag as the man who sells the plans of a fortress.[28]

The *Daily Standard* added its voice to the patriotic cause:

The Standard has made up its mind that in so far as it is able it is going to put a stop to the shameful tactics of some of the landlords in Kingston who, now that the breadwinners of families are away, are taking advantage of the ignorance and timidity of the women of the house who are left behind and are resorting to intimidation and cowardly threats to exact immediate payment of rent which they must know will be paid as soon as the husband's money is forthcoming from the Militia Department. ... The only remedy that this paper can see to put an end to this kind of tyranny and injustice is publicity.[29]

KINGSTON RALLIES TO THE FLAG

Canada was automatically committed to the global struggle. English-speaking Canadians throughout the country were enthusiastic at the prospect, and eager to volunteer for service. It was generally assumed that the war would be short and decisive. Nothing ominous was read into Prime Minister Sir Robert Borden's immediate pledge "to put forth every effort and to make every sacrifice necessary to ensure the integrity and maintain the honour of our Empire."[30]

Kingstonians, with their long military tradition and close identification with things British, shared the general enthusiasm. Their commitment did not diminish even when it became clear that the war would be long and costly of lives and money.

RMC cadets and graduates enlisted *en masse*; between 80 and 95 per cent of those available for service volunteered for active duty.[31] By 1918, twenty-eight RMC graduates were generals in the British army. G.M. Kirkpatrick and C.M. Dobell held the rank of lieutenant-general. The commandant of the college was correct

Gunners racing into action at RMC, 15 April 1915. (QUA)

when he noted in 1919 that "the Royal Military College of Canada has worthily carried out its part in the Great War, and ... has carved for itself a niche in the Empire's 'Hall of Fame' which will always remain as a proud tribute to the cause of justice and freedom."[32]

The point is well illustrated by the spectacular number of honours and decorations earned by the gentlemen cadets, including one Victoria Cross, five KCBs, seventeen CBs, fifty-one CMGs, ten OBEs, 118 DSOs, six DSOs with one bar, two DSOs with two bars, 126 Military Crosses, twelve Military Crosses with one bar, four DFCs, eighty-five (approximate) 1914 Stars, and 275 (approximate) 1914-1915 Stars. Major foreign decorations also came in numbers: eighteen Legion of Honour medals (France), eleven Croix de Guerre (France), three Ordre de Léopold medals (Belgium), eight other Croix de Guerre (Belgium), six White Eagles (Serbia), and three St Stanislas medals (Russia). Other exotic decorations were the Crown of Italy, St Maurice, and St Lazarus (Italy), St Sava (Serbia), Karageorge (Serbia), St

Vladimir (Russia), St Anne (Russia), Sacred Treasure (Japan), The Redeemer (Greece), and the Order of Lafayette (USA). Some 128 RMC men were mentioned in despatches once, fifty-seven twice, twenty-seven three times, six four times, six five times, three six times, and two seven times.[33] And 142 RMC graduates died in the war. The historian of the college was perfectly correct when he noted that "R.M.C. had proved its worth when Canada was at war."[34]

Queen's had little in the way of a military tradition by 1914, although organized military activity on campus was a part of university life. Students and staff responded immediately and impressively to the needs of the war. The Fifth Field Company, a Queen's group, was quickly pressed into service in August 1914 and prepared Valcartier Camp for 30,000 trainees. Other Queen's men served in a wide variety of units and capacities. By 1914, 40 per cent of the undergraduates were in the services, and by 1918 over 1,500 university men were in uniform.[35] Students and professors in the medical faculty were particularly visible. Kingston and Grant halls were converted into military hospitals in 1916. A Queen's medical unit established itself in Egypt in 1915, where it opened a hospital and treated 10,000 patients. It was moved to France in 1916, where it developed into a huge medical facility that had 2,290 beds by early 1917. Some 35,783 persons were treated between 15 November 1916 and 31 August 1917.[36] At least 187 Queen's men died in the war, 271 received decorations, and 114 were mentioned in despatches. The First World War also confirmed the university's sense of mission. Wilhemina Gordon, in her biography of her father, Daniel Miner Gordon, Queen's war-time principal, notes that "there was now no question of [Queen's] being sectional or denominational in its interests; it was a national university, helping to serve and defend the Empire."[37]

The Great War affected Kingston in other ways. The Royal Canadian Horse Artillery left for Valcartier before the middle of August,[38] but other recruits were trained at the Kingston Armouries or Barriefield Camp, where the men lived in tents from May to November (although permanent buildings were used for administrative purposes). The size of the Barriefield contingent underwent substantial fluctuation. Total strength (all ranks) went from 2,506 in August 1915 to 3,249 a month later. Only 805 men were in camp in June 1917, but 8,000 men was the average throughout the summer of 1916.[39] An early estimate of the value to the city of these trainees was $150,000 per month.[40]

Overall figures for wartime enlistments from Kingston are not available, but within eight days of the outbreak of war, 399 Kingstonians had volunteered and their names were published in the Kingston *Standard*.[41] By the end of the war over 65,000 men from Kingston's Military District 3 had volunteered.[42]

Kingston was the home-base of the 21st Canadian Infantry Battalion.[43] On the 19 October 1914 authority was granted to Lieutenant-Colonel (later Brigadier-General) William St. Pierre Hughes, to organize a battalion of infantry with personnel drawn from eastern Ontario, including Ottawa, Kingston, Belleville, Picton, Cobourg, Brockville, Lanark, Perth, Smith's Falls, Carleton Place, Almont,

RMC's Memorial Arch commemorates the Royal Military College men who died during the First World War. Stonework by James Alexander Rea, mason. (RMC)

Arnprior, Renfrew, Pembroke, Lindsay, Port Hope, Bowmanville, Trenton, Prescott, Peterborough, and Cornwall. According to the battalion's "Historical Calendar," the "volunteers exceeded the establishment by hundreds." Drafts started arriving at the battalion's headquarters at Kingston on 3 October 1914, and the unit was organized into eight companies. Accommodation was provided at the Armouries, the stables of the Royal Canadian Horse Artillery, the adjacent Artillery Park, and a cereal mill at the foot of Gore Street.

The battalion trained until 4 May 1915, and the next day, having been presented with its own colours by Kingston's Army and Navy Veterans' Association, was given a rousing send-off by Kingston, Brockville, and Cornwall *en route* to Montreal. On 6 May, the battalion boarded the *Metagama*, together with hospital units from

Queen's, McGill, and Laval universities. By 16 May, the battalion was encamped at West Sandling Camp, Kent, as a unit of the 4th Canadian Infantry Brigade, 2nd Canadian Division. On 14 September of that year it received the order to embark at Folkestone, and the 21st Battalion became identified with the British Expeditionary Force. From 14 September 1915 to 4 April 1919, when the battalion returned to camp in Britain, it participated in all the major engagements of the war. The battalion's colours include battle honours for St Eloi (1916), Somme (1916), Vimy (1917), Hill 70 (1917), Passchendaele (1917), Amiens (1918), Arras (1918), Cambrai (1918), and Mons (1918). With some thirty officers and 795 other ranks killed in action, Kingston's battalion returned to its home-city.

Of the thousands who served in the First World War from the Kingston district, three individuals may be taken as representative of the community's participation in that war. William Avery "Billy" Bishop represents RMC; Arthur Edward Ross stands for the Queen's contingent; and Sergeant W.P. Doolan serves for the many otherwise anonymous Kingstonians who rallied to the colours.

BILLY BISHOP was not a local boy, but Kingstonians identified with the contentious war hero because of his RMC connection. A winner of the Victoria Cross who became the Allies' leading flying ace,[44] Bishop served initially with the Canadian cavalry. But in 1915 he joined the Royal Flying Corps, and by 1918 he had destroyed seventy-two German airplanes. He became an air marshall in 1936 and took charge of RCAF recruiting during the Second World War. Ever a controversial figure, Bishop nonetheless stands as one of Canada's outstanding military heroes and national figures.

ARTHUR EDWARD ROSS is another war hero with Kingston connections. A medical doctor and professor at Queen's, prior to the war Dr Ross served as alderman from 1905 to 1908, mayor in 1908, and as MPP for Kingston after 1911. Ross was in South Africa from 1899 to 1902. Within days of the outbreak of the First World War he was appointed permanent medical officer of the Valcartier Camp.[45] His stay at Valcartier was brief and he was soon in Europe, where he served for the duration. Ross commanded the First Canadian Field Ambulance in France from 1914 to 1915, served as assistant director of medical services in the First Canadian Division from 1915 to 1917, was deputy director of medical services in the Canadian Corps from 1917 to 1918, and was director of medical services with the rank of brigadier-general when the war ended. Militia Minister Sir Sam Hughes claimed that Ross "deserved the Victoria Cross a score of times while he was at the front."[46] While never awarded that decoration, Ross was made companion of the Order of the Bath, and companion of the Order of St Michael and St George. He was also awarded the Croix de Guerre (Belgium) and was mentioned in despatches.[47] Ross was probably the most visible Kingstonian in Europe. His war-time leadership was of material assistance to his political career. Ross was still the provincial member for Kingston

A Sergeant of the 21st. (Brian S. Osborne)

HOSPITAL SHIP CASUALTY CARD.

Unit *21 Bn* No. *45454 9* Rank *Sgt*

Name *Doolen, W.P.*

Disability *Gsw Head* or Conv't.

Military District

Original *3*

To be left at *3*

M. F. W. 2541.
10M.—5-18.
1772-39-1318.

Hospital ship casualty card. Sgt. Doolan returns from battle wounded and misspelled. (Brian S. Osborne)

when the war ended. He was reelected by acclamation in 1919, and although a Conservative, joined the Farmer-Labour government of E.C. Drury as minister of Health. In 1921 he won Kingston for the federal Conservatives, and remained in the House of Commons until the Liberal sweep of 1935.

WILLIAM P. DOOLAN is a more enigmatic figure. Little is known of Sergeant W.P. Doolan other than a collage of postcards, memorabilia, and official records. His was the citizen's war.[48] In 1914, he received a postcard from his brother Teddy at Shorncliffe that noted that "It wont be long before you will be here to [*sic*]." Soon after, he enlisted and was trained at Camp Borden, and on 11 April 1916 he wrote from Liverpool to his wife in Kingston, assuring her that he had "Arrived safely. Cannot cable. Dont know where we are going." By 30 September 1916 he was a casualty somewhere in France, his Field Medical Card and Hospital Ship Card recording that he had been wounded in the head and face. Mrs Doolan had followed her husband to England and she received a Field Service Post Card in November of that year reporting that "I am quite well. ... I have received your letter. ... Letter follows at first opportunity." On 4 December 1916 she was notified that Sergeant Doolan had suffered "gunshot wounds in the hip, shoulder and face." There was silence until Christmas 1917, when a programme for the 21st Canadian Battalion celebration referred to a "Song (If Sober) from Sgt W.P. Doolan." Early in 1918 he was back in action and a citation dated 15 March 1918 described the events for which he was recommended for a Military Medal:

Sgt. Doolan's invitation to Windsor Castle. (Brian S. Osborne)

For conspicuous gallantry and devotion to duty. In connection with a raid on the enemy trenches, this Sgt showed great initiative and daring in house to house fighting. He led his section with great determination against an occupied house, and owing to his gallantry and personal braverness [sic], succeeded in occupying it. He personally killed several of the enemy, thus allowing the second party to advance. It was largely owing to his gallant action that the raid was a great success.

In July he wrote to his daughter Mary from the Canadian Convalescent Hospital at Clarence House. Doolan's stay there was interrupted by a formal invitation from Sandhurst, the Lord Chamberlain, "By Command of the King," to attend the State Apartments, Windsor Castle, on 27 August 1918 to receive his award. By October he was shifted to the 4th Canadian General Hospital at Basingstoke. A flurry of postcards from Liverpool in November announced his return home, and on Friday, 20 December 1918, he wrote to his wife from Halifax to say: "Arrived O.K. Expect to start for Kingston tomorrow (Saturday), and get home Monday." This ended the war for Sergeant W.P. Doolan, No. 45449.

November 1918 did not quite mark the end of the Great War for Kingstonians. On 11 November 1931, an elaborate program of events marked the unveiling of the War Memorial for the 21st Canadian Infantry Battalion, CEF. The memorial was unveiled by mothers of sons killed while serving with the 21st, the colours were escorted by ex-members of the battalion, and the memorial dedicated by Lieutenant-Colonel J. Stewart, DSO. The pipe band of the Princess of Wales Own Regiment – the regiment perpetuating the 21st Battalion – played "Flowers of the Forest," and the "Last Post" and "Reveille" were played by former buglers from the 21st Battalion.[49] Appropriately, at the banquet held that night at the La Salle Hotel, the toast to "Canada and the British Empire" was proposed by one of Kingston's heroes, Brigadier-General A.E. Ross, CMG, MP; the toast to "Our Guests" was proposed by another, William P. Doolan, MM, Esq.

A MILITARY PRESENCE

While the actual strategic significance of Kingston may have diminished, the military fact remains as strong as ever. Point Frederick, Fort Frontenac, and even Fort Henry serve to underscore the military presence. Moreover, the 1,900 acres of military land at Barriefield in Pittsburgh Township were central to several aspects of the development of the Canadian military.[50] Thus, in 1903 the Militia Signalling Corps was formed. Founded by Major Bruce Carruthers of Kingston, it consisted of eighteen officers and eighty-four men and was the first independent signal corps in the British Empire. It was the precursor of the Royal Canadian Corps of Signals, and in 1937, with the official opening of Vimy Barracks, it became based at Kingston. The school of the Royal Canadian Electrical and Mechanical Engineers joined RCCS at Barriefield in 1944, and the amalgamation of the two in 1968 produced the Canadian Forces School of Communications and Land Ordnance Engineering. The unification of the Canadian Armed Forces in 1968 resulted in the all-service unit, the Canadian Forces School of Communications and Electronics Engineering.

By the late 1980s Canadian Forces Base Kingston comprises the First Canadian Signals Regiment, HMCS *Cataraqui*, The Princess of Wales Own Regiment, and the Brockville Rifles. Together, these elements constitute Kingston's single largest employer.

Furthermore, of all Kingston's institutional functions, the military have contributed most to Kingston's townscape. The memorials for the 21st Battalion and the Royal Canadian Horse Artillery, the Cross of Sacrifice, and Memorial Hall in city hall all serve to commemorate the 254 Kingstonians who died during the Great War. This is not all: some would argue that the military's most important bequest to the city has been the generous expanses of open lands and vistas that were once military reserves and Ordnance lands. The lawns and buildings of the Royal

War Memorial for the 21st Canadian Infantry Battalion, City Park. (George Innes)

Military College, Fort Henry, the grounds surrounding the Martello towers, the remnants of the Market Battery, and City Park all serve as visual prompts recalling some three hundred years of military presence at Kingston.

Double ship-launching at the Kingston yards during the Second World War. (Marine Museum of the Great Lakes at Kingston)

FOURTEEN

Industry, Growth, and Expansion

AN ECONOMIC TRANSFORMATION

What the War of 1812-1814 did for Kingston in the nineteenth century, the Second World War did in the twentieth. More people were added to the city's population, and long-established enterprises experienced a considerable stimulus. Even more important was the addition to the economic structure of new industries, industries associated with the most modern technological developments of the day in metallurgy and synthetic textiles. With scarcely concealed pride, the *Whig-Standard* boasted of Kingston as a "Boom Town" in 1940:

The expansion program of the Canadian Locomotive Company, calling for the erection of their larger new buildings, is well under way. When these new buildings are ready many more men will be needed for the munitions work that is to be carried on. The Kingston Shipbuilding Company has one naval vessel launched and another on the ways, the two providing employment for hundreds of steel workers. ... [T]he outstanding feature of this city's spectacular growth of the past two years has been the erection and now full operation of the new plant of the Aluminum Company of Canada Limited, now employing over 700 persons. Further extension of this huge industry is also being made at the present time.[1]

The article went on to comment on the pressure on housing occasioned by the influx of labour: "every vacant house in the city has been rented, many older ones having been renovated to help provide accommodation." The local building industry was experiencing "an all time peak of activity," and by 1942 talk was in the air to incorporate into the city the 250 houses that had been constructed to the north of the city limits.[2] As the war progressed and as Kingston's population increased, it was claimed that the city's rents were higher than the national average, the cause said to be infusions of military personnel and industrial labour.[3] Under these circumstances, growth was inevitable; and between 1939 and 1943 alone, Kingston's

One of the Kingston yards' corvettes, HMCS *Frontenac*, and her first crew. (Marine Museum of the Great Lakes at Kingston)

population increased by 9,000 persons, with 506 houses erected to alleviate the acute housing shortage.[4]

Moreover, the war years and the generation immediately following them witnessed a significant change in the economic structure of the city and area. The Second World War served to stimulate the well-established industries as well as to attract new ones. Thus, the local dockyards contributed to the war effort by the construction of several classes of warships. Between 1940 and 1944, the yards specialized in Revised Flower Class corvettes for duty on the North Atlantic. In all, some twelve of these vessels were launched at the Kingston yards, including the *Honesty* and *Rosebay* for the Royal Navy, and one, the *Brisk*, for the Americans. The Canadian corvettes were distinguished by such local names as HMCS *Napanee, Prescott, Sudbury, Frontenac, Trentonian, Peterborough, Belleville*, and *Smiths Falls*. Two Western Isles Class trawler-minesweepers and seven Warrior Class tugs were also constructed. The shipyards were busy during the war, and the local economy benefited accordingly from the $9.7-million-worth of contracts.[5] Indeed, this aspect of Kingston's war effort came to be of considerable public interest. The launching of HMS *Flax* and two minesweepers prompted the headline, "New Record Set At Shipbuilding Yards As Three Naval Vessels Christened in 9 Minutes."[6] With such activity, it was not surprising that there was much talk that the yards were to be soon expanded and employment increased from 150 men to over 400.[7] The required extra manpower was not available, however. The shipyards – like other local industries – turned to female labour, and in May 1943, the local newspapers reported on another first for the shipyards: "Women To Work At Shipyard."[8] The Kingston community maintained an interest in "their" vessels even after they were launched. The sinking of the corvette *Charlottetown* in 1942 did not go unnoticed,[9] and the fortunes of the locally-sponsored vessel, the corvette *Frontenac*, were of particular interest.[10] Long before the war ended, however, the activity at the shipyards started to wane. In August 1944, the launching of the *Smiths Falls* marked the termination of that program and the onset of the peace-time level of production.[11]

Unfortunately, orders fell off rapidly following the war and, moreover, the radical increase in the size of the vessels operating on the Great Lakes rendered the traditional function of repair and construction of lakers impossible without considerable investment in improved facilities. Owned by the Canada Steamship Lines, the yards were closed in 1968 amid bitter political controversy and desperate attempts to save the plant and the 270 jobs it offered the community.

The Second World War also directed much business to the other major employer, the old locomotive works, now in the hands of Fairbanks Morse (Canada) Ltd., a subsidiary of Colt Industries of New York. During the war the plant employed as many as 1,800 hands producing various war-time products as well as locomotives, scales, mixers, dryers, and a variety of metallurgical and chemical equipment. Again, orders declined precipitously after 1945, and with increasingly difficult labour problems, the company lost money for most years in the 1950s and 1960s. By 1967 employment had fallen to a mere 327 hands. With the closure of the works in 1969, the city lost $3.5 million a year in payroll, taxes, and local purchases. Close on the heels of these closures, another hundred or so jobs were lost when the old Davis Tannery closed, leaving behind a site that was to become one of Kingston's several ecological conundrums from the nineteenth century.

If the old wards of Sydenham, St Lawrence, and Cataraqui lost these long-established enterprises, the Second World War had brought to Kingston new light industries that served to stimulate growth in both the city and adjoining townships.

In particular, Alcan and Du Pont had made the principal contribution to the 34-percent increase in the Kingston Urban Area's population between 1941 and 1951, from 36,772 to 49,246. Prompted by demands stimulated by the outbreak of the Second World War, Alcan and Du Pont located in the adjacent municipality of Kingston Township, albeit close to the municipal boundaries of the city. Space, lower taxes, and access to road and rail transport determined their precise locations, while proximity to Kingston assured a labour force and urban facilities.

Alcan was the first of the new arrivals in Kingston's second phase of industrial development. After considering several alternative sites in Ontario and Quebec, the firm acquired 311 acres just outside the city limits in 1939. Construction began immediately, equipment was installed in January of the following year, and by August 1940 the plant had produced its first ingots and sheets of aluminum.[12] The initial growth of the plant was directed to meeting the war-time needs of the Allies, and it produced the aluminum tubing, sheets, and mouldings for the air-frames and propellors of Spitfires, Lancasters, and other war-time aircraft. By 1944, 40 per cent of all Allied war planes were constructed of Canadian aluminum, much of it from the Kingston plant. Naturally, employment peaked during these years and reached a high of 2,479 men and 1,270 women in 1944. By the end of that year, however, employment had dropped to 2,311, and at the close of 1945 there were only 1,479 workers at the plant. This post-war retrenchment was felt most by the female proportion of the work force, which decreased from the war-time peak of 35 per cent to a mere 4 per cent.[13]

As other war-time industries turned from swords to ploughshares, so Alcan switched from planes to pots and pans. Despite the drop in employment, the Kingston plant had by 1946 doubled its war-time production, directing its products to the domestic household market. With the introduction of aluminum foil in 1946 another profitable dimension was added to the plant's line of products. The renewed military demands occasioned by the Korean War increased employment to over 2,500 in the 1950s, and there were even plans for a new sheet-metal mill to be constructed on some 660 acres that had been acquired to the west of Kingston at Millhaven. However, Oswego was selected as the preferred site for this development, and the Canadian site was sold. By the 1960s, the plant was restricted to its earlier site, which, after 1952, was located within the expanded municipal limits of the city of Kingston. Employment continued at about 2,000 hands in the 1960s, dropping to about 1,700 workers by the late 1970s.[14] The forerunner of Kingston's "new industries," Alcan constituted one of the city's most important economic elements during this post-war period of economic expansion.

Close on the heels of Alcan, Canadian Industries Limited – later to be called Du Pont – opened a nylon plant on a 313-acre site to the west of the city limits. Voters in the Township of Kingston unanimously passed a by-law that guaranteed the CIL company a fixed assessment for ten years, noting that such was the local support for attracting industry that the one negative vote against a similar by-law the previous year "was an accident"![15] "Well Done, Kingston Township," trumpeted the *Whig-Standard*, as "it means that this appreciation of the value of industry is on a permanent basis."[16] A week later, it was announced that CIL was to erect a $1.5-million plant on one hundred acres, two miles to the west of the city limits. Designed to manufacture nylon yarn, "the new synthetic fibre," it was expected that production would commence in the fall of 1941, requiring some 150 workers.[17]

Kingston's tradition of textiles went back to the cotton mill and hosiery plant of the late nineteenth century, but the arrival of the CIL works marked a new initiative. Opened in 1942, the plant utilized the same spur-line that had been constructed for the Little Cataraqui Bay elevator development. Originally producing nylon cloth for parachutes, the plant was subsequently developed as a combined production and research establishment, its products including nylon yarn for panty-hose, carpets, and tires.

In 1954, another textile factory located on another lakeshore site some twenty miles to the west. Celanese Canada, the third-largest producer of polyester in Canada, was constructed on a site at Millhaven that afforded water from Lake Ontario, proximity to good road and rail transport, and of course a location half-way between the major clothing producers in Quebec and western Ontario.

Finally, in 1971, a $34-million industrial plant was located on a 230-acre site in Kingston Township's new Industrial Park by Northern Telecom Limited. This company's production of wire and cables added another element to the city's new metallurgical industrial base.

These four industries dominate the private sector of the Kingston Urban Area's economic scene. The remainder of Kingston's manufacturing enterprises that continued in the post-Second World War period were predominantly small-scale operations. Of the 59 industrial units in 1962 and 82 units in 1976, over 50 per cent employed fewer than twenty-five hands.[18]

Moreover, if the principal private- and public-sector employers are compared, the importance of the public-service sector as a major employer becomes apparent. By 1970, only 5,280 of Kingston's 12,948 employees were in the private sector and some 7,428 in the public sector.

Top Ten Major Employers in the Kingston Urban Area, 1970[19]	
Employer	No. Employees
Du Pont of Canada	2,294
Queen's University	1,871
ALCAN Canada Products	1,820
Kingston General Hospital	1,443
Frontenac County Board of Education	1,410
Canadian Industries Ltd., Millhaven	1,406
Kingston Psychiatric Hospital	1,092
Hotel Dieu Hospital	836
Royal Military College	450
Canadian Penitentiary Service	326

While the major industrial employers shared in the general economic recession of the late 1970s and early 1980s, Du Pont of Canada, Alcan, and Northern Telecom continued to be major employers. By 1987, however, the "Big Four" manufacturing dominants of Du Pont (1,459), Alcan (860), Celanese Canada (792), and Northern Telecom (597), accounted for only 3,698 employees, a decline of close to 40 per cent since 1970.[20]

In the interim, Kingston has continued further to develop its dominant institutional-employment pattern with the growth of its several "white-collar" operations. The concentration of military, educational, medical, and other service functions is reflected in proportions of teachers, medical personnel, and service workers that are significantly higher than the national average.

Thus, the National Defence establishment of Canadian Forces Base Kingston consists of the Royal Military College, the National Defence College, the Staff College, and the various units at the Barriefield establishment. These units employ some 5,700 people, consisting of approximately 4,000 military personnel and 1,700 civilian support staff, as well as providing accommodation for an additional 1,800 dependants. The old Kingston garrison component is very much part of the economy and society of modern Kingston.

Education at all levels was a major employer in 1987; Queen's University dominated, with 3,492 academic and support staff. Furthermore, the Kingston-based Frontenac County Board of Education and the Frontenac, Lennox, and Addington Roman Catholic school boards employed some 3,097 and 488 personnel respectively. These several educational organizations, together with the 287 employed by St Lawrence College, accounted for a total of 7,364 employees.

The concentration of several major medical facilities in Kingston is also an important dimension of the local employment picture. Kingston General Hospital (2,350), Hotel Dieu (1,175), Kingston Psychiatric Hospital (673), Ongwanada Hospital (403), and St Mary's of the Lake Hospital (447) account for a stunning 5,048 personnel employed in medical services in Kingston.

Finally, the prevailing presence of the penitentiaries continues to contribute much to the local economy, and has come to constitute a local "growth industry" as the population of the penitentiaries burgeons and as associated services like the Staff College and Parole Service have also been added to the establishment. The several institutions administered by the Correctional Service of Canada throughout Kingston and environs employed some 1,954 staff.

Clearly, Kingston is predominantly a "service-industry" city much dependent upon infusions of federal and provincial pay-rolls. Many of these institutions reflect the largesse of politicians of previous decades who favoured Kingston for the location of now-important employers. That this process continues is evidenced by the attraction to the city of yet another government employer – the Ontario Health Insurance Plan offices. Cynics have claimed, unjustly perhaps, that the new initiative was announced on the eve of one election, construction commenced on the eve of another, and the official opening of OHIP's "Macdonald-Cartier Building" in 1983 marked the prospect of yet another. Certainly, Keith Norton, a Kingston cabinet minister in the provincial Conservative government at the time, could not have been expected to argue against a decision that contributed an additional 812 government positions to the economy of the Kingston area! In this way, Kingston's political connections have continued to provide inputs into the local economy to supplement the limited industrial and commercial dimensions.

CITY AND REGIONAL POPULATION TRENDS

The Second World War ushered in a new phase of urbanization for Kingston. Growth continued to be slow overall, but the urban form was changing. The area of the old city had filled up slowly over the preceeding century, and the outer limits of the city wards experienced most of the new construction. Now a more extensive development was to take place in the adjoining townships of Kingston, Ernestown, and Pittsburgh, with the new phenomenon of suburbanization. The old town limits, together with the newer suburbs, have increasingly come to be thought of – if not administered as – the "Greater Kingston Area." While somewhat reminiscent of the expansionary aspirations of the later nineteenth century, this grandiose title does, however, recognize that the region now includes a functioning urban unit that is best considered as a unified region for many administrative purposes. During the 1950s and early 1960s, this Kingston-centred region was growing more rapidly than the population of Ontario as a whole. But this changed in the mid-sixties: the annual growth rate dropped from over 2.0 per cent to a no-growth situation in the 1970s. Moreover, it is clear that there were also major differences within the sub-region with significant differences in rates, forms, and processes of growth.

| | Kingston Area: Population Growth, 1941-1986[21] | | | |
	Kingston City	Kingston Township	Pittsburgh Township	Ernestown Township
1941	30,126	4,436	2,210	2,669
1951	33,459	10,214	5,573	3,210
1956*	48,618	6,795	6,966	4,233
1961	53,526	10,442	9,024	5,704
1966	59,004	12,985	10,210	6,926
1971	59,045	17,387	9,443	8,849
1976	56,032	24,737	9,972	10,935
1981	52,616	27,860	9,812	12,485
1986	55,050	31,539	9,884	12,029

* 1952 annexation of Township of Kingston lands by city.

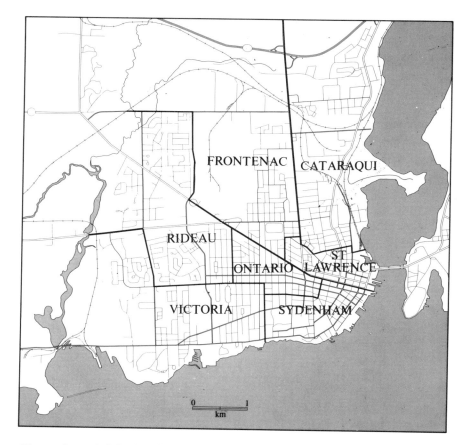

Kingston's wards following the annexation of 1952.

Between 1941 and 1971 the population of the city increased from 30,000 to 59,000. But this apparent doubling is somewhat misleading since the city also experienced a considerable increase in both the area and population by means of annexation. In 1952, the city's western limits were pushed out from Palace Road to Little Cataraqui Creek, thus incorporating the village of Portsmouth and the city properties of Lake Ontario Park and the Cataraqui grain elevator – both of which had hitherto been outliers surrounded by Kingston Township. Similarly, the same annexation advanced the city limits north from Concession Street to Highway 401, integrating the industrial lands occupied by Kingston's newest large industry, Alcan, and at the same time providing a considerable area of relatively undeveloped land that could accommodate future residential expansion. With this annexation of 1 January 1952, Kingston not only gathered in several industrial and commercial ventures that were very much part of the city's economy and society but also added close to 10,000 people to its population.

During the balance of the 1950s, Kingston's population increased at a rate of approximately 2 per cent per annum, reaching 53,526 by 1961. Even this modest growth rate slackened in the ensuing decade, the population increasing slowly to 59,004 by 1966 – and with only 41 more persons in 1971. The seventies were even worse in demographic terms. Between 1971 and 1981, the city's population decreased from 59,045 to 52,616 persons, a loss of some 11 per cent of the population over the decade. [22]

Within the city, a significant demographic shift has occurred. In 1941, the core downtown wards – Ontario, St Lawrence, and Sydenham – held most of the total city population. The more outlying wards of Victoria, Rideau, Frontenac, and Cataraqui were most affected by the war-time and post-war housing boom and the annexation of 1952, and by the 1980s they accommodated over 60 per cent of the city's population. The newer housing, the provision of retail and commercial facilities in both strip and shopping-mall developments, and the reliance upon a "commuting" way of life demarcate Kingston's inner zone of suburbs.

More recently, another trend has emerged. During the 1960s, the old Sydenham Ward lost over a thousand people. Its nineteenth-century buildings were losing families to the newer subdivisions being constructed in Kingston's inner and outer zones of suburban construction. This trend stopped and was actually reversed in the 1970s. Since 1971, when a low of 5,000 people was reached, Sydenham Ward has experienced a revitalization – with the addition of over 2,000 new people, for a population of 7,118 in 1982.

Three trends may be said to account for this remarkable reversal. First, even though Queen's University established a "steady state" of 10,000 students during this decade, the trend to off-campus living occasioned much subdivision of properties to accommodate students, many of whom located throughout Sydenham Ward. Second, for many people, suburbia offered few attractions, whereas the aesthetically-pleasing older homes and the ambiance and convenience of downtown living in a "pedestrian" rather than "commuting" community attracted another component of the growth. Renovation of older homes did much to "face-lift" several sections that were rapidly deteriorating and becoming dilapidated. Third, and finally, a new mode of living was introduced into this oldest of the wards. The Simcoe Apartments had attracted the first nucleus of high-rise tenants to the ward, but the late 1970s saw the first pioneers of "condominiumland" establish themselves along the waterfront of Ontario Street. Two large condominiums and two apartment buildings added close to 400 new units alone, while other developments such as apartments for senior citizens and smaller residential units allowed for the infusion of another thousand additional residents. Sydenham Ward's experience underscored the trend in housing-provision for the city as a whole. Of the 3,000 or so building permits issued for the period 1975-1980, over 2,000 were for apartment units, and only 529 were issued for single-family dwellings.

Such developments amount to more than a mere demographic shift. They were also accompanied by a considerable revitalization of Kingston's downtown as the increased population attracted new retail and commercial outlets and encouraged the refurbishing of older ones. The old city has experienced an infusion of life into the very heart of the downtown and waterfront area.

THE OUTER SUBURBS

Kingston's loss was suburbia's gain. In 1941, the combined population of the city of Kingston and the two adjoining townships of Kingston and Pittsburgh amounted to 36,772, the city containing some 82 per cent of that total. By 1951, the total had increased to close to 50,000 for the combined urban, suburban, and rural areas, with the city's share falling to 68 per cent. The annexation of 1952 temporarily checked this trend so that by 1956, 78 per cent of the Kingston Urban Area's population of 62,379 was located within the city's limits. Over the ensuing thirty years, however, the shift in emphasis to suburban living was to continue. By 1986 only 51 per cent of the 108,502 persons living in Kingston and the adjoining townships lived in the city itself; some 29 per cent lived in the Township of Kingston, 11 per cent in Ernestown Township, and the remaining 9 per cent resided across the Cataraqui River in Pittsburgh Township.

For two decades prior to the 1980s, it was the growth to the west that was most prominent. Originally, Pittsburgh Township suffered from the disadvantages of having less land amenable to rapid development and being on the wrong side of the bottleneck of the La Salle Causeway across the Cataraqui River. Kingston Township, on the other hand, was linked to the city by three roads and contained land well suited to developers' needs. It was also served by a reeve and council who viewed rapid and unfettered suburban growth as desirable and pursued this objective aggressively.

The dominance of apartment-condominium construction in the city was matched by the emphasis on single-family units throughout the adjoining townships. The word township became synonomous with "suburbia," and the communities of "Collins Bay," "Henderson Place," "Bayridge," and "Lakeland Acres" became part of the toponymy of the "Greater Kingston Area."

The economic recession of the late 1970s, the generally slow growth rate of the area, the increased preference for downtown rather than suburban living, and the impact of the energy crisis on commuting – all tended to decrease the rate of suburban development. But with the dramatic surge of housing and other development of the 1980s – with the townships of Ernestown and Pittsburgh challenging Kingston Township's growth rates – the Greater Kingston Area has continued to expand to the west and east along the Lake Ontario-Rideau-St Lawrence fronts. Indeed, rumours of yet another round of annexation, or experiments in regional government, periodically surface to challenge the continued existence of the suburban municipalities. Several factors argue for a regional government: the problem of control of the city of Kingston's remaining outlier, the Norman Rogers Airport; the question of duplication of municipal government and various services; and the general rationale of an already-existing functional integration of the outlying dormitory suburbs with the centre of their economic and social activity, Kingston itself.

But a regional government is strongly opposed by others, especially the Township of Kingston. The relocation of its municipal offices, the construction of a large modern shopping centre, and the development of an ambitious recreation and cultural centre are all intended to provide a functional nucleus and an improved sense of community identity for the township itself. The very name of a new retail project emphasizes this search for an independent identity: "Cataraqui Town Centre," with its over one hundred retail outlets, is intended to attract other commercial developments around it and stimulate further residential growth. Even more recently, some are even advocating that renaming the township "Cataraqui" would serve to further assert the municipality's sense of community and differentiate it from the city.

While not a region of major population growth, the Greater Kingston Area has been experiencing significant realignments and redistributions over the last thirty years. Kingston's old urban core of the 1940s had added to it a zone of newer houses in the 1950s and 1960s – a zone that can be labelled Kingston's "inner suburbs." The late 1960s and 1970s witnessed the addition of "outer suburbs" that are beyond the bounds of the municipality, but are clearly functionally dependent upon it in many important ways. At the same time, the downtown zone experienced a degree of revitalization that culminated in a considerable shift in population and investment back to the traditional urban centre.

In the 1980s, therefore, the Kingston region is witnessing two countervailing forces, each symbolic of different images of urban life and organization. A vital downtown development and an aggressive suburban expansion are designed better to serve the varied needs of the local population. In the light of the statistics of regional growth over the last few decades, it is clear that significant *redistribution* of population rather than rapid overall *growth* is the dominant pattern of development. It is the specific location of the pressure points generated by these trends that need to be monitored to ensure that they do not disrupt the distinctiveness of the city and its surrounding region.

View of the waterfront by G.H. Andrews, 1862. (QUA Library)

FIFTEEN

Preservation Versus Progress

THE HERITAGE OF THE NINETEENTH CENTURY

In one of his Kingston novels, David Helwig provides a vivid word-picture of Kingston's townscape and comments on the architectural symbolism of the institutional presence:

It was a city built around institutions, the university, the mental hospital, the two cathedrals, the army camp, the prisons. They gave a sense of the large dramatic possibilities of life, and the streets were haunted by their presence. ... each day as the ferry approached the shore, Wayne saw the prison in the distance, the dome of St. George's, the spire of St. Mary's, Fort Henry on its hill, the Royal Military College. ...[1]

It is this architectural fabric and its historical and aesthetic significance that, after a century of considerable structural change and development, elicited Kingstonians' pride and concern in the latter quarter of the twentieth century. There were diverse interests and mixed motives involved in this experience. On the one hand, some preservationists were actual residents of particular areas who wished to protect the ambiance and property values of their chosen community. Other preservationists were motivated by a concern for heritage and the uniqueness of Kingston's legacy of nineteenth-century architecture and urban form.

At the same time, those favouring development and renewal viewed "preservation" as an obstacle to "progress," a non-cost-effective approach to business, or else as a dreary view of urban design when compared with the more modernistic projects being developed in cities elsewhere. Such conflicts over different urban visions, different vested interests, and different sets of aesthetic principles resulted in much debate. The 1960s and 1970s witnessed the two groups at loggerheads over several particular buildings and sites such as Plymouth Square, the county jail, and the market square. And there were considerable successes on the part of preservationists in the defence of heritage and the assertion of community consciousness in such victories as the recognition of Barriefield Village as a protected area and Portsmouth Village's resistance to high-rise development.

Perhaps the most prolonged and contentious issue has been that of the concept of Kingston's new waterfront. The demise of waterfront commerce and industry presented the city with the opportunity to conceive of a new development appropriate to the values of the community in the late twentieth century, just as the wharves, railroads, and factories had been appropriate to those of the late nineteenth century. This turned out to be no simple task, and the identification of these values has been as problematical as their implementation.

Kingston grew as a commercial and administrative centre, and its skyline of city hall, St George's dome, and St Mary's spire overlooking the waters of the Great Cataraqui and Lake Ontario constitutes a unique urban prospect. Across the Great Cataraqui, the skyline is dominated by that other institutional presence: the military. The historic village of Barriefield, the Royal Military College in its manicured setting on Point Frederick, and the imposing fortifications of Fort Henry across Navy Bay – all these present themselves to the the eye of a person standing at Kingston's waterfront. And all are framed by the softer waterscape of the lake, with its backdrop of Cedar, Wolfe, Garden, and Simcoe islands.

Kingston had an active port, and if nineteenth-century Kingstonians built elegant houses, fine churches, and a magnificent city hall, they paid little attention to the aesthetics of the city's waterfront setting: this was neither an issue nor a concern. The "penny bridge" across the Cataraqui River, and its replacement, the La Salle Causeway, divided the waterfront into two sections: Kingston's "Outer Harbour," extending from the Causeway for over a mile to the southwest, fronting onto the open waters of Lake Ontario; and the "Inner Harbour," consisting of the sheltered waters of the estuary of the Great Cataraqui River, cut off from the lake by the limited access provided by the lift-bridge at the Causeway. Throughout the nineteenth century, the prevailing ethos assumed that the waterfront was a commercial, shipping, and industrial area. It was the appropriate locus for wharves, grain elevators, warehouses, railroad sidings, and industrial enterprises. The view of the lake was screened from the townspeople and visitors by this barrier of commercial and industrial development.

Indeed, attractive open spaces were few, and were rarely the product of any civic initiative. The magnificent parcels of land east of Queen's University that now constitute Macdonald Park, City Park, and the Cricket Field were Crown property over which the city never had full control, although public access was not restricted. Again, the military preserved the properties on the east side of the outer harbour and adjacent to the Causeway on the west side. After the military demolished the grimly picturesque market battery, which had been built in 1848 on the shoreline in front of city hall, the town acquired the property as a public park. Ten years later, it leased these prime 2.2 acres to the Kingston & Pembroke Railway as a switching yard and passenger station. The CPR acquired the site when it absorbed the K&P in 1912. Similarly, when considering possible sites for the much-vaunted "Terminus of the Great Lakes," the beautiful Tête-du-Pont site, Lake Ontario Park, and the

Cataraqui Golf and Country Club were all advanced as possibilities for "development." The city's initiatives in such cases were the diagnostic mark of Kingston's philosophy of municipal planning: the private sector could have virtually *anything* as a gift of the city fathers if it promised "growth" in return. As with urban centres elsewhere throughout North America, municipal politicians continued to be mesmerized by the dream of a vibrant waterfront economy.

This became increasingly unrealistic as the twentieth century advanced. Transshipment prosperity had become golden-age mythology by the first decade of the century. The First World War breathed some life into ship-building, locomotive enterprises, and other harbour-related activities, but only for a brief period. Shipping activity was minimal during the 1920s, and in the Depression years the waterfront was marked by under-used elevators and row upon row of empty ships. The Second World War provided another spurt of temporary activity, but the reality was that Kingston was finished as a port.

The problem of the waterfront district was compounded by a number of ancillary factors. Development during and after the Second World War tended to be on the western side of the city: Alcan, Du Pont, and CIL all located to the west of the city or in the northwest corner. This was also the area of sustained population growth and fairly steady suburbanization. Kingston Township to the west of the city became the scene of rapid growth. Shopping and other business activities in western Kingston and the township expanded and challenged the commercial and social supremacy of the historic waterfront-downtown district.

This area faced further problems. It was physically deteriorating at an alarming rate. Docks were ramshackle and dangerous. Industrial establishments were under-used and falling into serious disrepair. Ancient hotels were dominated by sleazy drinking establishments frequented by derelicts and worse. Substantial amounts of fire-trap slum housing emerged behind the Outer Harbour. Sydenham Ward, in which most of the old harbour is included, is the most historic part of Kingston and contains one of the most beautiful assemblages of nineteenth-century residential architecture in Canada. Waterfront blight and commercial activity invaded this area and threatened its destruction.

By 1960 Kingston was a city whose historic balance was in danger. A dynamic area of new residences, businesses, and suburbs to the west threatened to become the city's new focus, in place of a mouldering, deteriorating, uneconomic, and occasionally dangerous waterfront-downtown district. A redevelopment report in 1964 stated the situation succinctly: "Citizens were almost wholly excluded from the more enjoyable functions of the waterside, and in a true sense, the 'city' became introverted."[2]

THE OPPORTUNITY OF THE TWENTIETH CENTURY

The decade of the 1960s offered the opportunity for remarkable change and realization of potential. Kingston could revitalize its downtown; save the historic section of Sydenham Ward; reclaim the waterfront from its derelict state; reestablish the beauty of the city for the enjoyment of its residents as well as tourists. The opportunity did not go unnoticed. In 1964 a group of Kingstonians made this prophetic statement

The removal of warehousing, of coal storage, of rail freight loading, is either completed, or in the offing for much of the central waterfront. It is imperative that the city take advantage of this rarest of opportunities, that of developing plans for the integration of downtown and waterfront, so that the potential of the site and situation of Kingston may be realized.[3]

Economic logic and fortuitous circumstance combined to open up for redevelopment virtually the entire Outer Harbour shoreline. This unusual opportunity became manifest during the late 1950s and 1960s. Competition from fuel oil rendered obsolete the Richardson coal-yard, which occupied the waterfront between Simcoe and West streets. A new water-filtration plant built a half a mile to the west on the site of yet another redundant coal-yard superceded the municipal pumping station to the east of West Street. The radical increase in the size of Great Lakes shipping vessels made the drydock-shipyard facilities owned by the Canada Steamship Lines uncompetitive, and they were closed in 1968. While a major economic blow, the demise of the shipyard reopened the historic Mississauga Point for redevelopment after some one hundred and fifty years of ship-building activities there.

Close by, the old locomotive works occupied a 400,00-square-foot site covered by aged and dilapidated buildings and industrial plant. With the closing of this plant in 1969 the city was presented with yet another area for imaginative waterfront development. Similarly, the elevator built at Little Cataraqui Bay to compete with the new facilities at Prescott may have failed eventually, but it did serve to render redundant Kingston's downtown elevators at the foot of Johnson and Princess streets. Finally, the old Kingston & Pembroke Railway, owned by the CPR since 1912, had ceased its regular train service to the waterfront area in 1957. This made available the property between city hall and the water, an area used as a switching yard and passenger station since 1885. Other vestiges of the old docks and wharfs of the nineteenth and early twentieth centuries were to be found to the the northeast of city hall, along the waterfront of the Inner Harbour. Between these two areas of nineteenth-century commerce and industry lay the attractive grounds of Tête-du-Pont Barracks, an enclosed preserve of lawns and trees.

It is doubtful that any other old Canadian city has ever before been given such an opportunity for creative redevelopment. The entire Outer Harbour, with the exception of a couple of small parcels of property, was available for holistic treatment. As Warren Stanton, a journalist and unusually astute observer, commented when Fairbanks Morse announced its decision to close its Kingston operation: "Hurray! That land is now available. Let's make the most of it. ... It can be the location of a municipal-commercial development that has almost unbelievable possibilities."[4]

Kingston is a natural tourist centre. Its surviving military installations and impressive number of fine pre-Confederation buildings make it unusually attractive. Large numbers of boaters visit the city because of its location at the junction of Lake Ontario, the St Lawrence, and the Rideau Waterway, with the splendid sailing waters of the Bay of Quinte near by. A sustained attempt to develop a water-based tourist industry would seem so logical for Kingston that an observer might assume that such would be one of the city's highest priorities. The collapse of the old commercial waterfront underscored that opportunity.

Unfortunately, creative redevelopment was not to be. The waterfront district was not to become an attractive combination of low-rise waterside housing, mooring facilities for tourists, open areas, boardwalks, parks, leisure centres for Kingstonians, and stores and hotels – all designed to be compatible with a waterfront location. The town's old skyline of domes and spires, a skyline that has always impressed visitors approaching Kingston by the water, was to be lost.

Two factors explain the bungling of this unique opportunity. First, it is clear that the civic leaders of the period ignored the excellent advice given them by several officials and committees and failed to realize that the opportunity existed. They never resolved to use the full weight of government to obtain complete planning control over the entire district. As a consequence, early in the process, *ad hoc* and piecemeal decisions were made that rendered comprehensive and creative planning impossible. Hence the Richardson coal-yard was replaced by a high-rise apartment house of a standard and undistinguished design. Its only redeeming virtue is that it is slightly more aesthetically acceptable than the sixty-foot pile of lignite it replaced. This decision was particularly unfortunate and prophetic because it placed an entire block of shoreline in private hands.

Similarly, the Richardson property at the foot of Princess Street was alienated. It became the site of a large motor hotel, complete with outdoor and indoor swimming pools and a huge parking lot. Inexplicably, the fact that it was built on what had been a dock in a town noted for its water-borne tourism did not seem to merit the incorporation of mooring facilities in the design. Even more importantly, W.J. Coyle commented on another dimension of this development, one that would continue to incense citizens concerned with later projects:

One important point that seems to have been overlooked in approving the plans for this waterfront hotel is that the five storey brick building will seal off completely the view of the harbor [*sic*] and the Royal Military College which residents and visitors now enjoy from lower Princess street. When city council sold the water rights for $8,000 it parted with a valuable asset.[5]

A second chain hotel was built on Ontario Street diagonally across from city hall. It does not have a waterfront location, but it is clearly visible from the lake and helps to disfigure Kingston's skyline. The third chain hotel, built at the foot of Johnson Street, has a waterfront setting, but makes no compromise with its locale, other than a nominal public walkway. All three of these developments fail to maximize their location and could easily have been designed for suburban Calgary or Detroit.

A local developer purchased the shipyard property west of the drydock and built a large apartment complex that is thoroughly undistinguished and inconsistent with the character of the old portion of the town. It is complemented by three equally unattractive apartment houses on Ontario Street that are now salient features of the skyline. Eric Thrift, a prominent and prize-winning town planner, made a pointed statement concerning buildings of this sort. His comment on one of the numerous proposed apartment houses was that it was "out of scale" and in "direct conflict with what's next to it, whether it's one block away or six."[6]

These several *ad hoc* decisions were not all foolish. The city's old pumping station was retained as the Pump House Steam Museum, which is well designed and very popular with the public. The chief buildings at the drydock site, which are of nineteenth-century limestone construction, opened in 1976 as the Marine Museum of the Great Lakes at Kingston. It is a fine museum, with an extensive and valuable collection of documents and artifacts. The museum is the only waterfront property that is used in a major way for traditional water-based activities or displays.

The city had never sold the property between city hall and the shoreline. In 1961, the CPR agreed to abandon it for a site on the north side of the town and the city subsequently transformed it into Confederation Park, a good concept, but one of somewhat questionable taste and appropriateness. A public marina was opened in front of the park in 1967, and by 1987 it could accommodate 144 boats. It proved to be a major success and is heavily used during the long boating season by craft from all over eastern North America. Boaters enjoy the opportunity to moor within walking distance of shops, restaurants, and historic buildings. In fact, the public marina, which is supplemented by additional city-controlled berths at the Marine Museum and Portsmouth's Olympic Harbour, is a signal demonstration of the enormous, but only partially realized, tourist potential of downtown and waterfront Kingston.

ATTEMPTS AT INTEGRATED CONCEPTS

Failure to understand the existence of the opportunity to create a unique waterfront district explains much about the inept and haphazard evolution of the area during the 1970s. A second factor of equal importance was the city's inability to accept and support creative projects evolved by others for the central portion of the Outer Harbour's shoreline. Two such concepts merit brief analysis.

Wyllie Unfal Weinberg and Scheckenberger, a planning firm from Rexdale, Ontario, published a redevelopment scheme for Sydenham Ward in 1970.[7] Its two major concerns were the rehabilitation of the historic residential area in old Kingston and

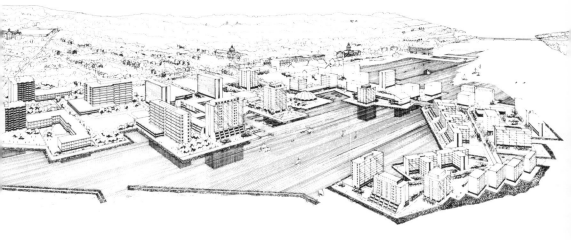

Downtown redevelopment, including a dramatic "Kingston Laguna," proposed by Wyllie Unfal Weinberg and Scheckenberger in 1970. (City of Kingston)

the transformation of the waterfront. The main feature of the waterfront portion of the plan was the construction of a huge landfill site using Carruthers Shoal as a base. The granite shoal had always been a key impediment to the use of Kingston harbour for deep-water shipping. The result would have extended Johnson Street in a westward arc until it approached the foot of Gore Street. The central part of the old Outer Harbour would then have fronted on the new "Kingston Laguna." Further protection was to be provided by a breakwater running west from the landfill to the Kingston Yacht Club, with an entrance a little east of the foot of West Street.

This imaginative plan, which was designed to rehabilitate old Sydenham Ward as well as revolutionize the harbour area, addressed itself directly to key and obvious concerns. Substantial new construction would have shifted the population balance to the waterfront. Needed low-cost and student housing was part of the plan, as were tasteful school, shopping, parking, hotel, and convention facilities. Above all, the plan was designed to make the revitalized harbour area a mecca for water-based leisure activity. Townspeople and tourists would have benefited equally from extensive, first-rate marina and mooring facilities.

The plan, while breathtaking in some respects, was not without its problems. The historic skyline and streetscape as viewed from the water would have been destroyed by modernistic and excessively tall buildings scattered along the shoreline and landfill. There was also some concern over the extent of the landfill proposed

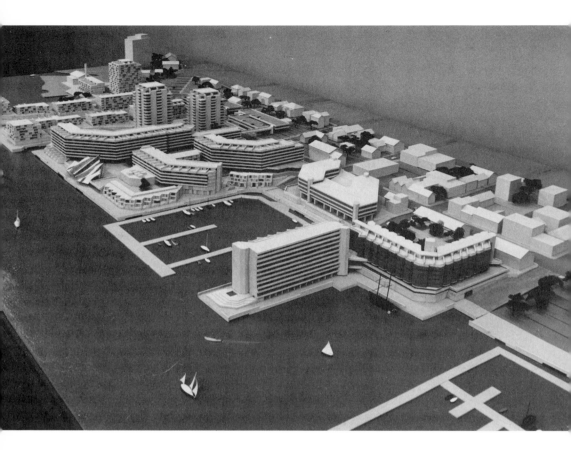

"Marina City," waterfront redevelopment proposed by William Teron in 1970. (George Muirhead)

and the complexity of the changes recommended for the residential area behind the harbour. For example, King Street would have been closed at West Street and the portion of the street to the westward connected with Ontario Street to create a new major thoroughfare. In any event, the Laguna project sank into oblivion with scarcely a ripple.

The lack of a ripple was no accident. A mere two months prior to the publication of the Laguna plan in May 1970, a much more substantial scheme had been announced to the public. It was not more advanced in terms of conceptualization, but by the time it was announced, its proposer had purchased most of the central waterfront district. Thus, in March 1970 Kingstonians learned that William Teron, an Ottawa developer with a first-rate reputation for high-quality and tasteful housing design and construction, had purchased the Fairbanks Morse property and the Swift dock on the eastward side. This gave William Teron Associates control over eleven acres bounded by Confederation Park, Ontario Street, Gore Street, and the waterfront. Teron's plans for the site were ambitious. He proposed to fill it with shops, theatres, office accommodation, walkways, restaurants, hotels, leisure facilities, housing, and an "Atlantic City-type boardwalk for use along the shoreline. ..."[8] Moreover, all this was to be integrated with the salvageable historic buildings that had survived throughout the area. Teron emphasized the need to populate the district and make it live again. "We want an alive downtown, not some place that vacates at 5:30 every night," he said. "Anyone who says this area should be made into a park is not being realistic. ... However, we are interested in the ability of people of the city to participate in the waterfront area – to walk by it, sit by it and drive by it."[9] The Teron proposal was modified from time to time, but during the early period of its life it included 750 apartment units, 185,000 square feet of commercial space, 120,000 square feet of office space, a 250-unit hotel, and a 150-unit apartment hotel. Construction was to cost some thirty million dollars. Although Teron Associates owned the vast bulk of the property on the "Marina City" site, it did not own it all. The missing pieces were to cause substantial complications for the project and for the city.

The Marina City project immediately became extremely controversial, and the controversy became quite byzantine. Full documentation is not yet available, and the motives and activities of the various actors cannot be definitively explained. Yet some things are clear.

Kingston's political establishment was not united in support of the project. J. Edgar Benson, Kingston's Liberal MP and federal minister of Finance, wanted the shipyard resurrected – a proposal that would have restored a noisy heavy industry to the waterfront adjacent to a residential area. This policy made so little sense that a senior official of Canada Steamship Lines, which owned the site, wrote to Mayor E.V. Swain: "I was most surprised ... since I cannot help feeling that any such move would be entirely opposed to the City of Kingston's best interests and would in all probability seriously affect the plans of Mr. Teron and would, in our opinion, prejudice the best development of those areas of Kingston's waterfront not already covered by Mr. Teron's proposed project."[10] Notwithstanding this good advice, the powerful and now extremely irritated minister pursued his policy insistently, and did manage to inspire a brief and final flourish of activity at the drydock in the early 1970s.

Citizen opposition to Teron was persistent and noisy but most certainly far from widespread. The Labour Council opposed the project and sought to obstruct it through the imposition of complicated terms: it asked city council to block construction until Teron had agreed to deed a fifty-foot strip around the project to the city and build 2,400 parking spaces. The labour leaders also wanted a variety of other zoning and timing conditions imposed.[11] The local branch of the New Democratic Party, then controlled by the radical "Waffle" left wing centred in the

Queen's graduate school, entered the fray for reasons that are far from clear. The NDP was flatly opposed to Teron and wanted a completely new project owned by a Crown corporation. A party spokesman argued that "the provincial government is spending $500 million to develop the Toronto waterfront and is prepared to make a similar arrangement with Kingston if City Council requests it."[12] The unlikeliness of a miniscule group of radicals in Kingston speaking for Ontario's Conservative government was evident to even the most naïve observer; but the NDP was able to generate a fair amount of publicity and add to the growing perception that Marina City was a misguided project.

Other opposition came from a different and more conservative perspective. Conservationists and local historians were appalled at the suggestion that some fine pre-Confederation structures along Ontario Street might have to be destroyed. They were not reassured by the commitment that destruction would be kept to a minimum and limited to structurally unsound buildings or buildings that could under no circumstances be incorporated into the project's concept. Their worst fears were realized when Plymouth Square, built in 1832 and for many years the residence and commercial establishment of John Counter (mayor of Kingston, 1841-1843, 1846, 1850, 1852-1853, 1855), was demolished. These critics were also concerned, and properly so, that Marina City was too large in scale, and would ruin the general proportions and arrangement of buildings in the area, which constituted much of the nineteenth-century charm and ambiance of that part of the town.

Sporadic opposition came from a variety of additional sources. Some local residents did not want any extensive commercial or residential construction between their properties and the waterfront. Others wanted the very reverse. John Meister, an NDP alderman, wanted a return of heavy industry and its concomitant employment of unionized labour, and was opposed to hotel and leisure facilities. Various other objections were heard.

The concept of a huge waterfront park attracted some support, even if such a scheme was hardly necessary in a district that already possessed substantial amounts of very attractive parkland. Teron's housing proposals irritated those who wanted only low-density, low-rise, and (by implication) high-income properties. Even the Kingston Fire Department entered the debate with a series of complaints about the fire-safety provisions for Marina City.

Strident opposition clearly irritated Teron Associates. Another irritant was a protracted negotiation concerning a small piece of property owned by the Royal Canadian Horse Artillery Club. The property was neither large nor of much intrinsic value, but Teron claimed that it was essential as an entranceway to his hotel. The veterans wanted substantial compensation and became increasingly upset and stubborn as they were portrayed as an obstacle to the implementation of this huge waterfront redevelopment project. Negotiations dragged on endlessly, with Mayor Swain acting as intermediary. Finally, an agreement was reached. At this point, however, a downtown activist intervened and challenged the proposed severance of the RCHA property. The outcome was uncertain and the appeal process promised to be lengthy.

William Teron took this occasion, in May 1972, to cancel the entire project. His motives are not known. The *Whig-Standard* claimed that he was frustrated by the federal government's insistence on attempting to revive the shipyard, the outpouring of bitterness over the clear threat to Plymouth Square, the protracted and nasty negotiations over the RCHA property, and the constant sniping from various activist groups and individual citizens. The newspaper was less than kind in its assessment: "William Teron ... packed in Marina City this week because, after more than three years of having much of his own way, he ran into a group that wouldn't play by his rules."[13]

It was no doubt a major tactical error for an outside developer to arrive in Kingston with a ready-made plan for massive redevelopment that would have changed the nature and character of the city. Such an approach was bound to generate hostility without a great deal of support at the same time. Nonetheless, the collapse of Marina City was unfortunate. It is true that it would have changed the city's skyline and produced relatively high-density residential areas. But this was to happen eventually, in any event. The plan was imaginative and sensitive to a number of aspects of the community. It made provision for public access to the waterfront and for a healthy diversity of land uses. Above all, it would have brought permanent dwellers to the waterfront within a framework of good landscaping and ancillary facilities that would serve the new residents, other Kingstonians, and tourists. This was much preferable to earlier and, indeed, later developments proposed for the area concerned, plans in which residential developers simply plunked down standard North American high-rises wherever possible, filled them with people, and left the new residents and the area to make whatever adjustments were possible.

William Teron built nothing in Kingston, but he demolished much, including the entire Fairbanks Morse property. Kingstonians were left with a huge area of cleared and desolate waterfront, and a grudging fear that neither politicians nor activists knew what they were doing.

THE SEQUEL

The sequel was even less encouraging. In 1973, Teron became chairman of the Central Mortgage and Housing Corporation. His various holdings, including all his Kingston lands, were placed in trusteeship under Urbanetics Ltd. The Kingston property remained empty and ugly until the end of the decade, when the Teron interests were liquidated and another group of developers and realtors entered the scene. Their plans called for two high-rise condominiums and yet another chain hotel on the eastern portion of the property. These projects were unimaginative in every respect.

There was some citizen opposition to the high-rises and the hotel, but city council, which seemed capable only of responding to proposals put to it, not of initiating its own concepts, was hungry for any downtown development. It let the developers have their way. As Mayor Ken Keyes put it when he supported one proposal, "It is time for Council to make up its mind whether to get on with it or watch weeds grow there for another seven years."[14] The result is another contemporary hotel of standard proportions and undistinguished design, juxtaposed with two monolithic condominiums that represent all that was feared by the opponents of earlier proposals. None of the developments incorporated the waterside location into their concepts in any meaningful way – except to provide for their occupants prime-quality vistas of the city's architecture and Lake Ontario's waterscapes. One official in fact commented that one of the condominium designs was "similar to one that the architect was building somewhere [else]."[15] They rise fortress-like above the adjacent parts of old Kingston, especially when viewed from the lakeside or the eastern approach to the city along Ontario Street. Architectural pearls like St George's and city hall are dwarfed and overshadowed by structures that are too tall, too close, and too independent of the dictates of their site.

Kingston entered the decade of the 1970s with an unparalleled opportunity to augment its uniqueness by developing a truly beautiful waterfront-downtown district that could have been both aesthetically pleasing and economically stimulating. The decade was spent dissipating that opportunity as the old policy (or perhaps more properly speaking, the old habit) of isolated and *ad hoc* decisions prevailed. Ten years later, when the town faced the 1980s, the damage had been done. The mile of Lake Ontario shoreline from the Kingston Yacht Club to the La Salle Causeway had suffered new and permanent disfigurement. The district had been chopped up and dotted with buildings that clashed with the neighbourhood, ruined the skyline, and possessed no architectural merit. Three chain hotels complemented the half-dozen apartment and condominium buildings that would have been more appropriate parts of some faceless city's urban sprawl. A portion of the central part of the waterfront that had been cleared by Teron's bulldozers remained as empty and unattractive as it had been ten years earlier.

The changes that came to Kingston during the 1970s were unfortunate because they failed to realize anything like the potential available at the beginning of the decade. This is not to suggest that the transformation of the seventies was completely negative. There were some redeeming features. In 1964 the *Whig-Standard* quoted Planning Officer Kurt Mumm's diagnosis of the "dormant" and "decaying" waterfront as a "cancerous growth." He went on to further define the problem:

the urban development of the city and its growth in other directions for other reasons, finds today's Kingston not facing the lake but actually having turned its back to it. ... But the waterfront is still there – part of it dormant, some parts lingering and a few prospering. The way the land is used is affecting the adjacent areas, in some parts adversely and in others favourably. This to me is the most important of all urban problems in the city. ...[16]

William Teron was all too correct when in 1970 he said, "Anything we do here will be better than what you have now."[17]

By the 1980s, much of the "cancerous growth" was gone and the downtown-waterfront district had been revitalized. The three chain hotels provided 428 units for visitors and between 275 and 415 downtown jobs for Kingstonians. Several hundred units of apartment or condominium housing had been built on or near the waterfront during the 1960s and 1970s. Two old and seedy hotels were restored to something like their original charm. They provided needed restaurant space and additional rooms for tourists. The Macdonald-Cartier Building, an office building for the Ontario Hospital Insurance Plan and other provincial agencies, brought over 800 workers into the downtown area in 1983. A variety of fine nineteenth-century structures were saved from mouldering decay and renovated into restaurants, bars, shops, bookstores, and boutiques. Virtually all slum housing in the downtown area was demolished, and substantial improvements have taken place in the residential areas of Sydenham Ward, again a thriving and attractive district of Kingston. Contrary to the views of many local politicians, the downtown shopping area has been rehabilitated without recourse to the alleged benefits of gigantic shopping malls, and it is crowded with people throughout the year.

Waterfront residential construction combined with some singularly unfortunate structures built by, or in alliance with, Queen's University, have deformed the city's nineteenth-century skyline. The two most unfortunate contributions by Queen's are its waterside smokestack to the west of Murney Tower, and Elrond College, as it was initially styled, on Princess Street. The smokestack is one of the two or three most egregiously ugly structures on the entire waterfront. Elrond, which was built with substantial assistance from the university as student housing, is a massive high-rise that manages to disrupt the skyline from whatever direction one looks.

However, for Kingstonians who frequent the downtown, the aesthetic situation has improved markedly. Confederation Park, in spite of its thoroughly inappropriate arch, is an attractive foreground for city hall. The public marina and the emergence of Kingston as a world-class sailing centre keep the harbour area filled with colourful sailing craft of all sizes and descriptions. The opening of street-ends has returned to Kingstonians some of the prospects afforded by the view across the bay to the Royal Military College and the islands. It is these perspectives that need to be protected against interruption by any further massive waterfront projects.

Above all, the balance of the city has been corrected. During the years after 1945, there was a real danger that growing suburbs and new shopping centres on the west side of the city and in Kingston Township would become the dynamic centres of the area in place of the historic downtown districts. The suburbs and their shopping malls remain, but they must now compete with the newly-energized downtown waterfront district and its substantial number of permanent residents and workers. The full potential of historic Kingston may not have been realized, but neither has it been destroyed. Kingston remains a public-sector town, a sub-capital, with a nineteenth-century flavour that is so strong that even the changes of the 1970s could not destroy its uniqueness among the cities of Ontario and Canada.

PARALLEL DEVELOPMENTS

The juxtaposition of beautiful buildings and streetscapes with lake and river has always helped to make Kingston unique. The finest illustration of this is the southern and eastern portions of old Sydenham Ward. But other major examples can be found in adjacent areas.

To the east, the village of Barriefield, which never became a part of Kingston, survives as a protected Heritage Conservation District. It remains a delightful relic of the nineteenth century, and is particularly significant because it constitutes a distinctive assemblage of homes representative of the living and social arrangements of a socially-diverse village community. However, Pittsburgh Township has recently experienced a significant increase in new construction that is expanding north of Barriefield along the Rideau waterfront, and to the east along the St Lawrence waterfront. These developments are now causing substantial concern among the citizens of Pittsburgh Township. South of Barriefield, however, the grounds of the Royal Military College and Fort Henry preserve a rich nineteenth-century heritage and constitute the finest view in the area for those who arrive in Kingston by water.

Portsmouth Village and areas farther west have evolved in substantially different ways. Portsmouth, which grew out of water-based activity at Hatter's Bay and employment provided by Kingston Penitentiary, was annexed to the city in 1952. This old and pleasant village has managed to retain much of its physical and social integrity, and remains a distinctive community. This social cohesiveness was strengthened by the need to monitor and contest developments that threatened to swamp the social fabric and drastically modify the architectural uniqueness of the village.

Kingston's planning department recognized the importance of Portsmouth's heritage by designating the village as a "Special Area" and urging that its water-front be protected and its commercial growth limited. Further, Kingston's Local Architectural Conservation Advisory Committee (LACAC) identified no fewer than seventy-five buildings that merited classification as of historic significance, and recommended that Portsmouth Village be designated a "Heritage Conservation District" under the Ontario Heritage Act of 1974. The rationale for this was recorded in the preface to their 1974 report: "it is the overall feeling of unity of the buildings as a group and the historic continuity of the Village as much as individual building merit which established the importance of Portsmouth as an area of architectural and historic significance."[18]

The preservation of the uniqueness of Portsmouth was no easy task. Early challenges to the village's distinctiveness were mounted in the 1960s, with little evidence of municipal or public concern. In 1963 a six-storey apartment building was constructed following a successful application to change the land-use designation from "Waterfront-Industrial" to "Multiple Family Residential." Another request for rezoning in 1964 resulted in a reclassification from "Two Family Residential" to "Multiple Family Residential" and the eventual construction in 1969 of Kingston's first condominium building, the Mowat Condominium.

These two developments occasioned little public stir, but the decision to site the 1976 Olympic sailing facilities in the village was controversial. As early as 27 April 1970 Kingston had offered to host the sailing events if Montreal were successful in its bid for the 1976 summer games. Recognizing the villagers' concerns for their community, an Olympic Users' Committee (OUC) was established in 1972 and a Portsmouth Villagers' Association came into being in the following year.

The OUC's report recognized the need to ensure that new waterfront construction and facilities would be compatible with the existing architecture and would have utility for the community once the Olympics were over.[19] While the requested tennis courts, swimming pool, and more extensive public spaces were not forthcoming, the progress and overall impact of the project were generally easy on the village. The Olympics did not affect the integrity of the community and did add facilities of benefit to the people of the general Kingston area. The subsequent annual program of the Canadian Olympic Regatta Kingston was another product of the 1976 initiative, but has proven to be substantially less welcome to the local community because of the pressures it produces on amenities and facilities.

In 1980, an application, known as the Cedak proposal, was filed to rezone the site of the Lakeview Manor Hotel to permit a high-rise, high-density condominium development. The developer assumed that village opposition to the Manor – a popular and noisy drinking place – would generate support for an alternative use for the property; indeed the Social Planning Council surveyed Portsmouth residents and found that support for the high-rise was vastly greater than support for the bar. Such, it turned out, was not the case. Opposition from the Portsmouth Villagers' Association was so intense that the proposal was withdrawn in 1980, following a heated public meeting.

The Cedak proposal came back in 1981, when it was argued that the development would be clean, would replace the Manor, would vitalize the village's economy, would generate employment, increase tax revenues, and provide more housing. The Villagers' Association rebutted this by pointing out that the Cedak development would contravene the official city plan on at least fourteen points. It reminded the city of its own published commitment concerning Portsmouth: "It is the City's intent to preserve the predominantly low density residential character of this area, therefore it shall be considered to be an Area of Stability and subject to the pertinent policies for such areas as set out in this plan.[20]"

Those coming to the defence of their community simply had to remind city planners and politicians of their own rhetoric, which had recognized that its historical development as a village and as part of the City proper, its continuity in residency, its old well preserved examples of Kingston limestone architecture and its retention of certain village characteristics makes Portsmouth an historic site of some importance and thus a policy of conservation is needed.[21]

The Cedak proposal was finally defeated by intelligent, informal, and focused opposition to a project that threatened valued qualities of community life.

Barriefield and Portsmouth are settlements that are ancillary to old Kingston. Nonetheless, they are fine historic communities on beautiful waterfront settings. They are particularly vulnerable because they are very small and on sites that are attractive to developers. Their preservation is of great value to their inhabitants and to the larger Kingston community.

THE FUTURE

In Kingston itself, the transformation of the old commercial waterfront continues apace in response to contemporary economic and social pressures, so that virtually nothing has survived from a hundred years ago. Such dramatic changes continue to energize an important and ongoing debate over the future of our waterfront. Indeed, the debate is really about the very nature and future of this city. Block D on Ontario Street, the last undeveloped section of the former Fairbanks Morse property, is the current centre of attention. Its future is very important to the evolving form of the waterfront since it represents a final large-scale opportunity to rectify the balance between development for its own sake and development concerned with a combination of aesthetics and good business. These are not irreconcilable. Opposition to massive projects for the site that disrupt both skyline and perspectives has been consistent, and has generated general popular agreement on the several considerations that should govern the use of Block D. Clearly, it must not be allowed to be yet another "high-rise" structure blocking off the city from its waterfront and causing further deterioration in the sensitive proportions of its skyline. Ideally, it should not be so massive that the street-end vistas of the lake are interrupted. Block D represents an opportunity to return to some of the earlier concepts that called for an appropriate mélange of water-based parks and marina facilities, commercial premises, and unobtrusive and tasteful residential accommodations. In this way, the revitalization of Ontario Street and the downtown in general will continue, and ensure that the area is a dynamic district accessible to the whole community and visitors – and not an enclave of condominiums, apartment houses, and chain hotels.

The most recent development is, appropriately enough, at the site of Kingston's last active commercial wharf. The Little Cataraqui-Elevator Bay site of grain transshipment became available for residential development with the closure of the Coverdale elevator in the 1980s and the sale of the property to private developers

Beautiful historic buildings like city hall and St George's Cathedral were dwarfed by inappropriate structures erected downtown during the 1970s. Kingston's nineteenth-century
ambiance was substantially damaged. (The authors)

Kingston's disfigured skyline in the 1980s. (The authors)

in 1986. Further, the last commercial vessel to use the adjoining Crawford dock sailed out in October 1987. As with much of the old Outer Harbour, this waterfront area is being dedicated to condominiums and marina slips. The critical questions are public access to the waterfront, ecological impact, disruption of the skyline, and the charge that, yet again, development is proceeding piecemeal without any consideration of an integrated waterfront plan.[22]

Finally, what Ontario Street has been through the 1970s and 1980s, Rideau Street and outer Montreal Street will be in the 1990s. The district of unsightly wharfs, oil tanks, and nineteenth-century factories and workshops is being looked to for development as high-price residential properties. Whatever the previous century of land-use and residential preference, the promised water aspect and access ensure a demand for residential properties there. Frontenac Village has led the move into the district, and while the city has shown some foresight in acquiring blocks of property along the former Inner Harbour, lands fronting the marshlands of the Great Cataraqui have already been turned over to massive high-rise tenements. While these lands are presently sufficiently far out to be of no concern to those more interested in the Sydenham Ward waterfront, their integrity will be increasingly of concern as population expands into these areas in the next decade.

In all these areas, Kingston and its adjoining municipalities would be well advised to follow the principles laid down in the city of Kingston's 1981 *Official Plan*.[23] This document recognizes that the "relationship of the City to Lake Ontario and the Great and Little Cataraqui Rivers is one of the great assets of Kingston, the benefits of which should be exploited to the advantage of the citizens at large as well as those living close to the waterfront." In order that these benefits "may accrue to as many persons as possible it shall be the policy of council to preserve and create views of the water" by zoning by-laws and also to "preserve unobstructed views of the water along those streets which terminate at the water's edge." Public access to the waterfront is to be ensured, public ownership of the waterfront is to be pursued, and public use and enjoyment are to be furthered. None would argue with the declaration in the *Official Plan* that

It shall be the policy of Council to co-operate with other municipalities in the preparation of plans for regional development of the waterfront. ... It shall be the policy of Council to encourage the enhancement of the environmental qualities of Lake Ontario. It is recognized that Lake Ontario provides the Kingston area with a large area of open space and is of great value with respect to (1) its use for recreation purposes, (2) the provision of distant views and (3) as a source of wind and fresh air.

Many Kingstonians would encourage the city's political leaders to read the *Official Plan* and to enforce it in both letter and spirit.

Building on the Past

Kingston is unique among the cities of Canada because it has been allowed to build on its past. Explosive urban growth and industrialization did not occur and hence did not lead to the general physical destruction of the nineteenth-century heritage. Also, the lack of massive growth has meant that what remains of the heritage has not suffered the relative diminution in scale that would have come had Kingston become a major metropolis. That is not to suggest that some architectural gems have not been destroyed or dwarfed by inappropriate and misplaced construction; such has occurred, but as a consequence of an inept civic leadership that has been consistently dedicated to outdated notions of urban and economic growth.[1]

Scale is central to the identity of Kingston and explains much about the importance of the city's continuities: everything would be different if Kingston had become a city of two or three or four hundred thousand people. For example, of important Canadian cities only two or three other locations possess more pre-Confederation structures than Kingston does. The relatively small size of Kingston makes this heritage substantially more dominant than would be the case had the city become large: scale has given Kingston the opportunity to retain the ambiance of a nineteenth-century town.

Scale ramifies in a wide variety of ways. This is true of the military presence. The military came first with Count Frontenac, returned with the Loyalists, and has been here ever since. One often reads about the departure of the garrison in 1870, and the traumatic effect that loss had on the city. Indeed the garrison did leave, but the military *presence* never left, and in relative terms it is probably as important in the 1980s as it ever was. In physical terms, military structures – Fort Henry, the Martello towers, Royal Military College, Tête-du-Pont Barracks – have as much to do with Kingston's physical appearance as any others. Indeed Kingstonians should be eternally thankful to the military. Had they not occupied the properties they do, and had the politicians of the area been in control of those properties, the entire entryway to the Rideau Canal would almost certainly be dotted with high-rise condominia and apartment structures.

The great institutions of Kingston are able to retain substantial influence and continue to play a major role in defining the character of the city because of scale. Kingston's three major institutions of post-secondary learning – Queen's University, Royal Military College, and St Lawrence Community College – are if anything relatively more important in the 1980s than has ever been the case. In comparative urban terms they provide Kingston with an unusually large community of writers, scientists, medical doctors, lawyers, artists, musicians, engineers, social scientists, and technicians. It is almost certainly the case that Kingston has, on a per-capita basis, more published authors than any other urban centre in Canada.[2] This pool of people – both teachers and students – clustered around these institutions has for generations contributed greatly to Kingston's cultural life. They have produced massive amounts of art, music, drama, fiction, non-fiction, and poetry for their fellow-citizens. They have also contributed vitally to all aspects of political and social life.

Kingston's relatively small size has permitted other defining institutions to retain unusual influence. It is true that the role of religion has declined over the years, but the Anglican Diocese and the Roman Catholic Archdiocese continue to perform important sub-capital functions.

As noted elsewhere, much research remains to be completed before we will be able to understand the precise nature of the influence exerted on the community by the Kingston area's massive penal system. In and about Kingston are hundreds upon hundreds of convicts and guards. This presence has been with us since the 1830s. We do not know how our guards are affected by devoting a career to incarcerating other people, but affect there must be. We also know, however, that since the 1830s Kingston has hosted a community of families one of whom – normally a father or husband – is in prison. We also know that some released convicts settle in Kingston; some are fully rehabilitated and contribute usefully to the community, while others continue less productive pursuits. One result of this facet of Kingston's identity is a police force somewhat unlike those in similarly-sized communities. The detectives of the Kingston Police Department are forced to deal with what is often essentially big-city crime.

Politics is another of Kingston's continuities, and politics too is influenced by scale. The city of Kingston has been a single constituency – really a political community – since 1820. This has applied to the Upper Canadian period (1820-1841), the United Province of Canada period (1841-1867), and, since 1867, to both provincial and federal politics. From 1820 on there has been a member for Kingston, and not just for a portion of Kingston. This has tended to make MPs and MPPs community leaders in a more obvious way than is usually the case in Canada. The sitting member is everybody's MP or MPP. Kingstonians tend to be familiar with their politicians and have usually found them highly accessible. A successful MP or MPP must know Kingston and its people extremely well.

Within the Kingston community, federal politics has normally been the dominant level of political activity. For the most part the member of parliament for Kingston has been the city's best known personality and most important single leader. Before Confederation this was obviously true of Christopher Hagerman and John A. Macdonald. Since 1867 Kingston's MPs have often been at or near the centre of power, and have almost always held an importance that extended far beyond the borders of their constituency. Sir John A. Macdonald, of course, was the founder of his country. William Harty was a key Liberal insider during the Laurier era. A famous Queen's political scientist, Norman McLeod Rogers, was an important member of the administration formed by Mackenzie King in 1935. Rogers, minister of Defence when war broke out in 1939, died in an accident in 1940. He was replaced as MP for Kingston by Angus L. MacDonald, premier of Nova Scotia, who remained as Kingston's MP and a Defence minister until 1945. The Honourable J. Edgar ("Ben") Benson served as minister of National Revenue under Lester Pearson and as minister of Finance under Pierre Elliott Trudeau.

Flora MacDonald holds the record as the longest-serving MP for Kingston since Confederation. She was a very senior minister in the short-lived government of Joe Clark and one of the most senior members of Brian Mulroney's cabinet. The Honourable Flora MacDonald is Kingston's best known citizen.

Continuity is central to Kingston's nature, and the city's continuities are as impressive as they are important. However, in one central area continuity is not the pattern: Kingston's present economy bears precious little relationship to what has gone before. Originally in the days of Frontenac, and then in the days of the Loyalists, the town's economy was based squarely on transshipment and infusions of government funds (the latter source of revenue does in fact represent a major continuity). The transshipment function died, as did virtually every single aspect of a water-based economy. Rafting, ship-building, ship-repair, waterfront warehousing, water-based transportation for people, and salvaging operations – all have vanished.

The town's municipal leadership sought to replace these vanishing functions in mundane and unimaginative North American ways. The answer, it was assumed, was industrial development and growth. The city sought these ends without success, and in the late nineteenth and early twentieth centuries – apart from a few atypical periods – Kingston exhibited either slow growth rates or actual absolute decline.

Later in this century, Kingston became one of Canada's most impressive illustrations of a public-sector town. The Crown contributed massive amounts of money to the city through its publicly-funded institutions, universities, assistance programs, restoration operations, and the military. Kingston acquired a disproportionately large number of civil servants (both federal and provincial) and a publicly-financed infrastructure that is the envy of other Canadian cities.

In the 1980s Kingston has emerged as a public-sector town with a population that has become more ethnically diverse due to the post-Second World War arrival of

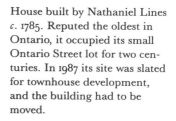

House built by Nathaniel Lines *c.* 1785. Reputed the oldest in Ontario, it occupied its small Ontario Street lot for two centuries. In 1987 its site was slated for townhouse development, and the building had to be moved.

Gutting: the house is shown on its original site; its fireplaces are being ripped out and thrown into dumpsters. (The authors)

Hauling away the heritage: the gutted house is taken east along Ontario Street. (Kingston *Whig-Standard*)

Going, going, gone: relocated to a deserted spot at the foot of North Street on the Great Cataraqui River, the house was destroyed by an arsonist in April 1988. (The authors)

new immigrant groups. Kingstonians now include substantial numbers of Canadians of Chinese, Greek, West Indian, Portuguese, Dutch, Jewish, and Scandinavian descent. This more mixed population has not, however, broken one of the town's most obvious continuities: it remains very much centred in Anglo-Celtic traditions and values.

The city's industrial base, never huge, diminished after the 1950s, and by the 1980s it was no longer of any major importance. What then emerged was a unique opportunity to utilize the city's location and natural beauty to allow Kingston to continue to build upon its past. Kingston is superbly convenient to such cities as Montreal, Toronto, Ottawa, and New York. Its setting is stunning in terms of recreational activities – virtually all of which relate to the water. Kingston has also emerged as a substantial retirement community and possesses the potential for an enormous water-based tourist industry. The town also has the potential to attract high-tech industry that is not dependent on location and that can utilize the substantial available intellectual resources.

This leads to the next of Kingston's economic-social challenges. Successful economic activity at the present time and probable developments in the future correlate with the city's ambiance and water-based setting. Kingston has no need to grow; but if it is to grow, such development will relate to retirement patterns, sailing and boating activities, amenities for the substantial body of public-sector employees, and high-tech industries that are locationally neutral.

In short, Kingston's future relates to scale, preservation, and beauty. Concerned citizens in the 1980s are bothered about civic decisions made in the 1950s and 1960s – decisions that have led to aesthetic and social imbalances in the 1980s. What judgements will the citizens of the early twenty-first century make of the leaders and planners of the 1980s? Did they – in adequate ways – consider the future?

Notes

In general, a conventional format has been used in footnotes and all bibliographical entries. Where more than one item by the same author occurs in the notes to a particular chapter, a short-title format is used. The fine articles in Gerald Tulchinsky, ed., *To Preserve and Defend: Essays on Kingston in the Nineteenth Century* (Montreal: McGill-Queen's Press, 1976) are cited so often that this book is always referred to simply as *To Preserve and Defend*. If an entry does not include a publisher, place of publication, or date of publication, such information was unavailable in the work cited. Unless indicated otherwise, newspapers referred to were published in Kingston. The following abbreviations are used:

AO	Archives of Ontario.
CE	*The Canadian Encyclopedia*
CKP	*City of Kingston Papers*, Queen's University Archives.
DCB	*Dictionary of Canadian Biography*.
f.p.	first published.
HK	*Historic Kingston*, the journal of the Kingston Historical Society.
NA	National (formerly Public) Archives of Canada.
n.d.	no date
n.p.	no publisher
OH	*Ontario History*
QU	Queen's University.
QUA	Queen's University Archives.

INTRODUCTION
The Personality of Place

1 Others have tackled this question. In geography, see Sir Cyril Fox, *The Personality of Britain* (Cardiff: National Library of Wales, 1932); Carl Orwin Sauer, "The Personality of Mexico," *Geographic Review*, XXXIII; E. Estyn Evans, *The Personality of Ireland* (Cambridge: Cambridge University Press, 1973). In history, see S.F. Wise, "A Personal View of Kingston," *HK*, 22 (1974); Arthur R.M. Lower, "The Character of Kingston," in *To Preserve and Defend*.

CHAPTER ONE
The French and Cataraqui

1 For a detailed discussion of this, see Victor Konrad, "An Iroquois Frontier: The North Shore of Lake Ontario During the Late Seventeenth Century," *Journal of Historical Geography*, 7 (1981), 129-144.

2 R.A. Preston and L. Lamontagne, eds, *Royal Fort Frontenac* (Toronto: Champlain Society, 1958), 103.

3 P.J. Robinson, *Toronto During the French Regime* (Toronto: Ryerson, 1933), 22.

4 Talon to Louis XIV, 10 October 1670, in Preston and Lamontagne, *op. cit.*, 102.

5 James S. Pritchard, *Journey of my Lord Count Frontenac to Lake Ontario in 1673* (Kingston: Downtown Business Association, 1973), xv-xvi.

6 Frontenac to Colbert, 13 November 1673, in Preston and Lamontagne, *op. cit.*, III-112; a league was approximately three miles or five kilometers.

7 W.J. Eccles, *Canada under Louis XIV, 1673-1701* (Toronto: McClelland and Stewart, 1964), 82.

8 Frontenac to Colbert, 13 November 1673, in Preston and Lamontagne, *op. cit.*, III-112.

9 Nicholas de La Salle, in *ibid.*, 128.

10 W. Bruce Stewart, "The Structural Evolution of Fort Frontenac," *Northeast Archaeology*, 14 (1985); Konrad, *op. cit.*, 137.

11 Robinson, *op. cit.*, 32, cited in Konrad, *ibid.*, 137.

12 J.P. Donelly, "The History of Brandy in Canada," *Mid-America*, 34 (1952), 53, cited in Konrad, *ibid.*, 137.

13 Cited in R.L. Jones, *History of Agriculture in Ontario, 1613-1880* (Toronto: University of Toronto, 1977; f.p. 1946), 11.

14 W.J. Eccles, *The Canadian Frontier, 1534-1760* (New York: Holt, Rinehart and Winston, 1969), 117.

15 Eccles, *Canada Under Louis XIV*, 150.

16 Preston and Lamontagne, *op. cit.*, 179.

17 *Ibid.*, 196.

18 *Ibid.*, "Plan of Fort Frontenac, c. 1740," following p. 66.

19 J. Douglas Stewart and Ian E. Wilson, eds., *Heritage Kingston* (Kingston: Queen's, 1973), 26.

20 Cited in Preston and Lamontagne, *op. cit.*, 250-251.

21 William Gerald Godfrey, *John Bradstreet: An Irregular Regular, 1714-1774*, Ph.D. thesis, Queen's, 1974, 347; see also Donald Chaput, "Payen de Noyan," *DCB*, IV, 611-613.

22 Cited in Godfrey, *ibid.*, 335.

23 *Ibid.*, 340.

24 *Ibid.*, 346.

25 *Ibid.*, 347.

26 Cited in Stewart and Wilson, *op. cit.*, 29.

27 Godfrey, *op. cit.*, 349.

28 Cited in Stewart and Wilson, *op. cit.*, 27.

29 Godfrey, *op. cit.*, 352.

30 Cited in Stewart and Wilson, *op. cit.*, 29.

31 Konrad, *op. cit.*, 143.

CHAPTER TWO
"A Poor Happy People"

1 E.A. Cruikshank, ed., *The Settlement of the United Empire Loyalists on the Upper St. Lawrence and Bay of Quinte in 1784: A Documentary Record* (Toronto: Ontario Historical Society, 1934), 1-2.

2 R.A. Preston, *Kingston Before the War of 1812: A Collection of Documents* (Toronto: Champlain Society, 1959), 22.

3 *Ibid.*

4 *Ibid.*, 23-24.

5 *Ibid.* 24.

6 *Ibid.*, xliii.

7 Victor Konrad, "An Iroquois Frontier: The North Shore of Lake Ontario During the Late Seventeenth Century," *Journal of Historical Geography*, 7 (1981), 142.

8 Pierre F.X. Charlevoix, *Histoire et Description de la Nouvelle France* (New York: Harper, 1900; f.p. 1721), I, 298.

9 R. Rogers, *The Journals of Major Robert Rogers* (Dublin: R. Acheson, 1769), 186-187.

10 Preston, *op. cit.*, 26.

11 *Ibid.*, 38.

12 *Ibid.*

13 Cruickshank, *op. cit.*, 21.

14 *Ibid.*

15 Preston, *op. cit.*, 360.

16 S.E. Dawson, *Indian Treaties and Surrenders* (Ottawa: Brown Chamberlain, 1891), I, 89.

17 *Ibid.*, 63.

18 Preston, *op. cit.*, 39.

19 *Ibid.*, 40.

20 *Ibid.*, 27.

21 *Ibid.*, xliv.

22 *Ibid.*, xiv, 89.

23 *Ibid.*, xlvi.

24 *Ibid.*, xlii.

25 *Ibid.*, xlvii.

26 *Ibid.*, 91-94.

27 QU, Government Documents, Department of Lands and Forests, Surveyors' Letter Books, vol. 1, f.2, John Collins, 12 August 1784.

28 *Ibid.*

29 *Ibid.*

30 *Ibid.*, vol. 1, 18 June 1785.

31 *Ibid.*, vol. 1, 7 May 1786.

32 Preston, *op. cit.*, 44.

33 *Ibid.*

34 *Ibid.*, lv.
35 The recent historical literature concerning the Loyalists is massive and filled with controversy. A very well written and competent synthesis of Loyalist material as it pertains to Ontario is Bruce Wilson, *As She Began: An Illustrated Introduction to Loyalist Ontario* (Toronto and Charlottetown: Dundurn Press, 1981).
36 *Ibid.*, 13.
37 *Ibid.*
38 *Ibid.*, 18.
39 Larry Turner, "Michael Grass: A Loyalist Founder of Kingston, 1783-1784," *HK*, 34 (1986),26.
40 Wilson, *op. cit.*, 109.
41 *Ibid.*, 10.
42 Larry Turner, *Voyage of a Different Kind: The Associated Loyalists of Kingston and Adolphustown* (Belleville: Mika, 1984), 35.
43 *Ibid.*
44 Larry Turner, "Michael Grass," *DCB*, V, 378.
45 Turner, *Voyage*, 42.
46 *Ibid.*.
47 Turner, "Michael Grass," *HK*, 25.
48 *Ibid.*
49 *Ibid.*, 27.
50 Turner, "Michael Grass," *DCB*, V, 378.
51 Donald B. Smith, "Mary Brant," *CE*, II, 215.
52 Barbara Graymont, "Mary Brant," *DCB*, IV, 416.
53 *Ibid.*, 417.
54 Turner, *Voyage*, 36.
55 Ian E. Wilson, "Molly Brant: A Tribute," *HK*, 24 (1976), 56.
56 Graymont, *op. cit.*, 416.
57 *Ibid.*, 417.
58 Wilson, *op. cit.*, 56.
59 Graymont, *op. cit.*, 418.
60 H.P. Gundy, "Molly Brant – Loyalist," *OH*, 45 (1953), 106.
61 A.H. Young, ed., *The Parish Register of Kingston Upper Canada 1785-1811* (Kingston: British Whig Publishing Company, 1921),32.
62 Ian Wilson, *op. cit*, 57.
63 T.R. Millman, "John Stuart," *DCB*, V, 785.
64 *Ibid.*, 786.
65 James Robertson Carruthers, *The Little Gentleman: The Reverend Doctor John Stuart*

and the Inconvenience of Revolution, MA research essay, Queen's, 1975, 45-46.
66 *Ibid.*, 69.
67 *Ibid.*, 82.
68 *Ibid.*, 115.
69 Millman, *op. cit.*, 787.
70 Carruthers, *op. cit.*, 130.
71 *Ibid.*, 128.
72 Marilyn G. Miller, *The Political Ideas of the Honourable Richard Cartwright 1759-1815*, MA research essay, Queen's, 1975, 16.
73 *Ibid*, 1.
74 George Rawlyk and Janice Potter, "Richard Cartwright," *DCB*,V, 169.
75 *Ibid.*, 170.
76 Carruthers, *op. cit.*, 97.
77 Miller, *op. cit.*, 21.
78 *Ibid.*, 63.
79 Rev. C.E. Cartwright, ed., *Life and Letters of the Late Hon. Richard Cartwright* (Toronto: Belford Brothers, 1876), 28.
80 Preston, *op. cit.*, liii.
81 *Ibid.*, 88.
82 *Ibid.*
83 *Ibid.*
84 Richard A. Preston, "John Ross," *DCB*, IV, 683.
85 William R. Riddell, *The Life of John Graves Simcoe* (Toronto: McClelland and Stewart, 1926), 155.
86 Mary Quayle Innis, ed., *Mrs. Simcoe's Diary* (Toronto: Macmillan, 1965), 72.
87 *Ibid.*
88 *Ibid.*, 73.
89 Patrick Campbell, *Travels in the Interior Inhabited Parts of North America in the Years 1791 and 1792* (Edinburgh: J. Guthrie, 1793), 142.
90 Cited in Richard A. Preston, "The History of the Port of Kingston," *HK*, 3 (1954), 5.
91 La Rochefoucauld-Liancourt, *Travels Through the United States, the Country of the Iroquois and Upper Canada in the Years 1795, 1796, and 1797* (London: R. Phillips, 1799), 279.
92 Sir David William Smyth, *A Short Topographical Description of His Majesty's Province of Upper Canada in North America* (London: W. Faden, 1799), 15.
93 Joseph Bouchette, *A Topographical Description of the Province of Lower Canada with Remarks upon Upper Canada* (London: W. Fadden, 1815), 598.

94 Preston, *Kingston Before the War*, 89.

95 *Ibid.*, 361-362.

96 *Ibid.*, 362-363.

97 Mary Quayle Innis, *op. cit.*, 72.

98 La Rochefoucauld, *op. cit.*, 292.

99 Isaac Weld, *Travels Through the States of North America and the Provinces of Upper and Lower Canada During the Years 1795, 1796, 1797* (4th ed.; London: Stockdale, 1807), II, 85-86.

100 *Gazette*, 27 November 1810.

101 NA, RG 5, A1, George Medley to Lt. Governor, 26 April 1819.

102 Preston, *Kingston Before the War*, 346-347.

103 *Ibid.*, 347.

104 *Gazette*, 20 April 1816.

105 *Ibid.*

106 Bouchette, *op. cit.*, 599.

CHAPTER THREE

Citadel Kingston

1 QUA, *Cartwright papers*, box 2, vol. 2, Cartwright to Todd, 21 October 1792.

2 J. Douglas Stewart and Ian E. Wilson, *Heritage Kingston* (Kingston: Queen's, 1973), 36-37.

3 Richard A. Preston, ed., *Kingston Before the War of 1812: A Collection of Documents* (Toronto: Champlain Society, 1959), 230.

4 *Ibid.*, 236.

5 *Ibid.*, lxxxi.

6 NA, RG 5, A1, 27 April 1812, Military Secretary Quebec to Major General Brock.

7 Preston, *op. cit.*, 248.

8 Preston, *op. cit.*, 255-256.

9 Cited in Gerald M. Craig, *Upper Canada: The Formative Years, 1784-1841* (Toronto: McClelland and Stewart, 1963), 284, note 16.

10 James A. Roy, *Kingston: The King's Town* (Toronto: McClelland and Stewart, 1952), 81.

11 Mackay Hitsman, "Kingston and the War of 1812," *HK*, 15 (1966), 50; see also John W. Spurr, "The Royal Navy's Presence in Kingston, 1813-1836," *HK*, 25 (1977).

12 NA, MG 24, "Diary of David Wingfield," 1813-1816.

13 Robert Gourlay, *Statistical Account of Upper Canada* (New York: Johnson Reprint Corporation, 1966; f.p. 1822), I, 128.

14 Brian S. Osborne, "The Settlement of Kingston's Hinterland," in *To Preserve and Defend*, 68.

15 Francis Hall, *Travels in Canada and the United States in 1816 and 1817* (London: Longman, 1818), 162-163.

16 James Strachan, *A Visit to the Provinces of Upper Canada in 1819* (Aberdeen: Chalmers, 1820), 27.

17 For more on the war of 1812 and Kingston see Hitsman, *op. cit.*; John W. Spurr, "The Kingston Gazette, the War of 1812, and Fortress Kingston," *HK*, 17 (1968); and "The Kingston Garrison, 1815-1870," *HK*, 20 (1971).

18 For the rationale for, and the construction of the Rideau Canal, see V.A. George, "The Rideau Corridor: The Effect of a Canal System on a Frontier Region, 1832-1898," MA thesis, Queen's 1972; Robert F. Legget, *Rideau Waterway* (Toronto: University of Toronto, 2nd ed., 1986); George K. Raudzen, *The British Ordnance Department and Canada's Canals* (Waterloo: Wilfrid Laurier, 1979); Brian S. Osborne and Donald Swainson, *The Rideau Navigation, 1832-1972: Its Operation, Maintenance, and Management* (Ottawa: Parks Canada Microfiche Report Series, No. 191, 1985), 2 vols.

19 The following discussion relies upon Ivan J. Saunders's excellent study, *A History of Martello Towers in the Defence of British North America, 1796-1871* (Ottawa: Information Canada, Canadian Historic Sites No. 15, 1976), 52-64. See also W. Patterson, "Fort Henry: Military Mistake or Defiant Deterrent?" *HK*, 29 (1981).

20 *Ibid.*, 40.

21 *Chronicle*, 15 October 1831.

22 For a summary of construction plans and estimates, see R.L. Way and B.W. Way, "Kingston's Defences, 1783-1871," *Fort Henry Source Material* (Kingston: Fort Henry, Part 1, 1965), 162.

23 NA, WO 55, 25 January 1841, vol. 876, Memo on the fortifications at Kingston and on the defence of the frontier.

24 *Ibid.*, 20 November 1841, Report on Defences.

25 *Ibid.*

26 *Ibid.*

27 NA, WO 55, vol. 866, Col. Durnford to Sir James Kempt, 10 October 1828.

28 Cited in John W. Spurr, "The Royal Navy's Presence in Kingston; Part 1, 1813-1836," *HK*, 25 (1977).

29 William Dewey, *Suggestions Urging the Construction of a Rail-Road from Rome to Watertown and Cape Vincent* (Watertown: J. Green, 1844), 26.

30 Way and Way, *op. cit.*, 227.

31 *Condensed Schedules of Authorized Pay and Allowances in Canada, 1841* (Quebec: T. Carey, 1841).

32 *Ibid.*

33 *British Whig*, 12 July 1844.

34 *Chronicle and Gazette*, 30 January 1846.

35 *British Whig*, 17 January 1846, cited in W.S. Lavelle, "The History of the Present Fortifications at Kingston," *Ontario Historical Society, Papers and Records*, 31 (1936).

36 NA, RG 5, A1, Commodore Barrie to Maitland, re. Enclosing Point Frederick, 4 February 1820.

37 *Chronicle*, cited in Bytown *Gazette*, 10 December 1840.

38 *Chronicle*, 10 December 1840.

39 P. Finan, *Journal of a Voyage to Quebec in the Year 1825, With Recollections of Canada during the late American War in the years 1812-1813* (Newry: A. Peacock, 1828), 323-324.

40 QU, Government Documents, Department of Lands and Forests, Surveyors' Letter Books, vol. 1, letter from A. Wells, 10 March 1846.

41 C.W. Cooper, *Frontenac, Lennox, and Addington: An Essay* (Kingston: Creighton, 1856), 16.

42 *Ibid.*, 19-20.

43 John W. Spurr, "Garrison and Community, 1815-1870," in *To Preserve and Defend*, 118.

44 In a personal letter, Professor Preston notes that "The last noon gun fired by the British garrison was in 1870. But when the Militia occupied the Fort, and perhaps afterwards, a caretaker fired a noon gun. One of the RMC Commandants used to check its accuracy and phone the caretaker if he was late or early."

CHAPTER FOUR:
Loyal in Rebellion

1 G.M. Craig, *Upper Canada: The Formative Years* (Toronto: McClelland and Stewart, 1967), 248.

2 *Ibid.*, 249.

3 Albert B. Corey, *The Crisis of 1830-1842 in Canadian-American Relations* (New York: Russell & Russell, 1970; f.p. 1941), 37.

4 *Ibid.*, 61.

5 *Ibid.*, 71.

6 Charles Lindsey, *The Life and Times of Wm Lyon Mackenzie* (Toronto: P.R. Randall, 1862), II, 199, note.

7 Corey, *op. cit*, 41.

8 *Ibid.*, 72.

9 Sir Charles Lucas, ed., *Lord Durham's Report on the Affairs of British North America* (Clifton, N.J.: Augustus M. Kelly, 1970; f.p. 1912), II, 4.

10 *Ibid.*, 148-49.

11 Frederick H. Armstrong, *Handbook of Upper Canadian Chronology and Territorial Legislation* (London: University of Western Ontario, 1967), 17, 110.

12 *Chronicle*, July 1838, cited in Corey, *op. cit.*, 91-92.

13 *Chronicle and Gazette*, 4 November 1837, cited in Donald Creighton, *John A. Macdonald*, (Toronto: Macmillan, 1952 and 1955), I, 44.

14 *Ibid.*, 46.

15 NA, WO 55, vol. 874, Bonnycastle to Colborne, 20 May 1839.

16 *Chronicle and Gazette*, 9 December 1837, cited in Creighton, *op. cit.*, 46.

17 NA, WO 55, vol. 874, Bonnycastle to Colborne, 20 May 1839.

18 Quebec *Gazette*, 12 November 1838, cited in Creighton, *op. cit.*, 60.

19 *Ibid.*

20 *Ibid.*, 61.

21 *Chronicle and Gazette*, 17 November 1838.

22 William R. Teatero, *"A Dead and Alive Way Never Does": The Pre-Political Professional World of John A. Macdonald*, MA thesis, Queen's, 1978, 158.

23 *Upper Canada Herald*, 25 September 1838, 2, cited in *ibid.*, 165.

24 Daniel D. Heustis, *Narrative of the Remarkable Adventures and Sufferings of Captain Daniel D. Heustis* (Boston: S.W. Wilder & Co., 1847), 57-58, cited in

Richard Pierce, "Nils Von Schoultz – The Man They Had to Hang," *HK*, 19 (1971), 61.

25 Heustis, *op. cit.*, 69, cited in *ibid.*, 63.

26 Cited in Edwin Guillet, *The Lives and Times of the Patriots: An Account of the Rebellion in Upper Canada, 1837-1838 and the Patriot Agitation in the United States, 1837-1842* (Toronto: University of Toronto, 1963), 140.

27 Pierce, *op. cit.*, 65.

CHAPTER FIVE

Capital of Canada

1 Fernand Ouellet, *Lower Canada 1791-1840* (Toronto: McClelland and Stewart, 1980), 312-313.

2 See S.F. Wise, "John Macaulay: Tory for all Seasons," in *To Preserve and Defend*.

3 W.P.M. Kennedy, ed., *Documents of the Canadian Constitution, 1759-1915* (Toronto: Oxford, 1918), 542.

4 Cited in David B. Knight, *A Capital for Canada: Conflict and Compromise in the Nineteenth Century* (Chicago: University of Chicago, Department of Geography Research Paper 182, 1977), 25.

5 Sir F.P. Robinson to J.B. Robinson, 20 January 1816, cited in Knight, *ibid.*, 33.

6 Cited in *ibid.*, 34-35.

7 *Ibid.*, 35-37.

8 *Ibid.*, 37.

9 Cited in David B. Knight, *Choosing Canada's Capital: Jealousy and Friction in the Nineteenth Century* (Toronto: McClelland and Stewart, 1977), 29-33.

10 Cited in *ibid.*, 33-34.

11 Margaret Angus, "Lord Sydenham's One Hundred and Fifteen Days in Kingston," *HK*, 15 (1967), 37.

12 Cited in Eleanor Herchmer Robertson, "The Herchmers of Kingston," *HK*, 15 (1967), 62.

13 *Ibid.*

14 Sydenham to Russell, 28 October 1840, in Paul Knaplund, ed., *Letters From Lord Sydenham, Governor-General of Canada 1839-1841, to Lord John Russell* (Clifton, N.J.: Augustus M. Kelly, 1973; f.p. 1931), 9.

15 Cited in Knight, *Choosing Canada's Capital*, 34.

16 6 February 1841, cited in *ibid.*, 34.

17 Sydenham to Arthur, 10 February 1840, in *ibid.*

18 Toronto *Examiner*, 10 February 1841, cited in *ibid.*

19 Montreal *Le Canadien*, 7 July 1841, cited in *ibid.*, 35.

20 Montreal *Morning Courier*, 10 February 1841, cited in *ibid.*, 34-35.

21 Angus, "Sydenham's One Hundred and Fifteen Days," 38.

22 Cited in *ibid.*, 39.

23 This description was that of James Buckingham, cited in *ibid.*, 40. The comment that follows by John Richardson is cited in the same article, 40.

24 Cited in *ibid.*, 48.

25 Thomson to Lord Russell, 22 May 1840, cited in Knight, *Choosing Canada's Capital*, 33.

26 Donald Creighton, *John A. Macdonald* (Toronto: Macmillan, 1952 and 1955), I, 42.

27 *Ibid.*, 79.

28 For Harrison, see George Metcalfe, "Samuel Harrison: Forgotten Reformer," *OH*, 50 (1958) and "Samuel Bealey Harrison," *DCB*, IX.

29 Jean-Charles Falardeau, "Étienne Parent," *DCB*, X, 579.

30 W.L. Morton, "William Agar Adamson," *DCB*, IX, 5.

31 W.A. Adamson, *Salmon-fishing in Canada*, ed., J.E. Alexander (London: 1860), 152-53, cited in J.E. Hodgetts, "The Civil Service When Kingston was the Capital of Canada," *HK*, 5 (1956), 21.

32 George Mainer, "Hamilton Hartley Killaly," *DCB*, IX, 403.

33 *Ibid.*, 404.

34 Sydenham to Russell, 12 June 1841, in Knaplund, *op. cit.*, 143.

35 Margaret Angus, *The Old Stones of Kingston: Its Buildings Before 1867* (Toronto: University of Toronto, 1966), 78.

36 Angus, "Sydenham's One Hundred and Fifteen Days," 41.

37 Angus, *Old Stones of Kingston*, 78.

38 Angus, "Sydenham's One Hundred and Fifteen Days," 41.

39 For an excellent assessment of Browne and his work in Kingston, see J. Douglas Stewart, "Architecture for a Boom Town: The Primitive and the Neo-Baroque in George Browne's Kingston Buildings," in *To Preserve and Defend*.

40 *Chronicle and Gazette*, 17 February 1841, cited in *ibid.*, 40.

41 *Ibid.*, 44.

42 *Ibid.*, 51-52.
43 W.H. Smith, *Smith's Canadian Gazetteer* (1846), p. 91, cited in Stewart, *op. cit.*, 58.
44 Sir Richard Bonnycastle, *Canada and the Canadians* (London: Colburn, 1849), II, 280-281.
45 *Ibid.*, I, 108-110.
46 A.R. Hazelgrove, *A Checklist of Kingston Imprints to 1867* (Kingston: Queen's, 1978).
47 Joseph Pope, *Memoirs of the Right Honourable Sir John Alexander Macdonald* (London: Edward Arnold, 1894), I, 25-26.
48 Toronto *Patriot*, 7 September 1841.
49 Cited in Angus, "Sydenham's One Hundred and Fifteen Days in Kingston," 39.
50 Cited in Knaplund, *op.. cit.*, 17.
51 Cited in John William Kaye, *The Life and Correspondence of Charles, Lord Metcalfe*, new and revised edition (London: Smith, Elder & Co., 1858), II, 328.
52 Cited in *ibid.*
53 Cited in *ibid.*, II, 399.
54 Metcalfe to Martin, 3 January 1845, cited in *ibid.*, II, 402.

CHAPTER SIX
Crisis

1 J.C. Dent, *The Last Forty Years: The Union of 1841 to Confederation*, ed. Donald Swainson (Toronto: McClelland and Stewart, 1972; f.p. 1881), 68-69.
2 Bagot to Stanley, 19 January 1842, cited in G.P. de T. Glazebrook, *Sir Charles Bagot in Canada: A Study in British Colonial Government* (Oxford: University Press, 1929), 35-36.
3 D.B. Knight, *A Capital for Canada: Conflict and Compromise in the Nineteenth Century* (Chicago: University of Chicago, Department of Geography, Research Paper 182, 1977), 48.
4 Arthur to Sydenham, 6 February 1841, cited in *ibid.*, 49, note 6.
5 Toronto *Examiner*, 10 February 1841, cited in *ibid.*, 50.
6 *Le Canadien*, 7 July 1841, cited in *ibid.*, 52, notes 4 and 5.
7 Charles Dickens, *American Notes for General Circulation* (London: Chapman and Hall, 1842), II, 194.
8 Wakefield to Girouard, 20 August 1842, cited in Knight, *A Capital For Canada*, 54.
9 Cited in *ibid.*, 55.
10 Cited in *ibid.*
11 David B. Knight, *Choosing Canada's Capital: Jealousy and Friction in the Nineteenth Century* (Toronto: McClelland and Stewart, 1977), 35-39.
12 *Ibid.*, 38-39.
13 Cited in Knight, *A Capital for Canada*, 62-66.
14 *Ibid.*, 76.
15 Donald Creighton, *John A. Macdonald* (Toronto: Macmillan, 1952 and 1955), I, 87-88.
16 Stewart in Ian E. Wilson, J. Douglas Stewart, Margaret S. Angus, and Neil K. MacLennan, *Kingston City Hall* (Kingston: City of Kingston, 1974), 4.
17 For a superb account of the fire and its influences on the development of Kingston, see John W. Spurr, "The Night of the Fire," *HK*, 18 (1970).
18 Margaret Angus, "John Counter," *HK*, 27 (1979), 19.
19 *Ibid.*
20 *Ibid.*, 19-20.
21 *Ibid.*, 20.
22 *Ibid.*
23 *Ibid.*
24 *Ibid.*
25 Angus in Wilson, Stewart, Angus and MacLennan, *op. cit.*, 11.
26 *Ibid.*, 6.
27 *Ibid.*.
28 *Ibid.*, 11. The following account of the building's use is based upon this excellent pamphlet.
29 *Ibid.*, 12.
30 *Ibid.*, 17.
31 Duncan McDowall, *Kingston in 1846-1854: A Study of Economic Change in a Mid-Nineteenth Century Canadian Community*, MA thesis, Queen's, 1973, III.
32 *Ibid.*, 109-110.
33 *Ibid.*, 110.
34 *Ibid.*, III.
35 *Argus*, 18 February 1845, cited in *ibid.*, 112.
36 *Ibid.*, 114.
37 *Ibid.*, 115.
38 See Angus, "John Counter," 21, 25, note 20.
39 *Daily British Whig*, 20 June 1850, cited in McDowall, *op. cit.*, 116.
40 CKP, *Report Book 1852-66*, Report 120, 11 December 1854, cited in *ibid.*
41 Robert Baldwin to his father, 4 August

1843, cited in Violet Margaret Nelson, *The Orange Order*, MA thesis, Queen's, 1950, 83 and 83, note 12.

42 Joseph Pope, *Memoirs of the Right Honourable Sir John Alexander Macdonald* (London: Edward Arnold, 1894), I, 33.

43 Cited in Knight, *Choosing Canada's Capital*, 53.

44 *Herald*, 12 September 1843, cited in Knight, *A Capital for Canada*, 71.

45 Cited in *ibid.*, 77.

46 *Ibid.*, 83.

47 *Herald*, 30 April 1844, cited in *ibid.*, 84. Clearly, the petition, to obtain 30,000 signatures, must have been circulated throughout the district as well as in Kingston.

48 *News*, 4 January 1844, cited in *ibid.*

49 *Herald*, 26 March 1844, cited in *ibid.*

50 *Chronicle and Gazette*, 30 January 1844, cited in Helen Nicholson, "Kingston and the Capital Question," research paper, Department of History, Queen's, 1979.

51 Knight, *A Capital for Canada*, 86.

52 Hopkirk to Arthur, 17 January 1844, cited in Knight, *Choosing Canada's Capital*, 65.

53 *Herald*, 11 June 1844, cited in Knight, *A Capital for Canada*, 86.

54 *British Whig*, 21 June 1844; *ibid.*, 86-87.

55 From *Chronicle and Gazette*, cited in James A. Roy, *Kingston: The King's Town* (Toronto: McClelland and Stewart, 1952),231.

56 Macdonald to his mother, 17 March 1856, in J.K. Johnson, ed., *The Papers of the Prime Ministers*, vol. 1 of *The Letters of Sir John A. Macdonald, 1836-1857* (Ottawa: Public Archives of Canada, 1968), 356.

57 Max Magill, "The Failure of the Commercial Bank," in *To Preserve and Defend*, 169.

CHAPTER SEVEN
From Village to City

1 *Gazette*, 30 December 1815.

2 *Ibid.*, 3 August 1816.

3 *Ibid.*, 30 December 1815.

4 *Chronicle*, 13 August 1819.

5 E.T. Coke, *Subaltern's Furlough: Descriptive Scenes in Various Parts of the United States, Upper and Lower Canada, New Brunswick and Nova Scotia During the Summer and Autumn of 1832* (London: Saunders and Otley, 1833), 318.

6 *British Whig*, 12 June 1835.

7 *Argus*, 20 January 1846, cited in G.M. Betts, "Municipal Government and Politics, 1800-1850," in *To Preserve and Defend*, 234-35.

8 *Argus*, 27 March 1846.

9 *British Whig*, 5 May 1846, cited in Betts, *op. cit.*, 237.

10 *Argus*, 7 August 1846, cited in *ibid.*, 240.

11 *Chronicle and News*, 14 October 1848.

12 *Ibid.*, 30 October 1839.

13 1851, Manuscript Census, Kingston Township.

14 *Ibid.*

15 *Daily British Whig*, 28 May 1850.

16 *British Whig*, 1 March 1848.

17 Betts, *op. cit.*, 235.

18 *Chronicle and News*, 16 May 1849, cited in *ibid.*, 243.

19 *Gazette*, 3 December 1819.

20 CKP, Box 1844-5, Letter, 29 September 1845.

21 *Gazette*, 12 August 1817.

22 *Chronicle*, 16 February 1827.

23 *Chronicle and Gazette*, 13 May 1837.

24 *Ibid.*, 15 May 1836.

25 *Chronicle*, 10 December 1831.

26 *Chronicle and Gazette*, 27 January 1841.

27 *Chronicle*, 31 October 1823.

28 *Argus*, 30 March 1847.

29 AO, Minutes of the General and Quarter Sessions, Midland District, 6 December 1836.

30 *Chronicle*, 18 January 1830.

31 T.R. Preston, *Three Years' Residence in Canada from 1837 to 1839* (London: R. Bentley, 1840), I, 126.

32 *Chronicle and Gazette*, 27 July 1839.

33 *Chronicle*, 17 April 1832.

34 H.C. Burleigh, *Forgotten Leaves of Local History – Kingston* (Kingston: Brown and Martin, 1973), 107.

35 *Chronicle*, 7 April 1832.

36 *Ibid.*, 5 May 1832.

37 *Ibid.*, 12 May 1832.

38 James A. Roy, *Kingston: The King's Town* (Toronto; McClelland and Stewart, 1952), 150.

39 *Chronicle*, 23 June 1832.

40 C.M. Godfrey, *The Cholera Epidemics in Upper Canada, 1832-1866* (Toronto: Secombe House, 1968) and Geoffrey Bilson, *A Darkened House: Cholera in Nineteenth Century Canada* (Toronto: University of Toronto, 1980); for Kingston see John W. Spurr, "The Town at Bay:

Kingston and the Cholera, 1832 and 1834," *HK*, 23 (1975).

41 NA, RG 5, A1, J.R. Forsythe to McMahon re: cholera in Kingston.

42 Walter Henry, *Surgeon Henry's Trifles: Events of a MilitaryLife* (London: Chatto & Windus, 1970; f.p. 1839), 231.

43 *Chronicle and Gazette*, 26 July 1834.

44 *Ibid.*, 2 August 1834.

45 *British Whig*, 12 August 1834.

46 *Ibid.*, 8 August 1834.

47 *Chronicle*, 23 June 1832.

48 *British Whig*, 8 August 1834.

49 Godfrey, *op. cit.*, 9.

50 Hallowell *Free Press*, 22 September 1834.

51 *British Whig*, 14 July 1847.

52 *Ibid.*, 10 July 1847.

53 *Ibid.*, 18 August 1847.

54 *Ibid.*, 6 October 1847.

55 *Ibid.*, 4 September 1847.

56 St Mary's Cathedral, *The First Registers, Internments, 1816-69*, V, 31-79.

57 Patricia E. Malcolmson, "The Poor in Kingston, 1815-1850," in *To Preserve and Defend*, 293.

58 *Chronicle and News*, 8 November 1848.

59 *Chronicle and Gazette*, 23 November 1839.

60 *Ibid.*, 3 November 1841.

61 *Ibid.*

62 *Ibid.*, 3 November 1841.

63 *Ibid.*, 19 November 1845.

64 12 Vict., cap. CLVIII, "City of Kingston Water Works Company" incorporated, amended by 14, 15 Vict., cap. 37; 18 Vic., cap. 217.

65 *Daily British Whig*, 21 November 1849.

66 *Chronicle and News*, 25 August 1849; see also Edwin E. Horsey, "Early Fire Regulation and Volunteer Firemen," (Kingston: no p., 1944), 22 pp.

67 John W. Spurr, "The Night of the Fire," *HK*, 18 (1970).

68 *Ibid.*, 65

69 *Ibid.*, 61-62.

70 CKP, Report Book E, No. 234, 25 January 1884; see also B. Rudachyk, "A Tempest in a Teapot: The City of Kingston and the City of Kingston Water Works Company," research paper, Department of History, Queen's, 1979.

71 *Ibid.*, Report Book E, no. 427, 4 October 1886.

72 *Chronicle*, reported in Bytown *Gazette*, 10 December 1840.

73 *Gazette*, 25 August 1818.

74 *British Whig*, 22 September 1835.

75 *Chronicle and Gazette*, 30 April 1843.

76 *Ibid.*, 30 April 1843.

77 *Chronicle and News*, 19 January 1841.

78 NA, RG 5, A1, Petition of Kingstonians to Sir Francis Bond Head regarding intemperance, 30 November 1836.

79 *Argus*, 17 November 1846.

80 *Chronicle and Gazette*, in Roy, *op. cit.*, 218.

81 Roy, *ibid.*, 265.

82 *Daily British Whig*, 7 December 1858.

83 B. Rudachyk, "City with a Heart of Stone: Fire in Kingston, 1838-73," research paper, Department of History, Queen's, 1979.

84 Prescott *Telegraph*, cited in *Daily British Whig*, 18 October 1858.

85 *Ibid.*, 13 December 1858.

86 CKP, City of Kingston By-Laws, vol. 103, 112-113.

87 *Daily British Whig*, 15 September 1855.

88 CKP, City of Kingston, *Papers of Council*, 1855.

89 Prescott *Telegraph*, cited in *Daily British Whig*, 4 November 1858.

90 Province of Canada, 22 Vic., cap. 99.

91 *Daily British Whig*, 3 March 1859.

92 *Chronicle and Gazette*, 1 September 1849.

93 *Ibid.*, 13 December 1843.

94 Resolution, Kingston Board of Commons School Trustees, December 1, 1865, cited in M. Campbell, "The Kingston Board of Common/Public School Trustees: Architect of the System of Public Education, 1850-1897," research paper, Department of History, Queen's, 1980.

95 Inspector's Report to KBPST, December 7, 1890, cited in *ibid.*

96 *Chronicle and Gazette*, 27 July 1839.

97 *Chronicle and News*, 13 November 1847.

98 *Ibid.*, 4 December 1847, cited in Malcolmson, *op. cit*, 293.

99 CKP, City of Kingston By-Laws, 31 January 1848, 78-79.

100 NA, RG 5, A1, A.B. Hawkes to J. Joseph, 14 May 1832.

101 *Chronicle and Gazette*, 14 July 1838.

102 Bytown *Gazette*, 10 December 1840.

103 Edwin E. Horsey, "Care of the Sick and Hospitalization at Kingston Ontario, 1783-1938," (Kingston: n.p., 1939), 2.

104 QUA, House of Industry Papers, box no. 2. Actually the House of Industry system as introduced in Kingston was consistent with the general principles of the Elizabethan Poor Law that was reaffirmed in the 1830s. This point was drawn to the attention of the authors by R.A. Preston.

105 Malcolmson, *op. cit.*, 293.

106 QUA, House of Industry Papers, Discharge Book, box no. 8.

107 *Chronicle and Gazette*, 11 September 1844.

108 *Ibid.*, 2 February 1848.

CHAPTER EIGHT

The Entrepot of the Great Lakes

1 Phillip Stansbury, *A Pedestrian Tour of Two Thousand Three Hundred Miles in North America, 1821* (New York: J.D. Myers and W. Smith, 1822), 147.

2 John Howison, *Sketches of Upper Canada, Domestic, Local and Characteristic* (Edinburgh: Oliver and Boyd, 1821), 43.

3 Edward Allen Talbot, *Five Years' Residence in the Canadas: Including a Tour Through Part of the United States of America in the Year 1823.* (London: Longman, Hurst, Rees, Orme, Brown and Green, 1824), I, 98-99.

4 T.R. Preston, *Three Years Residence in Canada from 1837 to 1839* (London: R. Bentley, 1840), 126.

5 Joseph Bouchette, *The British Dominions in North America; or a Topographical and Statistical Description of the Provinces of Lower and Upper Canada* (London: Longman, Rees, Orme, Brown and Green, 1831), I, 77.

6 QUA, Shanly Family Scrapbook, *c.* 1830-50.

7 Frederick H. Armstrong and N.C. Hultin, "The Anglo-American Magazine Looks at Urban Upper Canada on the Eve of the Railway Era," in Ontario Historical Society, *Profiles of a Province* (Toronto: Ontario Historical Society, 1967), 49.

8 G.D. Warburton, *Hochelaga: or England in the New World* (London: George Routledge, 1854), 97-98.

9 Sir Richard Bonnycastle, *The Canadas in 1841* (London: 1841), I, 123.

10 *Chronicle and Gazette*, 31 May 1837.

11 *Ibid.*, 31 December 1836.

12 *Ibid.*, 29 August 1830.

13 *Chronicle*, 17 July 1830.

14 Edward J. Barker, *Observations on the Rideau Canal* (Kingston: British Whig, 1834), 26.

15 James Marr Brydone, *Narrative of a Voyage with a Party of Emigrants, sent out from Sussex* (London: E. Wilson, 1834), 34.

16 For a detailed discussion of Rideau traffic flows, see V.A. George "The Rideau Corridor: The Effect of a Canal System on a Frontier Region, 1832-1898," MA thesis, Queen's, 1972.

17 *Chronicle and Gazette*, 22 July 1835.

18 George, *op. cit.*, 137-218.

19 *British Whig*, 6 May 1834.

20 W.H. Smith, *Smith's Canadian Gazetteer* (Toronto: H. & W. Rowsell, 1846), 91.

21 *Chronicle and Gazette*, 8 November 1845.

22 *Ibid.*, 5 October 1845.

23 *Ibid.*, 9 December 1846.

24 Niagara *Gleaner* 12 March 1825.

25 *Chronicle and Gazette*, 14 January 1837.

26 *Ibid.*, 28 January 1837.

27 William Dewey, *Suggestions Urging the Construction of a Rail-Road from Rome to Watertown and Cape Vincent* (Watertown: J. Green, 1844).

28 *Chronicle and Gazette*, 11 March 1848.

29 *Ibid.*, 24 October 1835.

30 *Ibid.*, 18 January 1837.

31 *Daily News*, 14 October 1851.

32 *Ibid.*, 13 April 1852.

33 *Ibid.*, 5 December 1853.

34 *Chronicle and Gazette*, 8 November 1845.

35 *Daily News*, 1 April 1854.

36 *Ibid.*, 27 October 1856.

37 *Ibid.*, 28 October 1856.

38 *Ibid.*

39 NA, RG 12, vol. 1995, "T.C. Keefer's Report upon the Preliminary Survey of the Montreal and Kingston Section of the Canada Trunk Railway," 30 January 1852.

40 *Ibid.*

41 *Chronicle and News*, 26 November 1858.

42 *Ibid.*, 5 August 1858.

43 *Daily British Whig*, 29 July 1853.

44 *Daily News*, 23 March 1859.

45 *Chronicle and Gazette*, 26 October 1839.

46 *Ibid.*, 14 April 1840.

47 *Ibid.*, 10 July 1840.

48 Cited in *ibid.*, 17 July 1840.

49 *Ibid.*, 21 August 1841.

50 *Chronicle*, 16 March 1844.

51 *Ibid.*, 6 December 1845.

52 *Chronicle and News*, 27 December 1848.

53 *Chronicle and Gazette*, 14 May 1845.

54 I.D. Andrews, *Report on the Trade and Commerce of the British North American Colonies and upon the Trade of the Great Lakes and Rivers* (Washington, D.C.: Exec. Doc. No. 136, 32, Congress, 1853), 472-475.

55 R.A. Preston, "The History of the Port of Kingston," *HK*, 3 (1954), 14.

56 Marvin McInnis, *Kingston in the Canadian Economy of the Late Nineteenth Century* (Kingston: Institute for Economic Research, Queen's University, Discussion Paper No. 132, n.d.), Table A-III.

57 *Sessional Papers*, "Tables of Trade and Navigation," 1860-1880.

58 J.R. Godley, *Letters from America* (London: J. Murray, 1844), I, 236.

59 *Chronicle and Gazette*, 11 July 1835.

CHAPTER NINE
The Search For A "Populous Back Country"

1 Robert Gourlay, *Statistical Account of Upper Canada* (New York: Johnson Reprint Corporation, 1966; f.p., 1822), I, 128.

2 QU, Government Documents, Department of Lands and Forests, Surveyors' Letters, vol. 9, Alexander Aitken to D.W. Smith, Surveyor General, 26 December 1792.

3 *Ibid.*, Samuel Wilmot's survey of Portland, vol. 34, 11 March 1809.

4 *British Whig*, 12 July 1835.

5 *Chronicle and Gazette*, 11 July 1835.

6 QU, Department of Lands and Forests, *op. cit.*, Field Note Book 1605, T.F. Gibbs' report on the resurvey of Oso, 1861-1862.

7 *Ibid.*, Field Note Book 1599, T.F. Gibbs' resurvey of Olden, 1860.

8 *Ibid.*, Field Note Book 1051, J.A. Snow's report on Clarendon, 11 August 1862.

9 *Chronicle and News*, 31 July 1857.

10 *Ibid.*, 18 April 1862.

11 Bobcaygeon *Independent*, 4 October 1858.

12 *Daily British Whig*, 20 January 1881.

13 NA, RG 5, A1, ff. 35776-35782, "Remarks on the Road from Perth to Kingston by the way of the Upper Narrows of the Rideau Lake, made in July 1824."

14 *Chronicle and Gazette*, 8 August 1835.

15 Quoted in W. Saywell, *The Building of the Kingston-Napanee Road* (Toronto: Department of Transport), 15-16.

16 *Chronicle and Gazette*, 26 November 1845.

17 Thomas Flynn, *Directory of the City of Kingston, 1857-1858 (Kingston: J. Robison, 1857)*, 272.

18 *Chronicle and Gazette*, 4 July 1842.

19 *British Whig*, 12 April 1844.

20 NA, RG 1, E8, Orders in Council, vol. 13, 5 May 1846. The "Owen Sound principle" was the model for settlement later applied to the colonization roads system.

21 *British Whig*, 14 July 1847.

22 *Daily News*, 7 April 1853.

23 Duncan McDowall,"Roads and Railways: Kingston's Search for a Hinterland, 1846-54," *HK*, 23 (1975), 32.

24 *Journals of the Legislative Assembly*, 1847, appendix LL, cited in G.W. Spragge, "Colonization Roads in Canada West, 1850-1867," *OH*, 49 (1957), 1-17.

25 *Journals of the Legislative Assembly*, Minister of Agriculture, Annual Report for 1856, Appendix No. 54 (1857).

26 For a fuller discussion of this see Alan Jay Nuttal, *The Success of Government Settlement Policy in the Ottawa-Huron Tract, 1853-1898*, MA thesis, Queen's, 1980.

27 QU, Department of Lands and Forests, *op. cit.*, Field Note Book 1479, J.S. Harper's report on Miller Township, 27 October 1860.

28 Province of Canada, *Sessional Papers*, 1863, vol. 5, no. 30.

29 *Chronicle and News*, 26 February 1864.

30 *Daily British Whig*, 1 September 1881.

31 Cited in *ibid.*, 12 September 1881.

32 *Ibid.*, 1 September 1881.

33 *Ibid.*, 20 September 1881.

34 *Census of Canada*, 1881.

35 Province of Ontario, *Sessional Papers*, (1901), Commissioner of Crown Lands, Annual Report for 1901.

36 Brian S. Osborne, "Frontier Settlement in Eastern Ontario in the Nineteenth Century: A Study in Changing Perceptions of Land and Opportunity," in

D.H. Miller and J.O. Steffen, eds., *The Frontier: Comparative Studies* (Norman: University of Oklahoma, 1977).

37 See Walter Lewis, "The Trials and Tribulations of the 'Kick and Push': A Business History of the Kingston and Pembroke Railway, 1871-1912," *HK*, 28 (1980), 95.

38 A. Murray, *Report of Progress of the Geological Survey of Canada, 1852-53* (Ottawa: 1854), 137-144.

39 *Canadian Illustrated News*, June 1876.

40 Montreal *Herald*, 11 January 1871.

41 *Daily British Whig*, 8 March 1871.

42 *Ibid.*

43 *Weekly British Whig*, 9 March 1871.

44 *Daily British Whig*, 19 February 1881.

45 CKP, City of Kingston By-Laws, Chap. 175, "A By-law to aid and assist the Kingston and Pembroke Railway Company by granting a Bonus thereto of Three Hundred Thousand Dollars"; City Council Minute Book, 30 January 1871.

46 *Daily British Whig*, 3 February 1881.

47 *Ibid.*, 9 February 1881.

48 *Ibid.*, 15 October 1881.

49 *Ibid.*, 1 February 1881.

50 NA, RG 12, K&P Papers, "Affadavit of J. Bauden, Receiver, filed in case of Folger vs. K. & P. Railway Co.," 2 May 1898; see also Annual Traffic Reports.

51 *Report of the Royal Commission of the Mineral Resources of Ontario and the Measures for their Development* (Toronto: Warwick and Sons, 1890), 128-135.

52 *Report of the Royal Commission [Canals], Sessional Papers*, 1871, no. 54, 101.

53 *Ibid.*,

54 *Ibid.*, 101.

55 *Ibid.*, 101.

56 *Ibid.*, 102.

57 *Ibid.*, 103.

58 *Ibid.* See also Brian S. Osborne and Donald Swainson, *The Rideau Navigation, 1832-1972: Its Operation, Maintenance and Management* (Ottawa: Parks Canada Microfiche Report Series, no. 191, 1985), II, 225-230.

59 NA, RG 43, vol. 479, Petition to Sir Charles Tupper, Minister of Railways and Canals, from residents of the Counties of Frontenac, Leeds and Addington, the City of Kingston, and the Town of Gananoque, 12 February 1883.

60 NA, RG 12, vol. 479, Superintendent Wise to Bradley, re: Gananoque Connections, 11 February 1884.

61 NA, RG 43, vol. 1465, Macdonald, President of Gananoque Water and Power Company, to George Taylor, February 1885.

62 Canals Commission, *op. cit.*, 104.

63 NA, RG 12, vol. 479, A.M. Chisholm to the minister of Railways and Canals, 8 August 1903; A.M. Chisholm to William Harty, 10 August 1903; Robert Rowan to William Harty, 12 August 1903.

64 *Ibid.*, Wise's memorandum, 19 April 1883.

65 *Ibid.*

66 *Ibid.*, City of Kingston to William Harty, 22 February 1904.

67 *Ibid.*, Petition of Kingston Board of Trade, 1910.

68 *Ibid.*, Macleod to Schreiber, 2 March 1905.

69 For a detailed examination of this rural out-migration, see Randy W. Widdis, *"With Scarcely a Ripple": The Eastern Ontarian Immigrant Experience in Northern New York at the Turn of the Century*, Ph.D. thesis, Queen's, 1984.

70 Lewis, *op. cit.*, 101-103.

71 The chorus of the "Ballad of the K & P" from M. Easton, *The Men and My Memories of the K & P* (Kingston: n.p., 1976), 21.

CHAPTER TEN

"Wake Up Sleepy Hollow!"

1 NA, RG 5, A1, ff. 64345-64348, James Nicholls, Clerk of Peace, to Provincial Secretary.

2 Marvin McInnis, *Kingston in the Canadian Economy of the Late Nineteenth Century* (Kingston: Institute for Economic Research, Queen's, Discussion Paper No. 132, n.d.), 14-15.

3 *Hutchinson's Kingston Directory for 1862-63* (Kingston: John Creighton, 1862).

4 QUA, Canada Shipping Registers for Kingston, 1846-1908.

5 For more details regarding shipbuilding in Kingston during the second half of the nineteenth century, see John D. Wilson, *The Economic History of the Kingston Port, 1853-1900*, BA thesis, Department of Economics, Queen's, n.d., 54-64.

6 George Richardson, "The Canadian Locomotive Company," in *To Preserve and Defend*, 160.

7 *Ibid.*

8 *Hutchinson's Kingston Directory, op. cit.*, 21.

9 For Garden Island and D.D. Calvin see two items by Donald Swainson: *Garden Island: A Shipping Empire/L'Empire Maritime Garden Island* (Kingston: Marine Museum of the Great Lakes at Kingston, 1984), and "Dileno Dexter Calvin," in *DCB*, XI.

10 For James Richardson and his business activities, see Donald Swainson "James Richardson" in *CE*, 2nd ed. See also *125 Years of Progress* (Winnipeg: James Richardson and Sons, Ltd., 1982).

11 *Daily British Whig*, 10 April 1869.

12 T. Naylor, *The History of Canadian Business, 1867-1914* (Toronto: Lorimer, 1975) 2 vols.

13 CKP, Section 2, "Constitution of the Board of Trade of the City of Kingston," 24 September 1864, Minute Book. John Counter was involved in an earlier venture at the Board of Trade. See Margaret Angus, "John Counter," *DCB*, IX, 163.

14 *Ibid.*

15 *Ibid.*

16 McInnis, *op. cit.*, tables AII, AIII.

17 *Daily British Whig*, 16 February, 1870; CKP, Board of Trade Minute Book, 10 January 1871; cited in Walter Lewis, "Towards a Progressive Kingston: Financial Inducements to Industries 1870-1883," research paper, Queen's Department of History, 1979, 17.

18 *Daily News*, 9 May 1871.

19 CKP, "Report of the Select Committee on Board of Trade," 13 May 1872.

20 *Daily News*, 8 March 1873.

21 *British Whig*, 19 December 1873.

22 CKP, City Council Minute Books, 9 June 1873; *Daily News*, 3 February 1874.

23 *Daily News*, 3 March 1874.

24 *Ibid.*

25 *Daily British Whig*, 16 October 1876.

26 McInnis, *op. cit.*, table A-II.

27 *Daily British Whig*, 24 January 1881.

28 *Ibid.*, 18 January 1881.

29 Heather Nicol, "Bonusing Railways and Industries in Eastern Ontario: 1851-1901," research paper, Queen's Department of History, 1988, Table II-3.

30 *Daily British Whig*, 5 April 1881.

31 *Daily News*, 9 July 1881.

32 *Ibid.*, 7 July 1881.

33 *Ibid.*, 12 July 1881.

34 *Ibid.*, 18 February 1885.

35 *Ibid.*, 30 June 1883.

36 *Daily British Whig*, 26 March 1881.

37 Richardson, *op. cit.*, 163.

38 Cited in *Daily British Whig*, 8 February 1881.

39 *Daily British Whig*, 26 March 1881.

40 Naylor *op. cit.*, II, 118.

41 Anne MacDermaid, "Kingston in the 1890s: A Study of Urban-Rural Interactions and Change," *HK*, 20 (1972), 36.

42 *Daily British Whig*, 4 November 1887.

43 See G. Levine, R. Harris, B. Osborne, "The Single Tax System in Kingston, 1881 to 1901," in *The Housing Question in Kingston, Ontario, 1881-1901* (Kingston: Queen's University, Department of Geography, June 1982).

44 Henry George, *Progress and Poverty* (New York: Modern Library, 1930; f.p. 1879), 10.

45 *Ibid.*, 10.

46 *Daily British Whig*, 1 February 1891.

47 *Daily News*, 20 November 1889.

48 *Daily British Whig*, 6 March 1890.

49 *Daily News*, 28 December 1888.

50 *Ibid.*

51 James Thomson to Alexander Thomson, 24 March 1847, in R.A. Preston, ed., *For Friends at Home: A Scottish Emigrant's Letters from Canada, California, and the Cariboo, 1844-1864* (Montreal: McGill-Queen's, 1974), 105-106.

52 NAC, RG 12, vol. 1985, Report upon the Preliminary Survey of the Montreal and Kingston Section of the Canada Trunk Railway, 30 January 1852.

53 NA, RG 3, Kingston Post Office Inspection, 4 October 1882.

54 Robert M. Pike, *Adopting the Telephone: The Social Diffusion and Use of the Telephone in Urban Central Canada, 1876-1914* (Kingston: Queen's Studies in Communication and Information Technology, Working Paper 15, March 1987), 11.

55 *Ibid*, 19.

56 *Montreal Gazette*, 7 October 1910, cited in *ibid.*, 22.

57 NA, RG 43, B4(a), Vol. 2006, Superintendant Slater to Braun, 4 December 1869.

58 Province of Ontario, 1875-76, "An Act to Incorporate the Kingston Street Railway Company," Chap. 74, assented to 10 February 1876.

59 *Ibid.*, amended 27 May 1893, Chap. 91, 1893, sec. 1.
60 *Daily British Whig*, 23 September 1893.
61 *Ibid.*, 26 October 1917.
62 *Daily Standard*, 12 September 1914.
63 *Ibid.*
64 *Ibid.*
65 CKP, Minutes of Kingston Board of Trade, 14 January 1915.
66 *Ibid.*, Minutes, Kingston City Council, 8 January 1917.
67 *Daily British Whig*, April 30 1918.
68 *Minutes of the Council of the Corporation of the City of Kingston, Ontario for the year 1928* (Kingston: Jackson Press, 1928), 63.
69 CKP, Kingston Industries Committee, 12 March 1920.
70 *Ibid.*, 1 December 1921.
71 *Daily British Whig*, 20 December 1920.
72 *Ibid.*
73 *Ibid.*, 29 June 1906.
74 *Ibid.*
75 KCP, Correspondence, Kingston Industrial Committee, W.W. Sands, Industrial Commissioner and City Clerk, 25 April, 1926.
76 See discussion in *Whig-Standard*, 29 July 1987.
77 *Census of Canada*, 1881–1941.
78 Toronto, *Globe and Mail*, 14 June 1881.
79 *Daily British Whig*, 13 August 1881.

CHAPTER ELEVEN
Revitalizing the Port

1 *Daily British Whig*, 20 May 1881.
2 *Ibid.*, 1 August 1881.
3 *Ibid.*, 29 July 1881.
4 John D. Wilson, *The Economic History of the Kingston Port, 1853-1900*, BA thesis, Queen's, Department of Economics, n.d., table XI, p. 52.
5 *Ibid.*, 76.
6 Communication from Maurice Smith, Director of the Marine Museum of the Great Lakes at Kingston.
7 For more details see QUA, Kingston Drydock Entry Book.
8 CKP, Minutes, Kingston City Council, Commission of Industry, 18 December 1923, 317-318.
9 *Ibid.*, Kingston Board of Trade Minutes, 28 March 1900.
10 G.P. de T. Glazebrook, *A History of Transportation in Canada* (Toronto: McClelland and Stewart, Carleton Library Series, 1964; f.p. 1938), II, 235.
11 For more on the late-nineteenth-century debate on canal and lock sizes, see Brian S. Osborne and Donald Swainson, *The Sault Ste. Marie Canal: A Chapter in the History of Great Lakes Transport* (Ottawa: Environment Canada, Parks Canada, Studies in Archaeology, Architecture and History, 1986).
12 NA, RG II, Acc. 83-84/356, Box 448, file 2660-1-A, R.F. Eliot, Acting Mayor of Kingston, 2 February 1911. This until recently "secret" file constitutes the basis for much of the following discussion. For an outline of the developments see Richard A. Preston, "The History of the Port of Kingston," *HK*, 3 (1954); for more detail see Sarah J. Drummond, *Kingston as the Foot-of-the-Great-Lakes-Terminus*, MA, Queen's, 1986.
13 RG II, *op. cit.*, Dominion Marine Association, 20 January 1911.
14 *Ibid.*, W. W. Sands, City Clerk of Kingston, 16 February 1911.
15 *Ibid.*, Chapleau to Lafleur, 22 March 1912.
16 *Ibid.*, clipping of House of Commons debate, 7 April 1915, 2244.
17 *Minutes of the Council of the Corporation of the City of Kingston, Ontario for the year 1915* (Kingston: British Whig, 1916), 10.
18 RG II, *op. cit.*, H.W. Newman, Mayor of Kingston, 24 February 1919.
19 *Ibid.*, J.M. Campbell, 31 March 1919.
20 *Ibid.*, Carvell to Nickle, 14 April 1919.
21 Preston, *op. cit.*, 21.
22 RG II, *op. cit.*, Carvell to Sands, 6 May 1919.
23 *Ibid.*, Corriveau, DPW, to Deputy Minister Hunter, "Memo. for the 15th. meeting re: Kingston Improvements," 14 March 1923.
24 *Ibid.*, Hunter to Campbell, 12 March 1923.
25 *Ibid.*, Campbell to King, Minister of Public Works, 22 May 1923.
26 *Ibid.*, Hunter to Wanklyn, General Executive Assistant, CPR, 25 June 1923.
27 *Ibid.*, Hunter to King, Dominion Marine Association, 28 June 1923.
28 *Ibid.*, McCarthy to Carvell, 21 May, 1919.
29 *Ibid.*, Ouelette to Madden, 11 December 1923.
30 *Ibid.*, Grant Hall, Vice President CPR, to Hunter, 8 August 1923.

31 NA, RG 30, vol. 7513, file 650-1, Thornton to Dalrymple and Hungerford, 4 July 1923.

32 *Ibid.*, Dalrymple to Hungerford, 20 July 1923.

33 *Ibid.*, "Report: Kingston or Prescott as Transhipping Point on Completion of the new Welland Canal," 12 October 1923.

34 RG II, *op. cit.*, Dunning to King, 22 May 1926.

35 *Ibid.*, King to Dunning, 28 May 1926.

36 *Ibid.*, Dunning to King, 24 June 1926.

37 *Ibid.*, Minutes of the Meeting of the Committee of the Privy Council, 8 September 1926.

38 *Ibid.*, Cameron to Chapleau, 15 January 1927.

39 *Ibid.*, Chapleau to Cameron, 14 January 1927.

40 *Ibid.*, Chapleau to Cameron, 2 March 1927.

41 *Ibid.*, Cameron to Deputy Minister of Public Works, 2 March 1927.

42 *Financial Post*, 25 October 1926.

43 Ottawa *Citizen*, 31 January 1927.

44 Toronto *Star*, 5 April 1927.

45 *Ibid.*, 22 May 1927.

46 Drummond, *op. cit.*, 112.

47 RG II, *op, cit.*, file 2660-1, "Report on Terminals for Use with the Welland Ship Canal," 21 December, 1927.

48 *Ibid.*, 28.

49 *Ibid.*, Corriveau, Chapleau, and Coutlee, Memorandum to Deputy Minister Public Works, 3 January 1928.

50 *Whig-Standard*, 14 January 1928, cited in Drummond, *op. cit.*, 135.

51 *Ibid.*, 17 April 1928, cited in Drummond, *ibid.*, 136.

52 RG II, *op. cit.*, J.E. Ouelette, Secretary Canadian Navigation Federation, to J. C. Elliot, minister of Public Works, 25 January 1928.

53 *Whig-Standard*, 8 March 1929.

54 *Ibid*

55 Osborne and Swainson, *op. cit.*, 101.

56 *Whig-Standard*, 8 March 1929.

57 Drummond, *op. cit.*, 171.

58 QUA, Kingston Elevator Company Correspondence, Howe to Craig, 20 May 1929.

59 *Ibid.*, Canadian Terminal System Ltd. to Craig, 16 May 1929.

60 *Ibid.*, Howe to Craig, 10 June 1929.

61 *Whig-Standard*, 4 June 1929.

62 *Ibid.*, 20 November 1929.

63 *Ibid.*

64 *Ibid.*, 25 October 1929, cited in Drummond, *op. cit.*, 184.

65 Drummond, *ibid.*, 197.

66 *Whig-Standard*, 23 October 1930, cited in *ibid.*, 198.

67 Fort William *Daily Times Journal*, 21 January 1932, cited in Drummond, *op. cit.*, 214.

68 *Whig-Standard*, 17 December 1931, cited in Drummond, 205.

69 Cited in Robert Gardiner, *The Port of Kingston: Past, Present and Future* (Kingston: 1955), 1.

70 Canada, Sessional Papers, Statements of Customs, Excise Revenue and other Services by Ports and Outports, Ontario, 1940, 1950, 1960.

71 Donald Swainson, "Chronicling Kingston: An Interpretation," *OH*, 74 (1982), 312.

72 *Whig-Standard*, 22 October 1987.

73 *Ibid.*

CHAPTER TWELVE

An Institutional Town

1 Marvin McInnis, *Kingston in the Canadian Economy of the Late Nineteenth Century* (Kingston: Institute for Economic Research, Queen's University, Discussion Paper No. 132, n.d.), 1, 3.

2 Arthur R.M. Lower, "The Character of Kingston," in *To Preserve and Defend*, 21.

3 For Macdonell, see J.E. Rae, *Bishop Alexander Macdonell and the Politics of Upper Canada* (Toronto: Ontario Historical Society, 1974).

4 Colborne to the Colonial Secretary, 23 September 1829, cited in *ibid.*, 116-17.

5 Information on the chapel was provided by Rose Mary Gibson.

6 F.A. Walker, *Catholic Education and Politics in Upper Canada* (Toronto: J.M. Dent & Sons, 1955), 22-23.

7 QUA, Edwin Horsey, *Cataraqui, Fort Frontenac, Kingston*, 1937, 205.

8 City of Kingston, *Buildings of Architectural and Historic Significance* (Kingston: City of Kingston, 1973), II, 40-41.

9 For George Okill Stuart see A.J. Anderson, "George Okill Stuart," in *DCB*, IX.

10 D.M. Schurman, "John Travers Lewis and the Establishment of the Anglican Diocese," in *To Preserve and Defend*, 301.

11 City of Kingston, *op. cit.*, I, 14.

12 D.D. Calvin, *Queen's University at*

Kingston (Kingston: Trustees of the University, 1941), 27 and *passim*.

13 Hilda Neatby, *Queen's University: To Strive, To Seek, To Find and Not to Yield* (Montreal: McGill-Queen's University Press, 1978), I, 63.

14 Hilda Neatby, "Queen's University: Town and Gown to 1877," in *To Preserve and Defend*, 335.

15 *Ibid.*, 339.

16 Neatby, *Queen's University*, I, 117, 206.

17 *Daily Standard*, 3 November 1913.

18 *Ibid.*

19 NA, RG 24, vol. 6518, file HQ 363-30-1, Officer Commanding 3rd Division to Secretary Military Council, 10 November 1913.

20 *Ibid.*

21 *Ibid.*

22 J. Edmison, "The History of Kingston Penitentiary," *HK*, 3 (1954), 243.

23 H.P. Gundy, "The Business Career of Hugh C. Thomson of Kingston," *HK*, 21 (1973), 62.

24 J.M. Beattie, ed., *Attitudes Towards Crime and Punishment in Upper Canada, 1830-1850: A Documentary Study* (Toronto: University of Toronto, 1977), 80.

25 *Ibid.*, 82, 85-86.

26 *Ibid.*, 86.

27 *Report of the Commissioners appointed for the purpose of obtaining Plans and Estimates of a Penitentiary to be erected in the Province* (1832), in *ibid.*, 89-90.

28 See Bryan Palmer, "Kingston Mechanics and the Rise of the Penitentiary, 1833-1836," *Histoire Sociale/Social History*, 13, 2 (1980).

29 W.G.C. Norman, *A Chapter of Canadian Penal History: The Early Years of the Provincial Penitentiary at Kingston, and the Commission of Inquiry Into its Management, 1835-1851*, MA thesis, Queen's, 1979, 206.

30 Charles Dickens, *American Notes for General Circulation* (London: Chapman and Hall, 1842), II, 194-195.

31 Beattie, *op. cit.*, 121.

32 *Ibid.*, 155.

33 *Ibid.*, 156.

34 *Ibid.*, 158.

35 *Extracts from the First Report of the Commissioners Appointed to Investigate into the Conduct, Discipline and Management of the Provincial Penitentiary* (1849), in *ibid.*, 159.

36 *Extracts from the RULES and REGULATIONS made by the Inspectors*, in *ibid.*, 128.

37 Cited in *ibid.*, 172.

38 Cited in Dana H. Johnson and C.J. Taylor, *Reports on Selected Buildings in Kingston Ontario* (Ottawa: National Historic Parks and Sites Branch, Ottawa, 1976-77), II, 413.

39 For an introduction to Roman Catholic involvement in politics in Eastern Ontario, see Rae, *op. cit.*, and Donald Swainson, "James O'Reilly and Catholic Politics," *HK*, 21 (1973).

40 H.P. Gundy, "Publishing and Bookselling in Kingston since 1810," *HK*, 10 (1962), 36.

41 *Chronicle and News*, 3 February 1849.

42 John W. Spurr, "Edward John Barker, M.D., Editor and Citizen," *HK*, 27 (1979), 113-114.

43 Cecil J. Houston and William J. Smyth, *The Sash Canada Wore: A Historical Geography of the Orange Order in Canada* (Toronto: University of Toronto, 1980), 38.

44 W. Stewart Wallace, *The Macmillan Dictionary of Canadian Biography* (Toronto: Macmillan, 1963, 3rd ed.), 290.

45 *Daily News*, 29 August 1872, and also Donald Swainson, "Kingstonians in the Second Parliament: Portrait of an Elite Group," in *To Preserve and Defend*.

46 Toronto *Globe*, 14 December 1899.

47 *House of Commons Debates*, 1891, II, 4190, 20 August 1891.

CHAPTER THIRTEEN
Changing the Guard

1 Richard A. Preston, "The British Influence of RMC," in *To Preserve and Defend*, 119.

2 *Ibid.*, 121.

3 Cited in Richard A. Preston, *Canada's RMC: A History of the Royal Military College* (Toronto: University of Toronto, 1969), 18.

4 Mackenzie to Dufferin, 5 August 1878, cited in *ibid.*, 18.

5 Cited in *ibid.*, 25.

6 Cited in *ibid.*, 46.

7 Kingston *Daily News*, June 1876, cited in *ibid.*, 47.

8 Cited in *ibid.*, 92.

9 Cited in *ibid.*, 204.

10 *Ibid.*, 53.

11 For an excellent exploration of the origins of hockey – and Kingston's role in its development – see J.W. Fitsell, *Hockey's Captains, Colonels and Kings* (Erin: Boston Mills, 1987).

12 *British Whig*, 2 July 1880.

13 Preston, "The British Influence of RMC," 136.

14 *British Whig*, 1890, in *Dixon Scrapbook*, Vol. 6, Massey Library, RMC, cited in *ibid.*, 133-34.

15 *Daily Standard*, 3 August 1914.

16 *Ibid.*, 12 August 1914.

17 *Daily British Whig*, 7 August 1914.

18 *Daily Standard*, 19 August 1914.

19 *Ibid.*, 22 August 1914.

20 *Ibid.*, 26 August 1914.

21 *Ibid.*, 5 August 1914.

22 *Ibid.*

23 *Ibid.*, 6 August 1914.

24 *Daily British Whig*, 2 August 1914.

25 *Daily Standard*, 15 August 1914.

26 *Ibid.*

27 NA, RG 24, vol. 513, HQ 54-21-43, Nickle to Brown, Militia Department, 2 January 1915.

28 *Daily Standard*, 18 September 1914.

29 *Ibid.*, 21 August 1914.

30 Cited in Robert Craig Brown and Ramsay Cook, *Canada 1896-1921: A Nation Transformed* (Toronto: McClelland and Stewart, 1974), 212.

31 Preston, *Canada's RMC*, 220.

32 *Annual Report of the Commandant Royal Military College of Canada for the Year 1919*, Sessional Paper No. 36, 1919, 25.

33 Ibid.

34 Preston, *Canada's RMC*, 222.

35 Kathryn M. Bindon, *Queen's Men, Canada's Men: the Military History of Queen's University, Kingston* (Kingston: Trustees of the Queen's University Contingent, Canadian Officers' Training Corps, 1978), 46.

36 *Ibid.*, 41.

37 Wilhelmina Gordon, *Daniel M. Gordon, His Life* (Toronto, Ryerson, [c. 1941]), 267, cited in Bindon, *op. cit.*, 38.

38 *Standard*, 14 August 1914.

39 NA, RG 24, vol. 340, files 33-6-121, 33-6-130, 33-6-135, 33-6-139, 33-6-143, 33-6-149 refer to the annual training and commandant's reports for 1915-1918.

40 QU, Special Collections, Claire McCallum, "Kingston and the War: August 1914-December 1914," citing Kingston *Standard*, 4 December 1914.

41 *Standard*, 12 August 1914.

42 *Ibid.*, 15 November 1918. See also James A. Roy, *Kingston: The King's Town* (Toronto: McClelland and Stewart, 1952), 316-18.

43 Much of the following is derived from *Historical Calendar: 21st Canadian Infantry Battalion (Eastern Ontario Regiment)* (Aldershot: Gale & Polden, 1919).

44 Preston, *Canada's RMC*, 222.

45 *Standard*, 26 August 1914.

46 Sir Andrew Macphail, *Official History of the Canadian Forces in the Great War; The Medical Services* (Ottawa: F.A. Ackland, 1925).

47 *Ibid.*

48 Brian S. Osborne and Geraint B. Osborne, "Doolan's War: A Family Experience," ms., 1988. Documents in possession of the authors.

49 *Ibid.*, program, *Unveiling and Dedication of the 21st Canadian Infantry Battalion CEF War Memorial*, 11 November 1931.

50 G.D. Smithson, "Pittsburgh," in Bryan Rollason, ed., *County of a Thousand Lakes: The History of the County of Frontenac, 1673-1973* (Kingston: Frontenac County Council, 1982), 457-471.

CHAPTER FOURTEEN

Industry, Growth, and Expansion

1 *Whig-Standard*, 15 November 1940.

2 *Ibid.*, 17 August 1942.

3 *Ibid.*, 9 April 1943.

4 *Ibid.*, 29 March 1944.

5 QUA, Canada Steamship Lines, vol. 109, Kingston Shipbuilding Company Ltd., Minutes, 1940-1945.

6 *Whig-Standard*, 16 June 1942.

7 *Ibid.*, 19 June 1942.

8 *Ibid.*, 7 May 1943.

9 *Ibid.*, 18 September 1943.

10 *Ibid.*, 26 October 1943.

11 *Ibid.*, 21 August 1944.

12 For more details on the origin and early years of Alcan in Kingston see C.J. Graham, *History of Kingston Works, 1940-1965* (Kingston: Aluminum Company of Canada Ltd., 1967); Sheldon MacNeil, "Inside Alcan," *Whig-Standard Magazine*, 16 January 1982, 5-7.

13 *Ibid.*

14 *Ibid.*

15 *Whig-Standard*, 9 November 1940.
16 *Ibid.*
17 *Ibid.*, 18 November 1940.
18 These data are derived from *Scott's Industrial Directory, Ontario, 1962 and 1976*.
19 Richard Harris, *Class Struggle in the Domain of Social Production*, PhD thesis, Queen's, 1981, Table 9.1.
20 The following employment data are based upon a 1987 survey conducted by the authors.
21 City of Kingston, *Kingston and Region Statistics, 1982*, (Kingston: City of Kingston Planning Department, 1982), 28; *Census of Canada, 1986*.
22 *Ibid.*

CHAPTER FIFTEEN
Preservation versus Progress

1 David Helwig, *It Is Always Summer* (Toronto: Stoddart, 1982), 203.
2 *Report of the Committee on Waterfront and Downtown Redevelopment* (Kingston: City of Kingston, 1964), 8.
3 *Ibid.*
4 *Whig-Standard*, 8 May 1969.
5 W.J. Coyle, "Wharves along Kingston Waterfront Links with the Past," in *ibid.*, 8 July 1966.
6 *Whig-Standard*, 27 July 1979.
7 *Sydenham Ward Urban Renewal Scheme, Kingston, Ontario* (Rexdale: Wyllie Unfal Weinberg and Sheckenberger, Town Planners, 1979).
8 *Whig-Standard*, 18 March 1970.
9 *Ibid.*, 10 March 1970.
10 *Ibid.*, 7 July 1970.
11 *Ibid.*, 17 June 1970.
12 *Ibid.*, 16 June 1970.
13 *Ibid.*, 31 May 1972.
14 *Ibid.*, 24 February 1978.
15 *Ibid.*
16 *Ibid.*, 28 October 1964.
17 *Ibid.*, 10 March 1970.
18 City of Kingston, *Buildings of Architectural and Historical Significance* (Kingston: City of Kingston, 1975), III, preface.
19 Olympic Users' Committee, *Summary of Briefs and Comments Submitted by Organizations and Institutions Concerning the Post-Olympic Use of the Portsmouth Harbour Site* (Kingston: 26 November 1973).
20 City of Kingston, *Consolidated Official Plan of the City of Kingston* (Kingston: City of Kingston Planning Department, 1976), Specific Area No. 9 (Portsmouth Village), Amendment No. 78.
21 City of Kingston. *Specific Area No. 9, Portsmouth Village* (Kingston: City of Kingston Planning Department, 1974), 3.
22 *Whig-Standard*, 1 December 1987.
23 City of Kingston, *The Official Plan for the City of Kingston Planning Area* (Kingston: City Hall Planning Department, 1981), sections 73-84.

CONCLUSION
Building on the Past

1 This is in no way to suggest that there is unanimity among civic politicians either now or in the past. Some, like the mayors E. Valorie Swain and John Gerretsen, have shown some sensitivity to the heritage and have provided – or at least have attempted to provide – leadership in this area. Unfortunately, the civic leadership as a decision-making apparatus has been differently-motivated over the years and, as is suggested in the text, has been consistently dedicated "to outdated notions of urban and economic growth."
2 A somewhat crude index that supports this view may be found in Albert and Theresa Moritz, *The Oxford Illustrated Literary Guide to Canada* (Toronto: Oxford Press, 1987). Kingston earns the tenth largest entry, exceeded by, in order, Toronto, Montreal, Vancouver, Ottawa, Quebec City, Winnipeg, Halifax, St John's, and Fredericton. Seven of these cities are capitals; others are major metropolitan centres. All are much larger. Kingston ranks ahead of such cities as Victoria, London, Calgary, Edmonton, Regina, Saskatoon, St John, Sherbrooke, and Hamilton. In short, Kingston's place in the urban literary hierarchy is *very* high.

Chronology
of the History of Kingston

Kingston: Building on the Past is organized along both chronological and thematic lines. This chronology is included to assist those who want to know the order of events, regardless of thematic concept. It is not designed to be either comprehensive or a summary of the book. Items are included that are not necessarily discussed in the text. The chronology is designed to give the reader a quick and reasonably representative overview of some four centuries of history.

THE SEVENTEENTH CENTURY

1615   Champlain traversed Kingston area.

1673   Fort Frontenac founded.

1675   La Salle secured extensive seigneurial rights and privileges in Cataraqui area.

1683   La Salle's Cataraqui estates seized by the Governor of New France.

1689   Fort Frontenac abandoned by the French.

1695   Fort Frontenac reestablished as a French military base.

THE EIGHTEENTH CENTURY

1756   Montcalm used Fort Frontenac as his base in his campaign against Fort Choueguen (Oswego).

1758   Fort Frontenac captured by the British under Colonel Bradstreet.

1763   Cataraqui became part of the Province of Quebec, a British colony.

1783   Cataraqui selected as site for a Loyalist settlement and a British naval base.

The acquisition of lands from the Mississauga by the Crawford Purchase (also known as the Gunshot Treaty).

The preparation of the site for a town and military base by units under the command of Major John Ross.

1784   Arrival of main body of Loyalists.

Richard Cartwright settled at Cataraqui in 1784 or 1785.

1786   Reverend John Stuart opened a school with thirty pupils.

1788   "Kingston" replaced "Cataraqui" as the town's official name.

1789   Name "Tête-du-Pont Barracks" (sometimes "Tête-de-Pont") came into use. This date is inscribed on the arch leading into the complex now known as Fort Frontenac. 1787 is sometimes suggested as the correct date.

1792   St George's Church (now known as St George's Cathedral) founded.

Lieutenant-Governor Simcoe proclaimed Upper Canada a separate constitutional jurisdiction in St George's.

Simcoe held his first meeting with his Executive Council, again in St George's.

Richard Cartwright appointed to the Legislative Council of Upper Canada.

Origin of the facility now known as the Kingston Collegiate Vocational Institute. Hence KCVI is the oldest institution of learning east of the Ottawa River.

1796   Death of Molly Brant.

1799   Honourable Richard Cartwright brought John Strachan to Kingston to serve as a teacher.

THE NINETEENTH CENTURY

1801   Establishment of a market.

1802   Commencement of ferry service between Kingston and Wolfe Island.

1808   St Joseph's Church, called "the French Church," built on the corner of Bagot and William streets.

1810   Stephen Miles began publication of the *Gazette*.

1811   Formal designation of the market square.

1812   Outbreak of the War of 1812-1814.

Commodore Isaac Chauncey led an unsuccessful expedition against Kingston.

Escape of the *Royal George*.

1813   Arrival of Sir James Lucas Yeo, commodore and commander-in-chief on the Lakes.

Stephen Miles established the Kingston Social Library. This was the origin of the Kingston Public Library.

1814   The *St. Lawrence* launched. With 112 guns it was the most powerful warship on the Great Lakes.

1815   Death of Honourable Richard Cartwright.

1816   Passage of Kingston Police Act.

1817   The Rush-Bagot Treaty was signed and the Great Lakes virtually demilitarized.

1819   John Macaulay and J.A. Pringle began the publication of the *Chronicle*.

Hugh Thomson began the publication of the *Upper Canada Herald*.

1820   Establishment of Female Benevolent Society of Kingston.

The Stone Frigate completed.

Kingston became a single constituency, a status that has continued to the present and has included the following constitutional régimes: Upper Canada, the Province of Canada, the Province of Ontario, and the Dominion of Canada.

Christopher Alexander Hagerman, a Compact Tory, elected as member for Kingston. He served 1820-1824 and 1830-1840.

Consecration of St Andrew's Presbyterian Church.

1822   Charles Sangster, a significant Canadian poet, born at the naval yard on Point Frederick.

1825   The James Carmichael Smyth commission recommended to the British government the construction of the Rideau Canal and a substantial strengthening of Kingston's fortifications.

1826   Construction of the Rideau Canal commenced.

Alexander Macdonell was appointed Bishop of Regiopolis, with Kingston as his diocesan seat.

1828   Major-General Sir Alexander Bryce's commission on Kingston's defence appointed. In 1829 it recommended the construction of five redoubts to complement Fort Henry, together with five Martello towers.

Cataraqui Bridge (Penny Bridge) constructed across Great Cataraqui and so prevented use of inner-harbour by large lake vessels.

1832   Navigation of Rideau Canal (Rideau Waterway) officially commenced, with Kingston as its "upper" terminus and "Bytown" as its "lower" terminus.

Several mothballed vessels from the War of 1812-1814 auctioned. The *St Lawrence* fetched £25.

Outbreak of cholera in Kingston.

1833   *Chronicle and Gazette* (later the *Chronicle and News*) commenced publication.

1834   Bishop Macdonell took up residence in Kingston.

Kingston naval-yard was closed.

Dr Edward John Barker commenced publication of the *British Whig*.

Kingston Mechanics' Institute founded. It absorbed the Kingston Social Library.

Another severe visitation of cholera.

1835   Foundation of the Midland District Land Company to promote settlement to the north.

Kingston Penitentiary at Portsmouth received its first inmates. This was the commencement of the major prison complex that was to develop in Kingston in the twentieth century.

1836   Fort Henry completed.

Construction of Summerhill started, to be completed in 1839.

Dileno Dexter Calvin began his extensive Garden Island operation.

1837   Christopher Alexander Hagerman appointed attorney-general of Upper Canada.

William Lyon Mackenzie led an Upper Canadian rebellion that was a dismal failure.

Over five hundred Kingstonians were armed to protect the town from rebels and raiders.

1838   Americans sympathetic to Mackenzie launched an unsuccessful invasion directed at Kingston.

Acquittal of John Ashley, who was defended by John A. Macdonald.

American invaders, led by Nils Von Schoultz, defeated at the Battle of the Windmill.

Incorporation of the Town of Kingston.

Thomas Kirkpatrick became town's first mayor.

Kingston General Hospital founded.

Von Schoultz hanged at Kingston.

1839   Publication of Lord Durham's *Report*.

Cornerstone of Regiopolis College laid. Original college is central portion of the old Hotel Dieu Hospital.

First establishment of Kingston Board of Trade under presidency of John Counter.

1840   Hagerman appointed to the court of king's bench.

Great fire devastated Kingston's downtown and waterfront.

Act of Union passed by the Imperial Parliament. It created the Province of Canada, a legislative union of Upper and Lower Canada.

1841   Official announcement that Kingston to be capital of the Province of Canada.

Arrival of Governor-General Charles Edward Poulett Thomson, Baron Sydenham of Kent (in England) and Toronto (in Canada).

Proclamation of Province of Canada.

John Counter elected mayor of town of Kingston.

Anthony Manahan elected to represent Kingston in first parliament of the Province of Canada.

First parliament met at the hospital.

Manahan resigned and was replaced as Kingston's member by Samuel Bealey Harrison.

Hale's Cottages constructed.

Death of Lord Sydenham and internment at St George's.

Establishment of Queen's University by royal charter.

Passage of "An Act to establish a Police Force ..." in Kingston.

Between 1841 and 1843 George Brown's three famous round-corner buildings were constructed. The Commercial Mart is now the S & R Department Store. Wilson's Buildings is the Victoria and Grey Trust Company. Mowat's Round Corner Building has been demolished.

Nuns from the Notre-Dame Convent of Montreal settled in Kingston to provide Catholic education for young girls.

1842   Governor-General Sir Charles Bagot arrived to take office in Kingston.

LaFontaine-Baldwin government in power.

The Assembly repudiated Kingston as capital.

Queen's opened its doors to students in building on Colborne Street.

Rockwood built as John Solomon Cartwright's country villa.

1843   Mayor John Counter negotiated large English loan to finance construction of city hall.

Cornerstone of city hall laid. Designed by architect George Browne, building completed in 1844.

Arrival of Bagot's successor as governor-general, Sir Charles Theophilus Metcalfe.

Death of Bagot at Alwington House.

City hall offered to government of the Province of Canada, if Kingston remained the capital.

Parliament resolved to remove capital to Montreal.

Anti-Catholic riot.

John A. Macdonald elected as alderman.

1844   Departure of Governor-General Metcalfe for Montreal.

St Mark's Anglican Church in Barriefield opened.

John A. Macdonald elected as Kingston's member in the Union parliament.

1845   Formation of the Wolfe Island, Kingston & Toronto Railway Company.

1846   Substantial violence between military and Kingstonians.

Kingston incorporated as a city.

John Counter elected first mayor of the city.

Britain adopted policy of free trade, which damaged Kingston's transshipment function.

Construction of four Martello towers (Cedar Island, Fort Frederick, Shoal Tower, Murney Tower), 1846-1848.

1847   Act passed to "Regulate the Public Market in the City of Kingston."

A peak immigration year also associated with severe outbreak of typhus fever.

Passage of "An Act to Prevent Wooden Buildings being erected in the thickly built parts of the City. ..."

Sisters of Providence of St Vincent de Paul arrived to assist Irish immigrants.

The Religious Hospitallers of St Joseph, or sisters of the Hotel Dieu, arrived to care for sick and orphaned immigrants. Their legacy is the major medical facility Hotel Dieu Hospital.

Midland District Colonization and Emigration Society established to promote settlement of Kingston's hinterland.

1848   Completion of major canal works along St Lawrence between Kingston and Montreal, which struck another blow against Kingston's transshipment function.

St Mary's cathedral consecrated.

Construction of bishop's residence to the west of St Mary's.

1849   Robert Baldwin's Municipal Act passed. On implementation in 1850 it established basic nature of Kingston's municipal government for over a century.

1850   Lot 24 ("Stuartsville") annexed to the city.

City council established the Kingston Board of Common School Trustees.

House of Industry established.

1851   *Daily News* commenced publication.

Sydenham Street United Church constructed in 1851-1852 as a Methodist church.

New Board of Trade established.

1852   Land that became City Park and Macdonald Park released by the military for park use, although not formally acquired by the city until 1865.

Construction of Wolfe Island Canal commenced.

1853   Queen's purchased Summerhill.

1854   Departure of garrison for service in Crimean War.

1855   Contracts let for the construction of the Frontenac County Court House, one of John A. Macdonald's many patronage gifts to Kingston.

James Morton purchased the Ontario Foundry at Mississauga Point and commenced manufacture of locomotives. Under a variety of owners and names, the locomotive works continued as a major Kingston industry for over one hundred years.

Formation of The First Volunteer Militia Rifle Company, which was reorganized as 14th Princess of Wales' Own Rifles in 1863, and renamed The Princess of Wales Own Regiment after the First World War.

1856   Grand Trunk Railway commenced Kingston service to Montreal and Toronto.

Building of Custom House commenced (completed in 1859) with financial assistance from James Richardson.

Old Post Office constructed 1856-1859.

Province of Canada purchased Rockwood from the estate of John Solomon Cartwright. This became the Kingston Psychiatric Hospital.

1857   Orphans' Home and Widows' Friend Society established an orphanage and school.

James Richardson and Sons Ltd. entered business and developed into Kingston's most successful and influential enterprise.

1858   Ontario Foundry became the largest single employer in Kingston.

1859   Grand Trunk Railway opened its downtown station.

1860   Prince of Wales refused to enter Kingston because of prominent presence of an Orange Order arch on proposed route.

1861   Sisters of Providence of St Vincent de Paul established the House of Providence.

John Travers Lewis elected first bishop of the Diocese of Ontario (Anglican), with St George's as his cathedral. He was consecrated in 1862.

Military tensions with United States resulted in the arming of the four Martello towers between 1861 and 1863.

1864   James Morton went bankrupt and died in the same year.

The most important of the Confederation conferences was held at Quebec and attended by three Kingstonian Fathers of Confederation: John A. Macdonald, Alexander Campbell, and Oliver Mowat.

1865   City hall's market wing destroyed by fire; it was eventually replaced by the present wing.

1867   John A. Macdonald, the chief architect of confederation, elected as MP for Kingston. He served as prime minister 1867-1873 and 1878-1891.

John A. Macdonald knighted.

M.W. Strange (Conservative) elected as Kingston's first MPP for the provincial parliament of Ontario.

Sir Henry Smith, a Kingstonian and Tory MPP for Frontenac, served as speaker of the Ontario parliament 1867-1868.

1870   Imperial garrison left.

Last noon gun to be fired by a British garrison at Fort Henry, although subsequent guns fired during militia years – by a caretaker.

1871   Kingston and Pembroke Railway, the "Kick and Push," was incorporated.

William Robinson elected MPP for Kingston.

1872   Construction of K&P commenced.

1873   Richard Cartwright, a Kingstonian and Liberal MP for Lennox, appointed as minister of Finance and held the post until 1878.

1874   Kingston selected as site for the Royal Military College.

1876   RMC admitted its first class.

1877   Kingston Street Railway Company commenced operations.

George Munro Grant became principal of Queen's and held the post until 1902.

1878   Sir John A. Macdonald defeated in Kingston by Alexander Gunn (Liberal).

1879   Kingston obtained its first telephone – to connect Rockwood Mental Asylum with the superintendent's residence.

James H. Metcalfe (Conservative) defeated William Robinson and was elected MPP for Kingston.

1881   Great fires to north of Kingston.

1882   Kingston Cotton Mill commenced production.

Free home-delivery of mail provided for Kingstonians.

James Richardson built "Richardson No. One" – a 60,000 bushel-capacity grain elevator on the Princess Street wharf.

1883   James Richardson and Sons Ltd. exported the first prairie grain destined for offshore consumption.

1886   First K&P train entered Pembroke.

1887   Voters approved by-law permitting city to purchase the Kingston Water Works Company.

Sir John A. Macdonald defeated Alexander Gunn and restored Kingston to Conservative ranks.

Sir Alexander Campbell, a Kingstonian and long-time Tory senator, appointed lieutenant-governor of Ontario.

From 1887-1891 three Kingstonians who had worked together in the same law office, simultaneously held three of the highest posts in Canada: Sir John A. Macdonald was prime minister of Canada; Sir Alexander Campbell was lieutenant-governor of Ontario; Sir Oliver Mowat was premier of Ontario.

1890   Sir John A. Macdonald laid the "first stone" at the Kingston Dry Dock, his last major "gift" to the city.

1891   Sir John A. Macdonald died and was buried in Cataraqui Cemetery.

1892   G.A. Kirkpatrick, a Kingstonian and Conservative MP for Frontenac (1870-1892) appointed lieutenant-governor of Ontario.

James H. Metcalfe replaced Macdonald as Kingston's Tory MP.

William Harty (Liberal) replaced James H. Metcalfe as MPP for Kingston. Harty served as a cabinet minister.

1893   Kingston Street Railway Company operations electrified.

Kingston Historical Society founded.

1895   Kingston Ice Yachting Club established.

1896   Richard Cartwright, Sir Richard after 1879, appointed minister of Trade and Commerce in Sir Wilfrid Laurier's régime and held the post until 1911.

         Kingston Yacht Club built its club-house on its present site.

         Byron Moffatt Britton elected Liberal MP for Kingston.

1897   Board of Public Schools amalgamated with the High School Board to form the Board of Education.

1899   Disastrous fire gutted St George's Cathedral. Rebuilt by 1901.

THE TWENTIETH CENTURY

1901   Edward J.B. Pense (Liberal) elected MPP for Kingston.

1902   William Harty (Liberal) elected MP.

1903   Dominion Marine Association founded in Kingston.

1908   *Daily Standard* commenced publication.

         Agnes Maule Machar's *The Story of Old Kingston* published.

         William Folger Nickle (Conservative) elected MPP.

1909   City purchased the Kingston Light, Heat, & Power Company.

         Kingston Mechanics' Institute renamed the Kingston Public Library.

         Prince of Wales visited Kingston.

1911   William Folger Nickle (Conservative) elected MP.

         Arthur E. Ross (Conservative) elected MPP.

1912   K&P absorbed by the CPR.

1914   Calvin firm on Garden Island closed its ship-building and transshipment activities.

         Within eight days of outbreak of First World War, 399 Kingstonians volunteered for military service.

         During First World War, Fort Henry used to confine prisoners of war.

         21st Canadian Infantry Battalion organized and based at Kingston.

1916   City signed a contract with Hydro Electric Power Company of Ontario for the supply of power to Kingston.

         Kingston Hall and Grant Hall converted into military hospitals on Queen's campus.

1917   La Salle Causeway opened, replacing the original "Penny Bridge."

1919   Arthur E. Ross served as minister of Health in the United Farmers of Ontario government, 1919-1921.

         Honourable Sir Henry Lumley Drayton (Unionist) elected MP and served as minister of Finance, 1919-1921.

1921   Arthur E. Ross (Conservative) elected MP.

1922   William Folger Nickle (Conservative) elected MPP for Kingston.

         Queen's won the Grey Cup.

1923   Executive office of Richardson and Sons Ltd. moved to Winnipeg.

1926   Origins of the *Whig-Standard*, a direct descendant of Dr. Barker's *British Whig* and Canada's oldest daily newspaper.

         Thomas Ashmore Kidd (Conservative) elected MPP.

1927   Large gathering of Kingston-area supporters of the Ku Klux Klan.

1928   Federal government selected Prescott over Kingston as site for the foot-of-the-lakes shipping terminal.

Establishment of Kingston Chamber of Commerce.

1930   City purchased the street railway company and thus acquired Lake Ontario Park.

Canada Steamship elevator at Little Cataraqui completed.

Thomas Ashmore Kidd, MPP, speaker of the Ontario parliament, 1900-1934.

1935   Norman McLeod Rogers (Liberal) elected MP and entered William Lyon Mackenzie King's Cabinet as minister of Labour.

1938   President Franklin Roosevelt received honourary doctorate from Queen's University at ceremony at Richardson Stadium.

Official opening of restored Fort Henry.

Centennial of the incorporation of Kingston as a town.

1939   Winnipeg replaced Kingston as the official headquarters for James Richardson and Sons Ltd.

Alcan began construction of its Kingston plant.

King George VI and Queen Elizabeth visited Kingston.

Norman McLeod Rogers appointed minister of National Defence.

1940   Fort Henry again served as military prison camp during Second World War.

Alcan commenced production of aluminum ingots, sheets, and various components for military aircraft.

Honourable Norman MacLeod Rogers killed in air crash.

Honourable Angus L. MacDonald, Liberal premier of Nova Scotia, parachuted into Kingston as Roger's successor as MP. Served throughout the war as minister of National Defence for Naval Services.

1942   Canadian Industries Limited (Du Pont) began production of synthetic fibres.

1944   Employment at Alcan peaked at 3,749 men and women.

1945   Thomas Ashmore Kidd (Progressive Conservative) elected MP.

1949   William James Henderson (Liberal) elected MP.

1951   William McAdam Nickle (Progressive Conservative) elected MPP.

1952   Annexation of lands by city from Township of Kingston to incorporate Portsmouth Village, Lake Ontario Park, Elevator Bay, and Alcan site within city boundaries.

Publication of James A. Roy's *Kingston: The King's Town*.

Commencement of publication of scholarly periodical *Historic Kingston*.

1954   Celanese Canada began production of synthetic fibres at Millhaven plant.

1957   The termination of the CP service between Kingston and Pembroke along the old K&P tracks.

1958   Portico on City Hall ripped down.

Fire seriously damaged Alwington House and it was demolished in 1959.

Publication of Richard A. Preston's and Léopold Lamontagne's *Royal Fort Frontenac*.

Benjamin Graydon Allmark (Progressive Conservative) elected MP.

1959   St Lawrence Seaway opened and effectively destroyed Kingston's function as a commercial port.

Publication of Richard A. Preston's *Kingston Before the War of 1812*.

1962   Edgar John Benson (Liberal) elected MP and held cabinet posts in governments of Lester B. Pearson and Pierre Elliott Trudeau.

1963   Syl Apps (Progressive Conservative) elected MPP and held cabinet rank.

1966   City Hall's portico rebuilt.

Publication of Margaret Angus' *The Old Stones of Kingston*.

1967   St Lawrence College opened.

1968   Kingston dry dock and shipyards closed.

1969   Kingston locomotive works closed.

Construction of the Mowat Condominium in Portsmouth Village, Kingston's first condominium building.

1970   William Teron proposed to build "Marina City."

Wyllie Unfal Weinberg and Scheckenberger published a development plan for Sydenham Ward.

1971   Northern Telecom Ltd. located in Township of Kingston.

1972   Teron's Marina City project cancelled.

Flora MacDonald elected Progressive Conservative MP. She is Kingston's longest-serving MP since Confederation and held senior posts in the governments of Joe Clark and Brian Mulroney.

1973   Kingston celebrated tercentenary of founding of Fort Frontenac.

1975   Keith Norton (Progressive Conservative) elected MPP and member of cabinet, 1977-1985.

1976   Sailing Olympics held in Kingston at Portsmouth Village.

Marine Museum of the Great Lakes at Kingston opened.

Queen Elizabeth II visited Kingston.

Publication of Gerald Tulchinsky's *To Preserve and Defend: Essays on Kingston in the Nineteenth Century*.

1978   Kingston Public Library moved into its present quarters on Johnson Street.

1979   Ken Keyes (Liberal) elected MPP and served in government of David Peterson, 1985-1987.

Construction of Harbour Place commenced, closely followed by extensive additional downtown construction.

1980   Agnes (Richardson) Benidickson appointed chancellor of Queen's, reaffirming traditional ties between Richardson family and both Queen's and Kingston.

1982   Opening of Cataraqui Town Centre.

1984   Kingston celebrated its bicentenary of Loyalist settlement.

1986   Kingston Brewing Company Ltd. reestablished one of Kingston's traditional industries.

1987   The last stretch of the original K&P railway track torn-up between Kingston and Tichborne.

The *Algo-Soo* docked at Kingston and was the last vessel to use Elevator Bay as a commercial shipping facility.

McAllister Towing and Salvage Company closed, bringing to an end the traditional shipping function of Kingston's Outer Harbour waterfront.

The "Big Four" manufacturing operations (Du Pont, Alcan, Celanese, and Northern Telecom) employed only 3,698 persons. The public-sector employers of the military, education, hospitals, OHIP, and prisons employed some 20,878 persons in the Greater Kingston Area.

Lines House, reputed to be the oldest building in Ontario, ripped from its Ontario Street site and moved to a site at the foot of North Street in order to make way for townhouse construction.

1988   Lines House destroyed by arson.

Two designated heritage buildings at foot of Princess Street demolished by developer without permit.

Sources for the
History of Kingston

PLACES TO LOOK

Kingston is unusually rich in historical sources. Several local institutions hold vast quantities of primary and secondary materials as well as paintings, prints, photographs, and artifacts. The Kingston Public Library has a special collection of Kingston materials that includes a first-rate selection of local newspapers. Both the Anglican diocese and the Roman Catholic archdiocese hold extensive quantities of valuable research materials. The Marine Museum of the Great Lakes at Kingston, in addition to possessing numerous marine-related artifacts, holds substantial collections of manuscript and other materials and is developing into a research centre of some substance. The Massey Library at the Royal Military College holds much material, especially items that relate to the military and to the history of RMC.

By far the largest and most important holdings are on the campus of Queen's University. The overwhelming bulk of this material is held by the Douglas Library (especially in these units: Special Collections, Periodicals, and Government Documents), the Agnes Etherington Art Centre, and the Queen's University Archives (housed in Kathleen Ryan Hall). Further details concerning the QUA will be supplied below. The Agnes Etherington Art Centre's extensive holdings include a substantial number of paintings and sketches of Kingston scenes and people.

Artifacts have also been collected and are displayed at Bellevue House, the Pumphouse Steam Museum, the International Hockey Hall of Fame, and the Kingston Historical Society's Martello Tower Museum. Those who wish to learn more about Kingston can be given major assistance by two vibrant organizations: the Kingston Historical Society and the Kingston Branch of the Ontario Genealogical Society.

The serious student of Kingston's history will have to visit non-local collections. Crucial Kingston materials – manuscripts, art work, photographs, travel books, pamphlets, military records, architectural material, maps, census data, and artifacts – are held by the National Archives of Canada, the National Library, and the National Gallery of Canada in Ottawa. The Archives of Ontario in Toronto are not as rich, but they are still indispensable to the study of Kingston.

The student of Kingston's history must also turn to the city itself. Here are still to be found many grand architectual statements interspersed with other vernacular forms and the homes of diverse classes and occupations. Together, these constitute a remarkable record of nineteenth-century streetscapes, a unique collage of institutional, ecclesiastical, and domestic architecture. Particularly notable assemblages are to be found in the adjacent communities of Barriefield and Portsmouth, and around Kingston's distinctive market square.

AIDS TO RESEARCH AND SOME MAJOR PRIMARY SOURCES

There is a vast body of sources, both primary and secondary, that relate to Kingston and its place in Canadian history. Some of this material is listed in Alan F.J. Artibise and Gilbert A. Stelter, *Canada's Urban Past: A Bibliography to 1980 and Guide to Canadian Urban Studies* (Vancouver: University of British Columbia, 1981), which includes 140 items specifically concerned with Kingston. Deborah Dafoe, *Kingston: A Selected Bibliography* (Kingston: Public Library Board, 2nd ed. 1982) and A.R. Hazelgrove, *A Checklist of Kingston Imprints to 1867* (Kingston: Queen's, 1978) are valuable starters for the serious student. Of course the most important sources are primary, and a key depository is the *City of Kingston Archives*, held by QUA. This collection is of some 1,700 linear feet (and growing constantly); it runs from 1838 to the present and includes minutes and proceedings of city council and its committees, correspondence, by-laws, assessment rolls, petitions, board of health records, board of works records, and much more. *A Guide to the Holdings of the Archives of Kingston* (Kingston: City of Kingston, 1979) facilitates the use of this large collection and lists those portions available on microfilm.

Numerous additional manuscript materials are available, and (along with photographs) have been listed in Anne MacDermaid and George F. Henderson, eds., *A Guide to the Holdings of the Queen's University Archives*, 2nd ed., and *A Guide to the Holdings of Queen's University Archives, Volume 2: Audio Visual Collections* (Kingston: Queen's, 1986 and 1987). Only a few will be mentioned to illustrate the nature of such collections. Queen's University Archives holds the voluminous collections that relate to the university. QUA also holds numerous collections of important academics whose careers made a substantial impact on Kingston, including Adam Shortt, Norman Rogers, Arthur Lower, John Deutsch, and George Whalley. Queen's University Archives is also rich in local business and political papers, and holds a microfilm copy of the papers of John A. Macdonald.

Some Macdonald material has been published. Of particular interest here is J.K. Johnson, ed., *Affectionately Yours: The Letters of Sir John A. Macdonald and his Family* (Toronto: Macmillan, 1969).

Newspapers are a basic source, and the town has been blessed with a wide array of lively and often highly-committed papers. Less important because of shortness of runs or narrowness of focus are the *Canadian Watchman*, 1830-1832, continued as *Kingston Spectator*, 1833-1840; Kingston *Statesman*, 1836-1845; Kingston *Herald*, 1844-1848; *Barker's Canadian Monthly Magazine*, 1846-1847; *The Age*, 1849; *Argus*, 1846-1851, 1862-1867; *The Magnet*, 1847-1848; *New Era*, 1865; Kingston *Evening Times*, 1897-1908; *Daily Standard*, 1908-1926; and *Canadian Register*, 1942-1974, continuing to the present as the *Catholic Register*. The more important newspapers are the Kingston *Gazette*, 1810-1818; *Upper Canada Herald*, 1819-1851; *Daily British American*, 1849-1873; Kingston *Chronicle and Gazette*, 1833-1847, continued as *Chronicle and News*, 1847-1899; Kingston *Daily News*, 1851-1908; and, most important of all, the *British Whig*, 1834-1849, continued as *Daily British Whig*, 1849-1926, and continued as *Whig-Standard*, 1926 to the present. The *Kingston Public Library Newspaper Index* is an unusually fine research tool. This ongoing project has provided an index of Kingston's newspapers that is now complete to 1848.

It goes without saying that the history of Kingston cannot be studied without recourse to published official documents. Of prime importance are the journals, debates and sessional papers of Upper Canada, the Province of Canada, Ontario and Canada. Census material is also crucial. A variety of city directories are also helpful: Queen's University's Douglas Library holds a run (broken for the early years) from 1855 to the present.

Adequate official and manuscript sources are not available for portions of the town's early history. Books by military officers, diarists, travellers, and chroniclers of various types do much to fill these gaps, even though they usually include only a few pages on Kingston. This kind of material is vast. Only the more famous and important are listed. Most have been used in this book. They appear roughly in the order of writing: Mary Q. Innis, ed., *Mrs. Simcoe's Diary* (Toronto: Macmillan, 1965); Isaac Weld, *Travels Through the States of North America and the Provinces of Upper and Lower Canada During the Years 1795, 1796, 1797*, 4th ed. (London: Stockdale, 1807); John Ogden, *A Tour of Upper and Lower Canada* (Litchfield: n.p., 1799); Sir David William Smyth, *A Short Topographical Description of H.M. Province of Upper Canada in North America* (London: Faden, 1799); George Heriot, *Travels Through the Canadas* (London: Phillips, 1807), 2 vols; Francis Hall, *Travels in Canada and the United States in 1816 and 1817* (London: Longman, 1818); Robert Gourlay, *Statistical Account of Upper Canada* (New York: Johnson Reprint Corporation, 1966; f.p. 1822), 3 vols; James Strachan, *A Visit to the Province of Upper Canada in 1819* (Aberdeen: Chalmers, 1820); John Duncan, *Travels Through Part of the United States and Canada in 1818 and 1819* (Glasgow: Glasgow University, 1823); Basil Hall, *Travels in North America in the Years 1827 and 1828* (Edinburgh: Cadell & Co., 1829), 2 vols; J. MacTaggart, *Three Years in Canada: An Account of the Actual State of the Country in 1826-7-8*, (London: Colburn, 1829), 2 vols; Joseph Bouchette, *The British Dominions in North America* (London: Longman, Reese, Orme, Brown, Green, and Longman, 1831), 2 vols; Charles Dickens, *American Notes for General Circulation* (London: Chapman and Hall, 1842), 2 vols; *Smith's Canadian Gazette, Comprising Statistical and General Information Respecting All Parts of the Upper Province or Canada West* (Toronto: Rowsell, 1846); Sir Richard Bonnycastle, *The Canada's in 1841* (London: Colburn, 1841), 2 vols, and *Canada and the Canadians*, new ed., 2 vols, (London: Colburn, 1849); Johann G. Kohl, *Travels in Canada and Through the States of New York and Pennsylvania* (London: Manwaring, 1861); Sir William H. Russell, *Canada: Its Defences, Conditions and Resources* (London: Bradbury and Evans, 1865). For a twentieth-century example of the *genre*, see Nicholas Monsarrat, *Canada: Coast to Coast* (London: Cassell 1955). Excerpts from a wide variety of travel literature are reprinted in Arthur Britton Smith, ed., *Kingston! Oh Kingston* (Kingston: Brown & Martin, 1987).

SECONDARY SOURCES

What follows is a highly selective list of secondary sources, designed to illustrate the quality and scope of writing about Kingston and its people, and to enable readers to examine in greater detail the major topics dealt with in *Kingston: Building on the Past*. The footnotes to this book and the bibliographies listed above should be consulted for additional readings.

Among general references, a nineteenth-century source that retains substantial utility is C.W. Cooper, *Frontenac, Lennox and Addington: An Essay* (Kingston: Creighton, 1856). The *Illustrated Historical Atlas of the Counties of Frontenac, Lennox and Addington* (Toronto: J.H. Meacham, 1878; repr. Belleville: Mika, 1972) includes much useful information relating to the history, economy, and society of nineteenth-century Frontenac County.

There are several survey histories of Kingston, but none is by a professional historian: Agnes Maule Machar, *The Story of Old Kingston* (Toronto: Musson, 1908) was produced by a major nineteenth-century Kingston intellectual. General but dated surveys are James A. Roy, *Kingston: The King's Town* (Toronto: McClelland and Stewart, 1952); Edwin Horsey, *Cataraqui, Fort Frontenac, Kingston*, (ms, QUA, 1937) and *Kingston a Century Ago* (Kingston: Kingston Historical Society, 1938); and T.R. Glover and D.D. Calvin, *A Corner of Empire: The Old Ontario Strand* (Cambridge: Cambridge University, 1937), chaps. 1 and 2. Nick and Helma Mika, eds., *Kingston: Historic City* (Belleville: Mika, 1987) is a multi-author coffee-table-type book. A comprehensive, if diverse, collection of some 82 essays on Kingston is to be found in *Kingston 300 – A Social Snapshot* (Kingston: Hanson and Edgar, 1973).

Several articles by professional scholars provide overviews of the history of the town: Brian S. Osborne, "Kingston in the Nineteenth Century: A Study in Urban Decline," in J. David

Wood, ed., *Perspectives on Landscape and Settlement in Nineteenth Century Ontario* (Toronto: Macmillan, 1975) and "Kingston," *CE*, 2nd ed. (Edmonton: Hurtig, 1988); Gerald Tulchinsky's Introduction to the book he edited on nineteenth-century Kingston, *To Preserve and Defend: Essays on Kingston in the Nineteenth Century* (Montreal: McGill-Queen's, 1976) hereafter cited as *To Preserve and Defend*; Richard A. Preston, "Kingston, Where Genealogy Meets History," *Families*, 19, 4 (1980); Donald Swainson, "Chronicling Kingston: An Interpretation," *Ontario History*, 74, (1982). Rose Mary Gibson, "An Historical Chronology of Kingston," *Historic Kingston*, 18 (1970) is filled with data that are often missed by students of the city. Two delightful and evocative views of Kingston are S.F. Wise, "A Personal View of Kingston," *Historic Kingston*, 22 (1974) and Arthur R.M. Lower, "The Character of Kingston," in *To Preserve and Defend*. J. Douglas Stewart and Ian E. Wilson, *Heritage Kingston* (Kingston: Queen's, 1973) was prepared as a catalogue for an exhibition at Queen's University "to honour the 300th anniversary of European settlement in the Kingston area" (Foreword). It includes massive amounts of data on all aspects of Kingston's development and is one of the major studies of the city.

Too many general and specialized works say something important about Kingston to permit even an illustrative list. However, two are so contextually important that they must be listed: Gerald M. Craig, *Upper Canada: The Formative Years 1784-1841* (Toronto: McClelland and Stewart, 1963) and Donald Creighton, *John A. Macdonald*, (Toronto: Macmillan, 1952 and 1955), 2 vols.

Aspects of Kingston's past are discussed in numerous ongoing publications. Five are of special importance. The *Dictionary of Canadian Biography*, while yet far from complete, includes several dozen first-rate biographies of Kingstonians or persons with important Kingston involvements. The *Canadian Encyclopedia*, 2nd ed., also includes much Kingston material. *Ontario History* and its predecessor, the Ontario Historical Society's *Papers and Records*, include numerous articles concerning the town. *Freshwater: A Journal of Great Lakes Marine History*, published by the Marine Museum of the Great Lakes at Kingston, includes much Kingston material.

Most important of ongoing publications is *Historic Kingston*, "Being the annual publication of the Kingston Historical Society." The first ten volumes (1952-1962) of this journal have been reprinted in one volume as *Historic Kingston* (Belleville: Mika,1974) and an index to 1972 has been provided: A.R. Hazelgrove, *Historic Kingston, Volumes 1-20 (1952-1972): Cumulative Index* (Kingston: Kingston Historical Society, 1973). *Historic Kingston*, hereafter cited as *HK*, is a publication of impressive quality. Only the more important articles are listed below. The journal should be examined carefully by any serious student of the town.

French Period and Continuity

Apart from the references cited in this book, there are few sources relating to the native population of the Kingston region. Among the few works that do relate to this topic are Wallace Havelock Robb, "Indian Folk Lore of the Bay of Quinte," *HK*, 2 (1953); Gerald Stevens, "Recent Archaeological Discoveries at Toniata," *HK*, 7 (1958); and Reverend B.P. Squire, "The Indian Site at Consecon," *HK*, 7 (1958). For a more scholarly treatment see Victor Konrad, "An Iroquois Frontier: the North Shore of Lake Ontario During the Late Seventeenth Century," *Journal of Historical Geography*, 7 (1981) and Gordon G. Taylor, *The Mississauga Indians of Eastern Ontario, 1634-1881*, MA thesis, Queen's, 1981.

Much general and biographical material relating to French expansion westward discusses Kingston's French period. W. George Draper, *History of the City of Kingston* (Kingston: Creighton, 1862) is essentially a compilation of documents concerning Fort Frontenac. Richard A. Preston and Léopold Lamontagne, eds., *Royal Fort Frontenac* (Toronto: Champlain

Society, 1958) is a superb collection of documents on the pre-Loyalist period, preceded by an extensive and excellent survey-history of the French period. James S. Pritchard, *Journey of My Lord Count Frontenac to Lake Ontario* (Kingston: Downtown Business Association, 1973) is a translated document relating Frontenac's journey to the site in 1673. Two articles that perforce deal with the issue of continuity between the French and Loyalist periods are Léopold Lamontagne, "Kingston's French Heritage," *HK*, 2 (1953) and Neil A. Patterson, "The Mystery of Picardville and the French Church," *Families*, 19, 4 (1980).

Loyalists and Loyalist Town

Alfred Leroy Burt, *The Old Province of Quebec* (Toronto: Ryerson Press, 1933) establishes the early context for Loyalist Kingston. Ernest A. Cruikshank, *The Settlement of the United Empire Loyalists on the Upper St. Lawrence and the Bay of Quinte in 1785: A Documentary Record* (Toronto: Ontario Historical Society, 1934) includes necessary documentation on the settlement period. Loyalists as a group have received a very substantial amount of attention.

A very *small* selection of recent books that are oriented toward Ontario and/or Kingston include Bruce Wilson, *As She Began: An Illustrated Introduction to Loyalist Ontario* (Toronto and Charlottown: Dundurn, 1981); Dennis Duffy, *Gardens, Covenants, Exiles: Loyalism in the Literature of Upper Canada* (Toronto: University of Toronto, 1982); Larry Turner, *Voyage of a Different Kind: The Associated Loyalists of Kingston and Adolphustown* (Belleville: Mika, 1984); Walter Stewart, *True Blue: The Loyalist Legend* (Toronto: Collins, 1985); Jane Errington, *The Lion, the Eagle, and Upper Canada: A Developing Colonial Ideology* (Montreal: McGill-Queen's, 1987). Richard A. Preston, *Kingston Before the War of 1812: A Collection of Documents* (Toronto: Champlain Society, 1959), with its extensive Introduction, was the most important single work on Kingston's Loyalist period until Kathryn M. Bindon, *Kingston: A Social History, 1785-1830*, Ph.D. thesis, Queen's, 1979.

Some representative biographical studies are C.E. Cartwright, *Life and Letters of the Honourable Richard Cartwright* (Toronto: Belford, 1876); Donald C. MacDonald, *Honourable Richard Cartwright, 1759-1815* (Toronto: Ontario Department of Public Records and Archives, 1961); Marilyn G. Miller, *The Political Ideas of the Honourable Richard Cartwright*, MA research paper, Queen's, 1975; James Robertson Carruthers, *The Little Gentleman: The Reverend Doctor John Stuart and the Inconvenience of Revolution*, MA thesis, Queen's, 1975; George A. Rawlyk, "The Honourable Richard Cartwright, 1759-1815," *HK*, 33 (1985); Larry Turner, "Michael Grass: A Loyalist Founder of Kingston, 1783-1784," *HK*, 34 (1986); H.P. Gundy, "Molly Brant – Loyalist," *OH*, 45 (1953); Jean Johnson, "Molly Brant: Mohawk Matron," *OH*, 56 (1964); Ian Wilson, "Molly Brant: A Tribute," *HK*, 24 (1963).

The Military

Some good general and introductory items on Kingston and the military are George F.G. Stanley, "Historic Kingston and its Defences," *OH*, 46 (1954) and his "Kingston and the Defence of British North America," in *To Preserve and Defend*; and Richard A. Preston, "R.M.C. and Kingston: The Effect of Imperial and Military Influence on a Canadian Community," *OH*, 60 (1968) and his "The British Influence of RMC," in *To Preserve and Defend*. Morris Zaslow, ed., *The Defended Border. Upper Canada and the War of 1812* (Toronto: Macmillan, 1964) is essential for the War of 1812-1814, as is J. MacKay Hitsman, "Kingston and the War of 1812," *HK*, 15 (1967). See also Jane Errington, "British American Kingstonians and the War of 1812," *HK*, 32 (1984) and "Friend and Foe: Kingston Elite and the War of 1812," *Journal of Canadian Studies*, 20 (1985). William Patterson, "Fort Henry: Military Mistake or Defiant Deterrent?" *HK*, 29 (1981) is a fine introduction to the most important of Kingston's military relics. For Fort Henry, see also George F. Henderson's two articles "Fort Henry During the Troubled Days of 1837 to 1839," *HK*, 30 (1982), and "Fort Henry During the Second World War," 34 (1986). Another useful contribution is Stephen D. Mecredy, *Some Military Aspects of Kingston's Development During the War of 1812*, MA thesis, Queen's, 1982. A valuable work in which Kingston's defences figure large is Ivan J. Saunders, *A History of Martello Towers in the Defence of British North America, 1796-1871* (Ottawa: Canadian Historic Sites, 1976).

John W. Spurr made major contributions to Kingston military history, including: "The Kingston Garrison, 1815-1870," *HK*, 20 (1972); "Garrison and Community, 1815-1870," in *To Preserve and Defend*; "The Royal Navy's Presence in Kingston, Part I:1813-1836," *HK*, 25 (1977); "The Royal Navy's Presence in Kingston, Part II: 1813-1853," *HK*, 26 (1978); "The Kingston Gazette' the War of 1812, and 'Fortress Kingston,'" *HK*, 17 (1969); "Sir Robert Hall (1778-1818)," *HK*, 29 (1981); "Sir James Yeo, A Hero on the Lakes," *HK*, 30 (1982). An unusual foray into twentieth-century military history is Claire McCallum, "Kingston and the War: August 1914-December 1914," ms, Special Collections, Douglas Library, Queen's.

The Capital Period

Some general works on this subject are: David B. Knight, *A Capital for Canada: Conflict and Compromise in the Nineteenth Century* (University of Chicago, Department of Geography, Research Paper 182, 1977) and his *Choosing Canada's Capital: Jealousy and Friction in the Nineteenth Century* (Toronto: McClelland and Stewart, 1977); Fred Cook, *The Struggle for the Capital of Canada* (Ottawa: nd); D.J. Pierce and J.P. Pritchett, "The Choice of Kingston as the Capital of Canada, 1839-1841," Canadian Historical Association *Annual Report, 1929*; George F.G. Stanley, "Kingston, and the Choice of Canada's Capital," *HK*, 24 (1976); and James A. Gibson, "The Choosing of the Capital of Canada," *The British Columbia Historical Quarterly*, XVII (1953) and his "Sir Edmund Head's Memorandum on the Choice of Ottawa as the Seat of Government of Canada," *Canadian Historical Review*, 16 (1935). Some glimpses of life in Kingston during the capital period can be found in John William Kaye, *The Life and Correspondence of Charles Lord Metcalfe*, new and rev. ed., 2 vols (London: Smith, Elder and Co., 1858); G.P. de T. Glazebrook, *Sir Charles Bagot in Canada: A Study in British Colonial Government* (London and Toronto: Oxford , 1929); Paul Knaplund, (editor), *Letter from Lord Sydenham, Governor-General of Canada 1839-1841, To Lord John Russell* (Clifton, N.J.: Augustus M. Kelley, 1973; f. p. 1931); J.E. Hodgetts, "The Civil Service When Kingston was the Capital of Canada," *HK*, 5 (1956); Margaret Angus, "Lord Sydenham's One Hundred and Fifteen Days in Kingston," *HK*, 15 (1967).

The Port and Economic Development

Some good overviews of economic development are Marvin McInnis, *Kingston in the Canadian Economy of the Late Nineteenth Century* (Kingston: Institute for Economic Research, Queen's University, Discussion Paper No.132, n.d.); and Anne MacDermaid, "Kingston in the Eighteen-Nineties: A Study of Urban-Rural Interaction and Change," *HK*, 20 (1972). The port, at least until the early 1950s, has been carefully analysed: R.A. Preston, "The History of the Port of Kingston," *HK*, 3 (1954); Robert Gardiner, *The Port of Kingston: Past Present Future* (Kingston: n.p., n.d.); John D. Wilson, *The Economic History of the Kingston Port, 1853-1900*, BA thesis, Queen's, 1977; and Sarah J. Drummond, *Kingston as the Foot-of-the-Great Lakes-Terminus: A Study in Urban Boosterism*, MA thesis, Queen's, 1986.

Closely related to the port is the Rideau Waterway, which has received substantial attention. In particular see Robert Legget, *Rideau Waterway*, 2nd ed. (Toronto: University of Toronto, 1986); V.A. George, *The Rideau Corridor: The Effect of a Canal System on a Frontier Region, 1832-1895*, MA thesis, Queen's, 1972; George Raudzens, *The British Ordnance Department and Canada's Canals 1815-1855* (Waterloo: Wilfrid Laurier University, 1979); Robert W. Passfield, *Building the Rideau Canal: A Pictorial History*, (Don Mills: Fitzhenry & Whiteside, 1982); and

Brian S. Osborne and Donald Swainson, *"Dividing the Waters": A Preliminary Overview of Water Management on the Rideau, 1832-1972* (Parks Canada: Microfiche Report Series, Number 179, 1985), and their *Rideau Navigation, 1832-1972: Its Operation, Maintenance and Management* (Parks Canada: Microfiche Report Series, No. 191, 1985), 2 vols. For a discussion of the distinctive art work recording the early years of the Rideau Corridor, see Brian S. Osborne, "The Artist as Historical Commentator: Thomas Burrowes and the Rideau Canal," *Archivaria*, 17 (1984).

Some individual industries and entrepreneurs are analyzed in Anna G. Young, *Great Lake's Saga: The Influence of One Family* [Gildersleeve] *on the Development of Canadian Shipping on the Great Lakes, 1816-1931* (Owen Sound: Richardson, Bond & Wright, 1965); H.P. Gundy, "The Business Career of Hugh C. Thomson of Kingston," *HK*, 21 (1973); Joan MacKinnon, *Kingston Cabinet-makers, 1800-1867*, (Ottawa: National Museums of Canada, 1976); M.L. Magill, "James Morton of Kingston – Brewer," *HK*, 21 (1973) and his "The Failure of the Commercial Bank," in *To Preserve and Defend*; George Richardson, "The Canadian Locomotive Company," in *ibid.* ; Ian R. Dalton, "The Kingston Brewery of Thomas Dalton," *HK*, 26 (1978); and the anonymous *125 Years of Progress* (Winnipeg: James Richardson and Sons, Ltd., 1982). The title of Neil A. Patterson's "Why Kingston Did Not Become a Major Industrial Centre," *HK*, 34 (1986) is self-explanatory.

Adjacent Communities and Kingston's Quest for a Hinterland

Bryan Rollason, ed., *County of a Thousand Lakes: The History of the County of Frontenac 1673-1973* (Kingston: Frontenac County Council, 1982) is a massive multi-author history of Frontenac County. There is an enormous variation in the quality of the chapters, but this volume should be consulted and selected portions read. The distinctive community of Portsmouth has been described in Margaret Angus, "Portsmouth Village," *HK*, 21 (1973) and in her *Buildings of Architectural and Historic Significance*, III (Kingston: City of Kingston, 1975). The "township," as it is usually called, has received indifferent and multi-author attention in Neil A. Patterson, ed., *History of the Township of Kingston* (Kingston: Township of Kingston, 1985). A history of Pittsburgh Township is currently in progress: in the interim, readers should consult various issues of *Talks of Historical Interest* (Kingston: Pittsburgh Historical Society, n.d.).

Garden Island has received substantial attention. T.R. Glover and D.D. Calvin, *A Corner of Empire: The Old Ontario Strand* (London and Toronto: Cambridge, 1937), chaps. III-VI, is a charming and evocative account. D.D. Calvin, *A Saga of the St. Lawrence: Timber and Shipping Through Three Generations* (Toronto: Ryerson, 1945) is a neglected but important book. Illuminating works are Marion Calvin Boyd (ed. Margaret A. Boyd), *The Story of Garden Island* (Kingston: n.p., 1972); Margaret A. Boyd, *Island Summer* (Kingston: n.p., 1983); John David Calvin, *A Canadian Gentleman: A Biography of Jonathan David Calvin* (n.p., n.d.). Donald Swainson has written "Garden Island and the Calvin Company," *HK*, 28 (1980); *Garden Island: A Shipping Empire/L'Empire Maritime Garden Island* (Kingston: Marine Museum, 1984); and "Dileno Dexter Calvin," *DCB*, XI.

Transportation, hinterland problems, and the search for economic alternatives can be studied in: Brian S. Osborne, "The Settlement of Kingston's Hinterland," in *To Preserve and Defend*, his "Frontier Settlement in Eastern Ontario in the Nineteenth Century," in D.H. Miller and J.O. Steffen, eds., *The Frontier: Comparative Studies* (Norman: University of Oklahoma, 1977), and his "The Farmer and the Land," in *County of a Thousand Lakes*. See also Neil A. Patterson, "Kingston's Industrial Hinterland," *HK*, 29 (1981); Duncan McDowall, *Kingston, 1846-1854: A Study of Economic Change in a Mid-Nineteenth Century Canadian Community*, MA thesis, Queen's, 1973 and his "Roads and Railways: Kingston's Mid-Century Search for a Hinterland 1846-1854," *HK*, 23 (1975); Walter Lewis, "The Trials and Tribulations of the 'Kick and Push': A Business History of the Kingston and Pembroke Railway, 1871-1912," *HK*, 28 (1980). For a folk-history of the Kingston and Pembroke Railway, see Mel Easton, *The Men and My Memories of the K & P* (Kingston: n.p., 1976).

Some Key Institutions

There are many specific studies of Kingston's several institutions and their impact on the local society. For the penitentiaries see J. Edminson, "The History of Kingston Penitentiary," *HK*, 3 (1945); W.G.C. Norman, *A Chapter of Canadian Penal History: The Early Years of the Provincial Penitentiary at Kingston, and the Commission of Inquiry Into its Management, 1835-1851*, MA thesis, Queen's, 1979; Bryan Palmer, "Kingston Mechanics and the Rise of the Penitentiary, 1833-1836," *Histoire Sociale/Social History*, 13 (1980); J.M. Beattie, *Attitudes Towards Crime and Punishment in Upper Canada, 1830-1850: A Documentary Study* (Toronto: Centre of Criminology, University of Toronto, 1977).

Kingston's medical institutions have also received some attention: Rose Mary Gibson, *St. Mary's of the Lake in Kingston* (Kingston: n.p., 1971); Margaret Angus, *Kingston General Hospital: A Social and Institutional History* (Montreal: McGill-Queen's, 1973); Catherine Anne Sims, *An Institutional History of the Asylum for the Insane at Kingston, 1856-1858*, MA thesis, Queen's, 1981.

Information concerning Kingston's schools, colleges, and universities are to be found in the following: Donald A. Lapp, *The Schools of Kingston: Their First Hundred and Fifty Years*, MA thesis, Queen's, 1937; D.D. Calvin, *Queen's University at Kingston* (Kingston: Trustees of the University, 1941); Hilda Neatby, "Queen's University: Town and Gown to 1877," in *To Preserve and Defend* and *Queen's University: To Strive, to Seek, to Find and not to Yield*, I, *1841-1917* (Montreal: McGill-Queen's, 1978); Frederick W. Gibson, *Queen's University : To Serve and Yet be Free*, II, *1917-1961* (Montreal: McGill-Queen's, 1983); Richard Arthur Preston, *Canada's RMC: A History of the Royal Military College* (Toronto: University of Toronto, 1969); Kathryn M. Bindon, *Queen's Men, Canada's Men: The Military History of Queen's University, Kingston* (Kingston: Trustees of the Queen's University Contingent, Canadian Officers' Training Corps, 1978).

There are several published studies of Kingston's religious institutions and leading religious figures: Lothrop George Starr, *Old St. George's* (Kingston: R. Unglow and Company, 1913); A.H. Young, *The Parish Register of Kingston Upper Canada 1758-1811* (Kingston: Whig Publishing Company, 1921); D.M. Schurman, "John Travers Lewis and the Establishment of the Anglican Diocese," in *To Preserve and Defend*. Some are discussed in part or tangentially in J.E. Rea, *Bishop Alexander Macdonell and the Politics of Upper Canada* (Toronto: Ontario Historical Society Research Publication no. 4, 1974); Louis J. Flynn, "Bishop Edward John Horan," *HK*, 24 (1976); A.H. Young, "The Rev'd George O'Kill Stuart, M.A., LL.D.," Ontario Historical Society *Papers and Records*, 24 (1927); P. Lloyd Northcott, "The Financial Problems of the Reverend John Stuart," *HK*, 13 (1965).

For some insights into Kingston's institutions of entertainment, see John W. Spurr, "Theatre in Kingston, 1816-1870," *HK*, 22 (1974); Erdmute Waldauer, *Grand Theatre, 1879-1979* (Kingston: The Grand Theatre, 1979). More prosaically, for details on the operation of Kingston's market see Brian S. Osborne, "Trading on a Frontier: The Function of Peddlers, Markets and Fairs in Nineteenth Century Ontario," *Canadian Papers in Rural History*, II, 1980; and Quentin P. Chiotti, *The Evolving Food Distribution Network: An Analysis of Conflicting Agrarian, Commercial and Municipal Interests in Kingston, Ontario, 1879-1906*, MA thesis, Queen's, 1984.

The Urban Landscape

Margaret Angus has published several works concerned with Kingston's physical heritage, including *The Old Stones of Kingston: Its Buildings Before 1867* (Toronto: University of Toronto, 1966); "Some Old Kingston Homes and the Families Who Lived in Them," *HK*, 4 (1955); "Architects and Builders of Early Kingston," *HK*, 11 (1963); "The Old Stones of Queen's, 1842-1900," *HK*, 20 (1972); and "Loyalist Buildings in Kingston," *HK*, 33 (1985).

Two major studies of local architecture are *Buildings of Historical and Architectural Significance*, (Kingston: City of Kingston, 1971, 1973, 1975, 1977, 1980, 1985), 6 vols; Dana H. Johnson and C.J. Taylor, *Reports on Selected Buildings in Kingston, Ontario* (Ottawa: National Historic Parks and Sites Branch, Manuscript Report Number 261, 1976-1977), 2 vols. Gerald Finley, *In Praise of Older Buildings* (Kingston: Frontenac Historic Foundation, 1976) is a first-rate shorter study. Blake and Jennifer McKendry, *Early Photography in Kingston* (Kingston: n.p., 1979) includes some unusual and important photographs of buildings and streetscapes.

Some individual architects and buildings can be studied in Ian E. Wilson, J. Douglas Stewart, Margaret S. Angus, and Neil K. MacLennon, *Kingston City Hall* (Kingston: City of Kingston, 1974); J. Douglas Stewart, "Architecture for a Boom Town: The Primitive and the Neo-Baroque in George Browne's Kingston Buildings," in *To Preserve and Defend* and "Some of Kingston's Old Bricks, Sticks, and Stones: a First Essay on the Architecture of William Newlands (1853-1926)," in Christina Cameron and Martin Segger, eds., *Selected Papers from the Society for the Study of Architecture in Canada Annual Meetings, 1975 and 1976* (Ottawa: Society for the Study of Architecture in Canada, 1981); Mary Winnett Fraser, "William Coverdale, Kingston Architect 1801-1865," *HK*, 26 (1978); Joan Mattie, *100 Years of Architecture in Kingston: John Power to Drever and Smith* (Ottawa: Public Archives of Canada, 1986); Jennifer Margaret McKendry, *Selected Architectural Drawings and Buildings of John and Joseph Power, Kingston, Ontario, 1850-1900*, M. Phil. thesis, University of Toronto, 1986; Fern Elizabeth Mackenzie Graham, *The Wooden Architecture of William Newlands*, MA thesis, Queen's, 1987; John W. Spurr, "The Night of the Fire," *HK*, 18, (1970) explains why much of early Kingston was built of limestone.

Public reports are necessary to any serious study of the development of Kingston's urban landscape. In particular see George Stephenson and G. George Muirhead, *A Planning Study of Kingston, Ontario. Prepared for the City Council* (Kingston: City of Kingston, 1961); *Report of the Committee on Waterfront and Downtown Redevelopment* (Kingston: City of Kingston, 1964); *Proposal for 1967 Centenary of Confederation* (Kingston: City of Kingston, n.d.); Wyllie Unfal Weinberg and Scheckenberger, Town Planners, *Sydenham Ward Urban Renewal Scheme, Kingston, Ontario* (Rexdale: n.p., 1970); *A Study of the City of Kingston Waterfront: Property Ownership, Land Use, and Buildings and Property Descriptions* (Kingston: Kingston Area Planning Board, 1971); *Mayor's Waterfront Committee 77 Report* (Kingston: City of Kingston, n.d.); graduate students, School of Urban and Regional Planning, *Planning Kingston's Future Waterfront* (Kingston: School of Urban and Regional Planning, Queen's, 1979).

The Urban Community: Society, Culture and Politics

There is no systematic study of Kingston's poor, but glimpses of life among the lower classes can be had from: Robert Francis John Barnett, *A Study of Price Movements and the Cost of Living in Kingston for the Years 1865 to 1900*, MA thesis, Queen's, 1963; Margaret Angus, "Health, Emigration and Welfare in Kingston, 1820-1840," in Donald Swainson, ed., *Oliver Mowat's Ontario* (Toronto: Macmillan, 1972); Patricia E. Malcolmson, "The Poor in Kingston, 1815-1850," in *To Preserve and Defend*; Alan G. Green, "Immigrants in the City: Kingston as Revealed in the Census Manuscripts of 1871," in *ibid*.; Harvey J. Graff, *The Literacy Myth: Literacy and Social Structure in the Nineteenth-Century City* (New York: Academic Press, 1979); Robert E. Elliott, *Working-Class Kingston: The Impact of an Industrial Economy on Working-Class Conditions and Union Organization During the 1880s,* MA thesis, Queen's, 1982 . For a discussion of Kingston's late-nineteenth-century social structure see R. Harris, G. Levine, and Brian S. Osborne, "Housing Tenure and Social Classes in Kingston, Ontario, 1881-1901," *Journal of Historical Geography*, 7 (1981) and *The Housing Question in Kingston, Ontario, 1881-1901* (Queen's Department of Geography, 1982). For more contemporary concerns see Richard Harris, *Democracy in Kingston: A Social Movement in Urban Politics 1965-1970* (Kingston and Montreal: McGill-Queen's, 1988) which is concerned with housing, urban developments, and various short-lived and largely ineffective protest groups.

Kingston's ethnic groups have received nothing like the attention that they deserve, but three studies stand out: Lubomyr Y. Luciuk, *Ukrainians in the Making: Their Kingston Story* (Kingston: Limestone Press, 1980); Marion E. Meyer, *The Jews of Kington: A Microcosm of Canadian Jewry* (Kingston: Limestone Press, 1983); Merle Koven and Gini Rosen, eds., *From Strength to Strength, 75th Anniversary Commemorative Book* (Kingston: Beth Israel Congregation, 1986). Some insights into the Irish and the Orange Order can be found in: Sean Gerard Conway, *Upper Canadian Orangeism in the Nineteenth Century: Aspects of a Pattern of Disruption*, MA thesis, Queen's, 1977; Cecil J. Houston and William J. Smyth, *The Sash Canada Wore: A Historical Geography of the Orange Order in Canada* (Toronto: University of Toronto, 1980); Donald H. Akenson, *The Irish in Ontario: A Study in Rural History* (Kingston and Montreal: McGill-Queen's, 1984). See also Anne MacDermaid, "The Visit of the Prince of Wales to Kingston in 1860," *HK*, 21 (1973) and J.D. Livermore, "The Orange Order and the Election of 1861 in Kingston," in *To Preserve and Defend*.

The élite have received more attention. Margaret Angus, "Doctor James Sampson: A Brief Biography," *HK*, 31 (1983) introduces us to Kingston's medical profession as well as to a leading nineteenth-century personality. A fascinating insight into some aspects of sport activity is J.W. Fitsell, *Hockey's Captains, Colonels and Kings* (Erin: Boston Mills Press, 1987). J. Douglas and Mary Stewart, "John Soloman Cartwright: Upper Canadian Gentlemen and Regency 'Man of Taste,'" *HK*, 27 (1979) is a fine study of a local aristocrat.

Several studies have analyzed Kingston's most famous resident – John A. Macdonald – and his relationship with the city: T.S. Webster, *John A. Macdonald and Kingston*, MA thesis, Queen's, 1944; Donald G. Creighton, "Sir John Macdonald and Kingston," *Canadian Historical Association Annual Report*, 1950; J.K. Johnson, "John A. Macdonald and the Kingston Business Community," in *To Preserve and Defend*; William R. Teatero, *"A Dead and Alive Way Never Does": The Pre-Political Professional World of John A. Macdonald*, MA thesis, Queen's, 1978; Donald Swainson, *John A. Macdonald: The Man and the Politician* (Toronto: Oxford, 1971) and his *Macdonald of Kingston* (Toronto: Nelson, 1979); Margaret Angus, *John A. Lived Here* (Kingston: Frontenac Historic Foundation, Occasional Paper No. 1, 1984).

Kingston's politics and politicians have not received systematic study and the twentieth-century phase has been largely ignored. However, there are numerous articles. Most focus on individuals. A representative sample is: Margaret Angus, "John Counter," *HK*, 27 (1979); S.F. Wise, "Tory Factionalism: Kingston Elections and Upper Canadian Politics, 1820-1836," *OH*, 57 (1965), "The Rise of Christopher Hagerman," *HK*, 14 (1966), and "John Macaulay: Tory for All Seasons," in *To Preserve and Defend*; and J.K. Johnson, "Anthony Manahan and the Status of Irish Catholics in Upper Canada," *HK*, 31 (1983). Donald Swainson has written several articles on Kingston politicians and politics; see in particular his "Richard Cartwright Joins the Liberal Party," *Queen's Quarterly* (Spring 1968); "Alexander Campbell: General Manager of the Conservative Party (Eastern Ontario Section)," *HK*, 17 (1969); "George Airey Kirkpatrick: Political Patrician," *HK*, 19 (1971); "James O'Reilly and Catholic Politics," *HK*, 21 (1973); "Richard Cartwright's Tory Phase," Lennox and Addington Historical Society *Papers and Records*, 15 (1976); "Sir Henry Smith and the Politics of the Union," *OH*, 66 (1974); and "Kingstonians in the Second Parliament: Portrait of an Elite Group," in *To Preserve and Defend*. W. Michael Wilson, "Eleven Years of Dissension: the Conservative Party in Kingston, 1867-1878," *HK*, 32 (1984) is a most useful contribution, as is Leslie H. Morley, "A Nickle For Change – The Political Career of W.F. Nickle, 1906-1926," *HK*, 32 (1984).

Publishing and politics have gone hand in hand in Kingston. George M. Betts, "Municipal Government and Politics, 1800-1850," in *To Preserve and Defend*, is a good survey of local government. For an introduction to Kingston's newspapers and journalists, see H.P. Gundy, "Publishing and Bookselling in Kingston since 1810," *HK*, 10 (1962) and "Hugh C. Thomson:

Editor, Publisher and Politician, 1791-1834," in *To Preserve and Defend*; John W. Spurr, "Edward John Barker, M.D., Editor and Citizen," *HK*, 27 (1979).

The Personality of Place

By reading the above references and by walking the streets of the contemporary Kingston, it is possible to approach an appreciation of this distinctive place. Clearly, Kingston has had several scores of authors writing about it but three novelists may be highlighted for their evocative reconstructions of the physical and social fabrics, harmonies and tensions, and continuities and changes.

The writings of Robertson Davies cast much light on Kingston society, and in particular on the educated, rich, and eccentric. See his novels: *Tempest-Tost* (Toronto: Clarke, Irwin, 1951); *Leaven of Malice* (Toronto: Clarke, Irwin, 1954); and *A Mixture of Frailties* (Toronto: Macmillan, 1958). Davies' play, *Fortune, My Foe* (Toronto: Clark, Irwin, 1949) focuses on a famous Kingston eccentric, Dollar Bill, who is also discussed in Mike Murphy's, *My Kind of People* (Westport: Butternut Press, 1987), Chapter 9, "Dollar Bill."

The characters in David Helwig's Kingston tetralogy move through the streets and institutions and their lives highlight the social milieu and cultural ambiance of the city: *The Glass Knight* (Canada: Oberon, 1976); *Jennifer* (Canada: Oberon, 1979); *It Is Always Summer* (Toronto: Stoddart, 1982); and *A Sound Like Laughter* (Toronto: Stoddart, 1983).

Finally, Matt Cohen's fictional Salem is set in the countryside of southern Ontario and his novels do much to evoke the sense of historical development, economic transformation, and social stress in that rural society. While much is artistic fabrication, the reader will learn a great deal about the landscapes and inscapes of Kingston's "backcountry" from Cohen's novels: *The Disinherited*, (Toronto: McClelland and Stewart, 1974); *The Colours of War* (Toronto: McClelland and Stewart, 1977); *The Sweet Second Summer of Kitty Malone* (Toronto: McClelland and Stewart, 1979); and *Flowers of Darkness* (Toronto: McClelland and Stewart, 1981).

Index